94
C

PARKING OF MOTOR VEHICLES

To
ANN

PARKING
of
MOTOR VEHICLES

Second Edition

JOHN BRIERLEY

O.B.E., C.Eng., F.I.C.E., F.I.Mun.E., F.R.T.P.I., F.G.S.

*Rees Jeffreys Prizeman, Richard Pickering Prizeman and Gold Medallist,
Consulting Civil Engineer*

APPLIED SCIENCE PUBLISHERS LTD
LONDON

APPLIED SCIENCE PUBLISHERS LTD
RIPPLE ROAD, BARKING, ESSEX, ENGLAND

FIRST EDITION PUBLISHED 1962

ISBN: 0 85334 528 7

WITH 187 ILLUSTRATIONS AND 13 TABLES

© 1972 APPLIED SCIENCE PUBLISHERS LTD

Printed in Great Britain by Galliard Limited, Great Yarmouth, Norfolk, England.

Preface to First Edition

This book is an attempt to reveal the growing problems of parking motor vehicles and to describe some of the methods that may be adopted to meet the difficulties. It is a problem which is growing imperceptibly day by day and is liable to be dealt with by expedients. It will be found that the expedients do not solve the problem; ultimately they make it more complex. There is no simple answer. There are many different ways of accommodating the stationary motor vehicle, and undoubtedly each city, town or village will have to work out a solution using the most suitable combination of methods to suit local circumstances. It is a subject which calls for a long, broad and balanced view of the situation today, tomorrow and 20 years ahead. It is inevitable that there will be some curtailment of the freedom and privileges that motorists have enjoyed in past years, and this will have to be sacrificed so that a greater number of people may have the advantage of private motor transport.

Great Britain has the advantage of being in a position to examine the parking problem in other countries where the use of motor vehicles has increased more rapidly than in this country. Therefore some of the errors of the pioneers should be avoided. It is hoped that this book will help those people who have the responsibility of finding a solution to the parking problem.

In writing this book I have received a great deal of kindness, help and advice, particularly from Mr D. G. England, M.A., A.M.I.C.E., who has corrected Chapter 7 on 'Parking Meters', the lawyer to the Automobile Association, who has corrected Chapter 3 on 'Legislation', and Mr J. L. Waldron, C.V.O., Assistant Commissioner, Traffic and Transport, Metropolitan Police, who has given me much information on the parking problem in London. I am also greatly indebted to Mr L. R. Suter, who has doggedly prepared the typescript at his home in the evenings.

Exeter   JOHN BRIERLEY
May, 1962

v

Preface to Second Edition

In the ten years that have passed since the first edition of *Parking of Motor Vehicles* was written, the number of licenced motor vehicles has increased by nearly 100 per cent in the United Kingdom and similarly there have been large increases of traffic in other developed countries of the world. The problems of providing facilities and managing the arrangements for stationary vehicles in urban areas, particularly in the central business areas, have become apparent to most people.

During this period we have had new legislation to help control parked vehicles; new methods, new ideas and new policies have been introduced and developed. These changes have made it necessary to rewrite the book almost completely, and introduce ten new chapters. Some chapters in the first edition have been omitted and some of the material included in the new chapters.

Chapter 17 entitled 'Security on Car Parks' is based on information supplied by John V. DuRose, O.B.E., a Director of National Car Parks Ltd, and formerly Deputy Assistant Commissioner (Criminal Investigation), New Scotland Yard, London. This is a growing problem, and I am very grateful for his help and advice. I am also indebted to Eric Dore, Senior Structural Advisory Engineer to the Cement and Concrete Association, London, who very kindly read the draft of Chapter 10 on the 'Design of Multi-storey Car Parks', and made several helpful suggestions which have been incorporated in the text.

Throughout my studies of car parking I have drawn heavily on the 'Digest of Literature' and 'Supplementary Review of Literature' on this subject, compiled by Mrs R. G. Knight, M.A., M.Sc., when she was Librarian at the Road Research Laboratory, Crowthorne, Berkshire. This information has proved to be an excellent foundation for a study on a new subject of this type, and without this help my task would have been much more difficult.

Finally, I wish to thank L. R. Suter who has given up very many evenings and weekends during the winter of 1970–71 to prepare the typescript, also Henry C. Jennings, H. C. Maunder and A. J. Rowe, who have devoted much of their leisure time to help produce some of the illustrations. It is only with their help and interest in this work that it has been possible to produce this second edition of *Parking of Motor Vehicles*.

JOHN BRIERLEY

Exeter
January, 1972

Contents

Chapter 1

Development of the Car Parking Problem

Parking is not a new phenomenon. History tells us that in Rome special off-street parking facilities were provided to get chariots off the travelled way, and that Julius Caesar forbade vehicles from entering the business districts of large cities in the Roman Empire during certain hours of the day because of traffic congestion. The following is a translation of an extract from Tabula Heracleensis:[1]

> 'Concerning those roads in the City of Rome which are or will be within well populated places, no one after the first of the Kalens of January, in the daytime, after sunrise or before the hour of 10 of the day, is to drive or lead a cart, unless that which is necessary to be carried or transported for building dwelling places of the immortal gods, or for doing public works, or things which by order of the State, are scheduled to be demolished, and for these reasons, this law permits carts to be driven or led by particular men, and for special reasons.
>
> On those days, for the furtherance of the common religion of the Roman people, when it is fitting to carry priestesses of Vesta, and priests into the City, and when it is fitting that triumphal carts on the day of a triumphal procession, or game carts which happen to be at Rome, or near to the City of Rome, on state occasions should be led, or if there is need of circus revels to be led or driven into the procession, only by reason of these things on these days may carts be led or driven in the City in the daytime, and by this law nothing is to be questioned.
>
> That carts may enter the City by night, but only empty carts or ox-carts for carrying out dung are allowed to be in the City of Rome, or within a mile of the City after sunrise or before the hour of 10 of the day, and this law is not to be questioned.'

Coming to more recent times, in the United Kingdom, the Industrial Revolution came in the 18th and 19th centuries, along with the development of railways, which started in 1825 with the opening of the Stockton to Darlington railway. Telford, Metcalf and Macadam became pioneers in new methods of road construction. During this period, 2800 miles of artificial waterways were brought into use. The population of England and Wales increased from 8,892,536 in

1801 to 32,527,843 in 1901, and the increase was largely concentrated in the newly developed industrial towns. These towns were built to meet the immediate requirements of the day, they were often developed on the site of a village, and the roads followed the pattern of the former village streets. The traffic on the roads was horse-drawn or pedestrian, the wealthy had their carriages, and goods were transported from the factories to the railway stations by horse-drawn lorries. The method of transport used by manual and factory workers was either on foot, public transport, such as stage coaches, wagonettes, horse-drawn tramcars, and later the steam tramcar. These were superseded by the electric tramcar at the end of the century. Comparatively few people travelled far from their homes. The houses in the towns were huddled together, with row after row of cottages clustering around the factories. The factory workers were employed for long hours, children started work at an age of eight or nine years, and all were given very short holidays. In the country districts transport was on horseback, by horse-drawn carriage or on foot. Each village was the market and meeting centre for the surrounding rural area, with a larger county town developing at the junction of main roads. The county town may have had its origin in Roman or mediaeval times and built with narrow congested streets.

The population of Greater London in 1901 was approximately 6,500,000, of which 4,500,000 were resident within the County of London. In London the first motor bus was licensed in 1897, the horse buses reached their maximum number of 1418 in 1905, and the last horse bus was withdrawn from the road in 1911. Trevelyan writes of the period 1832–67: 'In the capital, the convenient "landau", the light "Victoria", the smart "hansom" cab (called by Disraeli "the gondola of London"), the homely four-wheeler and the democratic omnibus held the streets.'[2] There was traffic congestion in those days with horse-drawn vehicles. We read in a diary of 1820: 'We left the play at 11 o'clock and in Piccadilly we got into a crowd of carriages caused by a party of Lady Charleville's, and were kept there unable to move either way for above two hours.'[3]

Throughout the country horse traffic became ancillary to the railway, which was used for long journeys. The highway became unpopular for long journeys until the coming of the motor car. This was how the people in England travelled, and this is how goods were transported on land at the end of Queen Victoria's reign when the internal combustion engine was introduced.

The cities had been planned and built for conditions quite different from those required for the automobile. Speaking at a public dinner in 1905, the late Sir Winston Churchill remarked that one of the most striking things to his mind was the extraordinary rapidity with which automobilism had overspread national life since the beginning of the century. 'Five years ago', he said, 'a motor car was an object of derision if it stopped for one moment; now, the asses have got used to them, and we see them on every road.'[4]

By the construction of canals, roads and above all railways, a new route network and new means of transport had been created in the United Kingdom. It would be misleading to infer that similar conditions were established generally on the Continent of Europe, even in its most western parts. Many of the distinguishing features of Britain in the age of coal and iron, made their appearance on the Continent rather belatedly and sporadically. It was not until the middle of the 19th century that the means of transport on the Continent had been revolutionised by the establishment of railways.

Railway construction, which began in England, was undertaken on the Continent first in Belgium, rather later in Germany and later still in France. In Scandinavia and Mediterranean Europe a system of trunk railway lines had been for the most part completed by 1870. In Germany by 1870 there were clear signs of drastic changes in the location of industry and growth of towns.[5]

In the United States of America by 1790, the population had centred itself in the main along the coast and the rivers. In the 1850–80s occurred the great age of railway building, and the population was drawn out along the railway lines to spill over the Western Plains. Growing communities of people developed at railway and road junctions, or at the crossing of railway and river. The immense growth of industry between 1890 and 1920 led to the concentration of population in the North East and the East North Central States. It was from New York, Philadelphia and Baltimore that the early roads in the late 18th and early 19th centuries were built to Ohio and the Old North West.

The 20th century has seen the explosion of the American Metropolis. The essentially vertical city of the last century, compact and intensive in its land use, has been surrounded by a sprawling suburbia. As a result the whole countryside is changing. Former villages have become important residential satellites of the larger industrial and commercial cities.[6]

Road transport came to challenge the railway's monopoly of freight and passenger traffic, and the railway's share of the national transport business has markedly declined. By 1955 it was estimated that 88% of all passenger miles were covered by private car.

As the United States has taken the lead in the production of motor vehicles, so it has been the first Continent to create a network of roads designed specifically for this form of transport. Around such cities as New York and Los Angeles, the congestion of arterial roads is becoming intense, and finding space for these broad highways is a great problem. Meanwhile the centres of cities have become virtually impassable and the significant feature of the motor age is the parking lot.[7]

Increasingly the internal combustion engine has changed the pattern of our lives. The motor car and omnibus have made transport from door to door not only possible but quick and easy. It has linked the villages of the countryside with the towns, and the whole population of a country is now mobile as it has never been before. In the development of towns we see the closely built-up areas of the pre-motoring days followed by the spread of the open development of the 20th century. A family now has much more choice of position for living in relation to work, schools and shopping.

The increased industrialisation and shorter working hours have given more leisure to the employees. The changes in the distribution of wealth have enabled more and more people to become the owners of some type of motor vehicle. Vast numbers of these vehicles can be seen on the roads leading to the coast and the countryside at week-ends. Coaches, cars and motor cycles pour out in their thousands from the cities and towns, to return in masses in the evening. This spectacle can be seen at its height on Public Holidays.

The motor car has made an incursion into our way of life very gradually over

the last 70 years. Whilst the number of cars in use was small, no great inconvenience was caused by parking on the highway. The motorist was able to
enjoy the maximum ease and convenience from the new invention by driving
from door to door. This is a privilege which cannot continue indefinitely, and
a stage will be reached when the roads will become choked with vehicles. In
some cities this has now happened, in others it is near at hand.

INDUSTRIAL TRAFFIC

An increasing population calls for increased business and office accommodation
in the city centres, which in its turn brings increased traffic and increased parking
requirements. Instead of people moving to the big industrial centres, encourage-
ment is given to establish new factories where the labour is available. The system
of specialisation, and sub-contracting, is developing very rapidly. The production
of component parts takes place in different factories, often situated in different
parts of the country, and transport is required to bring them to an assembly
point. Much time and thought is given to the movement of goods inside a
factory, and it is just as important to have efficient movement outside. Distribution is an important factor in the cost of production. Sir Geoffrey Heyworth,[8]
Chairman of Unilever Limited, in England, said: 'Our investment in transport,
handling equipment and warehouses amounts to £18,000,000, or nearly 15
per cent of our total investment in manufacturing and distribution facilities.
Our annual expenditure on transport is equal to nearly one-half of the total
wage and salary bill of our 250,000 employees. Transport also affects the amount
of working capital we need. The slower the movement of raw materials, intermediate products, and finished products, the larger the stocks that have to be
maintained and financed. A day's delay in our world-wide operations would tie
up another £5,000,000 working capital. All this shows why we take such an
active interest in transport, and why efficiency of transport is as important to us
as efficiency of manufacture.

'Distribution is an integral part of the production process, and its cost is a
significant factor in determining the retail prices of products. Transport is a
major part of the distribution process, and indeed a major element of cost. A
striking illustration of this is the fact that while the labour cost of producing a
ton of washing powder is 13 man hours, the cost of delivering it 200 miles from
factory to retailer may be equivalent to 19 man hours'.

Prosperity in industry is the basis for an improved standard of living, but
prosperity depends on efficiency to compete with overseas markets. Efficiency
includes efficient means of communication and transport, and this cannot be
brought about whilst there are inadequate means of loading and unloading
vehicles, and long and expensive delays on traffic routes caused by the haphazard
parking of cars on main roads.

The increased use of private cars has had its effect on public transport by
reducing the number of passengers, thereby adding an increased financial
burden on the passenger transport undertakings. The services provided could
carry a larger number of passengers for the same running expenses. In some
cases, especially in the rural areas, the services are curtailed, which encourages

more people to use private cars. The practice of using the private car for travelling to and from business, places a very heavy burden on the roads at the peak periods in the morning and evening. It also increases the demand for parking accommodation, because many of the cars used for travelling are parked all day.

FUTURE TRAFFIC VOLUMES

It is difficult to visualise what traffic conditions will be like in the future. Many people find it impossible to accept the figures put forward by research engineers for the estimated number of licensed vehicles 40 years hence. Even if the figures are accepted, it is extremely difficult to visualise what the effect will be on traffic conditions when there is a 200 per cent increase in traffic volumes above the present day figures (1970).

TABLE I

Number of Vehicles per 1000 Persons

Country	1965		1969		1965–69 Percentage Increase	
	Private Cars	All Vehicles	Private Cars	All Vehicles	Private Cars	All Vehicles
United States of America	386·7	464·4	433·2	524·0	12	12·9
New Zealand	269·0	330·3	304·0	365·3	13	10·6
Canada	266·0	334·0	293·0	368·0	10	10·2
Australia	258·0	336·0	292·0	368·0	13·2	9·5
Sweden	232·0	250·0	274·0	293·0	18·2	17·0
France	184·0	220·0	235·0	270·0	27·5	22·8
Germany	—	181·0	216·0	234·0	—	29·3
Denmark	156·0	206·0	209·0	262·0	34	27
Switzerland	155·0	172·0	208·0	229·0	34	33
Great Britain	169·0	200·0	208·0	239·0	23	19·6
Belgium	145·0	172·0	196·0	226·0	35	34·5
Norway	125·0	161·0	181·0	219·0	45	38·5
Netherlands	112·0	132·4	162·0	187·1	35·8	41·7

The number of licensed vehicles is increasing year by year, and in order to plan ahead intelligently it is necessary to have some indication of the number of vehicles likely to be using the roads in the years ahead. To forecast accurately the number of cars that may be licensed in ten or twenty years' time is very difficult. For instance, there may be a national economic crisis, which could seriously reduce the number of cars purchased at any one time. In spite of the variable factors which could restrict purchasing power, it is reasonable to assume that the present rate of increase will continue for some years ahead.

A study of the increase in licensed vehicles in other countries, especially the United States of America, Canada, Australia and New Zealand, gives a good guide to the number of licensed vehicles that may be expected in the United Kingdom and other European countries in the years to come.

Table I shows the number of vehicles per 1000 persons in a selected list of countries over the five years 1965–69. It shows the average annual growth in the United States of America during this period is approximately $2\frac{1}{2}$ per cent, whereas in the European countries it is much higher. It is quite clear that we have to think of an average of 2 persons per car or 500 cars per 1000 of the population in the future in the developed countries. In order to arrive at a true assessment we must also take account of the increasing population. The continuing increase in the number of vehicles using our roads presents a dual problem. How to keep vehicles moving on the roads, and how to park them satisfactorily off the roads.

THE IMPORTANCE OF PARKING

The importance of parking can hardly be over-estimated. There are 8760 hours in a year. If it is assumed that the average mileage per year per car is 16,000 km (10,000 miles) and the average speed is 40 km (25 miles) per hour, the total travelling time will be 400 hours. This leaves 8360 hours per year when the car is parked. Probably the greater part of this time the car will be parked in a private garage. This illustrates that the period over which a car is parked is very great compared with the time it is in motion.

The size of the average parking space is about $14\cdot0$ m^2 (150 sq ft). The average number of people using a car cannot be more than two, which gives an average of $7\cdot0$ m^2 (75 sq ft) of parking space per person. Because the motor car is a mobile and personal vehicle, it requires two parking spaces, one where it is normally housed when not in use, and the second in town or country when only temporarily out of use; the former space being left vacant when the car is in use.

A man standing will occupy a space of about $0\cdot18$ m^2 (2 sq ft); when walking or sitting he will occupy about $0\cdot55$ m^2 (6 sq ft). A house that will accommodate five people very comfortably will have an area of 140 m^2 (1500 sq ft) divided between two floors. The actual ground space taken per person for living accommodation is therefore $14\cdot0$ m^2 (150 sq ft). This is a generous allowance. If a subsidised house is taken as an example with 93 m^2 (1000 sq ft) floor area, the space per person will be reduced to $9\cdot3$ m^2 (100 sq ft) of ground space. A single-deck omnibus when parked will occupy an area of $33\cdot5$ m^2 (360 sq ft), which is an average of $1\cdot02$ m^2 (11 sq ft) per person, and this figure is almost halved for a double-deck omnibus. Therefore it will be seen that a motor car when measured against the service it provides and the space it occupies is one of the most extravagant inventions in land use in modern transport.

That the motor car has come to stay there can be no doubt, and it must be accommodated. The advantages that it offers in convenience, comfort, speed, conservation of energy and effort, are so great and attractive that they outweigh the disadvantages. Modern professional, business and social life has now been integrated with the use of the motor car so much so that it has become an essential part of this life.

The problem that has to be solved for our towns and cities which were laid out for a pattern of life in the 18th or 19th century, or even earlier, is how to adapt them to meet the demands of the late 20th century, when the car/population ratio will be 1 in 3 at least.

The United States of America has led the world in the use of the motor car, and it is possible to gain valuable information from the methods that have been adopted to meet the traffic and parking problem. No two countries are alike, and the United States of America is a new country with comparatively new towns, whereas in Europe there are many old towns and cities.

Parking control has become the chief means available to cities all over the world to limit congestion. It is not the particular problem of any one country. The problem is not that of providing suitable equipment and legislation to control parking. It is the enforcement of laws and regulations.

In Tokyo, the world's second largest city, illegally parked cars can be seen on the streets at any time. Parking meters have been tried once and abandoned, and are to be re-introduced. Parking is a problem in West German cities and they look to Britain for new ideas. In Flensburg, near the Danish frontier, too many parking infringements may cause a motorist to lose his driving licence.

In New York, the Mayor is dedicated to the idea of banning all cars from Manhattan. San Francisco claims to have the world's worst parking problem with roughly one car to every two inhabitants and another 343,000 streaming into the city every day. Rome disputes San Francisco's claim, and reports that a monstrous parking problem is only one aspect of the traffic anarchy.

In France, Strasbourg, Nice and Menton have meters, but not Paris. In Paris, 950,000 cars enter the city every day, and the Prefect of Police has a strong case for introducing meters but the authorities will not have them. In their place they have the 'blue zone' where discs are used, but there is a formidable backlog of uncollected fines.

In London, where meters are used, the chances of avoiding a fine for street parking are increasing every day. In England, discs have been introduced in a few genteel towns such as Cheltenham, Devizes, Harrogate and Ruislip. There are also important cities which have set their face against parking meters. Cardiff is one, Swansea, Exeter and Leicester are others. On the other hand, many of the largest cities in Britain have introduced meters with varying degrees of success.[9]

Traffic congestion is like a malignant disease which, unless arrested, will surely bring death to the heart of the city. Where there is traffic congestion, and a lack of car parking facilities in the centre of cities, land values will tend to fall. European countries are in the fortunate position of being able to study the traffic problem in American cities where the car/population ratio is perhaps 15 years ahead of Europe. America has resorted to large departmental store or supermarket establishments in suburban areas with extensive surface car parking space immediately around the buildings. This is now beginning to be adopted in Europe.

The ideal would be to rebuild our cities to the requirements of the motor car age. Such proposals may be included in a long term plan, but the problem is too urgent to wait for a long term plan to be carried out. Something must be done, and done quickly, to accommodate motor vehicles in our cities, otherwise the consequences may be very serious in the loss of business and property values.

The provision and siting of car parks should be related to the future traffic flow of the roads that will be carrying the traffic to the city or town. The wise siting of car parks can make it possible to increase the number of cars that can be parked in a city centre, without causing congestion, whereas the converse will apply if the siting is bad and not related to the traffic flow.

It should be remembered that even in this motor car age there will always be a large and probably an increasing number of pedestrians in our city centres. Pedestrians require reasonably compact shopping and business areas, and it is a great disadvantage and time waster if the area is broken up by extensive car parks. Therefore when considering the adaptation of city centres to accommodate the motor car the pedestrian must also be considered.

The problem is basically the same in the centre of a village or a large city, and it varies only in degree. Too many people wish to park their vehicles at the same time in too small an area. To ban all vehicles in the congested urban centre is unnecessary and unwise. It would create great inconvenience. Goods have to be delivered by motor vehicles, and there are many times when private cars must be taken into the inner city area. Until the last few years vehicles have been able to circulate in the centre of cities easily. Whilst cars are permitted to circulate in our city centres, there must be some regulation and control which will give the maximum use of the space available. Ultimately this will be to the advantage of everyone concerned. The approach to the problem should be to give the motorist as much advantage as possible from the use or ownership of a motor vehicle. The motor vehicle was invented for the use and convenience of man, and the cities and roads should be adapted to accommodate it in its proper place after giving consideration to other claims on a city's resources. If the car parking problem is to be solved, it is necessary to get it in the true perspective. There is no doubt that we must plan for at least one car per family or one car to every three people.

It is completely out of date and inadequate to rely on using undeveloped sites in our cities for car parking which are sacrificed for building development as soon as a favourable offer is received. Adequate, planned and organised car parking is as essential to the life of our cities as a railway station, an omnibus station, or a departmental store. The same care, thought and consideration should be given to their planning, siting and operation as to other traffic termini. It means that local authorities must be strong minded on this subject. Car parks are not likely to make big profits, and a business house will be in a more favourable position to offer higher ground rents for a site than could possibly be considered as an economic proposition for a car park. Nevertheless adequate car parking is a necessary part of development in a city centre, and without it trade cannot prosper.

REFERENCES

1. ABBOT, F. F. and JOHNSON, A. C. 'Municipal Administration in the Roman Empire', Princetown University Press, 1926.
2. TREVELYAN, G. M. 'English Social History', Longmans, Green & Co., 1946.

3. WALKER, STELLA A. Letter in *Sunday Times*, 6th December, 1959.
4. KEIR, D. and MORGAN, B. 'The Golden Milestone', Automobile Association, London, 1955.
5. EAST, W. G. 'Historical Geography of Europe', 4th Edition, Methuen, 1966.
6. WATSON, J. W. 'North America—its Countries and Regions', 2nd Edition, Longmans, 1968.
7. PATERSON, J. N. 'North American Regional Geography', Oxford University Press, 1960.
8. HEYWORTH, SIR GEOFFREY, Chairman, Unilever Ltd, Annual General Meeting, 26th May, 1955.
9. 'Parking—an Insight Investigation', *Sunday Times*, 5th April, 1970.

Chapter 2

Parking Surveys and Assessment of Demand

Most cities have a parking problem, and before any recommendations can be made for its solution it is necessary to have all the basic information that affects parking in the area under consideration. This can be done by making a series of surveys.

PARKING HABITS SURVEY

The object of this survey is to ascertain the use that is being made of space for street parking. It should give information on the vehicles that are legally parked and those that are causing some obstruction, those parked in the wrong place, and overstaying the time limit, and also the type of vehicle, *e.g.* private car, heavy lorry, etc. An example of the field sheet is shown in Fig. 2.1. On the top of the sheet information is written indicating the type and numbers of the property fronting on one side of the street. Underneath, any restrictions operating in any part of the street can be marked by cross hatching and writing, *e.g.* 'bus stop', 'no waiting', 'street junction'. The vertical columns cover a space on the kerbside about 5·48 m (18 ft) long, and the horizontal lines divide the time into half-hour units or other time interval that may be selected. Each small square is further divided into two where the car registration number is written, and underneath a letter or number indicating the type of vehicle. Illegal or dangerous parking, or overstaying permitted waiting periods, should be given a distinctive mark such as an × or a ring ○, preferably with a coloured pencil. The observer should go round his area on foot and complete a tour in less than half an hour if this is the unit of time taken between surveys. The information revealed by this survey should give a good indication of the existing conditions— the extent to which regulations are being ignored, areas of dangerous parking and the length of time cars are parked.

PARKING INVENTORY

This is a survey of existing facilities and a 1/1250 ordance map is suitable for recording the information. The survey should be made on foot; lengths of

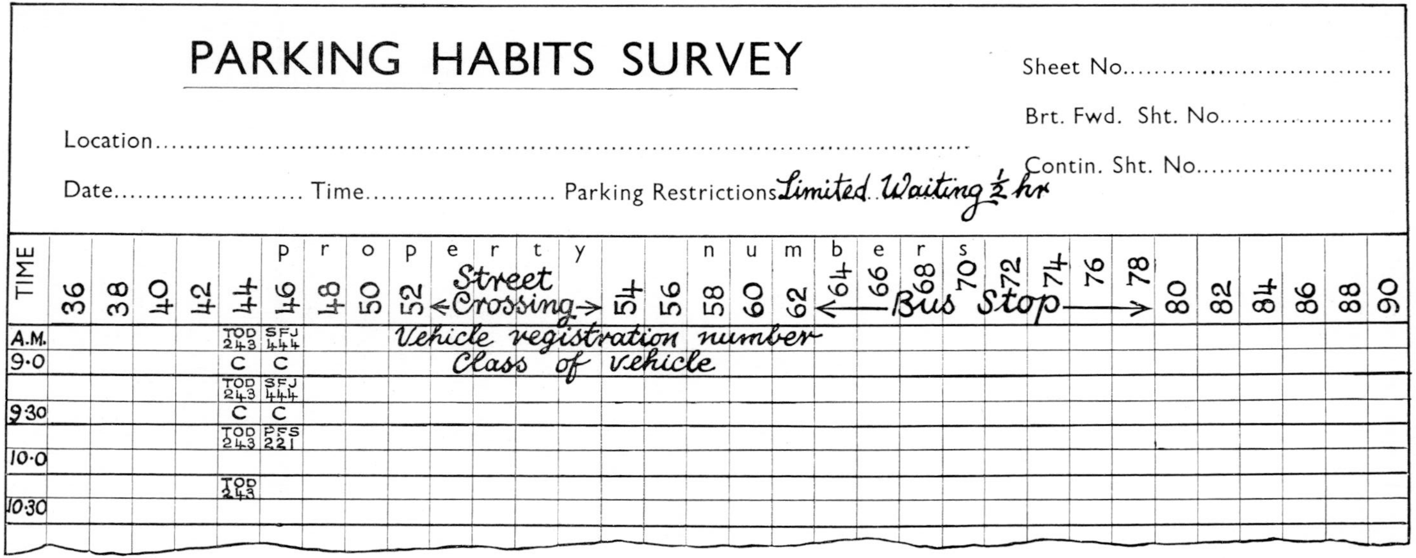

PARKING HABITS SURVEY

Location...

Date................. Time................. Parking Restrictions *Limited Waiting ½ hr*

Sheet No................

Brt. Fwd. Sht. No................

Contin. Sht. No................

TIME	36	38	40	42	44	46	48	50	52	54	56	58	60	62	64	66	68	70	72	74	76	78	80	82	84	86	88	90
A.M. 9·0					TOD 243 SFJ 444																							
					C C																							
9·30					TOD 243 SFJ 444																							
					C C																							
10·0					TOD 243 PFS 221																							
10·30					TOD 243																							

p r o p e r t y *Street Crossing→* *←* *n u m b e r s* *Bus stop →*

Vehicle registration number
Class of vehicle

Fig. 2.1 Parking habits survey form. *Note*—Illegal or dangerous parking, or overstaying permitted waiting periods, should be given a distinctive mark such as a × or a ring ○, preferably in a coloured pencil.

kerb could be measured or paced where space is available for parking or for limited waiting, loading and unloading or no waiting. Details should be obtained of private parks at the rear of buildings, or in basements, courtyards and alleys, garages, multi-storey car parks, and all other types of parking space either in buildings, on or below the ground, whether permanent or temporary. All this information when collected should be recorded on a map, using symbols and colours to indicate different classes of information. It may be considered preferable to use two maps for clarity; one for street parking and one for off-street parking.

PARKING CONCENTRATION

Information on the concentration of parking may be required at any particular time of the day, or the time when it is likely to be at or near a maximum. The procedure to follow is to take a map of the area, about 1/1250 scale, and mark out a route to be followed for the street survey. A driver and an observer in a car can drive around slowly recording the number of cars parked on the roads in figures on the map. Cars parked in public car parks can be counted by the attendant or other observers at the same time, and the cars in side streets, alleys, vacant building sites and private garages can be counted by observers on foot. The information can be presented on a map, using colour and symbols, or in tabular form.

PARKING DURATION

It is important when planning a parking scheme to know the length of time that vehicles are parked so that plans can be made for long and short term parking. This survey is usually made by the observer on foot, because it is necessary to record car registration numbers, which takes more time than a simple count. A time interval is selected which may be a quarter of an hour, half an hour, one hour or any other period, but half an hour has been found by experience to be very suitable for reliable results. The observer goes round the area allotted to him at the selected time intervals and makes a record of the car registration numbers. When the records are analysed at the end of the survey the length of time the cars have been parked in any particular place can be found.

There is bound to be some degree of error in this survey. Some cars will arrive after a count has been taken, park for a short period, and move away before the next count is taken. Other cars may be parked just after a count has been taken, and move away just before another count, *e.g.* a car seen on three successive counts at half hourly intervals will be assumed to have been parked for $1\frac{1}{2}$ hours. It may have been parked for a period varying from 1 to 2 hours.

In order to allow for those vehicles missed on patrols, the City Engineer's Department, Birmingham, have used a correction factor ranging from 0·8 to 1·3, depending on the type of frontage concerned, which is applied to the number of vehicles counted once. The results are transferred from the analysis sheet to the summary sheet which gives the number of vehicles parked and the duration.

PARKING BY CUSTOMERS AND EMPLOYEES

This survey is to ascertain the parking habits of both customers and employees. It should reveal with other information whether the kerbside is being used for long term parking, and the distance travelled from car parks to the store or other business premises. Whilst making the survey the opportunity may be taken to find out the place of residence of the customers, which will give an indication of the catchment area served by the retail store. The survey should be made on normal weekdays and may extend over several weeks. The information should be collected at the store doors, including staff doors. One observer should be on the inside of the door interviewing people going out, and one on the outside of the door interviewing those going in.

The information required from each person is (*a*) their activity, *i.e.* merchant, employee, salesman or customer; (*b*) means of transport; (*c*) if by car, where it has been parked and, if possible, the approximate length of time it will be parked; and (*d*) place of origin of their journey.

ESTIMATING UNRESTRICTED PARKING DEMAND

Future parking demand is very difficult to assess accurately, because it depends on many variable factors, such as increase in car ownership, increase in population, development in business areas, and the extension of the shopping catchment area due to increased mobility of population. Where a land use/transport survey is to be carried out it is advisable to collect information on parking from the cordon surveys and the home interviews, in addition to the counts of parked vehicles in the central business areas. From the cordon and home interview surveys a check can be made on actual usage against the shown demand, and by means of using appropriate growth factors future demand can be assessed. When it is not possible to make a land use/transport survey, estimates have to be made of future extensions and development in the area, and the additional parking facilities required. One method is to ascertain the number of persons working in the central area, and the number of shoppers and visitors likely to be in the area during working hours plus the number of residents. This is a long and involved task. The total number of cars parked in the area will be known from the parking surveys, and these figures can then be related to the number of people in the area. The future demand can be estimated by allowing a growth factor for the increased number of vehicles registered, plus an allowance for either increase or decrease in population.

Another method is to take the gross floor space of different building uses in the whole of the central business area, and relate it to the number of cars parked. The future floor space area can be estimated together with a growth factor for vehicles. From these figures the parking demand can be estimated.

A third method is to take the parking situation as a basis, and estimate the future demand by applying an average growth factor for the whole area.

A further simple method spread over a period of years is to plot a graph showing the number of vehicles registered nationally and locally, and the number parked in a given area at peak periods. The latter may be divided into short term and long term parking. In a few years these graphs will show the relationship of the rate of increase both in parking usage, and in car registrations. The parking demand can then be estimated for any future date.

The above methods of predicting parking demand are approximations only; therefore, it is advisable to use two or three methods, and compare the results before deciding which figures to take.

In the United Kingdom the accepted forecast for traffic growth is based on traffic figures for 1963 when there were 10·5 million vehicles registered, and it is estimated that there will be 18 million vehicles (including 12 million cars) by 1970, 27 million vehicles (including 19 million cars) by 1980, and perhaps 40 million vehicles (including 30 million cars) by 2010. By this date it is estimated that the population will have reached 74 million, and that the ratio of the number of vehicles to the population will have stabilised at 1·8 persons per vehicle. By 1969 it now appears that the assessment of 12 million cars by 1970 will prove to be correct, although the estimated total of 18 million vehicles is likely to be rather high.

The total demand for parking in the central business area of many cities is likely to be greater than it is possible to satisfy, and a policy decision will have to be made as to what type of transport should be discouraged from using the central area. Transport may be grouped into two main groups: (*a*) operational, and (*b*) non-operational. In the former group are commercial and other vehicles used for supplying goods and are essential for the day to day working of a business. The second group may be sub-divided into two classes: (i) long term parking, and (ii) short term parking. The former will consist mostly of employees in the central area, and the latter shoppers, business callers, sightseers, and visitors with other requirements. Cars used by employees are the ones usually regarded as the least essential, because public transport is usually available as an alternative means of transport.

The amount of car parking that can be permitted in the central business area must also be related to the traffic capacity of the road system and the amount of traffic flowing at peak periods.

BUILDING REDEVELOPMENT

In the redevelopment of the congested central business areas of cities, the height and size of new buildings seem to be greater each year. Small, old buildings of two or three storeys high, formerly used for shops and residential purposes, are being demolished, and in their place large stores, office blocks, or flats are being erected. The day-time population housed on the site may be increased by 200–300 per cent or more and, in addition, the business conducted in the new buildings may attract a further increased number of visitors during the day-time. A portion of the visitors, and staff employed in the buildings, will have their own cars, which will be an added load to the roads already heavily loaded with traffic. The position may be further aggravated by cars being parked for long periods by the kerbside, thereby reducing the effective width of the carriageway for moving traffic.

The purpose for which the building is used is important. For instance, a block of flats will not generate as much traffic as a departmental store, or the administrative headquarters of a large trading organisation.

On the other hand in a new development there may be, and certainly should be, some special provision made for loading and unloading vehicles and parking cars off the highway. The problem is to find out the parking requirements that will be created by the users of a new building, and the amount of space that should be allocated for parking purposes. It may be found to be more economical to use cheaper 'back land' for a public car park rather than allocate a portion of an expensive site which could be used to better advantage for the main business purposes.

FLOOR SPACE INDEX

In central urban areas which are likely to be redeveloped, the 'floor space index' may be used as a guide in assessing the change in parking demands. A floor space index is the ratio between the total area of the floors contained within a

CALCULATION FOR FLOOR SPACE
INDICES

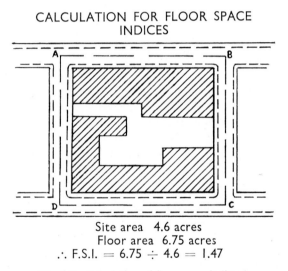

Site area 4.6 acres
Floor area 6.75 acres
∴ F.S.I. = 6.75 ÷ 4.6 = 1.47

Fig. 2.2   Calculation of floor space indices.

building (or buildings), and the area of the plot on which it stands. The floor space index for any building or buildings is obtained by dividing the total area of all the floors within the buildings by the area of the land plus half the width of the adjoining streets. The floor area should include all wall thicknesses, corridors, staircases and basements. When calculating the index for a street block of property, internal access roads, pedestrian ways, and small planted areas, mainly used by the occupiers of the block, should be included in the gross area of the street block. Figure 2.2 shows an example where the site area is that contained within ABCD, and the small open spaces are included in the site area.

Where a street block is only partially built-up, and the remainder used as a permanent public open space, the built-up area only is included in the site area, and the remainder is measured separately and included with other open spaces. The floor space index is not a guide to the number of storeys in a building. A site may have buildings on all the street frontages five storeys high with a central loading and parking space, and a floor space index of 2, whereas the same site may have buildings of eight or ten storeys high and still a floor space index of 2. It is a simple means of determining, comparing and controlling the building density to be provided on any area of land down to a single plot. Therefore, if an area is being redeveloped, and the use is not changed, the floor space index of the old development, and the proposed development, will give some indication of the change that may be expected in the car parking requirements when the development has been carried out. A change of use is an added complication and should be taken into consideration.

SHOPPING CENTRES

In the United States of America and Canada since World War II, and to a lesser extent in England, the increase in traffic congestion and the difficulties of providing adequate parking facilities have led the proprietors of large or multiple trading establishments to consider building shopping centres in the suburbs of large cities rather than near the city centre. These shopping centres fall into two groups: (a) regional centres, and (b) suburban centres. They both follow the same general pattern. The regional centres are usually situated near an express highway and draw on a catchment area over a radius of 30 minutes' driving time. The population that a regional centre will serve is governed by travelling facilities, the size of income and purchasing power available and may vary from 750,000 to 1,500,000. The smaller centres may cover 8–16 hectares (20–40 acres) and serve the suburban area of a large city. If a suitable site is selected it may be possible to provide all the necessary space required for car parking, but the question that immediately arises is, how much car parking space is required now and in the future?

This has to be assessed for each store individually. One store may be dealing in low-priced goods and have a large number of individual sales per day. In this case a large amount of parking space will be required. Another store may have an equal annual turnover, but dealing in expensive goods with a smaller number of customers, and a less demand for parking space. In practice there is usually a variety of stores in a shopping centre, and the high demands of one store may be offset by the smaller demands of another. If in a mixed shopping centre 74,320 m^2 (800,000 sq ft) of floor area was devoted to the store, then according to USA standards the car parking space required will be $3{\cdot}0 \times 74,320$ m^2 (800,000 sq ft) = 222,960 m^2 (2,400,000 sq ft), including roadways, or sufficient space to park 10,000 cars. It should not be assumed that all customers to regional and suburban stores travel by private car. It is estimated that 50 per cent only use private cars, and as a shopping centre becomes established public transport services become more frequent and more passengers use omnibuses.

There is no simple method of ascertaining the parking demand for a shopping centre. A careful scientific study is required which takes into account topography, population density of the catchment area, public transport services, road access from catchment area, travelling time and the type and class of stores in the shopping centre.

There are peak periods for shopping business—there is the weekly peak, often on market day or Friday and Saturday, and there is also a seasonal peak which may be during the weeks before Christmas.

If parking spaces are provided for the peak volume of cars, on most days of the year there will be ample vacant spaces. The partially filled car park may be a joy to the would-be parker, but it does give an air of quiet and slack business, which any trader will deprecate. It is better to strike a balance and provide for a good average demand.

The cost of providing parking space to the extent required for shopping centres can be expensive, and if the area is reduced by erecting multi-storey car parks the cost is increased.

CAR PARKING IN OFFICE AREAS

The activities carried on by people in the centre of a city are so intermingled that it is impossible to completely unravel and isolate any one of them from the remainder.

The structure of a city is constantly changing, and it is necessary to have an approximate idea of the effect that the changes will have on, amongst other things, traffic flow and car parking. Some offices will have few visitors and will require all-day parking for a portion of the staff, others will have a large number of visitors requiring short term parking, and there are members of office staffs who use cars for several short visits during working hours.

It is not difficult to make a simple survey of the car parking requirements by firms in a block of offices. This could extend over a few weeks and give information on the number of spaces required for all-day parking, number for short term parking and the distribution over the working day; also the requirements of those members of the staff who must have a car available at any time of the day and know that there is a parking place available when they return.

There is still the problem of estimating the requirements for the future. There are the statistics quoted in Chapter 1 for the future increase in car registrations which may be used as a guide, but there is also an unknown factor. Owing to traffic congestion and parking difficulties, some motorists will avoid taking their cars into the congested business centre of a city, either voluntarily or to comply with the city's general parking plans. If this occurs, then parking in the office area may not increase as fast as the number of cars registered each year.

It is desirable that office blocks should, as far as possible, make provision within the site for operational requirements. In densely built-up areas of old city centres this is not always possible, but if the facility of having a parking space available at any time is required, it must be provided by the firm or private arrangements made with a garage or privately controlled car park.

CAR PARKS AS TRAFFIC GENERATORS

From the motorist's point of view the ideal position for a car park is in front of his or her office or other building that has to be visited. This is now becoming a rare privilege. The siting of business premises and the floor space requirements are usually given careful and detailed consideration, and much research work is undertaken before a final decision is reached. When selecting a site for an omnibus station much consideration is given to the traffic routes, so that 'dead' mileage and delays in heavily trafficked streets are reduced to a minimum. Convenience of pedestrians in relation to shops, offices and business premises is considered. This kind of detailed consideration and planning is required for the siting of a car park.

In determining the location of a car park of whatever type it may be, the size and possible capacity is only one consideration. A survey carried out on several occasions in Exeter showed that of the cars parked in the centre of the city immediately before 5.0 pm, 66 per cent moved to join the traffic routes between 5.0 pm and 6.0 pm, and 46·2 per cent moved between 5.15 pm and 5.45 pm. These figures indicate that in Exeter a car park should be capable of discharging 50 per cent of its load within half an hour, and that the roads adjoining the car park should be capable of absorbing this amount of traffic at peak periods without any difficulty. It should not be difficult to make arrangements inside a car park to discharge vehicles at this rate, but the success of the arrangements outside will depend on the position of the car park in relation to the busy traffic routes. The most desirable position for a car park from the traffic point of view is near the city terminus of the radial roads leading into the city centre. Motorists should be encouraged to use these car parks in preference to traversing busy shopping streets, either when entering or leaving the city. This should help to ease the load on the city centre roads, and help the discharge of cars from the car parks at peak periods.

The size of the car park is also an important factor in relation to the discharge and flow of traffic. Whilst a small park would have little effect, the influence of a large one on traffic flow at peak periods could be disastrous. It is not just the volume of traffic from the car park that should be considered; the arrangement of the entrance and exit should provide for a free flow of traffic from and to the car parks without crossing other traffic streams on the adjoining roads.

PARKING SATURATION IN CENTRAL BUSINESS AREAS

The problem that has to be solved is how to adapt the central area of a city, built in another age, to satisfy future conditions when the motor car will be used much more than at the present time. Cities are in a continuous state of change and renewal, but the process is slow compared with the rapid increase in the use of the motor vehicle. Even if the capital were available it is not possible to rebuild our city centres to cope with the demands of the motorists. There is also much that is of great value in some of our old cities that we have been privileged to inherit, and should preserve, even at the expense of some inconvenience to the motorist.

Whilst the increasing requirements of the people with activities in different classes of building have to be considered, there is also a limit to the number of cars that should be parked in the central area of a city, if serious congestion is to be avoided. The demand is for more and more parking places. In an attempt to meet the demand all available sites are taken for car parking, and the number of parking spaces on some of the sites is increased by building multi-storey or underground car parks. The roads and streets are also lined with cars.

Whilst there is a general increase in traffic flow, the traffic arteries are gradually being reduced in effective width because the kerbs are lined with parked vehicles. At the same time a reservoir of cars is being stored up in the car parks to be released when the traffic flow is at its peak and the roads are overloaded with vehicles and pedestrians. The result is chaos and stagnation. This leads to accidents, loss of time, money, business and ultimately decay in the city centre. Each city must find the parking saturation figure in relation to the traffic capacity of the roads.

If all kerbside parking on traffic routes through the city were forbidden, and all loading and unloading of goods confined to off-peak periods, the traffic capacity of the roads would be greatly increased if there were no restrictions on waiting vehicles. This should make more traffic accommodation on the roads available for cars leaving car parks, and permit an increased amount of off-street parking to be provided without causing traffic congestion. In other words, the parking saturation figure should be raised by banning kerbside parking. Road junctions are well known as 'bottle-necks' on traffic routes, and the traffic capacity at these points is usually well below that of the roads feeding the junction. If these junctions could be improved by constructing underpasses, or increasing the traffic capacity in other ways, then this will be reflected in an increased figure for parking saturation in the city. Again it may be necessary to construct a new urban motorway which could have the same effect as increasing the traffic capacity of roads in other ways. The parking saturation figure may or may not equal the parking demand. If it is less than the demand then some restriction or deterrent is called for to reduce the concentration of parked cars, and enable each parking space in the central area of the city to be used by several motorists each day.

The difficulty is in encouraging motorists to use car parks as intended and avoid the heavy concentration of cars at the hub of the city. If a parking space is used to park a car all day, it serves one vehicle and satisfies one motorist. If it is restricted to short period use, of say not more than two hours, it is available for at least four cars in the course of an eight-hour day. It is reasonable and in the interests of the motoring public that public parking sites within the inner shopping and business area should not be occupied by one vehicle all day. The system of imposing high parking fees for periods over two hours is perhaps the most effective, provided that free or low fee parking is available at a reasonable distance from the hub of the city.

Conditions in the United States of America give some idea of what the future demand may be when there is a 1 to 2 car/population ratio. Regional and suburban shopping centres require three times the floor area of the shop for parking, and even so it is estimated that 50 per cent of the customers travel by public transport or on foot. It should not be thought that with the increasing use of the motor car the motorist alone should receive consideration. There are still many pedestrians, and in London it is estimated that 93 per cent of the people who travel into the central area do so by public transport. If there is no restriction or limit on the parking places to be made available and if the parking demand in a city centre is to be met in the future, then it will mean that after allocating land for roads and public open spaces, one-quarter of the area of land available for building development will be for business premises and three-quarters for car parking. The actual area of land required could be reduced by building multi-storey car parks. Even this would give a city centre looking like a huge car park with isolated business premises towering above the sea of parked cars. This is a theoretical view of the future assuming that all motorists wishing to park their car in the city centre would find suitable accommodation available. Nevertheless there will be the demand. Imagine London if instead of the 1970 conditions when 93 per cent of the people travelling into the central area daily do so by public transport, only 50 per cent used public transport and the remaining 50 per cent came by private cars. The demand for parking space would increase by six or seven times and the conditions would not be far removed from the theoretical city centre of a sea of cars. A business centre under these conditions would be quite intolerable for the pedestrian.

If the car parking demand continues to increase, as it will, and attempts to satisfy the demand are isolated, haphazard, unplanned and not co-ordinated, the result will be disastrous. The motorist will attempt to find his or her own solution by supporting regional and suburban shopping centres, leaving the city centre to decline. If this is to be avoided, and every local authority will wish to have a prosperous town or city centre, then some overall parking plan to direct and control the parking must be prepared and followed.

The surveys are necessary to give detailed information of the existing conditions in the area studied. They will reveal the space available, the extent to which it is used, whether there is a surplus or deficiency of parking accommodation, whether further restrictions are necessary for street parking, number of long term and short term parkers and their distribution.

This information will assist in formulating a plan for an orderly system of parking at the present time. Motorists can be prevented from leaving their cars in dangerous places—steps can be taken to prevent long term parking and encourage short term parking in certain areas. Generally, parking demand in central business areas has followed fairly closely the increase in the number of motor vehicles licensed, and future plans should allow for this overall rate of increase, but it is the detailed distribution of the car parks for long term and short term parking that must be studied. Redevelopment must be watched carefully, and change of use or trade in buildings must be under constant observation. The relationship between car parks and traffic routes and the time taken for a motorist leaving a car park to join a traffic route must be carefully watched.

Finally, the demand for car parking in the central business district should be controlled in such a way that it will not be permitted to exceed the supply.

REFERENCES

1. CHARLESWORTH, G. and GREEN, H. 'Parking Surveys', *Roads and Road Construction*, May, 1953.
2. 'Manual of Traffic Engineering Studies'. The Accident Prevention Department of the Association of Casualty and Surety Companies, New York, 1953.
3. CHAMBERLAIN, S. J. 'Tall Buildings—the Traffic and Parking Problems', *Proc. Institution of Civil Engineers*, August 1955 (No. 2), Vol. 4, Part III.
4. DANT, NOEL, 'The British Floor Space Index Use in Calculating Parking Demand', *Traffic Quarterly*, USA.
5. ARMSTRONG, W. H. 'The Effect of Off Street Parking Garage as a Traffic Generator', *Traffic Engineering*, USA, Jan. 1950, Vol. 20, No. 4.
6. BECKET, W. 'Shopping Center Traffic Problems', *Traffic Quarterly*, USA.
7. INWOOD, J. 'Parking', Research Note No. RN/3398/JI February, 1959, Road Research Laboratory, England.
8. ROTH, G. J. 'Parking Space for Cars—Assessing the Demand', Cambridge University Press, London, 1965.

Chapter 3

Parking in Relation to Town Planning

The Buchanan Report,[1] Traffic in Towns, published in 1963, was an excellent study in depth of the problems which have to be tackled in replanning our towns for the safe movement of people and vehicles. It drew attention to the impact of a great and rapid increase in the growth of traffic in towns over the next 40 years, and to the ways and means of reconciling two conflicting objectives—the efficient movement of traffic, and good urban living conditions.

From time to time there are suggestions that the motor vehicle will be superseded by some new form of transport. We have only to contemplate the wide variety of uses that have been found for the motor vehicle to appreciate how difficult it will be to replace. Consider the private car, which is available for door to door transport in all weather conditions; the passengers may be dressed for any occasion and travel in comfort. Similarly, door to door transport is available for commercial vehicles with a minimum amount of loading and unloading. In addition we have speed, costs compare favourably with other forms of transport, and for many journeys there is more comfort and greater convenience.

At the present time (1971) there does not appear to be a practical alternative to the motor vehicle. There will no doubt be many variations of the present designs, and maybe a change of fuel or the source of power; there may be developments in the use of travelators, escalators, pipes and ducts which could relieve motor vehicles of some of their functions, but the combined effect of these developments is likely to be small in proportion to the whole problem. There is the possible development and extension of air travel, but there does not appear to be any practicable proposal for people taking to the air *en masse* in their own private planes.

The motor vehicle appears to have thoroughly established itself, and is likely to be with us for very many years. Therefore, we must plan for the motor vehicle to be used in our cities, our towns, our villages and in the countryside. It is fundamental to our planning that we accept the motor vehicle as a beneficial invention with an assured future.

There are two aspects of the traffic problem—accessibility and environment. By accessibility is meant the general freedom of vehicles to penetrate to destinations and stop on arrival. Environment means the maintenance of acceptable conditions in relation to the adverse effects of motor traffic; this is to say, in relation to danger, anxiety, intimidation, noise, fumes, vibration and visual intrusion. Inefficiency in circulation is costing the country considerable sums of money, and environment is being affected in a way which is rapidly building up a major social problem.

The cause of these conflicting problems is in the physical form of towns, that is, the way buildings and streets are put together, and therefore the conventional layout of streets should give way to new designs for buildings and streets. If an urban area is to handle large amounts of motor traffic successfully, it must consist basically of areas where consideration of environment predominates, and these areas must be served by a network of roads to effect the primary distribution of traffic from area to area. This is called the primary network of roads, and its pattern and dimension can be worked out reasonably accurately.

In the United Kingdom the Town and Country Planning Act 1968[2] states that the local planning authority shall prepare a structure plan for their area. Section 2(3) states: 'The structure plan for any area shall be a written statement:

(a) formulating the local planning authority's policy, and general proposals in respect of the development and other use of land in that area (including measures for the improvement of the physical environment and the management of traffic);

(b) stating the relationship of those proposals to general proposals for the development and other use of land in neighbouring areas which may be expected to affect that area; and

(c) containing such other matters as may be prescribed or as the Minister may in any particular case direct.'

The structure plan will provide for the full integration of land use and transport planning and the movement between the different land uses. It will therefore be concerned with the principles that will be applied to the management and control of road traffic, for maintaining a balance between public and private transport and provision for and control of stationary vehicles.

Local plans are needed to apply the strategy of the structure plan in detail, and Section 6(3) of the Act states that a local plan shall consist of a map and a written statement and shall formulate proposals including such measures as the authority think fit for the improvement of the physical environment and the management of traffic. Local authorities have also been asked by the Minister of Transport (now Secretary of State for the Environment) to prepare traffic and transport plans showing how they intend to relate their traffic and parking policies to their available road capacities and to their immediate and longer term policy objectives. Along with other matters detailed in 'Traffic and Transport Plans'[3] the plan should be accompanied by a statement of the action to be taken to put the policy decisions into effect. This should include, for example:

(a) The creation of controlled parking zones.

(b) Provision for parking, on and off street.

(c) Clearway programmes for radial routes.

(*d*) A programme of junction improvements.

(*e*) Specific measures to improve road safety, to aid public transport, and to preserve or improve the environment.

THE LAND USE/TRANSPORT SURVEY[4]

Traffic and transport studies are an essential part of the physical planning process. It is these studies that provide the essential factual basis for the development and evaluation of plans, whether they are town or regional. Transport studies may be based on the simple origin and destination surveys, but the broad and integrated approach to land use and transport planning now requires a much more detailed and comprehensive study which is provided by the land use/transport survey. This was developed originally in the United States of America in the late 1950s.

The procedure for a land use/transport survey is first to define the study area, and plot the cordon and screen lines. The area is then divided into zones and separated into internal zones and external zones. Each zone has a reference number for coding, as names of locations could not be used with a computer. The surveys usually include home interview surveys, commercial vehicle surveys, taxi surveys, parking surveys, roadside interviews, public transport data and registration number surveys. Then comes the survey analysis—coding, editing, expansion, accuracy checking, and analysis programmes. This is followed by trip forecasting, trip generation, trip distribution growth by using growth factors, inter-area travel, modal split and assignments. These surveys take full account of future land use proposals, and trends in population and employment growth. It is then possible to assess future demands for urban transport, and its distribution between public and private transport and, where necessary, between road and rail. From all this detailed information a new road network is evolved, and it will indicate whether it is economic and practicable to provide for the full and free use of motor vehicles in the central area of a city, or whether the detrimental effect on the environment would be too serious, and restraint on the use of the motor vehicle has to be introduced.

THE ROAD NETWORK

The road network is the skeleton of any town plan. The principles set out by Sir Colin Buchanan in 'Traffic in Towns' have been accepted by the British Government as a basis for future planning. The basic proposition, which is not new and has been used in planning new towns, suggests that an urban area be divided into a series of sub-areas, each comprising a block of development served by an interlacing network of roads for the primary distribution of traffic. The network is to have strictly limited access and dedicated to movement of traffic. The sub-areas are to be dedicated to development and environment, as it is in these areas where people live and work, and are now referred to as environmental areas.

The size of an environmental area is governed by the need to prevent its own traffic building up to a volume that would in effect necessitate sub-division by the insertion of a further distributor. A road network exists to serve the environmental areas, and its capacity must be related to the areas. It would be unwise, for instance, to redevelop a central environmental area with office blocks including huge car parks if the road network could not deal with the resulting traffic.

A primary distributor road network consists of roads for motor traffic only, with no frontage access, and with limited connections with other roads. It involves concentrating the longer movements of vehicles on to a comparatively limited number of roads.

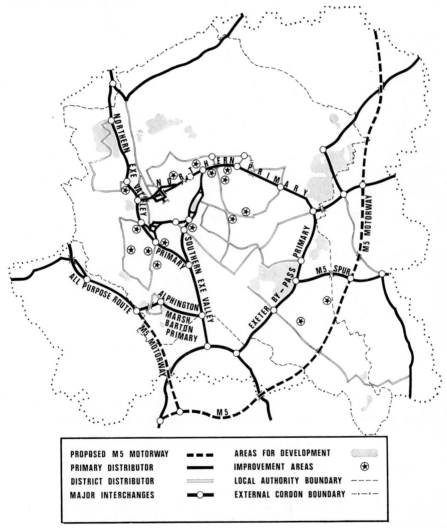

Fig. 3.1 The primary distributor road network for the City of Exeter based on a land use/ transport survey.

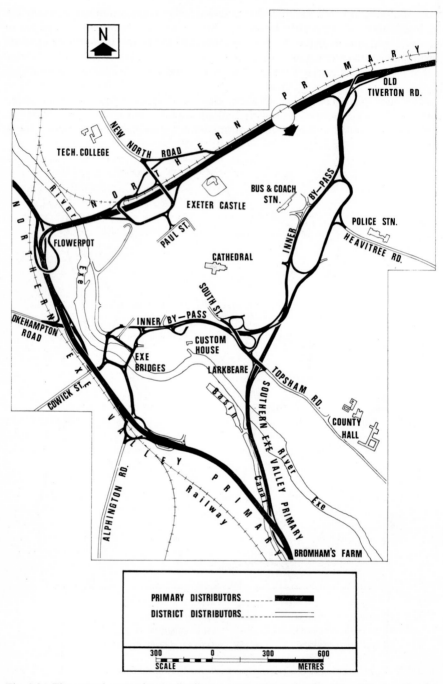

Fig. 3.2 The central area primary distributor road network for the City of Exeter, showing
connections with district distributor roads.

In closely developed areas there are likely to be definite limits to the amount of traffic that can be accommodated. These limits are likely to be below and in some cases well below the full potential demands for vehicle usage in the future. This is where a policy of restraint has to be exercised.

An example of a primary distributor road network which has been planned for the old Cathedral City of Exeter, and based on a land use/transport survey is shown in Fig. 3.1. Traffic on the north east; east; south; and south west is very heavy, as this is in the direction of London and the industrial areas of Bristol and the Midlands. To the north and north west, traffic is comparatively light. The city has also developed extensively on the north east and easterly sides, leaving the central business area on the westerly side of the city. Because of these factors and the area being very undulating and in places hilly, the primary distributor road network follows an unusual and irregular pattern. The connections to the M5 on the national motorway network are also shown. Figure 3.2 shows the central area primary distributor road system and the connections with the district distributor roads which for the most part are existing roads.[5]

THE SITING OF CAR PARKS

The siting of car parks is an essential part of town planning, and this cannot be done efficiently and effectively until a comprehensive parking policy has been defined. Therefore it is necessary to adopt a parking policy before completing a town plan.[6]

The land use/transport survey and the more detailed parking surveys will indicate the distribution of the demand for parking and the amount of very short term, short term and long term parking required. It will be possible to make an assessment of the future demand from the land use/transport studies. Parking accommodation will be related to peak hour traffic volumes and the traffic capacity of the roads. It may be that the traffic capacity of the feeder roads will be sufficient to accommodate peak hour traffic volume without exercising any restraint on the flow of traffic. On the other hand it may be that it will not be possible to satisfy the demand without building roads that would destroy the character of the environment, and restraint on traffic using the central environment area becomes necessary. When a policy of restraint has to be exercised, the first consideration is to determine which traffic is essential for the functions of the area. This is usually industrial, business and shopping traffic; whilst optional traffic consists mainly of the use of cars for personal movement and particularly the journey to work.

In smaller towns it is possible that full motorisation may be provided, but this presents a serious problem for public transport, and it is not possible to see how public transport can be an economic proposition if in the future there is complete freedom to use private cars in the smaller towns.

In exercising a policy of restraint the first step to take is control of car parking by segregating the short term from long term users, in other words shoppers and business callers from the commuters. To carry this out successfully it is essential for the public authority to retain control of the amount, location and policy of car parking in the city and use the price mechanism to restrict central area parking to short periods. Parking policy is considered in more detail in Chapter 19.

When the ultimate amount of car parking accommodation that can be provided has been determined, the zones for very short term, short term and long term parking should be defined. The ideal is for car parks to be sited near the inner ring or primary distributor roads connected by a district distributor road which would give easy access to the car park and a quick route to the primary road network from the car park. The ideal size for a car park is about 500–700 car capacity and if distributed round the central business area in proportion to the demand the walking distance should not be unreasonable. In practice, however, this is not always possible. Sites may not be available where required, and other less desirable sites may have to be used. In central business areas land values are usually very high, and in order that a car park may be a viable proposition it is often necessary for it to be linked with some other use in the same building, e.g. ground floor for shops, and upper floor and roof for parking. This of course determines the siting of the car park. Every car park siting problem is different, therefore the basic principles should be kept in mind, and the problem solved as near to the ideal as possible. There should, however, be no compromise on the facilities for easy and quick ingress and egress to and from the car park.

PARKING STANDARDS FOR NEW DEVELOPMENT

When new development is proposed it has been common practice in the United Kingdom and other countries for local planning authorities to insist that car parking accommodation be provided up to certain standards based on the use of a building. This means that ultimately there would be a large amount of private parking space provided, and the local authority would have no control over its use and operation. On trading estates in commercial areas, residential districts and rural areas there is much merit in this policy, but in central environmental areas the position is different. In future it is expected that most large towns and cities will have to adopt some policy for the restraint of traffic in the central areas. This means that there will be a tight schedule between parking accommodation and traffic capacity of feeder roads at peak periods. For this to operate successfully the local authority must have control of the car parks in the central area either directly or through an agent. Parking control cannot operate successfully if there are numerous privately owned car parks over which the local authority has no control. In central areas land is usually expensive and in short supply. If private car parks are attached to a building they have a limited use during normal working hours and are not available in the evenings and at weekends. Car parks in a central area should not be limited in use—they should be available to the public at all times when there is the demand. The changed policy which planning authorities are beginning to adopt, is to allow within the curtilage of the development, provision for parking a limited number of cars required for the proper and efficient conduct of the business. Allowance is made for this provision when assessing the number of parking spaces to be provided by the local authority in public car parks.

DECENTRALISATION

The movement of people and goods to and from buildings is a source of traffic generation. If the traffic so generated is too much for the environment to absorb it can be reduced or removed by resiting the traffic generators. This means siting new, or resiting old, industries, offices, shops, warehouses and other buildings that might contribute to the build-up of peak traffic volumes. Resiting should mean that the traffic will be able to move quickly to the primary distributor road network or the private car quickly dispersed among the local road network. From the car parking point of view this means taking away the need to park a vehicle in the central area and therefore reduce the demand.

Where redevelopment is taking place on a comprehensive scale, decisions about decentralisation or concentration can be taken without affecting in any way the overall cost of the development proposals, unless it resulted in vacant sites being left in important areas. Where uses are not likely to be disturbed for any reason other than their traffic generating capacities, the cost of removal would be prohibitive.

When preparing a plan for a city centre, consideration should be given to the decentralisation of industry. This may then leave more land for the expansion of the shopping area to develop as a specialised centre; other shopping being decentralised to the major district centres, and day to day shopping to neighbourhood centres.

Reduction of traffic and parking in a central area by means of a decentralisation policy is a long term policy even when there is large scale redevelopment contemplated. This does not mean that a policy of decentralisation should not be pursued. On the contrary, city centres have to be redeveloped, and this should be on sound and attractive principles. Traffic and parking problems have been developed by small contributions from numerous sources and the solution will need a similar variety of contributions and help.

ENVIRONMENT

We are all becoming conscious of the detrimental effects that carelessness, and the misuse of some of our technological developments are having on the environment. The motorist is not free from guilt. The detrimental effects that parking the motor vehicle may have on the environment are discussed in some detail in other chapters and it is a subject about which we should be fully conscious. We should seize every opportunity to reduce if not remove any detrimental effects that the parked vehicle may have on our environment.

REFERENCES

1. 'Traffic in Towns', HMSO, London, 1963.
2. Town & Country Planning Act, 1968. HMSO 1968.
3. 'Traffic and Transport Plans', Roads Circular No. 1/68, HMSO 1968.

4. DAVIES, E. (Editor) 'Traffic Engineering Practice', E. & F. N. Spon Ltd, London, 1968.
5. BRIERLEY, J. 'Transportation Problems in West Country Towns—The County Town Problem', Annual Conference Report, 1970, The Institution of Municipal Engineers.
6. 'Parking in Town Centres', Planning Bulletin No. 7. HMSO, London, 1965.

Chapter 4

Street Parking

In the United Kingdom, the Report of the Departmental Committee on Traffic Signs, 1933,[1] states that the Committee 'carefully considered whether or not they should recommend a sign for the purpose of indicating that parking on the highway is prohibited. They came to the conclusion that it should be assumed that parking is prohibited in the absence of a sign to the contrary, and that consequently it would be undesirable for such a sign to be authorised'.

Nevertheless, the parking of vehicles on city streets, especially traffic routes, has become a major problem in most cities. The practice has developed from a small beginning when there were few motor cars on roads which had sufficient traffic capacity to permit some street parking without causing inconvenience to other road users. This was a great privilege for the motorist who was able to travel by car from door to door. Shops and other business premises have relied on goods vehicles being permitted to wait in front of the premises, and along the kerbside whilst goods have been loaded and unloaded. As traffic volumes have increased there have arisen conflicting demands on the space available on the carriageway. Traders usually support kerbside parking, the police and others interested in expediting the movement of traffic through a city are opposed to it.

Roads are built primarily for the movement of traffic, and when there are conflicting claims, priorities must be established. Without doubt, traffic flow should have the prior claim on the use of a traffic route, but waiting vehicles cannot be completely eliminated from our roads, except in exceptional circumstances. In adapting an existing city to the motor car age, many concessions, relaxations and deviations from the ideal have to be made. For instance, it is often impossible without considerable major reconstruction to make off-street accommodation for loading and unloading vehicles, and stopping places for public service vehicles.

There is, however, a great difference in the traffic capacity of a street when cars are parked indiscriminately along each kerbline, compared with the traffic capacity when waiting is restricted to vehicles giving an essential service and for which a limited amount of kerbside waiting should be permitted. It is much better to have off-street accommodation so that no 'bottlenecks' on a carriageway are created by even one waiting vehicle. On the whole, a balance has to be made between the claims of vehicles for essential waiting at the kerbside and for free movement along the carriageway. It is not possible to make a rule which will apply to all streets because the circumstances and difficulties vary.

First of all the volume of traffic may vary between different times of the day, different days of the week and even different weeks of the year. A waiting vehicle, or one being loaded or unloaded, may cause a serious hold-up at one period on a road and cause no obstruction at another time or on another road. If restrictions have to be imposed they must be related to the actual conditions on the road under consideration. The first essential requirement to reduce kerbside parking is to provide adequate off-street parking. It is difficult to reduce kerbside parking if there is no alternative means of parking within a reasonable distance.

Parking on the carriageway is an extravagant way of using valuable land. The actual value of land in the centre of cities varies considerably, but a parking place for a car could cost £750–£1500 or more. In any city, sections of road may be seen that have been widened to the widths recommended by the Ministry of Transport, now the Department of the Environment, only to find that the added width is occupied by parked cars, and as far as traffic flow is concerned the same effect could have been achieved by prohibiting vehicles from parking or waiting on one side of the road. The Ministry of Transport, now the Department of the Environment, has made its recommendations for the width of traffic lanes, but if a line of cars is permitted to park along the kerbside it makes nonsense of any recommendation for the width of traffic lanes or carriageways.

A carriageway 9 m (30 ft) wide designed to take two lanes of traffic and have an overtaking lane is reduced to 7 m (23 ft) or 7·3 m (24 ft), which is enough for two lanes of traffic, and it becomes dangerous to overtake. With parking on two sides, the width is reduced to 4·8 m (16 ft), which is dangerous for two heavy vehicles to pass at a normal speed for the road and, therefore, traffic moves at walking pace. Roads of other widths are similarly reduced in capacity with kerbside parking.

Street parking is a contributory cause of accidents (Fig. 4.1). The dangers are with pedestrians, and especially children, stepping from behind a vehicle, obstruction to the line of vision at street junctions, and drivers pulling vehicles out from a parking place into the traffic stream. Fire hazards may be created by improper parking which impedes the movement of fire-fighting apparatus and prevents access to water hydrants and buildings.

Angle parking is more convenient for the motorist than parallel parking against the kerb, but invariably it produces a higher accident rate than parallel parking. The length of kerb space required for parking a vehicle is at its maximum with parallel parking, and decreases as the parking angle increases until it reaches a minimum when the parking angle is 90° with the kerb. Right-angle parking will accommodate nearly two-and-a-half times the number of vehicles as parallel parking. As the angle increases so does the amount of space required for manoeuvring the vehicle on the carriageway.

Parallel parking usually involves a backing motion which some drivers find difficult to carry out without two or three attempts, and this is likely to hold up the flow of traffic. Angle parking is easy and simple for the driver and causes a minimum of interference with moving traffic when entering the parking space. When leaving, it is more difficult, as the driver has to back out into the traffic stream. Drivers have different habits; some back out slowly, some quickly, some a minimum distance, others allow themselves ample space. Consequently there is a variable demand on the carriageway space, and the area at the rear of angle parked vehicles is a danger zone. One other disadvantage is that the bumper may overhang the footpath, restricting the available width for pedestrians, and the sharp angles can easily be caught by articles of clothing or a leg.

Parking is sometimes permitted in the centre of extremely wide streets, and it is more common in smaller towns. Angle parking is usually adopted, and whilst it may be convenient it is not a satisfactory or safe parking place. It has the disadvantage of vehicles being backed out into traffic streams, and drivers and passengers have to cross the traffic stream when going to or leaving the parking place.

Fig. 4.1   Uncontrolled street parking.

Where there is a busy traffic route passing through a business or shopping area it is frequently desirable to introduce some means of control so as to attain an equitable balance between the needs of the moving and waiting vehicles.

Restrictions should not be imposed if they would have the effect of preventing reasonable access by vehicles to any premises situated on or adjacent to the road. In practice, orders are normally drafted to permit the picking up and setting down of passengers, and the loading and unloading of goods, and access for the maintenance of the normal services of the road. Where the demand for the loading and unloading of vehicles at the kerbside is heavy, it may be necessary to introduce a time limit of 20 or 30 minutes in order to check unnecessary obstruction. When traffic and the demand for loading and unloading are both very heavy it may be necessary to impose additional restrictions such as the prohibition or restriction of loading and unloading up to six hours in any period of twenty-four hours. The period of six hours may be divided into shorter periods to cover peak traffic flows such as the rush periods in the morning, at midday and again in the evening. It should be remembered that loading and unloading restrictions may have an effect over a very wide area, and if the restrictions are for an unnecessarily long period they could be a great time waster with a serious effect on the business. Vehicles carrying goods from a long distance, with perhaps several calling places, will require the journey to be programmed so as to lose as little time as possible by having to comply with loading and unloading restrictions. It is helpful, therefore, for the restricted period to be as short as possible. Restrictions are usually unpopular measures with local traders because of their alleged effect on retail trade, and the loading and unloading prohibitions arouse opposition because of the interference with delivery schedules. It is often helpful to have prior consultation with traders' organisations, and explain the object and the anticipated effect of the restrictions. In this way, misconception and opposition may be avoided. It is significant that where there is strong opposition initially to restrictions it appears to die away very quickly after the restrictions come into operation. Experience usually shows that the benefits outweigh the disadvantages. A congested and overloaded road with traffic frequently coming to a standstill cannot be helpful to traders.

Residents in a street in the vicinity of a cinema or public hall may be disturbed at night by noise caused by the starting up of parked cars, in what may be a perfectly safe parking place on traffic grounds. There may be cases where it is necessary to impose restrictions on amenity grounds on a residential road, but before doing so consideration should be given to:

(a) the alternative parking place, and
(b) restrictions would also apply to residents in the street.

It may prove that the loss of some amenity in a residential street is the least evil that is created in that district by the increasing use of the motor vehicle.

The time and days when waiting restrictions should be applied must be carefully studied. It may be possible to relax the restrictions on Sundays, early closing day or several hours in the middle of the day, leaving the restrictions to apply at periods of peak traffic flow in the morning and evening. Local conditions will determine the times when the restrictions should apply, but it is usual for them to apply from 8 am or 9 am to 6 pm or 7 pm. It is confusing to the motorist if the times vary in adjoining streets, and confusion should be avoided.

When considering the imposition of waiting restrictions, it is necessary to have alternative parking facilities within a reasonable distance for both long and short periods.

NO WAITING

This restriction means what it says except that 'No Waiting' orders normally provide exemption for vehicles stopping to pick up or set down passengers or loading and unloading of goods. The need for this restriction on a road is usually very apparent. When a road is carrying traffic in two directions it is essential to maintain two through traffic lanes and allow sufficient width of carriageway for loading and unloading of goods, or a vehicle stopping to pick up or set down passengers. When this is not possible except by 'double banking' and blocking one lane of traffic then some restriction to prevent waiting on one (*i.e.* unilateral waiting) or both sides of the road is clearly necessary.

Road junctions, particularly those controlled by traffic lights, control the traffic capacity of the approach roads, and it is considered necessary to impose 'no waiting' restrictions for at least 15 m (45 ft) on both sides of the road and on both the approach and leaving sides of the intersection. On busy roads it may be necessary to restrict the waiting of vehicles for 40 m (120 ft) on both sides of the road and on both the approach and leaving sides of the intersection.

Consideration should be given to imposing similar restrictions to side roads where they join the main road. Where there are no traffic signals 15 m (45 ft) is usually a suitable distance on which to apply this restriction.

LIMITED WAITING

Vehicles may be restricted to 'limited waiting' by applying it to certain times of the day, certain parts of the road or to specified periods. These restrictions regulate the parking of vehicles on a road rather than facilitate the flow of traffic along the road.

It is not usually practicable to have a limited waiting period for less than 30 minutes as it becomes impossible to control. In business areas a period of 30 minutes or 1 hour is useful for free short period parking, where parking for longer periods, say up to 2 hours, is provided for in off-street car parks in the business area. In some residential areas commuter parking has become a serious problem, preventing service vehicles, doctors' cars, delivery vans and private cars from gaining access to domestic property. Here a 2 hours limit from 9 am to 6.0 pm would permit residents to have parking facilities until 11.0 am and from 4.0 pm. Commuters find this arrangement inconvenient. Space is then available for the motorist making normal calls to domestic property.

Where it is possible to permit waiting by the kerbside, the main purpose of this regulation is to ensure where there is a heavy demand for parking that a kerbside parking place is used to the best advantage, and by as many motorists as possible, and not by one car parked in one place all day.

UNILATERAL WAITING

This method restricts waiting to one side of the road, and is not normally suitable for two-way roads. It has the effect of encouraging motorists to pull across the traffic stream, which is an extra hazard. There are often objections from residents and business people in the road to parking being permitted or not permitted on their side of the road, which may be overcome by operating a unilateral control system on alternative sides of the road from day to day, but this is confusing, and not to be recommended.

CLEARWAYS

Clearway restrictions are applied 24 hours per day to important traffic routes where standing vehicles would seriously interfere with the even flow of traffic, and cause a serious hazard to traffic on a main carriageway. This restriction can have serious consequences to people occupying premises on the traffic route if they have not an alternative means of access. These restrictions are mainly applied to traffic routes in rural areas.

URBAN CLEARWAYS

Clearway restrictions covering a period of 24 hours are not usually practicable on urban roads. Peak periods tend to be limited to a few hours during the day, *i.e.* a morning peak from 8.0 am to 9.30 am, and an evening peak from 4.30 pm to 6.30 pm.

The restrictions which are normally used are:

(1) 'No waiting' restrictions on the whole length of road for at least the working day.
(2) Loading and unloading restrictions on the whole length of road during the morning and evening peak periods, and for longer periods where necessary at selected points such as road junctions.
(3) Clearway regulations applied during peak hours only.

Traffic signs and road markings are used to indicate the basic restrictions which are required in the normal way.

LOADING AND UNLOADING

It is usual for waiting restriction orders to include exemption for loading and unloading operations and a period of 20 minutes is a suitable time to allow. When longer periods are required, it is usually preferable for the trader or supplier to get permission from the police.

Loading and unloading restrictions usually have a wide influence, and may affect times of delivery of goods, night deliveries, and multiple deliveries, all of which affect the working hours of staff for both supplier and trader. It is essential to have consultation with both suppliers and traders and their trade associations, when loading and unloading regulations are in the formative stage.

AREA STREET PARKING CONTROL

Parking restrictions for a street should not be considered for one street in isolation. Restrictions in one street will immediately have an influence on parking in other streets. Therefore it is usually necessary to define an area where waiting and parking on streets is to be considered, and this should also include the facilities in the area for off-street parking. The central business area of a town or city is usually the first area to be considered.

The area parking control plan may contain proposals for:

(1) 'No waiting'.
(2) 'Limited waiting' under traffic warden supervision (no charge).

(3) Parking discs (no charge).

(4) Parking meters or ticket machines (fee paying).

All street parking proposals must be related to and considered with the existing and proposed off-street parking facilities. It is most important that all parking facilities should be complementary to each other.

Parking meters and parking discs are considered in more detail in Chapters 5 and 6.

PROCEDURE FOR MAKING AN ORDER FOR STREET PARKING WITHOUT CHARGES

The detailed democratic procedure for making orders for street parking without charges in the United Kingdom, together with specimen orders, is contained in 'Traffic Management and Parking'[2] and the following is a summary of this procedure.

The power for certain authorities to make orders for street parking without charges is contained in Section 28 of the Road Traffic Regulations Act, 1967,[3] as amended by the Transport Act, 1968.[4] An order may also be made under Section 31 of the Act, specifying which vehicles or classes of vehicles may use the parking places, the period for which vehicles may be parked, and other conditions on which parking places may be used. The local authorities outside the Greater London area authorised to use these powers are a County Borough, a Non-County Borough, an Urban District and a Rural District. Within the Greater London area, the Common Council of the City of London, the Greater London Council (subject to Section 7), and in Scotland, the County Council and Town Council. Reference should be made to new legislation after the reorganisation of Local Government in the United Kingdom in 1974.

Procedure.—It is essential that the proposals for regulation of street parking should be thoroughly prepared, and consideration given to the needs of the motorist, and the inconveniences that may be caused to other people, residents, traders, shoppers, etc.

Consultation.—The police and highway authority and representative organisations who may be interested must be consulted.

Public Inquiries.—It is not likely that it will be considered necessary to hold a public inquiry into proposals to establish free street parking places. If it is necessary, the Inspector should be selected from a panel maintained by the appropriate Minister.

Publication of Proposals.—After consultations have taken place, the Council must publish a formal notice of its intention, at least once in the local newspaper circulating in the area, and once in the London Gazette. The details to be specified in the press notice are:

(*a*) Name of authority and title of proposed order.

(*b*) A statement of the general nature and effect of the proposed order.

(*c*) Names of the roads affected.

(*d*) The address and times at which a copy of the order may be seen.

(*e*) The address to which objections should be sent within a period of 21 days.

Throughout the whole period, notices should be displayed at each end of the street referred to in the order. A copy of the order, and plan, must be available for inspection at the Council Offices.

Making the Order.—The Council must consider all objections to their proposals and, if a public inquiry is held, the reports and recommendations of the Inspector. Where it is possible to meet reasonable objections, the Council should do so by amending their original proposals.

When the Council decide to make the order, the police must be notified in writing, and also any objector who has not withdrawn his objection. Within 14 days of the date when the order was made, a notice must be published at least once in the local newspaper, and once in the London Gazette. The form of the notice is similar to the notice of intention, but it also includes the date of the order.

Traffic signs may then be erected in accordance with the Traffic Signs Regulations and General Directions 1964.[5]

ROAD MARKINGS AND SIGNS

The United Kingdom Ministry of Transport, now Department of the Environment, 'Traffic Signs Manual'[6] states:

'The signs to denote restrictions on waiting and on loading are the yellow carriageway and kerb markings, and associated time plates. The yellow markings show the type of restrictions, where they apply. The plates give precise details of when they apply.'

'All these signs, including time plates and carriageway markings may be used only to indicate the effect of an order imposing restrictions.'

'At or near the main points of entry to any area in which there are waiting restrictions, signs shown in Fig. 4.2 must be erected on both sides of the road to face traffic entering the area. Only one size—508·0 mm (20 inches) diameter—is prescribed. This sign is not repeated along a restricted length or to mark the terminal points of individual restricted lengths within the area. It is not used where less important side roads on which there are no restrictions join a road with restrictions.'

'Small replicas of this sign appear on all yellow time plates indicating waiting restrictions.'

'A transverse mark must be placed at each end of a continuous sequence of longitudinal carriageway lines and at any point where one type of line changes to another type. Where a continuous line (single or double) changes to a broken one, the first 1·0 m (3 ft) mark follows immediately after the transverse mark.'

'For all alternating unilateral waiting restrictions and for all limited waiting, regardless of hours of operation, the broken line is used.'

'The marks on the kerb to indicate a prohibition on loading and unloading must be laid so that the first and last marks in the series correspond with the

Fig. 4.2   Road signs in use in the United Kingdom. (*a*) No waiting. (*b*) Supplementary plate for use with (*a*). (*c*) No stopping on carriageway. (*d*) All vehicles prohibited in both directions, and supplementary plate. (*e*) Parking place. (*f*) All motor vehicles prohibited, and supplementary plate. (*g*) Entrance to controlled parking zone. Legend may be varied to Disc Zone or Controlled Zone according to type of control. (*h*) Exit from controlled parking zone, and supplementary plate. (*Reproduced by permission of The Controller, Her Majesty's Stationery Office.*)

limits of the prohibition, but where two different types of prohibition meet, the marks should be laid as shown in the manual.[6] The marks should be repeated at approximately 3·0 m (10 ft) intervals, but this may be varied between 2·5 m (8 ft) and 3·5 m (12 ft) so as to avoid a very short odd spacing at the end of a length. The marks are not used when an order restricting waiting has an exemption to allow vehicles to load or unload for a stated maximum period.'

'For restrictions on waiting, the plates have a yellow background; for restrictions on loading and unloading, they have a white background. For both types of restriction together, a composite sign is used. Where there is a time limit on waiting, the plates have a blue background as in Fig. 4.2(b).'

'The plates should be erected parallel to the kerb and facing the carriageway on every lamp column on the footways or verges within the restricted length of road. Where there are no such lamp columns and no other suitable posts, special posts will have to be provided at approximately 60·0 m (200 ft) intervals. As the letter size is small the plates must be mounted close to the kerb and should not normally be mounted at the back of the footway or verge. If there is no lamp column within about 18·0 m (60 ft) from the end of the restricted length, a plate should be erected at or close to the terminal point within the length.'

'There will normally be no need for arrows on the plates. Where markings change it is not essential to have plates at the point of change, but if plates are so sited they must contain arrows and should be mounted side by side. If the restrictions change but the markings do not, e.g. a change from 8.0 am start to 8.30 am start, two plates with arrows must be erected side by side at the point of change.'

'Alternating unilateral restrictions tend to be confusing because they cannot be so clearly signed as fixed restrictions. Authorities should therefore try to avoid imposing such restrictions and consider eliminating existing ones. Where alternating restrictions remain, they should be indicated by the broken yellow line, and flap type plates showing the hours of current restrictions or a blank face as appropriate. Alternating loading and unloading restrictions can be indicated by the single kerb mark and flap type signs.'

'Yellow markings should not be interrupted for bus stops or taxi ranks; the white carriageway markings for these should be used as well if appropriate.'

LIGHTING OF PARKED VEHICLES

In the Metropolitan Police Area and the City of London, the Road Vehicles Lighting (Standing Vehicles) (Exemption) (London) Regulations, 1955,[7] permit vehicles being parked without lights on any road where there is a speed limit in force, unless it is an omnibus or trolley vehicle route, provided that no part of the vehicle is more than 23·0 m (25 yards) from an illuminated street lamp.

The nearside (or in a one-way street, either side) of the vehicle must be close to and parallel with the kerb. The vehicle must be more than 14·0 m (15 yards) from a road junction.

There is provision in relation to the single parking lamp which may be used, if it is fitted to the offside of the vehicle. It is required that a red light be shown to the rear, and a white light to the front, but the lamp must not be more than

305 mm (12 in) from the offside edge of the vehicle, and not less than 381·0 mm (15 in) or more than 2·0 m (6 ft) from the ground.

Vehicles which are fitted with special parking lamps may be parked within 91·5 m (100 yards) of a street lamp (lit or unlit), providing they are not within 14·0 m (15 yards) of the road junction.

In those areas where the street lighting is extinguished during the hours of darkness (usually at midnight), the lighting of the vehicle must then conform to the ordinary requirements, *i.e.* two white lights forward, indicating the width;

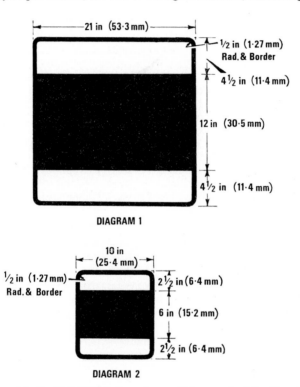

DIAGRAM 1

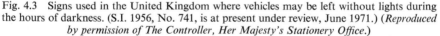

DIAGRAM 2

Fig. 4.3   Signs used in the United Kingdom where vehicles may be left without lights during the hours of darkness. (S.I. 1956, No. 741, is at present under review, June 1971.) (*Reproduced by permission of The Controller, Her Majesty's Stationery Office.*)

red to the rear, and illumination of rear number plates, unless a single parking light as referred to above is in use.

The Road Vehicles Lighting (Standard Vehicles) (Exemption) (General) Regulations, 1956, came into operation on June 5, 1956.[8] The Chief Constable in each district outside the Metropolitan Police Area and the City of London, is empowered to approve roads where vehicles may be left without lights during the hours of darkness. As in the London area, parking is allowed only on roads which are subject to a speed limit, and no part of the vehicle must be more than 23·0 m (25 yards) from an illuminated street lamp.

The approved roads are indicated by a special traffic sign in the form of a horizontal black band without wording on a white background, attached or adjacent to a lamp post (Fig. 4.3).

Parking with special parking lamps is permitted in the same way as in London.

The Road Transport Lighting Act, 1957,[9] requires that all vehicles on a road during hours of darkness should have two lamps in front of the vehicle showing white lights, and two lamps at the rear of the vehicle showing red lights. These lights are additional to lights required for reversing and illuminating number plates. There are powers of exemption and variation of requirements for vehicles standing or parked as well as for other conditions.

REFERENCES

1. 'Report of the Department Committee on Traffic Signs', HMSO, London, 1933.
2. 'Traffic Management & Parking', Ministry of Transport, (now Department of the Environment), HMSO, London, 1969.
3. Road Traffic Regulations Act, 1967, HMSO, London.
4. Transport Act, 1968, HMSO, London.
5. 'Traffic Signs Regulations & General Directions', SI 1964 No. 1857. HMSO, London.
6. 'Traffic Signs Manual', HMSO, London, 1965.
7. The Road Vehicles Lighting (Standing Vehicles) (Exemption) (London) Regulations, SI 1955 No. 1363. HMSO, London.
8. The Road Vehicles Lighting (Standing Vehicles) (Exemption) (General) Regulations, SI 1956 No. 741. HMSO, London.
9. Road Transport Lighting Act, 1957, HMSO, London.

Chapter 5

Parking Meters

Parking meters were invented by Carl Magee, and were used for the first time in the streets of Oklahoma, USA in 1935. Since then the use of parking meters has spread rapidly, first in the United States of America, and later in Europe and the British Commonwealth. It was not until 1951 that meters were used by New York City, and not until the Road Traffic Act, 1956, came into force on January 1st, 1957, that parking meters could be installed in London and elsewhere in the United Kingdom.

Parking meters are the most widespread and well known of the methods for imposing charges and time limits for parking on the highway. Each country or state in which parking meters are permitted has its own regulations, and these should be consulted before a scheme is prepared.

In determining which parking places are to be designated for control by parking meters, consideration must be given to the traffic volumes and the interests of the owners and occupiers of adjoining property. The matters which require special attention are:

(*a*) the need for maintaining the free movement of traffic,
(*b*) the need for maintaining reasonable access to premises, and
(*c*) the extent to which parking accommodation (whether open or covered) otherwise than on highways is available in the neighbourhood, or the provision thereof is likely to be encouraged by the designation of parking places.

The installation of parking meters could create orderly parking for a smaller number of cars in one area, and at the same time could intensify the congestion in neighbouring roads. It is essential that a scheme for parking meters should form part of a comprehensive scheme for parking which must include 'no waiting' regulations and preferably one-way streets, and off-street parking proposals.

PROCEDURE IN ENGLAND, WALES AND SCOTLAND

In England, Wales and Scotland, local parking authorities can make their own parking meter Orders.[1] The powers to do this stem from Section 35 of the Road Traffic Regulation Act, 1967,[2] as amended by the Transport Act, 1968.[3]

A parking meter Order will not be legally valid unless it has been made in accordance with the procedure laid down in the Statutes, and in their subordinate instruments. These procedural obligations are imposed by the Fourth Schedule of the Road Traffic Regulation Act, 1967, as amended by the Transport Act, 1968.

'1. Before applying for the consent of the appropriate Minister to the making of a designation Order, a local authority shall consult with the appropriate Minister and the Chief Officer of Police.

2.1. After such consultation as aforesaid and before applying for the consent of the appropriate Minister to the making of a designation Order, a local authority shall publish in the London Gazette and in at least one newspaper circulating in the locality an advertisement:

(a) stating the general effect of the proposed Order, the highways in which parking places are to be designated thereby, the classes of vehicles for which they are to be designated, the charges to be made for the use of the parking places and the provisions of the proposed Order as to the times when the parking places may be used;

(b) specifying a place or places where a copy of the proposed Order, and a plan showing what parts of the carriageway of any highway are comprised in the parking places to be designated, may be inspected at reasonable times specified in the advertisement during a period so specified of not less than twenty-eight days from the publication or first publication of the advertisement;

(c) stating that any person wishing to object to the making of the Order may do so by sending to the Minister, within the said period, notice in writing of his objection, stating the grounds thereof.

2.2. Sub-paragraph 2.1 above shall, in relation to a designation Order containing such provisions as are authorised by Section 39(1) of this Act,* have effect as if:

(a) particulars of the road affected by those provisions were included among the matters mentions in head (a) of that sub-paragraph, and

(b) the reference in head (b) thereof to the parts of the carriageway of any highway comprised in the parking places to be designated included a reference to the said roads.

2.3. Before applying for the consent of the appropriate Minister to the making of a designation Order a local authority shall post such notices in highways in the neighbourhood as appear to the authority to be sufficient for the purpose of bringing specifically to the knowledge of persons likely to be specially affected, as the occupiers of land adjacent to the parking places, information as to the matters specified in sub-paragraph 2.1 above and may take such other steps for

* Road Traffic Regulation Act, 1967.

that purpose as they think fit; and for the purposes of this sub-paragraph a local authority may post notices on any traffic sign, lamp-post or other structure in a highway whether or not belonging to that authority.

2.4. On the expiration of the period specified in the advertisement under sub-paragraph 2.1 of this paragraph the local authority shall apply to the appropriate Minister for his consent to the making of the Order and shall on making such application refer to him (as regards England both at the Head Office of the Department of the Environment and at the office of the Regional Controller of Roads and Transportation for the area in which are situate the highways in which parking places are to be designated) copies of any objections duly made to the making of the Order which have not been withdrawn and to the local authority's replies to these objections: provided that where the local authority proposes that the Order should designate parking places on, or otherwise make provision with respect to, a highway for which they are not the highway authority, the application shall not be made unless the consent of the highway authority has been obtained to the making of the Order.

2.5. Where it appears to the appropriate Minister that, before the application is further dealt with, the local authority should take further steps for the purpose mentioned in sub-paragraph 2.2 of this paragraph, he may direct the authority to take such further steps for that purpose as he may specify, and if he does so the period within which a copy of the Order and plan may be inspected, and objections may be made, shall be deemed to be extended by such time as the appropriate Minister may direct.

3. The appropriate Minister shall, after the period for objecting to the making of the Order has expired, consider the application and any objections duly made thereto which have not been withdrawn and may hold a public inquiry.

4.1 After compliance with the provisions of the last foregoing paragraph the appropriate Minister may consent to the making of the Order, either as proposed by the local authority or with such modifications as he may direct.

4.2 The power of the appropriate Minister under the foregoing sub-paragraph to consent to the making of the Order with modifications includes power to consent to the making of the Order with additions, exceptions or other modifications of any description; but where the appropriate Minister proposes to consent to the making of the Order with modifications which appear to him substantially to affect the character of the Order as proposed by the local authority at the time when they published the advertisement referred to in paragraph 2.1 of this Schedule he shall, before giving his consent, inform the local authority and take such steps, or direct the local authority to take such steps, as appear to him to be sufficient and reasonably practicable for informing other persons likely to be concerned.

4.3 On making the Order the local authority shall forthwith send a copy to the appropriate Minister.'

Before proposals for the control of parking are put forward, an assessment must be made of the parking needs, and the needs of moving traffic in any area where a more orderly control of parking is needed. The way to do this is to conduct a parking survey and prepare a parking and traffic regulation plan.

THE SURVEY

A parking meter scheme may be considered to be necessary when street parking is getting out of control under existing 'limited waiting' or 'no waiting' Orders, when it is preventing access to premises, causing double banking for the loading and unloading of goods, and becoming a serious obstruction to the flow of traffic. If the area to be controlled by meters is too small, there will be an excess in concentration of parked cars around the perimeter of the parking meter zone, which means that the congestion has been transferred from one area to another. On the other hand it may be that the meters would not be fully used if there was ample parking space on the fringe area. There must also be a demand for short term parking, usually made by shopping public, and visitors to offices. The parking zone, therefore, should be large enough to ensure that there will be a sufficient demand for short term parking, and that the congestion caused by parked cars will not be transferred to another area on the fringe of the zone.

To ascertain this information a survey will be necessary to give the number of cars parked; and the duration of parking over a much larger area than that contemplated for use as a meter controlled zone. The field survey should be carried out on foot. It is not sufficient to rely on information from an ordnance map. Much detailed information is required before the parking bays can be fixed; such as, position for loading gaps where they will be of greatest benefit, the nature of the goods to be loaded, position of entrances to buildings, cellar flaps, oil fuel intakes, opening pavement lights, and the position of fire hydrants, clear space for sight lines at road junctions, bus stops, cab ranks, and pedestrian crossing places, where loading and unloading should be prohibited, and suggestions for cycle parking places.

Consideration should be given to the type of vehicle that will be permitted to use a metered parking bay. It may be that the parking place should be reserved for passenger vehicles, motor cycles and invalid carriages, or it may be advisable to include hackney carriages, and certain commercial vehicles, such as vans used in repair and servicing work to equipment in building or window cleaning, and chimney sweeping equipment. If there is a café or restaurant in the vicinity it may cater for drivers of light commercial vehicles and, therefore, create a short period parking demand. Unless particular restrictions or prohibitions are specially indicated, loading and unloading of vehicles may take place anywhere in the zone for so long as is necessary to load and unload a vehicle up to a limit of 20 or 30 minutes as specified in the Order, and longer with police permission. This includes unoccupied metered parking places and gaps left between such spaces.

It is also necessary to consider the exemption of certain vehicles when being used for various statutory or special purposes. These are fire engines, ambulances, police vehicles, local authority vehicles (other than passenger vehicles) and statutory undertakers' and builders' vehicles being used in connection with operations in or adjacent to a parking place, funeral coaches and furniture removal vans.

There may be some areas where it is not necessary to limit all the meters to short term parking, *i.e.* maximum of two hours. In these cases it may be desirable to allocate a portion of the meters for longer term parking, and say, five hours' parking for 12½p (2/6). Long term meters should be made distinctive from the short term meters either by position or colour.

The use of parking meters is not confined to kerbside parking on a highway.

There are instances where off-street parking in the heart of a city will be better controlled by parking meters than by an attendant. It may even be the only way that short term parking can be operated successfully when the area cannot be completely controlled at the entrances and exits because of the rights of people to enter the area with a motor vehicle without using the official car park.

As the introduction of a parking meter scheme invariably reduces the number of cars that may be parked on the roads included in the scheme, there will be an increased demand for parking in the neighbouring area. It should therefore be considered how this can best be controlled. It may be that a system of one-way streets could be adopted, both within and without the parking area, with advantage to the flow of traffic. By directing traffic in one direction only, parking on two sides of a road may be practicable, whereas with traffic in two directions parking on one side only may be the maximum that can be permitted. 'No waiting' Orders may be necessary for some streets, and it may be deemed necessary to designate certain lengths of streets at junctions as non-loading areas. Loading and unloading may also have to be controlled on other streets.

THE PARKING METER PLAN

From the information collected in the survey, a plan of the area where parking meters are to be introduced should be prepared to a scale of not less than 1/1250 Ordnance. Each parking place will be a length of carriageway on one side of the street normally 2·25 m (7 ft 6 in) wide and coloured red. The limits of the parking place should be clearly defined. The parking place should be divided to show the position of each parking bay and the area within the parking place that will not be occupied by parking bays. A convenient length for a parking bay is 6·0 m (20 ft), but this may be reduced to 5·5 m or 5·8 m (18 ft or 19 ft) if local conditions and requirements can be fulfilled with a reduced length. Spaces between groups of parking bays are necessary for picking up and setting down passengers, loading and unloading goods, outside entrances to important buildings, opposite carriageway crossings, and the lengths of kerbside against which loading and unloading will be prohibited; also for cycle parks. It is advisable to consult the police as soon as the draft scheme has been prepared.

For each parking place there should be a reference on the plan in a rectangle which contains three figures. The top figure is the number of the parking place on the schedule. The second figure (shown on a red background) gives the maximum number of parking bays in a parking place. The third figure (on a green background) gives the minimum total length in metres (feet) not to be occupied by parking bays.

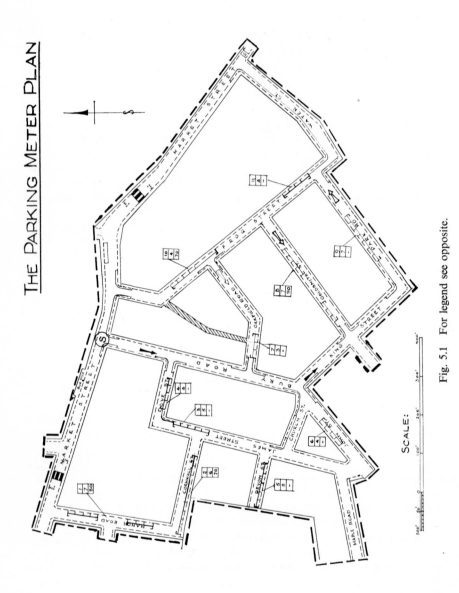

Fig. 5.1   For legend see opposite.

LEGEND

BOUNDARY OF CONTROLLED
          PARKING ZONE

ONE-WAY STREETS

          PERMANENT

          EXISTING TEMPORARY

          SUGGESTED (COLOURED RED)

SMALL STREETS & AREAS NOT
INCLUDED IN SCHEME

SIGNAL CONTROLLED JUNCT.

SIGNALLED PED. CROSSINGS

UNCONTROLLED PED. CROSSINGS
WITH ASSOCIATED AREAS.

BUS STOPS

LOADING BANS :- ALL DAY (COLOURED YELLOW)

  ,,   ,,   PEAKS (ALTERNATE BAYS COLOURED YELLOW)

CAB RANKS (COLOURED BROWN)

                                 see note — 42 / 5 / 30

METERED PARKING PLACES
          SHORT TERM (COLOURED RED)

          LONG TERM (COLOURED BLUE)

                                see note — 91 / 4 / 50

MOTOR-CYCLE PARKING AREA (COLOURED GREEN)

NOTE:-

Reading downwards these figures refer to:-

No of parking place in schedule

Maximum no of parking bays in parking area

Minimum total length in feet
within parking place not to be
occupied by parking bays.

Fig. 5.1 The parking meter plan.

PRELIMINARY SCHEME AND CONSULTATION

The draft scheme should consist of the following documents:

  (i) the plan,
  (ii) explanatory pamphlet,
  (iii) schedule of proposed parking places, cycle parking places, non-loading areas and one-way streets.

When this has been prepared it is essential that consultation should take place with people and organisations whose interests are involved with the proposals. In addition to the Minister through the Regional Controller of Roads and Transportation, and the Chief Officer of Police, the interested parties that might be consulted could be:

  (a) General Post Office, Fire Services and Statutory Undertakers.
  (b) Road haulage and road transport businesses.
  (c) Commercial trading firms, industrial concerns, businesses concerned with distribution.
  (d) Particular local interests affected, e.g. residents' associations, educational establishments, hospitals, etc.

The purpose of this consultation is to ensure that the proposals which are eventually included in the draft parking meter scheme are generally acceptable, and cater for the major needs and the problems involved. It is advisable that the explanatory pamphlet should contain a full explanation of the scheme and an objective appreciation of the wider field of influence and benefits to be derived from the proposals.

If the authority proposing the scheme is not also the highway authority, then the highway authority should be consulted.

DRAFT SCHEME

When the draft scheme has been prepared with additions or amendments to the preliminary proposals as a result of consultations with interested parties, it should then be formally advertised, and brought to the notice of the public. It would be helpful if it were also brought to the notice of known interested parties. The notice should inform the public that the scheme is available for inspection, and there should be available detailed descriptions of the effect of the Order with such maps and diagrams as are necessary. The full text of the draft Order should also be available for inspection together with explanatory information.

The consideration of objections is an important public relations exercise, and each objection should be given careful consideration. These will probably fall within one of the following three groups:

  (a) genuine and reasonable requirements that have not been met,
  (b) misunderstanding of the proposals, and
  (c) frivolous.

A great deal of patience is required in answering objectors, but nevertheless the exercise should be pursued and in the end it will be well worth while if some of the objectors can be satisfied.

In practice it is rarely found that all objections are withdrawn, and it becomes necessary to hold a public inquiry. The most effective way is to appoint an independent Inspector as Chairman. This enables the objectors to explain their reasons for objecting to the proposals, and also gives the parking authority an opportunity of giving further and perhaps a more detailed explanation to the public.

If the Council wishing to make the parking meter Order is not also the highway authority, then the consent of the highway authority must be obtained.

The final approval that is required to the making of the Order is from the Minister. The application for this consent should be sent with triplicate copies of the relevant documents, and reports that have been produced as the scheme and inquiry have proceeded, including details of any outstanding objections. The approval of the Minister is also required for the type of parking meter to be installed.

Whilst the foregoing is the procedure that must be followed in England, Wales and Scotland, it could be used as a basis for the preparation of a parking meter scheme in other countries, and adapted to satisfy the local regulations and legal procedure.

OPERATION AND TYPES OF PARKING METER

Parking meters consist of a clockwise mechanism which is contained in a metal casing, and mounted on a post or bracket 1·06 m to 1·52 m (3½ ft to 5 ft) high.

In England, Wales and Scotland there are two basic types of meters authorised for use, automatic and manual.[5] The automatic type is wound up periodically (about once per week) by an attendant. When the motorist inserts a coin in the slot provided, a needle will show in the time scale, the time bought, and will then move across the time scale on the face of the meter until the period of time paid for by the coin has expired, when a flag or other indication appears on or above the face of the meter indicating that the authorised period has now expired. In London, the excess charge period then comes into operation. Another flag, usually red, appears when the excess charge period has expired, indicating that the motorist is liable to prosecution, and the vehicle may be towed away at the owner's expense.

The meter which is in general use in the United States of America indicates the maximum time a motorist is allowed. This is either 30 minutes, 60 minutes or two hours, depending on variable conditions. At the end of the parking period, a flag or other device indicates that the time has expired, and it is the responsibility of the motorist to vacate the space and make it available to someone else. Those that overstay know that they are liable to pay a fine and run the risk of having their vehicles towed away at their expense. This type of meter may be used under the Ministry of Transport, now Department of the Environment, Regulations.[6]

The manually operated type is similar to the automatic type except that it is set in motion by the motorist by moving a lever or turning a knob on each occasion he inserts a coin.

Meters may be divided into two groups:

(*a*) The 'cumulative' type, where the mechanism is so designed that at the time of insertion of a coin for the payment of an initial charge any unexpired time displayed on the time scale of the meter is added to the time for which payment was made by the initial charge, but so that the total time shown on the time scale after the payment of that initial charge does not exceed the standard period;

(*b*) the 'non-cumulative' type of meter, where the mechanism is so designed that the unexpired period displayed on the time scale is cancelled when a coin is inserted for the payment of an initial charge.

In some cities, when a vehicle is parked at a metered parking bay, the initial charge must be inserted in the meter even if there is an unexpired period left by the previous occupant. In others, the unexpired period may be used by a motorist, free of charge, but if he stays longer than the unexpired period the excess charge becomes operative. The cumulative meter appears to be more fair to the motorist, and most meters can be easily changed from one type to the other if the authority so decides.

Some manufacturers market twin parking meters so that two parking bays can be controlled by a twin meter mounted on one post. They claim that they are cheaper, simplify the attendant's work, and are less unsightly than single meters on a post at each parking bay. On the other hand other manufacturers prefer to have two independent meters mounted on one post. Experience of erecting posts in an existing footpath shows that there are often too many obstructions underground from service pipes and mains, and it is not always practicable to erect a pole at a precise point on a footpath. When a single pole is used for two parking bays it must be exactly on the dividing line between the two bays, otherwise it will lead to confusion with the motorist. There is also the danger of the motorist making a mistake, and placing the coin in the wrong meter. It is advisable to erect meter posts about 1·2 m (4 ft) from the forward end of the bay so as to be clear of the car door when the car is parked correctly. It is also advantageous to erect the meter heads at an angle of 45° to the kerbline, with the coin slot to the right hand of the motorist standing on a footpath facing the meter. The plate telling the motorist how to use the meter faces him standing in this position. He is also advised on this plate that on the reverse side of the meter is information on the operation of the scheme. When posts are erected, it is advisable to fix the meter cases and cover with hoods to indicate they are not yet in operation. This makes them more prominent and prevents people from walking into them. When the mechanism is fixed in the cases, it should be tested as near as possible to the day the meter scheme comes into operation.

Details of the description and testing of parking meters are contained in Statutory Instrument 1961, No. 705 'The Parking Meters (Description and Testing) (England and Wales) Order, 1961',[6] and Model Orders can be found in 'Traffic Management and Parking'.[8]

These regulations require that a parking meter shall display a time scale, graduated in intervals of not less than two minutes nor more than five minutes. After the insertion of a coin in the meter the scale should show at any instant, by means of a pointer or other device, how much unexpired time remains. At the end of the time paid for, plus any additional time permitted to be used on a cumulative meter, a flag or other device shall appear suddenly. Most meters have a separate flag which appears on the scale.

The maximum size of the slots is specified so that coins larger or thicker than the correct coin or coins cannot be inserted in the meter.

There are also requirements for ensuring the accuracy of operation. Where the standard period is two hours, the pointer has to reach zero mark on the scale in not less than two hours and must not exceed the period by more than two minutes for each hour. The sudden appearance of the excess flag must be at a time not less than one minute nor more than three minutes after the pointer has reached zero on the time scale, when the excess charge period does not exceed two hours. When the excess charge period exceeds two hours the tolerance is two minutes and six minutes respectively.

In the 'Parking Meters (Type and Design Approval) (Appointed Day) Order, 1962',[7] it is stated that meters offering two hour periods of parking will be grey, and those offering periods longer than two hours will be green.

The regulations attempt to set out a basic uniformity in operation of meters to safeguard the users, but local authorities are permitted considerable freedom in their choice of meters, and several manufacturers have produced different meters which comply with the Ministry of Transport, now Department of the Environment, regulations. The life of parking meters in this country is estimated to be from five to ten years so far as the amortisation of their cost by the local authority is concerned. In view, however, of the provisions of Statutory Instrument 1961, No. 705, as regards the annual overhaul of meter mechanisms, it is not unrealistic to speak of their life as 'infinite', since each year any worn or defective part must be replaced.

Before placing an order for parking meters it is essential to ensure that any parking meter installed, under the terms of a designation Order, shall be of a type and design which has been approved, either generally or specially, by the Minister of Transport, now Secretary of State for the Environment. For this purpose the Minister will be advised by the Council of Industrial Design.

EXAMPLES OF AUTOMATIC METERS

VENNER PARKING METER

The Venner Parking Meter is entirely automatic and known as the 'Park-O-Meter'. It is a two flag parking meter that has been designed to comply with the requirements of the Ministry of Transport, now Department of the Environment, for an excess charge period for metered car parking. This 'excess charge' type of parking meter incorporates independent signals visible from both sides of the meter. The yellow 'excess charge' flag appears when the time paid for has expired, and a red 'penalty' flag appears when this excess period has elapsed, indicating that the motorist has committed an offence. At all times the time scale indicates the amount of time the motorist has in hand or the time overstayed.

This meter is housed in a cast casing with a coin slot protected from the weather and covered with a machined metal hood which snaps shut immediately the coin is accepted by the meter. Coins cannot be inserted in a jammed meter. The windows are of toughened heat-treated safety glass.

Three keys are required to completely open this meter and coin box. The first provides access to the mechanism compartment and is usually issued to the maintenance mechanic. The second is the key to the coin box compartment which is usually issued to the collector who removes the full coin box and inserts an empty one. The third key is used to unlock the coin box and is usually kept by the cashier in the City or Borough Treasurer's Department.

There are three types of coin collecting systems that may be adopted. The first is a sealed box which is taken out and replaced by an empty container. The second is an open box from which the money is taken and the box returned to the meter. The third is an automatic system which consists of a container on a trolley which is placed under the meter. The coin compartment is unlocked, pulled

Fig. 5.2   Venner 'Park-O-Matic' single parking meter. (*Reproduced by permission of AMF International Ltd.*)

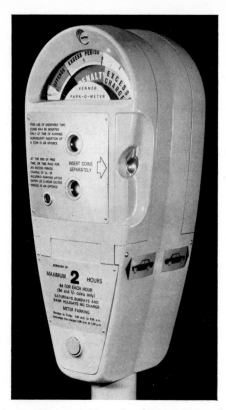

Fig. 5.3   Venner Duplex parking meter. (*Reproduced by permission of AMF International Ltd.*)

out and the money drops into a funnel and along a tube into the container on wheels.

The mechanism is operated by a main spring which is normally rewound about once per week. The time pointer can be arranged to stop at any point on the time scale and changed from 5p for one hour to 5p for two hours or other ratio. The maximum registration of, say, five hours can also be adjusted to, say, 10 hours, on site. The mechanism can be removed from the case in a few seconds for maintenance. When two meters are required on one post, a Duplex parking meter has been devised which is a back to back arrangement with two single parking meters. Two Duplex parking meter units may be mounted on a single post using a dual headed bracket. A meter may also be fixed on a bracket inserted in a wall. These two types are shown in Figs. 5.2 and 5.3.

This meter is manufactured by AMF International Ltd, Venner Division, Kingston By-Pass, New Malden, Surrey, England.

KIENZLE PARKING METER

The Kienzle Parking Meter 'PU.3' is a fully automatic meter with the entire mechanism made of stainless steel, and the movement is fully enclosed. The elastic and durable gasket and the screw type lock, prevent the entrance of rain, snow and dirt.

The large expiry flag shows when the parking time has elapsed and an excess parking time up to 12 minutes is shown on the dial. With long term parking meters excess time up to 20% of the maximum parking time is shown. The dual time indicator can be read from the front as well as from the back, which makes it easy for motorists and inspectors to read. The coin meter can also be read easily from above and through the dial window. The mechanism can be removed from its housing in one operation, which makes servicing quick and simple. The passage of coins to the coin box is simple and claimed to be trouble free.

This parking meter can be supplied with or without dump collection by means of the coin collecting cart and it can be built as a short term or long term meter. There are eight different time settings which can be made on the spot without having to exchange the mechanism or parts of it.

The Kienzle parking meter may be supplied as a single meter, twin meters, *i.e.* single meters mounted in one case back to back, or quadruple meters which are two twin meters mounted on separate brackets on one post.

The meters are manufactured and supplied by Kienzle Apparate GmbH, Villingen/Schwarzwald, Germany.

VDO PARKING METER

The VDO parking meter is manufactured in Germany, is entirely automatic and when wound up operates for a period of 100 parking hours. It is sufficient to wind the meter by means of a crank handle once per week when collecting the money.

The meter is housed in a dust and weather-proof casing which is an aluminium alloy die casting. The mechanism is made from stainless steel and brass. Two different sized coins may be used to operate the meter, *e.g.* two 5 pfennigs or one 10 pfennig. This meter can be supplied with a one coin system. The coin slot is at the side of the meter and there are two coin display windows which show the last two coins inserted. The pointer covers an arc of approximately 160° and the pointer position is also clearly visible from the back of the meter. There is a built-in coin counter which registers all coins inserted, and the excess time indicator shows the excess time in one minute intervals. On expiry of the parking time a red 'no parking' flag appears automatically. This flag is visible from both sides of the meter.

This parking meter is equipped with three different safety keys. Usually the cash box key is held by the Treasury Department where the cash boxes containing the money will be emptied. The cash compartment key will be held by the cash box collector, and the mechanism compartment by the Service Department. Each key fits only one particular lock. There is also available a collecting trolley which facilitates the money collection and prevents any possible theft. The use of the trolley is possible on an economical basis for any quantity of over 20 metres provided they are installed in close proximity to each other.

This meter is also available as a twin-head parking meter, which consist of two meters built in a single case and mounted on one standard, and as a double head parking meter which consists of two separate meters mounted on a cross bar and supported on one standard (Figs. 5.4 and 5.5).

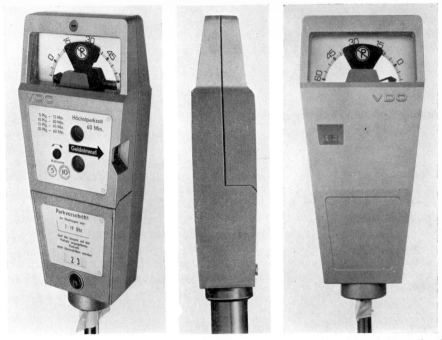

Fig. 5.4   VDO single parking meter showing front, side and rear view of meter. (*Reproduced by permission of Adolf Schindling GmbH, Frankfurt/Main.*)

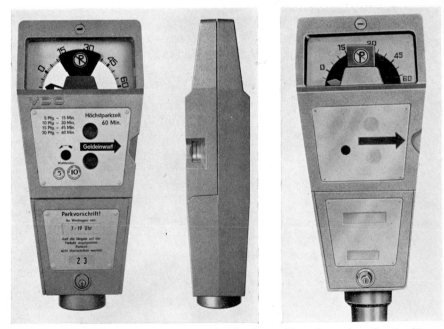

Fig. 5.5   VDO twin headed parking meter showing front, side and rear view of meter. (*Reproduced by permission of Adolf Schindling GmbH, Frankfurt/Main.*)

The VDO parking meter is manufactured by VDO Tachometer Werke, Adolf Schindling GmbH, Frankfurt/Main, Gräfstrasse 103, Germany.

KARPARK PARKING METER

The Karpark parking meter is an automatic type of meter and may be obtained as a single meter known as 'Unimatic' or as a twin meter known as 'Twin-O-Matic'. The twin meter has two entirely separate mechanisms which are identical to those used in the 'Unimatic' type.

The mechanism is housed in a cast aluminium alloy case which is resistant to corrosion. The windows are made from a shatterproof acrylic plastic and are sealed into the housing with a non-hardening waterproof compound.

The mechanism is constructed of brass, stainless steel and aluminium alloy, and the whole mechanism is appropriately treated to render it corrosion proof. It is removable and interchangeable, and service time is only a few seconds whilst a new unit is installed. One or two coins of appropriate size can be used and the meter can be quickly adjusted for any time combination from six minutes up to twelve hours with cumulative or non-cumulative operation. The clock

Fig. 5.6   The 'Unimatic' parking meter. (*Reproduced by permission of Fisher-Karpark Ltd.*)

Fig. 5.7   The 'Twin-O-Matic' parking meter. (*Reproduced by permission of Fisher-Karpark Ltd.*)

will run for 150 hours on one winding, regardless of the number of coins inserted. Inspection windows are provided in the clock case to enable attendants to see that the clock is working without having to open the meter casing.

The coin slot opening is placed on the side of the housing. On the insertion of a coin the clock mechanism starts and a pointer registers the duration of the parking time purchased. The coin box mechanism is independent of the clock mechanism, and the insertion of a coin by a motorist into a faulty clock will register the insertion and not deny the motorist the right to park. The coin box compartment has a separately locked door and contains the coin box from which the money can only be extracted by breaking the wire seal or unlocking the special lock. A second sealed box per meter can be supplied.

There is also an automatic system which consists of a container on a trolley which is placed under the meter. The coin compartment is unlocked, pulled out and the money drops into a funnel and along a tube into the container on wheels (Figs. 5.6 and 5.7).

The meter is manufactured by Fisher-Karpark Ltd, Luddendenfoot, Halifax, England.

DUNCAN PARKING METER

The Duncan Model '60' parking meter is a manually operated meter which has been used extensively in the United States of America. It has a simple mechanism, is easy to service and is adaptable to many different time and rate combinations. The mechanism can be lifted out of the housing very quickly for servicing, and is adjustable for the cumulative or non-cumulative operation as required. It consists of a clockwork timer employing a balance wheel and

Fig. 5.8   The Duncan Model '60' parking meter. (*Reproduced by permission of Duncan Parking Meters, Chicago.*)

lower escapement, and an interchangeable sealed coin box. It is housed in a corrosion resistant weatherproof casing.

The time expired flag, which consists of a large red flag with bold lettering on both sides is clearly visible from either side. Jammed mechanisms are easily noted by a large red flag displayed in the large dial window area. A coin viewing window can also be included if required.

There is a choice of three types of coin collection systems:

(*a*) open cylinder cartridge,
(*b*) open ejector,
(*c*) patented sealed cylindrical cartridge.

The sealed coin box system utilises one sealed cylindrical cartridge per meter. The filled sealed cartridge is removed from the meter and inserted into a sealed

Fig. 5.9   The Duncan VIP Model '70' parking meter. (*Reproduced by permission of Duncan Parking Meters, Chicago.*)

coin box receptacle mounted on a locked collection cart. This receptacle opens the sealed cartridge, releases the coins into the locked collection cart, closes the sealed cartridge, and the same sealed coin box is placed back into the meter. The collector cannot see the coins or remove the open cartridge from the receptacle.

The materials used are clock brass, stainless steel, aluminium stampings, Zamac castings, bonderised baked enamel finish.

The Duncan VIP Model '70', was designed to meet the request from some of the major cities for a meter that was resistant against vandalism. The VIP (vault insured protection) meter has the coin container housed in a malleable cast iron vault. It reduces to a minimum the possibility of being opened by prising or hammering with tools such as chisels, sledge hammers and crowbars. The same operating mechanism is used as in Model '60'.

The Duncan Duplex is designed to serve two car spaces utilising one standard. Both mechanisms are individually housed and separated from each other so that the motorist will not inadvertently insert coins into the wrong meter. To further eliminate confusion on the part of the motorist, the meter can be placed in one of three distinct positions. The same operating mechanism is used as in Model '60' (Figs. 5.8 and 5.9).

The Duncan Meters are manufactured by Duncan Parking Meters, 835 No. Wood Street, Chicago 22, Illinois, USA.

SUPERVISION

If a parking meter scheme is to succeed it is essential that the regulations for street parking must be strictly enforced. The Road Traffic and Roads Improvement Act, 1960, gives authority by Order to police authorities with the consent of the local authority to appoint traffic wardens to act as attendants at parking places, and also in certain circumstances a traffic warden may, on finding a person committing one of the following offences, affix to his vehicle, or give the driver, written notice offering him the option of paying a fixed penalty. If he pays this within 21 days or such other period as may be specified in the notice, he will not be liable to proceedings. This relates to:

  (i) using the vehicle on the road without lights or reflectors,
 (ii) obstructing the highway by waiting with or parking a vehicle, or by loading or unloading a vehicle,
(iii) the non-payment of a charge at a street parking place.

This means that parking meter schemes may with the agreement of the Minister, and the local authority, be controlled by one authority, the police, through the traffic wardens. If an Order under this Act is not applied for, or is refused, then two authorities are involved in the control of street parking. Firstly, the police are responsible for administering the law in connection with vehicles causing obstruction, loading and unloading, extended parking in streets where 'no waiting' and 'limited waiting' Orders are in force, whereas the car park attendants are usually under the control of the City or Borough Engineer, and are responsible for that part of the street where there are parking bays controlled by meters. It is not possible to say that one traffic warden or one attendant can look after a fixed number of parking meters. It is more dependent on the layout of the streets rather than the number of meters. It may be that two attendants would be required to supervise 100 meters in a difficult area, whereas they could supervise twice this number in a compact area where a large number of the meters could be seen from one vantage point.

CITY/COUNTY BOROUGH OF
ROAD TRAFFIC REGULATION ACT, 1967
SECTIONS 35 to 44
PARKING PLACES

To the driver* of vehicle, registration number...
which was left in parking bay No...in the parking
place at ....
At ....a.m./p.m. on...............................19.........., traffic
warden...first noticed that the parking
meter at the above-numbered parking bay duly indicated that the period
for which payment was made on the leaving of this vehicle had expired.
YOU ARE, THEREFORE, REQUIRED TO PAY AN EXCESS
CHARGE OF FIFTY NEW PENCE.

> *Name* ....
> *Address* ....
> ....

Please enter your name and address in the above space and enclose this form
intact with your remittance.

Under Section 42 of the Road Traffic Regulation Act 1967, it is an offence
for the driver of a vehicle who has left it in a parking place to:—

(*a*) fail duly to pay an excess charge, and/or

(*b*) leave the vehicle therein for longer than two hours after an excess charge
has been incurred.

The penalty is a fine up to £5 for a first offence or up to £10 for a subsequent
offence.

Payment of the excess charge should be made either by cheque or postal order
delivered or sent by post, or by cash in person, so as to reach the City/Borough
Treasurer,   , not later than 4 p.m. on
the 7th day following the date shewn above. When the City/Borough Treasury
is closed on the 7th day, payment must be made by 4 p.m. on the next full day
on which the Department is open. Cheques and postal orders should be made
payable to "Corporation of   " and crossed "A/c payee only".
Receipts for payments by cheque will be given only if specifically requested. IN
NO CIRCUMSTANCES SHOULD THE CHARGE BE PAID TO A TRAFFIC
WARDEN.

City/Borough Treasury, Hours of Opening:—

*The driver of the vehicle is the person driving the vehicle at the time it was left
in the parking place.

Fig. 5.10 Yellow ticket. Used when motorist leaves his car for longer than the time paid for,
and enters the two-hour excess period. First copy attached to windscreen of car. Second copy
returned to City/Borough Engineer or Police when Traffic Wardens are employed. Third copy
to City/Borough Treasurer. The second copy contains a space for the make, colour, also name
of Licensing Authority instead of name and address on first copy. *The third copy is shown
in Fig.* 5.11.

CITY/COUNTY BOROUGH OF
ROAD TRAFFIC REGULATION ACT, 1967
SECTIONS 35 to 44
PARKING PLACES

To the driver of vehicle, registration number..
which was left in parking bay No...in the parking
place at ....
At .... a.m./p.m. on.................................19............, traffic
warden..first noticed that the parking
meter at the above-numbered parking bay duly indicated that the period
for which payment was made on the leaving of this vehicle had expired.
YOU ARE, THEREFORE, REQUIRED TO PAY AN EXCESS
CHARGE OF FIFTY NEW PENCE.

Make ....
Colour ....
Licensing Auth.
From Licence ....

Date Paid	*Passed to*
Letter to	*Town Clerk* ....
Licensing Auth.	*Reply from*
Letter to	*Town Clerk* ....
Owner	*Written*
Letter to	*Off* ....
Driver	

NOTES:—

DATE	Ticket No.	RECT. No.	AMOUNT			BALANCE		

Fig. 5.11   Yellow ticket, third copy (*see* Fig. 5.10).

In Westminster, England, 35 uniformed attendants working an average of 44 hours per week controlled 1822 meters distributed over an area of 111 hectares (275 acres) containing 24·1 km (15 miles) of streets. In addition, three plain clothed supervisors were employed. It is necessary to have a few men additional to the basic number required, to cover sickness, holidays, meal times, extra hours over the eight-hour day, and absence to give evidence in attending court.

CITY/COUNTY BOROUGH OF
ROAD TRAFFIC REGULATION ACT, 1967
SECTIONS 35 to 44
PARKING PLACES

To the driver* of vehicle, registration number..
which was left in parking bay No...in the parking
place at ....
At .... a.m./p.m. on................................19........., traffic
warden..first noticed that this vehicle
had been left in the above parking place and that the initial charge payable
on the leaving of the vehicle in that parking place had not been duly paid.

Under Section 42 of the Road Traffic Regulation Act, 1967, it is an
offence for the driver of a vehicle who has left it in a parking place to fail
duly to pay the initial charge.

You are hereby given notice that the question of taking proceedings
against you for the above offence will be considered.

*The driver of the vehicle is the person driving the vehicle at the time it was left
in the parking place.

Fig. 5.12 Blue ticket. Used when motorist is seen by attendant to leave his car without inserting a coin in the parking meter. First copy attached to windscreen of car. Second copy returned to City/Borough Engineer or Police when Traffic Wardens are employed. Third copy returned to Town Clerk.

Note—The second and third copies have a space at the bottom of the ticket for the make and colour of the car, and the name of the Licensing Authority.

When parking meter attendants are employed as distinct from traffic wardens, three distinct tickets are used, each having a distinctive colour. The first (Figs. 5.10 and 5.11) is, say, a yellow ticket used when a car is parked against a meter showing the yellow flag, indicating that the driver has overstayed the time for the initial payment, or the unexpired period where it is permitted to be used.

The second (Fig. 5.12) is, say, a blue ticket used when it is known that the driver has failed to pay the initial charge.

The third (Fig. 5.13) is, say, a red ticket used when a motorist has used up the time for the initial payment plus two hours excess charge period. The red ticket should be added to the yellow one served earlier. This ticket informs the motorist that an offence has been committed. It is found to be an advantage to slip the tickets in a polythene envelope and attach them to the windscreen under the wiper by adhesive tape, the second copy being sent to the City or Borough Engineer, the third copy of the red and blue tickets to the Town Clerk, and the third copy of the yellow ticket to the City or Borough Treasurer. After the red

---

CITY/COUNTY BOROUGH OF
ROAD TRAFFIC REGULATION ACT, 1967
SECTIONS 35 to 44
PARKING PLACES

To the driver* of vehicle, registration number................................
which was left in parking bay No.........................in the parking place at ....

At .... a.m./p.m. on.......................19........, traffic warden...first noticed that this vehicle had been left in the above parking place for more than two hours after an excess charge of fifty new pence had been incurred.

Under Section 42 of the Road Traffic Regulation Act, 1967, it is an offence for the driver of a vehicle who has left it in a parking place to leave the vehicle therein for longer than two hours after an excess charge has been incurred.

You are hereby given notice that the question of taking proceedings against you for the above offence will be considered.

———————

*The driver of the vehicle is the person driving the vehicle at the time it was left in the parking place.

———————

Fig. 5.13   Red ticket. Used when motorist leaves his car for longer than the time paid for, plus the two-hour excess period, and enters the offence period. First copy attached to windscreen of car. Second copy returned to City/Borough Engineer or Police when Traffic Wardens are employed. Third copy returned to the Town Clerk for possible prosecution.
Note—The second and third copies should have the yellow ticket number written at the bottom of the ticket.

ticket has been issued, arrangements may be made for the vehicle to be towed or driven away to another park or pound. The owner of the vehicle is liable to be prosecuted for the offence, and charged for the cost of towage, and maybe, storage of the vehicle.

MAINTENANCE OF PARKING METERS

A very high standard of maintenance is called for in the United Kingdom and the requirements are set out in the Parking Meters (Description and Testing) (England and Wales) Order, 1961. 'Each meter shall be examined and tested as

PARKING METER·RECORD CARD

LOCATION (Name of Street) ....   Post/Bracket/Support Identification No................

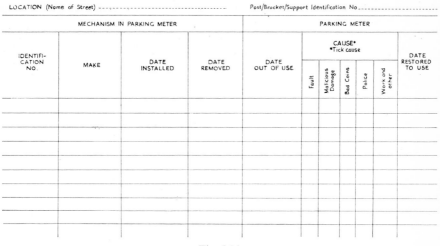

Fig. 5.14

to its accuracy once in each period of four weeks, and any work that is necessary to restore the meter to its proper working conditions shall be carried out.

In addition, the mechanism from each parking meter shall be removed for overhaul once in each year. The inspections, repairs and removal of mechanism shall be carried out in such a manner and at such times so as not to preclude the use of the mechanism or the parking place by the public. Detailed records have to be kept of all meters in use.

PARKING METER ROUTINE INSPECTION

INSPECTION DATE	WHETHER IN WORKING ORDER	INSPECTED BY	INSPECTION DATE	WHETHER IN WORKING ORDER	INSPECTED BY	INSPECTION DATE	WHETHER IN WORKING ORDER	INSPECTED BY

Fig. 5.15

TEST AND OVERHAUL CARD FOR PARKING METER MECHANISM

MECHANISM NO. ....   TESTED BY..................................

INITIAL TEST DATE ....   MAKE...................................

MECHANISM DATE BROUGHT INTO USE	ON POST/ BRACKET/SUPPORT IDENTIFICATION NO.	NAME OF STREET	DATE REMOVED

Fig. 5.16

The following headings for record cards have been found useful:

(*a*) Parking meter record card (Fig. 5.14)
(*b*) Parking meter routine inspection (Fig. 5.15)
(*c*) Test and overhaul card for parking meter mechanism (Fig. 5.16)
(*d*) Overhaul and test (Fig. 5.17)

OVERHAUL AND TEST

DATE	OVERHAULED AND TESTED BY	NATURE OF FAULT OR WORK DONE IF ANY *A.O. — Obligatory annual overhaul.

Fig. 5.17

A satisfactory method of maintaining parking meters in a working order is for the contractor supplying the meters to set up a maintenance depot locally. A short-wave radio communication system between the depot and the mobile maintenance mechanics ensures that no meter is out of commission for mechanical reasons for more than a very short period. In order for it to be economically possible to have a local maintenance depot, there should be not less than 500 meters to maintain in a locality.

ADVANTAGES OF USING PARKING METERS

The meter system of controlling street parking prevents all-day parking by the kerbside, and makes each parking space available for use by four or five cars in a 10-hour day. Parking bays are clearly marked on the carriageway so that each vehicle has adequate space in which to draw in or out of the parking bay. With uncontrolled street parking, a motorist often finds that he is either unable to move his car, or he moves it with considerable difficulty, because other cars have been parked too close to his car. Parking bays controlled by meters should be long enough to avoid this difficulty. Parking in front of important entrances, goods loading bays and street junctions, which may cause a great inconvenience, is avoided. Revenue is produced which can be used to finance off-street car parks. 'Double banking' is avoided. The motorist doing shopping or making business calls finds it a great convenience to be able to find a suitable parking place quickly. The amount of time that can be wasted in finding a parking place can be quite out of proportion to the length of time spent in making a business call.

DISADVANTAGES OF USING PARKING METERS

Motoring organisations have not favoured the introduction of parking meters in most countries when they have been first introduced on the grounds that:

1. Parking meters by themselves do not represent an easy solution to the bold solutions which are urgently required.

2. With the parking meter system every bay must be large enough to park the largest car, and in England there are very many small cars on the road. Therefore there would be a waste of suitable space for parking cars.

3. Householders may have to pay to park outside their own front doors.

4. From an aesthetic point of view they are not desirable.

5. The number of cars that may be parked along the kerbside is reduced considerably.

6. The motorist wishing to park for a long period is either compelled to go to a multi-storey car park, and pay a heavy parking fee, or leave the car outside the central area of the city, and have the inconvenience of using public transport or walking.

It is significant that in each country where parking meters have been introduced there has been initial opposition, but this has soon died away, and the scheme has been welcomed generally by the motoring public and extended. In London the traders were at first opposed to the introduction of meters, but later became in favour of them. The Banks were losing customers owing to car parking difficulties, but after the introduction of meters they found their customers returning.

Fig. 5.18   Parking meter scheme in operation at Hanover Square, London, W.1. (*Reproduced by permission of AMF International Ltd.*)

No one will claim that parking meters are the complete solution to the parking problem in our large city centres, but they are a helpful contribution towards establishing an orderly system of street parking where without them there is chaos.

REFERENCES

1. Local Authorities' Traffic Orders (Procedure) (England & Wales) Regulations, 1969. SI 1969, No. 463. HMSO, London.
2. Road Traffic Regulation Act, 1967. HMSO, London.
3. Transport Act, 1968. HMSO, London.
4. HOGG, A. W. 'Control of Street Parking', Report on Convention on Car Parking. Institution of Municipal Engineers, London. 1960.
5. DUFF, J. T. 'Parking Control', Paper presented to Traffic Engineering Study Group Institution of Civil Engineers. December 1960.

6. Parking Meters (Description & Testing) (England & Wales) Order, 1961. SI 1961, No. 705. HMSO, London.
7. Parking Meters (Type & Design Approval) (Appointed Day) Order, 1962. SI 1962, No. 947. HMSO, London.
8. 'Traffic Management & Parking', Ministry of Transport (now Department of the Environment), HMSO, London, 1969.
9. 'Clockwork Parking Meters', British Standard Specification No. 4684:1971. British Standards Institution, London, 1971.

Chapter 6

Parking Discs

Parking discs were first introduced in 1957 in Paris. Like many other large cities, Paris had a parking problem, but it could not be solved by parking meters or any other means of charging a motorist who wished to park on a highway. A parking tax was not legally possible in France, and presumably there was no desire or intention of changing the law to make it legally possible. The only solution appeared to be the strict enforcement of limited parking regulations.

Prior to 1955, parking was limited to 30 minutes in many streets in the central area of Paris, but owing to lack of manpower the regulations were not strictly enforced. Another reason was that the parking and traffic problem at that time was not acute. As the traffic volumes increased, the streets became lined with parked cars, and lorries had to 'double bank' in order to load and unload near buildings, which in turn temporarily blocked the road for other traffic.

In November 1955, an experiment was carried out on the Champs Elysées. Traffic wardens were appointed, and their duty was to paste coloured stickers on the tyres of parked cars. The colours were changed every hour, and when a car had three different colours on the tyres it was certainly parked over time. The warden's job was limited to pasting the stickers on the tyres, and any infringements were reported by constables. The Prefect of Police decided that all cars obstructing the highway could be loaded on a trailer and taken away.

This system gave good results, and in June 1956 it was extended to Place Vondâme. In November 1957, the Prefect of Police decided to limit parking in the central area of Paris to one hour. This area was called the 'Zone Bleue'. The sticker system now proved to be impracticable because it occupied the time of too many men. Therefore a new system was introduced based on the 'parking disc'. (Fig. 6.1).

The purpose of the parking disc system is to assist in the enforcement of the street parking regulations. The Paris disc consists of a thin piece of cardboard 100·0 mm (4 in) diameter—one side has times for morning and the other for afternoon parking. The left-hand half of each face is for the arrival times, and the other half has the expiry times, usually in red print. The disc is contained between two thin pieces of cardboard forming an envelope and secured at the centre. On each side of the 'envelope' are two windows—one for the arrival time and the other for the expiry time. When the motorist parks his car, the disc should be turned to the time of arrival, which is marked at half-hourly intervals, and the time of expiry is automatically shown at the right-hand window. The disc should then be placed behind the windscreen on the near side.

In Paris, all entrances to the 'Zone Bleue' are marked by special signs, and any motorist parking his car inside the 'Zone Bleue' must display the disc on his car indicating the time of arrival. The discs give from one hour to ninety minutes' parking time according to the time of arrival. A longer period is given for lunch

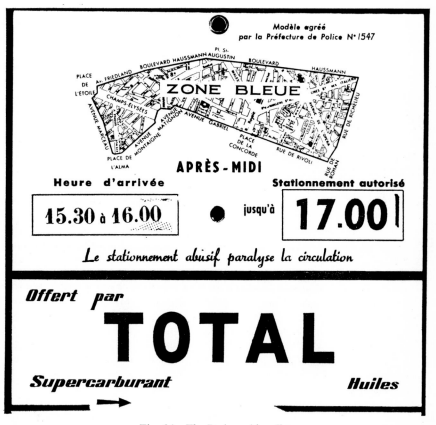

Fig. 6.1   The Paris parking disc.

time so that arrivals after 11.30 hours may park until 15.30 hours, and if a car arrives after 18.00 hours it may park until 9.00 hours next day.

When the 'Zone Bleue' system was put into operation, 418 policemen were used to check offences. The object of using this large number of men was to impress on the motorist that the new regulations were going to be enforced. When the system was working smoothly the number of men was reduced and constables were replaced by wardens. Each warden was responsible for 180 m (200 yards) of street, but it is considered that this may be reduced. The warden's task is to note infringements, and leave a notice under the windscreen wiper informing the offender that he will be reported to the Superintendent, whose task is to write down proceedings and forward them to Court, when the motorist will be liable to a fine of 9 francs, 62 p (12s 6d) or $1.75.

The only direct income derived from this system is fines imposed on the motorist. It is also claimed that by enforcing orderly parking there is also a saving of petrol and motorists' time. On the expenditure side the main item is the cost of employing traffic wardens. The difference between income and expenditure is bound to vary with each scheme and no general guide can be given. It is claimed that there has been an improvement in the parking and traffic conditions in the 'Zone Bleue' in Paris, and the system works well enough for it to be extended to other cities.

The chief disadvantages are caused where there are no other regulations preventing parking, and where space is required for loading and unloading vehicles, and bus stops. This encourages 'double banking', which may completely block a highway. Again there is little advantage gained and a lot of inconvenience created for the motorist if he can comply with the parking regulations by moving his car to another place on the road when the initial time has expired.

Apart from the extension of the disc system to Nice, Rouen, Bordeaux, Lyons and other principal French towns, it has been used extensively in other European countries.

In the German Federal Republic short time parking zones have been created in 78 cities and towns, making the use of parking discs obligatory. A standard parking disc has been designed and developed by the Federal Ministry of Transport in co-operation with the Allgemeiner Deutscher Automobil Club. The disc is illustrated in Fig. 6.2. It is intendes that this disc shall be used in all towns in the Federal Republic. It merely indicates the time of arrival and therefore may be used in places where the regulations permit waiting for different periods of time. To ascertain the parking time allowed, the motorist is referred to the relevant sign posts. False indication of the time of arrival or its subsequent alteration is prohibited.

The town of Kassel has provided a good example of the successful use of the parking disc system. The town centre has been built as one large shopping centre, in which different areas are reserved for use by long-term and short-term parkers. In the zones used for short-term parkers, the parking time is controlled by parking discs.

The use of parking discs was legally authorised in The Netherlands in March 1963, and there are about 1000 municipalities who are free to make their own choice in using them. The Netherlands parking disc indicates the time of arrival only on the front face, and each half hour interval is shown in different colours, five bright colours being in use. Colours are used to facilitate the work of the police and wardens. On the reverse side the time is indicated when a period of half an hour, one hour or one and a half hours expires. In order to simplify the task of checking the parking discs, the wardens carry a checking disc of their own. This is reset by the warden every half hour, and indicates to him the colours which will appear in the window of a disc in a car which has overstayed the permitted period.

Information on the use of the disc is printed on the reverse side. The disc is printed with black lettering on a yellow background. It is valid throughout The

Netherlands, which is a great advantage, as motorists can use the same disc in any town they visit. It was designed by the Royal Dutch Touring Club.

The disc used in Vienna and in a number of Austrian towns, consists of a rectangular piece of card on which is printed a clock face marked in quarter hour intervals. There are two movable indicators, one in black pointing to the time of arrival, and the other in red pointing to the time when the permitted parking period expires. The two indicators are linked together so as to give a uniform parking period of, say, one hour or one and a half hours.

Fig. 6.2   A standard parking disc designed and developed by the German Federal Ministry of Transport in co-operation with the Allgemeiner Deutscher Automobil Club.

The disc system is now in use in most principal Italian towns. The Italian Road Traffic Acts do not permit the use of parking meters. It is estimated that 50% of the available parking spaces in the centre of the historical towns are regulated by discs. The type of disc in use is based on the Paris pattern. Much of the possible benefit from the use of the disc system is jeopardised by the fact that the police, who are responsible for enforcing the system, have heavy demands on their time, and this permits the system to be abused. The off-street parking charges and penalties for parking offences are substantially the same.

In Switzerland, the Paris 'Zone Bleue' idea has been adopted, using a disc similar to the one in use in Paris. In some towns the Vienna type of disc is used.

Geneva has introduced a 'red zone' for parking on the outskirts of the town, where the time limit is 15 hours. This is being considered by other Swiss Municipalities together with the obligation to display a parking disc as they do in the 'Zone Bleue'. It is proposed to combine the two discs into one by using the front side for 'Zone Bleue' parking and the reverse side for 'red zone' parking.

The disc system appears to be favoured by motorists in Switzerland, but in some towns it is opposed by the police on the grounds that it is difficult to enforce the regulations, and supervision is expensive compared with meter parking.

At St Helier, in Jersey, the Paris disc is used to permit half hour parking in certain streets of the town between 9.0 am and 6.0 pm on weekdays except where a vehicle arrives between 12.30 pm and 2.0 pm parking is permitted until 2.30 pm. Unlike most authorities using the Paris disc system, St Helier makes a charge of 2·5p (6d) for the disc.

In England and Wales, subsection (3) of section II of the Road Traffic and Roads Improvement Act,[2] enables a Council to make provision in an Order for regulating street parking, that an apparatus be used for indicating the time during which a vehicle was left in, or should be removed from a parking place. In other words, the use of the parking disc is authorised but only if the apparatus is generally or specially approved by the Minister of Transport (now Secretary of State for the Environment).[9]

Cheltenham was the first town in England to adopt a parking disc system. The discs used are similar to the Paris discs. They are obtainable free at garages and shops and allow a maximum of 90 minutes waiting time between 9.0 am (9.00 hours) and 6.0 pm (18.00 hours). This system is used to tidy up the parking in the town centre, to drive all day parkers to the off-street car parks, to encourage motorist shoppers to visit the town in greater numbers, and also from the aesthetic aspect the disc system is preferred to parking meters.

Many offences can be created in a disc system, such as parking without a disc or setting the time scale incorrectly. They do not enable the time to be varied between one parking place and another, but discs can be designed to give variable periods in the same parking place. This operates in Paris where a longer period is permitted at midday than at other times. The difficulties experienced in enforcing the regulations are similar to those experienced in European cities and towns. A system which is very difficult to enforce strictly cannot be regarded as being completely satisfactory. Experience indicates that discs are more suitable for use in small towns where the demand for parking does not greatly exceed the space available, and where the bulk of the demand arises in a limited area of the town with fairly regular use of the space.

In 1970, the British Standards Institution issued a British Standard Specification for Parking Discs.[16] The disc is designed for national usage in order to avoid the necessity for a motorist to use a different disc for each town or area visited. The disc is in the form of an envelope in which is contained an indicating wheel for the time of arrival.

PUNCH CARD SYSTEM

This system of parking control is a Swedish invention and known as the 'Park System'. It was introduced in 1965 and is patented internationally. Cards are

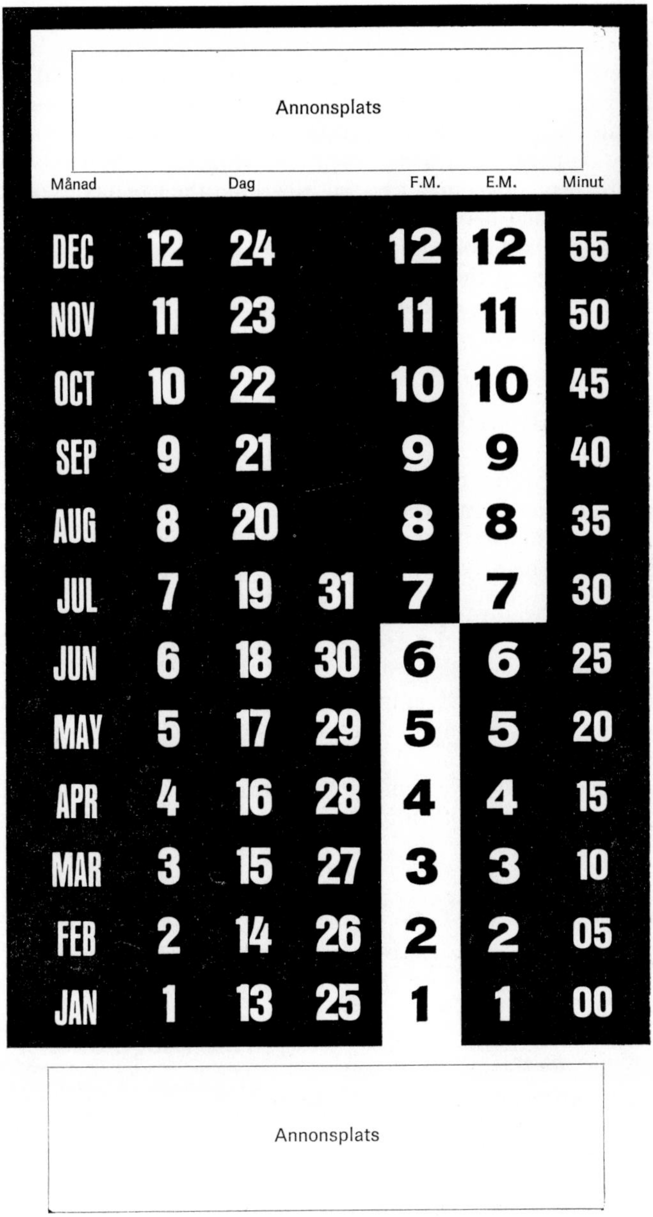

Annonsplats				
Månad	Dag	F.M.	E.M.	Minut
DEC	12	24		12	12	55
NOV	11	23		11	11	50
OCT	10	22		10	10	45
SEP	9	21		9	9	40
AUG	8	20		8	8	35
JUL	7	19	31	7	7	30
JUN	6	18	30	6	6	25
MAY	5	17	29	5	5	20
APR	4	16	28	4	4	15
MAR	3	15	27	3	3	10
FEB	2	14	26	2	2	05
JAN	1	13	25	1	1	00

Annonsplats

Fig. 6.3   The Swedish punch card park system.

used which the motorist buys in advance either in sets or singly. The cards are printed in different colours, each colour indicating the length of parking time permitted, *viz.*, half an hour, one hour, two hours, or more (Fig. 6.3).

The cards are printed with columns indicating the months, dates, hours and minutes. When the driver wishes to leave his car in an authorised parking area he selects the card appropriate to his length of stay, and pierces four holes in the card to indicate his time of arrival within five minute intervals. An ignition key or pencil may be used. The card is then placed against the windscreen so that the traffic warden or policeman can tell how long the car has been parked.

The main difference between this system and the disc system is that these cards must be purchased from the police station, petrol service garages, stationers' shops, etc. A charge is therefore made for parking, and the local authority receives the revenue. It is, of course, possible for a charge to be made for the Paris type disc, and there are places where this is done.

CAR BADGES FOR DISABLED DRIVERS

In England, the Secretary of State for the Environment encourages local authorities to adopt a scheme whereby disabled drivers can display an authorised badge on their car, so that they can be given all possible help with the parking of their vehicle.[11] The drivers with whom this scheme is concerned are:

(*a*) those who drive invalid vehicles supplied by the Government,
(*b*) those who drive vehicles specially adapted for persons with defects of locomotion,
(*c*) those drivers who have amputations which cause considerable difficulty in walking or who suffer defects of the spine, or the central nervous system which make control of the lower limbs difficult; and
(*d*) those drivers who have some other permanent and substantial disability which causes severe difficulty in walking.

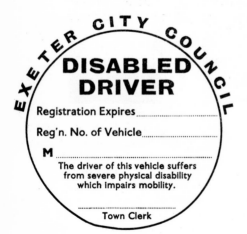

This badge does not confer any legal right on the driver to park in restricted areas.

Fig. 6.4   A disabled driver's disc showing front (left) and reverse (right) sides.

Some drivers are unable to make use of their cars unless they can find parking places close to their destination, where they can leave their cars as long as they need to stay, and some need extra space in which to manoeuvre crutches or wheel-chairs. Restrictions which have to be accepted by other drivers may cause great hardship to the disabled, but the extent to which they can be waived will depend on local traffic conditions.

In order to identify the disabled driver, a yellow disc is issued by the local welfare authority on condition that it is not used to relieve the parking difficulties of anyone other than the disabled driver. The disc or badge is illustrated in Fig. 6.4 and should be prominently displayed at the front and rear of the vehicle.

In addition to offering help and courtesy to disabled drivers, local authorities are asked to consider:

(a) whether the time limit should be waived when making or amending 'Limited Waiting' on-street traffic regulation Orders,

(b) what regular parking arrangements can be made for parking directly adjacent to his place of employment,

(c) what off-street parking places can be reserved at shopping centres, stations, cinemas, theatres, etc.

When considering the total prohibition of cars from shopping centres, consideration should be given to the needs of the disabled driver. It is desirable that the standard yellow badge should be used by all authorities throughout the country and, wherever it is possible, the recommendations of the Secretary of State for the Environment for waivers in the parking regulations should be accepted.

CAR BADGES FOR MEDICAL PRACTITIONERS

The Council of the British Medical Association has agreed to issue on hire special car windscreen badges to enable the police and local authorities to exercise discretion in favour of doctors using their cars in the course of professional medical practice. It is emphasised that the concessions afforded by the badge are entirely dependent on the goodwill of the police and local authorities, and that it is essential that they should not be abused. As the badges are easily transferable from one car to another, the Association only issues one per person. If, however, a medical practitioner has two cars an extra holder may be obtained (Fig. 6.5).

The badge is issued subject to the following conditions:

(a) The badge is to be used only by registered medical practitioners who are actively engaged in general medical practice, or use a car in the course of their professional medical duties for domiciliary visits or consultations, or for visits to establishments where provision for off-street parking is not available.

(b) The badge is to be displayed only in the course of professional medical duties.

(c) The badge will remain the property of the Association.

(d) In the event of the Association being satisfied that the badge has been used improperly it will be recalled and the police notified of its registration number.

Fig. 6.5 The medical practitioner's car badge. Crest, red on white; lettering, blue on white; P. 1916, black on white; background, blue; windows, white; border, black.

(e) The Association must be contacted immediately if a badge has been lost; and the badge must be returned immediately if, in the future, condition (a) no longer applies.

RESIDENTS' PARKING CARDS

In many cities where there are large blocks of terrace houses, many of which have been converted into flats, there is a growing problem of finding accommodation for residents' cars. These buildings are often in a built-up area, near the business centre, and in the absence of some form of on-street parking control there is a continuous line of parked cars along both sides of the road. Under these conditions, residents often find it impossible to park their car within a reasonable distance of their home, and being a heavily built-up area there are no facilities for enough private garages to satisfy the demand. This situation became very acute in the City of Westminster and the Royal Borough of Kensington and Chelsea.

In 1967, the Road Traffic Regulation Act was passed in the United Kingdom, and sections 35, 36, 37, 38 and 40 of that Act empowers local authorities to accept pre-payment of parking charges.[13] These powers were extended for Greater London by section 26 of the Greater London Council (General Powers) Act, 1967.[14]

In the City of Westminster a fundamental principle of the scheme is that residents should only be asked to pay when the vehicle has been physically parked since no resident can be guaranteed a parking space at any one time in any one place. The scheme must also be sufficiently flexible to allow a driver to pay for his next day's parking as he parks his vehicle overnight, and to make short trips during the day without the need to pay every time he returns to park his car.

The Westminster scheme allows a motorist to buy parking space for one or more full calendar days anywhere within the specified area, for as long ahead as he pleases. On any of those days he can come and go as he pleases, or leave his car unused. In order to do this, a parking card and a book of parking tokens are required. The parking card is a transparent sheet of plastic over-printed as a calendar. The back of the sheet is coated with an adhesive to which is stuck a sheet of backing paper. This paper is so cut that an individual square can be peeled off behind any of the dates, and a token inserted to show through in place of the peeled off square.

At the top of the card a permit is fixed by the issuing authority. This permit bears the vehicle registration number, together with the authority's internal reference number and a zone number. The authority checks the bona fides of residents before issuing cards, and used cards must be returned before new ones are issued. A card for one calendar month has proved convenient, both in size and for administration. At the authority's discretion several months' cards may be issued at one time to cut administrative costs, and to ensure that the motorist is not without a card for the following month. Parking tokens are simply receipts for the pre-payment of one day's parking, and are sold in books of £1 or £5 value. The tokens are not dated. Parking cards are issued by the authority with a holder in which they can be displayed on the inside of the car windscreen. Books of tokens are available from the office of the local authority or through local retail outlets, such as garages.

Before setting up a scheme, it is necessary for the authority to analyse the demand for parking and in particular the demand for on-street parking by residents. In Westminster, special parking places for residents have been allocated, and control operates during the normal working day by traffic wardens who are themselves controlled by the Metropolitan Police Force.

The Westminster scheme was originated by the City in conjunction with Thomas De La Rue and Co. Ltd, London, EC2.

In the Royal Borough of Kensington and Chelsea there is a similar problem for the provision of parking facilities for residents. The Council consider that their parking control scheme should amongst other things, provide for the reservation of a high proportion of parking places for the exclusive use of residents.[15]

Residents' parking places are clearly marked and are not divided into individual bays, as this type of marking is uneconomical. Resident permit holders are entitled to park in residents' parking places during permitted hours once they have paid their daily charge or are current season ticket holders. The provisions of the Parking Control Orders do not empower the Council to allocate parking spaces to individual residents. Parking permits are valid from zone to zone within the Royal Borough, and during permitted hours residents may park on any available residents' parking space within a controlled parking zone.

Residents are issued with self-adhesive holders free of charge. When affixed to the windscreen they form two pockets, which enable a permit holder to display (a) a parking permit, and (b) either a daily or season ticket. Only one permit and, if required, one season ticket can be issued to a resident in respect of a specified motor vehicle, and the registration mark must be shown on both documents. This is essential for enforcement purposes.

Payment by residents may be made in two ways:

(a) by purchasing a season ticket costing £26 for a period of 12 months or £7·50 for a period of 3 months, or
(b) by purchasing a daily ticket costing (1969) 12·5p (2s 6d) from a ticket machine. Such machines are sited at various points in the controlled zone.

Permits are obtainable from the offices of the local authority, and every resident who owns and uses a motor vehicle is entitled to a permit. Parking Control Orders are enforced by the Traffic Warden Service of the Metropolitan Police Force.

These two schemes are designed for similar problems, but whereas the Westminster scheme asks the motorist to pay for the day he uses a parking place only, with the Kensington and Chelsea scheme the motorist pays for a season ticket and there may be days when he does not use it. There is also provision for a daily parking ticket.

REFERENCES

1. WEHNER, B. 'Parking', International Road Safety & Traffic Review, 1959, Vol. VII. I.
2. Road Traffic & Road Improvement Act, 1960. S.II(3), HMSO.
3. WEGMÜLLER, K. 'The Parking Disc System', International Road Safety & Traffic Review. 1960, Vol. VIII. 2.
4. Memorandum No. 777, para 4–9. Ministry of Transport. March, 1961.
5. The Parking Places Order (Procedure) (England & Wales) Regulations 1961. SI 1961, No. 411.
6. Memorandum No. 792. Ministry of Transport, December, 1961.
7. Model Order for Parking Disc Schemes. Ministry of Transport Circular, No. Roads 3/62.
8. KUYSTEN, C. A. 'The Parking Disc System', International Road Safety & Traffic Review, 1964, Vol. XII. 2.
9. Parking in Town Centres. Planning Bulletin No. 7. HMSO 1965.
10. ANON. 'Parking Control: An International Survey'. International Road Safety & Traffic Review. 1965, Vol. XIII. 3.
11. Disabled Drivers' Car Badges, Ministry of Transport Circular, No. Roads 32/67.
12. Disc Controlled Parking. Ministry of Transport Circular, No. Roads 36/67.

13. Road Traffic Regulation Act, 1967 (as amended 1968). HMSO.
14. Greater London Council (General Powers) Act, 1967. HMSO.
15. 'Statement on Proposals for Controlled Parking in the South Kensington and Central Chelsea Areas', Royal Borough of Kensington & Chelsea, 1969.
16. 'Parking Discs', British Standard Specification No. 4631:1970. British Standards Institution, London.

Chapter 7

Parking in Residential Areas

EXISTING HOUSING DEVELOPMENT

The parking and garaging of cars in residential areas is becoming an ever increasing problem It is probably most acute in areas built prior to 1914 which consist of rows of terrace houses with small gardens in front and small yards and gardens at the rear. These houses were built either before or during the very early days of the motor car, and there are no facilities at all for parking or garaging a car, except on the street. This type of development is often on the fringe or reasonably near the central business area and, in order to avoid paying parking fees, commuters park their cars in these residential areas and complete their journey to town on foot or by public transport. The position can be aggravated when there are colleges, sports grounds or any facilities which attract people with cars to the neighbourhood, and no off-street parking facilities can be provided in the area. Residents in these areas are therefore deprived of the facilities for a garage, and if they move the car from the street, they usually find great difficulty in finding a parking place on their return unless it is late in the evening. Extensive street parking can restrict traffic flow along the streets. Congestion on main traffic routes encourages motorists to look for alternative 'short cuts' through the adjoining residential areas. This additional traffic coupled with extensive street parking causes more congestion.

Estates built during the inter-war years usually have more land allotted to each house. The medium and more expensive houses have either garages or space available for one to be constructed. On local authority estates the houses were built to a higher density and no garages were provided. With the immediate post war local authority housing the position became worse because the density of houses per acre was increased, and it is not until recent years in the United Kingdom that facilities have been provided for garaging cars on housing estates. With the medium priced to more expensive houses where single garages have been provided, we now find families with two cars, and two cars plus a caravan.

Parking on residential estates is not confined to private cars. Parking of commercial vehicles in residential areas at night and at weekends has reached gigantic proportions. In addition to the effect on the amenity of the area, when damage is caused to grass verges and open grassed areas, these vehicles are often

driven away at an early hour causing noise and waking people in the neighbourhood. Also, any parked vehicle on a residential road where children are moving
around is a potential danger.

The pre-1914 terrace houses in residential areas present the most difficult
problems. In seeking a solution, the needs of the residents must be considered
first, whilst remembering that no one has a legal right to park his car on a public
highway except in the special places authorised for that purpose. Streets in these
areas are usually rather narrow, and parked vehicles on both sides obstruct the
free movement of traffic in two directions. Traffic management cannot be

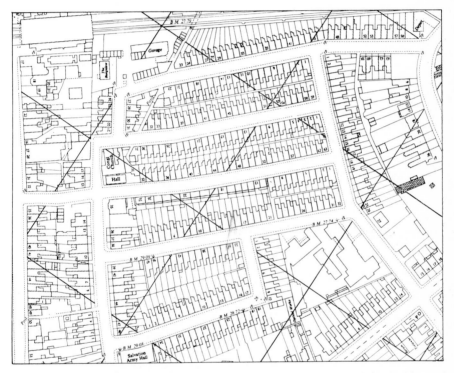

Fig. 7.1   Densely built up area of terrace houses where streets were used for parking and
'short cuts' for through traffic, causing danger to children.

divorced from parking. Therefore a traffic management exercise may help by
adopting a 'one-way' traffic system in certain streets, making other streets into
culs-de-sacs, and making it difficult if not impossible for through traffic to use
the streets for 'short cuts', thereby reducing the traffic to that which has a
destination in the area. The adoption of Traffic Regulation Orders would help
to control commuters or people from other areas who use the streets for long
term parking. By adopting a Traffic Regulation Order for 'Limited Waiting'
for a period of 2 hours from 09.00 hours to 18.00 hours, long term parking could
be prevented. This would enable residents to park from 16.00 hours to 11.00
hours, and enable facilities to be available during the daytime for tradesmen and

visitors to have a parking place. Excessive parking in a cul-de-sac may be controlled by making a Traffic Regulation Order prohibiting all motor vehicles except for access. The red ringed prohibitive sign indicating 'All Motor Vehicles Prohibited' with the supplementary plate 'Except for Access' should be erected at the entrance to the cul-de-sac. (*See* Chapter 4—Street Parking).

Figure 7.1 shows a densely built up area of terrace houses where roads were used for parking and by through traffic, causing danger to children attending the school in the area. By inserting three road blocks and arranging a system of 'one-way' traffic, through traffic has been eliminated (Fig. 7.2). The obstructions

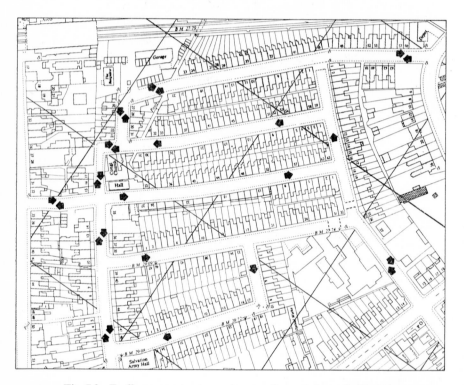

Fig. 7.2   Traffic management arrangements for area shown in Fig. 7.1.

used are sufficient to deter ordinary motor traffic from gaining access, but emergency service vehicles, such as fire engines, can easily overcome the obstacles if necessary.

In 1966, the Denington Report was published by the Ministry of Housing and Local Government and Welsh Office, entitled 'Our Older Homes—A Call for Action'. Following this report a few local authorities have carried out rehabilitation schemes for areas of domestic property built in the 19th century and capable of being improved and given a new lease of life. The work could include closing parts of existing streets to vehicular traffic except funeral cars, builders' vehicles, furniture removers' vans, and invalid carriages, also the provision of parking

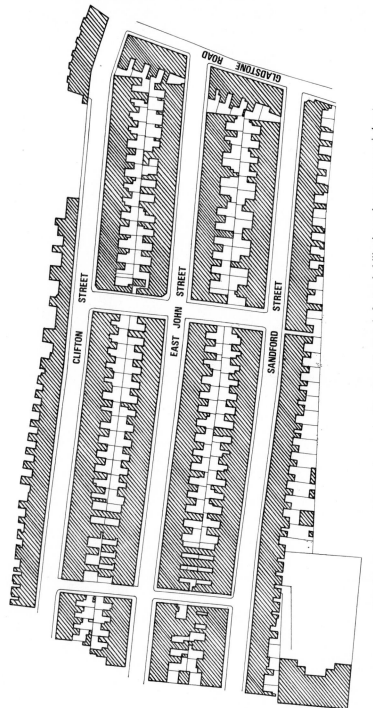

Fig. 7.3 An area of terrace houses in Newtown, Exeter, before rehabilitation scheme was carried out.

places, garages and small amenity areas. Powers to carry out these rehabilitation schemes are contained in the Housing Act 1969, the Town and Country Planning Act 1968, and the Road Traffic Regulation Act, 1967. The conversion of existing highways into pedestrian ways in areas of dense terrace property presents some difficulties because there are certain classes of vehicles which must have access to the properties. If exemptions are too wide, the road ceases to be a pedestrian way. Therefore, in the case of the Newtown Area in Exeter, the Order as made under Section 92(3) Town and Country Planning Act, 1968, contained specific exemptions for funeral cars, builders' vehicles, furniture removers' vans, and

Fig. 7.4   Parking in streets in Newtown, Exeter, before rehabilitation scheme was carried out.

invalid carriages only. It was considered that emergency service vehicles (police, fire, ambulance) would not need specific authority, and that lighting maintenance and road cleansing vehicles could gain access by virtue of Section 49 of the Public Health Act, 1961. An example of the rehabilitation scheme carried out at Newtown, Exeter, is shown in Figs. 7.3 to 7.6.

Some of the Inner London Boroughs, particularly Westminster and Kensington and Chelsea, have large areas of dense development with large Georgian or Regency terrace houses. Here there is the special problem of providing parking space for residents. Many of these houses have become flats, and there are several separate apartments in an original house, which has a comparatively narrow road frontage. The local authority's solution to this problem is described in Chapter 5—Parking Discs.

In Kensington and Chelsea, the Greater London Council have made a study in Environmental Management.[3] The area considered is 91 hectares (225 acres) in extent and bounded on the north by Kensington High Street and Kensington Road (A315), on the south by Cromwell Road (A4), on the east by Queen's Gate (B325), and on the west by Earl's Court Road.

The proposals consist of closing certain roads and arranging a system of 'one-way' traffic. This is with the object of preventing through traffic from using

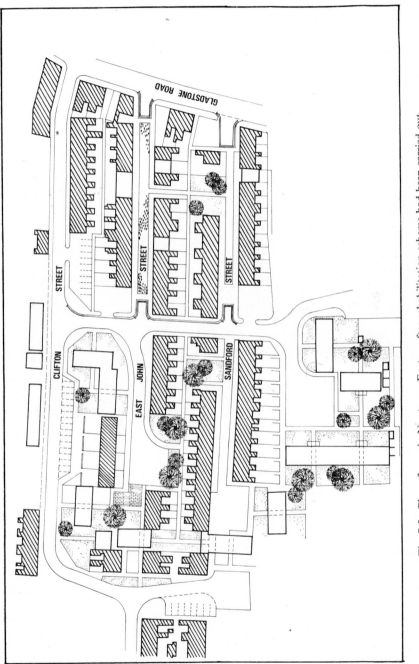

Fig. 7.5   Plan of area in Newtown, Exeter, after rehabilitation scheme had been carried out.

the unclassified roads. Parking places have been allocated on the roads and on small areas of land adjoining the roads.

One of the dangers of introducing a scheme of this type is the increased traffic which will be diverted to the surrounding main traffic routes. In this case it is estimated to vary between 5% and 190% and throwing an increased load on intersections which are already saturated at peak periods. Therefore in considering an exercise in environmental management, the side effects on other roads and areas must receive consideration.

In areas built up with large terrace houses, it is often possible for property owners to provide their own garage accommodation by making a basement into

Fig. 7.6   Illustration of parking arrangements in a street in Newtown, Exeter, after a rehabilitation scheme had been carried out.

a garage with a ramp down from the highway. Also it may be possible to convert the whole or part of the forecourt or garden into a paved open parking area, or convert a ground floor room into a garage.

On housing estates where no provision was made for garaging cars, there is now a parking problem. It may, however, be possible to satisfy part of the demand for garages and parking by providing blocks of garages and parking areas where cars may be left. It should be pointed out that this does not always provide a satisfactory solution. There are cases where new garages have been so severely damaged by vandals before they had been let, that they have had to be demolished. Also, car owners have refused to park their vehicles on a spare piece of ground out of sight of their dwelling for fear of damage by vandals. There are also many motorists who refuse to pay any rent or parking fee, and insist on using the highway as a permanent parking place; also for cleaning and carrying out repairs to the car. Commercial vehicle drivers often bring their vehicles home and park them all night and at weekends in front of their houses.

(*See* Chapter 14—Commercial Vehicle Parks.) Outside normal working hours the roads on Council housing estates are cluttered with vehicles of all kinds. This applies to other estates where there is inadequate garaging accommodation. This is a serious problem which affects the amenity of the estate and is not easily solved. The following are suggestions which may help to preserve the amenity of the district:

(*a*) The ideal solution is to build a garage within the curtilage of the house.
(*b*) Provide groups of garages.
(*c*) Provide parking space on spare land.
(*d*) Provide parking space by taking away part of gardens or even demolishing a house.
(*e*) Provide a rear access road by taking garden land and building garages in rear gardens.
(*f*) In wide streets with a grass verge, the grass verge could be removed to make a parking strip. This presents difficulties such as permanent parking in front of another person's house, and may cause difficulties with delivery vehicles.
(*g*) Provide for parking in front gardens.
(*h*) In revitalisation areas, certain properties may be demolished and parts of streets marked off to provide parking spaces.

NEW HOUSING DEVELOPMENT

The standard of one car per family has not yet been attained except in special areas or districts. There are, of course, small areas of residential development where there are now two or more cars per family. Nevertheless, for new development a garage should be provided or space reserved for one car per family, and two cars for more expensive houses. Hard standings and parking places must be provided for cars being used by residents during the day and for visitors at night. It is essential that new residential development should be planned to separate vehicles and pedestrians as much as possible.[4]

The United States has led the world in the use of the motor car, and consequently it is in that country that some of the problems of dealing with the motor vehicle have arisen first. The problem of planning for the motor car on residential estates was one of them, and as a possible solution the 'Radburn' system of planning for residential estates was developed at Radburn, in New Jersey. This was in 1928, and one of its aims was to secure safety from traffic without hampering the freedom of the car.

There are now many variations of this idea but, basically, a large area is selected on which the development is planned with a surrounding road from which cul-de-sac service roads radiate to feed the interior. There must be no through road in this area. In effect it is based on the traditional Garden City layout in reverse. The roads are for vehicles only—the houses face the interior and back on to the roads—the interior is an open space with a network of footpaths instead of the private back gardens in the Garden City plan. The footpaths link all the dwellings and places where people assemble without crossing the roads. These residential areas are linked by roads or footpaths which pass under or over main roads.

Main roads are controlled access roads and the circulatory roads link up all the culs-de-sac which give back access to dwellings for service deliveries, collection of refuse, car parking and garaging. An interesting scheme has been carried out at the New Town, Cumbernauld, near Glasgow, with complete vehicular/pedestrian separation. It is not necessary to provide footpaths for the culs-de-sacs, and they can be treated as garage courts.

In high density multi-storey housing, it is inevitable that the garages must be some way from the main building and grouped together. Whilst it is a great convenience to have a garage adjoining the dwelling, there are also some advantages in group garages with 'patios', and shared hosing facilities. In some areas multi-storey garages, as distinct from 'car parks', have been erected to serve high density housing areas. An example is described and illustrated in Chapter 11, page 203. On steeply sloping sites it may be economical to provide basement garages.

Cars, garages and surface car parks on housing estates do not, as a rule, contribute anything of value to the environment. Therefore in the first place they must be carefully sited so as to be easily obscured from the view from residential property and footpaths, carefully designed to be of as little offence to the eye as possible, and carefully screened by walls, trees or shrubs. The landscaping of surface car parks is discussed in more detail in Chapter 9—Surface Car Parks.

REFERENCES

1. 'Our Older Homes—A Call for Action', Ministry of Housing and Local Government and Welsh Office, 1966. HMSO, London.
2. 'Conversion of Highways into Footpaths or Bridleways (City of Exeter) (No. 1) Order, 1969', HMSO, London.
3. 'Kensington Environmental Management Study', Greater London Council. 1966.
4. 'Cars in Housing'/I. Design Bulletin No. 10. Ministry of Housing and Local Government, 1966. HMSO, London.

Chapter 8

Traffic Wardens

The primary function of a Police Authority is the prevention and detection of crime, and the preservation of public order. The increasing volume of traffic has called for an increased allocation of police manpower to be devoted to traffic control; whilst at the same time there has been no relaxation in the demands for manpower to fulfil the primary function of the police force.

The Road Traffic Regulation Act, 1967, Section 81,[1] provides that a Police Authority in England and Wales may appoint certain persons to discharge functions connected with road traffic, or road vehicles, or the enforcement of the law relating to road traffic, as may be prescribed as appropriate by order of the Secretary of State. These persons are to be known as traffic wardens, and are to act under the direction of the Chief Officer of Police.

The Functions of Traffic Wardens Order, 1960 (SI No. 1582)[2] which came into operation on September 15, 1960, provides that traffic wardens may be employed to enforce the law with respect to an offence:

(*a*) committed by a vehicle being left or parked on a road during the hours of darkness without the lights or reflectors required by law;

(*b*) committed in respect of a vehicle obstructing a road or waiting, or being left or parked, or being loaded or unloaded, in a road;

(*c*) created by Section 88 of the Road Traffic Act, 1960 (which relates to offences in connection with street parking places on highways where charges are made).

The Order provides that traffic wardens may exercise the functions conferred on constables to make use of the fixed penalty procedure to enforce the law in such areas that the Secretary of State may by Order specify. The effect of this is that the fixed penalty procedure may be used for any of the offences set out at (*a*) or (*b*) above (other than obstruction or leaving a vehicle in a dangerous position), and for an offence committed by the non-payment of the charge made at a street parking place.

The fixed penalty procedure is a means of enforcement; but it does not follow that a traffic warden must make use of this procedure when he sees a breach of the law with which he is empowered to deal. There are certain offences with which he will not be free to deal. Alternative possible actions he may take, subject to any direction from the Chief Officer of Police, are to give an informal warning, to report the matter to the police who may give an informal warning or a prosecution, or to call a police constable. A primary part of a warden's task is to help motorists by pointing out where they may or may not park a car.

Traffic wardens may be employed by the Police Authority, subject to arrangements being made between the Police Authority and the Local Authority, to act as parking attendants at designated street parking places, i.e. for parking meter zones. Arrangements should be made for payment to the Police Fund for the services of the warden, and for ancillary expenditure by the Police Authority.[2]

Where a Police Authority employs school crossing patrols, traffic wardens may be employed to act as patrols, either temporarily during the absence of a patrol because of sickness or any other reason, or at times of the day when the traffic warden is not required for warden's duties.[3]

During the debate in the House of Commons on the second reading of the Road Traffic and Road Improvement Bill,[4] the Minister of Transport emphasised that people were not to be fined on the spot or given a summons on the spot for a parking offence. The intention behind the Act is that persons committing certain minor traffic offences shall be punished without recourse to the courts, unless the offender wishes to go to the courts. A constable or a traffic warden may attach to a vehicle or hand to a person a notice informing him that an offence has been committed, and it will specify briefly the offence. The driver of the vehicle can decide whether he will pay the fixed penalty within a specified time, or he can wait to be prosecuted. If the penalty is paid within the specified time the police cannot prosecute, and there is no conviction, and no sentence. The Justices' Clerk is the person to whom the penalty should be paid. No money should pass to a constable or traffic warden.

A Police Authority shall not employ any person who is a police constable as a traffic warden. This provision has the effect that a special constable cannot become a traffic warden and remain a special constable. It is also stated that the Police Authority shall take steps to ensure that only persons adequately qualified are appointed as traffic wardens, and that the wardens are suitably trained before undertaking their duties.

The training required consists of a short course of about two weeks when the duties are explained to them, and afterwards they work for about one week with an experienced warden. Politeness and good manners in dealing with the public are stressed during the training period.

The following instructions were issued to traffic wardens in Leicester, and are reproduced by permission of Mr Robert Mark, a former Chief Constable of Leicester.[5]

INSTRUCTIONS TO TRAFFIC WARDENS[5]

1. YOUR PRIMARY ROLE—PREVENTION

You are clearly to understand that your primary function is to help vehicle drivers in streets in the centre of Leicester where waiting is prohibited.

You are to do so by:

(i) preventing the unwitting commission of 'waiting' offences; and
(ii) informing vehicle drivers of the parking facilities available to them.

Your efficiency will not be determined by the number of prosecutions you initiate, or by the number of fixed penalty forms you issue, but by the freedom of your patrol area from vehicles parked in contravention of the law.

2. COURTESY

You must always be polite to all vehicle drivers notwithstanding that at times you may feel that you are not accorded by them the civility and co-operation that you are entitled to expect. Remember that many of the people with whom you will deal will have little or no knowledge of the laws relating to parking and waiting. Some of them will have no knowledge at all of their own obligation to avoid causing inconvenience to others and some may consider that their own interests should prevail over those of the public. Try to maintain a courteous attitude notwithstanding that you may be subjected to much provocation. Never invoke for any retaliatory reason the power of enforcement with which you are invested by law. If you decide that it is your duty to invoke it, do so firmly but without departing from the high standard of politeness and good manners expected of a public servant.

3. YOUR SECONDARY ROLE—IMPARTIAL ENFORCEMENT

Your secondary purpose is to enforce the law in respect of waiting offences when you have not been able to prevent them; to that end you must be firm and impartial. You must remember that everyone in this country is equal before the law and that only when faced with a claim for diplomatic immunity need you be concerned about the identity of the person with whom you are dealing. You should invite the claimant to give his name and address and to specify the diplomatic mission to which he belongs. If you act firmly and politely when dealing with vehicle drivers, you are unlikely to give any serious cause for complaint.

4. 'NO WAITING'

Initially your work will relate only to those streets in the centre of Leicester in which waiting is prohibited by the Leicester (Traffic Regulation) Order, 1960. You must study the Order closely. Prohibition of waiting is clearly indicated by traffic signs. It extends from 8.30 am until 6.30 pm from Mondays to Saturdays inclusive; and in certain streets only between 8.30 am and 9.30 am and between 5.0 pm and 6.30 pm. A period of 20 minutes is allowed for the loading and unloading of vehicles so long as a period of not less than 40 minutes has elapsed since the termination of the last period of waiting (if any) of the vehicle outside the same premises.

On seeing a vehicle in a 'No Waiting' area, you should enquire whether the vehicle is being loaded or unloaded or whether it is there because the discretion vested in police by the Order has been exercised in its favour.

(i) *Loading and Unloading.*—The Order does not attempt to define loading or unloading. You will ordinarily not find it necessary at all to enquire about vehicles obviously built for the carriage of goods, *e.g.* lorries, vans, and so on, unless you have reason to believe that they are not actually being loaded or unloaded. When deciding whether private cars can reasonably be said to be loading or unloading, ask yourself if the car appears to be necessary—as distinct from convenient—for that purpose. In a large and wealthy city like Leicester, large sums of money are frequently deposited at banking houses by car or collected from them by the same means; it is obviously better for security and for crime prevention if motor transport can be used for this purpose. It is, therefore, the practice generally to extend the discretion vested in police in respect of loading or unloading to vehicles left outside banking houses for not more than 20 minutes for this purpose.

(ii) *Discretion.*—The Order confers on all police constables a discretion to set aside its provisions in respect of particular vehicles; that discretion is often exercised in accordance with principles well known to a regular force. You must not, therefore, attempt to issue a fixed penalty form if told by any police officer—man or woman—that his or her discretion is being exercised in that particular case; in the event of any doubt, you should report the incident briefly to your superintendent.

Police discretion is also exercised more generally by the senior police officers of the force in respect of loading or unloading that must of necessity take longer than 20 minutes, *e.g.* removals of furniture, deliveries of heavy equipment, and so on. Fixed penalty forms are not to be issued in any case of loading or unloading in respect of which the driver produces a letter or form showing that he has been granted permission by the police.

5. ENFORCEMENT

If you have been unable to prevent the leaving of a motor vehicle in a 'No Waiting' area in contravention of the law, you must adopt one of the following courses:

   (i) If the vehicle is on a main traffic route or near a road junction, or appears to be in a position likely to attract others to it, you should consider whether to notify the control room or the nearest police officer so that consideration can be given to removing it from the highway altogether. If you decide to follow that course, do not issue a fixed penalty form. The police will interview the driver when he collects the vehicle from police headquarters, will levy the fixed charge of £2.00 for removal and will institute proceedings. You should enter particulars of all such cases in your notebook because you may have to give evidence against the driver.

  (ii) If the driver returns to his vehicle or for any other reason you do not think it appropriate to arrange for its removal by police, you should issue a fixed penalty form. It will be helpful to the driver if you inform him that if he does not intend to avail himself of the opportunity to pay the fixed penalty, he can obviate delay in the subsequent proceedings by voluntarily giving you particulars of his name and address. Make sure that these are recorded correctly in your notebook, and in the case of a woman, that you insert correctly the prefix 'Miss' or 'Mrs'.

(iii) If a police officer happens to be in the vicinity and for any reason you think it would be better for the alleged offence to be dealt with by police, you should call upon the officer to assist you. He will then deal with the matter; if proceedings follow, you may be called to give evidence.

6. YOUR NOTEBOOK

You will be issued with a notebook. Whenever you see a vehicle stationary in a 'No Waiting' area, unless you are satisfied that no offence is being committed, enter in your notebook under the appropriate date, particulars of the time, place and registration mark of the vehicle. If you later issue a fixed penalty form, record also the number of the form and the time it was issued.

Remember that you have no power to require anyone to produce a licence or to give you his name and address, but that there is no objection to inviting drivers voluntarily to identify themselves.

7. DISABLED PERSONS

You will occasionally meet with claims by disabled persons for special consideration. The following statement published in the local press on April 23, 1959, will make clear to you the policy of the force with cases of that kind:

'In considering whether or not obstruction by an unattended motor vehicle is likely to be regarded by the courts as unlawful, police have always paid careful attention to any factors urged in mitigration by those reported for this alleged offence.'

'Severe physical disablement—whether resulting from war service or not—is obviously a factor of which police ought to be aware before deciding whether to institute proceedings.'

'It is for that reason that any member of BLESMA, and any other severely disabled driver, is asked to bring his disablement to the notice of police if he should be reported for unnecessary obstruction in the city.'

'It ought not, however, to be assumed that proceedings will necessarily not follow.'

If you are in any doubt in dealing with cases of this kind, do not issue a fixed penalty form; communicate with the nearest police station or police officer. You will then be given assistance by police as soon as possible.

8. MEDICAL PRACTITIONERS

Representations have been received from the British Medical Association and the Medical Practitioners' Union urging recognition of car badges provided by both organisations for display on windscreens of cars used by doctors. It is not open to police in law to agree to a general exemption from the provisions of the law relating to road traffic in respect of any road user or class of road user. No special significance can therefore be attached to any badge or emblem displayed on a motor vehicle.

If, however, a doctor puts forward reasons of professional urgency in mitigation of an alleged contravention of the laws relating to parking, it is possible that police discretion will be exercised in his favour. You must not, therefore, issue a fixed penalty form to a doctor who claims that he has left his car in a 'No Waiting' area for reasons of professional urgency; instead you should note carefully the particulars of the vehicle, invite the doctor voluntarily to give you his name and address, and report the incident to your superintendent.

9. CARE OF FIXED PENALTY FORMS

Each of the fixed penalty forms issued to you represents £2.00 in value and must be accounted for daily. You must, therefore, keep any forms accidentally damaged or marred and hand them in at the end of each day.

10. GENERAL

The police will do all that they can to help you to discharge your duties efficiently. Their power in law to deal with motoring offences of all kinds is much wider than the limited authority conferred upon you. Whenever a police officer is present, you must comply with his instructions in any matter relating to an alleged contravention of the law.

It is not expected that you will discharge your new and difficult duties without occasional errors of judgment or mistakes; these will, no doubt, lessen with experience. It is of the greatest importance that you should understand that mistakes and errors of judgment can always be put right if you reveal them frankly and without hesitation. Do not hesitate to say if you think you have acted wrongly for any reason. Concealment of errors of judgment or mistakes will give the motoring public good cause for complaint against the Traffic Warden Service and will do great harm to its reputation.

METROPOLITAN POLICE DISTRICT

Traffic wardens were appointed to operate in the Central London Area immediately after the Road Traffic and Roads Improvement Act, 1960, came into operation in September, 1960. With the exception of two Metropolitan Boroughs where parking meters have been installed, wardens are employed by the Commissioner of Police to the Metropolis, in the Traffic and Transport Department, as parking meter attendants, in addition to other duties as set out in the Functions of Traffic Wardens Order, 1960. The success of the traffic warden scheme in London can be judged best by the increasing number of wardens employed. Wardens are now employed in most large towns in the United Kingdom.

The Conditions of Service of Traffic Wardens in the Metropolitan Police District are as follows:

CONDITIONS OF SERVICE[6]

Traffic wardens will be members of the Civil Staff of the Commissioner's Office, which is not part of the Civil Service of the Crown although the general conditions of service, discipline, etc., are similar.

DUTIES

Candidates appointed will be liable for service in any part of the Metropolitan Police District. They will be required to discharge such functions in connection with the enforcement of the law relating to parked vehicles or with the control or regulation of road traffic as the Commissioner may direct. In particular, traffic wardens may be required to supervise parking of vehicles at parking meters and to attach tickets to cars which contravene the Parking Meter Order; also to advise members of the public where to park, to warn them against illegal parking and to attach tickets to vehicles which are illegally parked outside the parking meter bays.

HOURS

Normal working hours will be 44 (gross) over a week of $5\frac{1}{2}$ days; and duty will be performed on early and late hours.

TRAINING

There will be a short course of training (with pay).

UNIFORM

Traffic wardens will be required to wear the prescribed uniform on duty.

PROBATION

In the first instance appointment will normally be in an unestablished (non-pensionable) capacity and will be subject to the satisfactory completion of an initial trial period of three months. After a minimum qualifying period of two years a traffic warden will be eligible to be considered for appointment to the established staff. On appointment in an established capacity a traffic warden will be on probation for one year from the date of establishment.

ANNUAL LEAVE

Traffic wardens will be allowed three weeks annual leave (in addition to the usual public holidays or days in lieu thereof), increasing to three weeks and three days after 10 years' service.

SICK LEAVE

During the first year of service sick leave on full pay, less any National Insurance benefit received, may be allowed up to a maximum of one week for every month of effective service. After 12 months' effective service an officer may be allowed up to three months' sick leave on full pay in any period of 12 months, less any National Insurance benefit received. For established staff, sick leave on full pay, less any National Insurance benefit received, may be allowed up to a maximum of six months in any period of 12 months, and thereafter for a further period on reduced pay, subject to a deduction of National Insurance benefit in certain cases; provided that sick leave must not exceed an overall maximum of 12 months in any period of four years or less.

PENSION

The appointment, when established, will carry superannuation benefits similar to those which apply in the Civil Service. These benefits normally provide a pension and lump sum gratuity calculated on the number of years' service and the average salary over the last three years before retirement. No contributions are required to secure these benefits, but there is also a contributory pension scheme for widows and children.

INJURY ON DUTY

In the event of an injury to a traffic warden arising out of or in the course of his employment, he will be entitled to compensation only to the extent and in the circumstances prescribed by the National Insurance (Industrial Injuries) Act, 1946, or any amendments thereof.

TERMINATION OF APPOINTMENT

The engagement may be terminated at any time by a week's notice on either side, such notice to run from any day of the week; and in the case of misconduct notice or pay in lieu of notice. The engagement will be reviewed when a traffic warden reaches the age of 60 and, subject to annual review thereafter, will terminate when he reaches the age of 65.

Note: Salaries and conditions of service are liable to alteration.

LEICESTER [7]

Leicester was the first provincial city to appoint traffic wardens. The service commenced in March 1961, under Mr Robert Mark, who was then the Chief Constable. He commenced with nine wardens, and at the end of the first year the staff was 39 wardens, of which 19 were women.

Initially the duties of traffic wardens were confined to supervision of streets in which waiting is prohibited between 8.30 am and 6.30 pm. Subsequently their duties were extended to include supervision of streets in which unilateral waiting is permitted for 30 minutes between those hours. Enforcement of the traffic regulations was achieved by use of the fixed penalty procedure authorised by the Road Traffic and Roads Improvement Act, 1960, as now repealed by the Road Traffic Regulation Act, 1967.

Mr Robert Mark considers that the success of any measure for the regulation of traffic must depend on the extent to which the regulations can be enforced. No more prohibitions or restrictions should be imposed than are clearly necessary in the public interest, and are within the capacity of the staff available for enforcement. Relaxation of the enforcement of these measures would lead to inadequate, spasmodic or bad enforcement; resentment and criticism by vehicle drivers, and frontagers; and would tend to bring the system into disrepute.

The primary duty of wardens is the prevention of offences by helping motorists to find a suitable parking place. During the first year a record of the contravention of the Orders was closed on 6255 occasions with a word of warning, and without the issue of a fixed penalty ticket.

The second duty of enforcement was the issue of fixed penalty tickets, and 2908 were issued during the first year. This was only an average of 55·9 tickets per week or an average of 1·7 tickets per warden per week. Of the penalty tickets issued, 87·9 per cent were paid voluntarily, 4·4 per cent were excused, and 6·3 per cent were referred to the Justices. The remaining 1·4 per cent were cancelled owing to some defect or other in completion. The average delay between the issue of a fixed penalty ticket and the court proceedings following non-payment was eight weeks.

The staff employed in Leicester consisted of one inspector and one sergeant engaged on recruitment, training and supervision of traffic wardens, and two clerks engaged on the administration of the service, and the fixed penalty procedure.

The cost of operating a traffic warden scheme compared with an extension of the police force based on 1971 wages and salaries is as follows:

1. This is a comparison of the basic cost (*i.e.* pay, rent allowance and pensions) of 50 police officers with that of 50 traffic wardens in the provinces.

2. The cost of uniform, national insurance, etc., for both groups is roughly the same and can therefore be disregarded for this purpose.

3. The cost of police officers engaged wholetime in training and supervision of traffic wardens is offset by the difference in the cost of training traffic wardens as compared with the cost of training police; that factor has been disregarded also.

(A) POLICE   £

 2 inspectors ⎫ Pay at the minimum plus 20 per cent pension
 8 sergeants   ⎬ charge   70,050
 40 constables ⎭

 Rent allowances: 40 married men⎫   8,750
        10 single men   ⎭

                    78,800
 The same officers at the maximum pay scale   99,144

(B) TRAFFIC WARDENS

 44 wardens (minimum of pay scale)
 6 leading wardens (minimum of pay scale, plus 10 per cent
  pension charge)   51,156
 The same wardens (maximum of pay scale)   55,836

(C) DIFFERENCE IN ANNUAL COST

 At the minimum   27,644
 At the maximum   43,308

The Chief Constable gives the following summary of the first year's working of the traffic warden scheme in Leicester.[7]

'The new service can now be said to have ended its experimental stage and to have achieved unexpected success. It enjoys excellent public relations, has maintained very satisfactory traffic conditions and has allowed extensive saving of police manpower. It has also helped to lessen appreciably the work of the local Courts. So long as the traffic wardens continue to be employed on the enforcement of clearly advertised conventional methods of traffic regulation, not related to schemes offering facilities for street parking, in return for a monetary payment, it seems probable that they will continue to be acceptable to the motoring public, to afford a persuasive and effective system of traffic control and to allow the highest possible proportion of the force to concentrate on its most urgent task—the prevention and detection of crime'.

REFERENCES

1. Road Traffic Regulation Act, 1967. HMSO, London.
2. The Functions of Traffic Wardens Order, 1960. SI 1960, No. 1582. HMSO, London.
3. Home Office Circular No. 139: 2nd September, 1960. Home Office, London.
4. 'Hansard', Vol. 62. No. 96. HMSO, London.
5. MARK, ROBERT, Annual Report as Chief Constable of Leicester, 1961.
6. Regulations & Conditions of Employment of Traffic Wardens in the Metropolitan Police District. Commissioner of Police to the Metropolis, London, 1960.
7. MARK, ROBERT, 'Traffic Wardens—The First Year', March, 1962.
8. MARK, ROBERT, 'A Police View on the Control of Parking in Urban Areas', July, 1963.

Chapter 9

Surface Car Parks

A surface car park may be a spare piece of land on which as many cars as possible are crowded, or it may be a large car park of good design and layout surrounding a shopping centre and occupying three times as much land as the buildings occupy. Whatever the size, and wherever they may be, permanent surface car parks should be regarded as a piece of permanent development, and not left in an untidy, neglected condition.

In the heavily war-damaged cities in England and on the Continent of Europe, many 'blitzed' sites have been used as temporary car parks until permanent development has taken place. These sites have often had no special attention other than rough levelling, but they have given useful parking areas until more permanent car parks could be constructed.

As with other types of parking facilities and building development, a surface car park must be well designed, efficiently operated, and made as far as possible aesthetically pleasing.

LAYOUT OF CAR PARK

Sites for surface car parks are usually irregular in shape, and an individual layout has to be prepared for each site. There are certain basic principles which will help the designer to make most use of the land available. In preparing the design it should be remembered that if a compacted surface is to be laid it will be necessary to avoid awkward slopes and small corners where mechanical plant cannot operate. If these cannot be avoided it may be possible to use them for trees, shrubs or as flower beds.

Vehicles range in size from the small British Leyland mini cars to the large limousines. It is interesting to note that there has not been any appreciable change in the size of cars during the last ten years. The United Kingdom Ministry of Housing and Local Government have devised a 'standard design car', 4·78 m (15 ft 8 in) × 1·77 m (5 ft 10 in).[1] The dimensions cover 95 per cent of the cars in current use in the United Kingdom, which is a reasonable basis for design purposes. It has become common practice in the United Kingdom to design parking stalls 16 ft 0 in × 8 ft 0 in; suitable metric dimensions recommended by the

103

TABLE II
Dimensions of Cars, 1970[2]

Make and Model	Length			Width			Turning circle		
	metres	ft	in	metres	ft	in	metres	ft	in
Aston Martin									
DB6 Mk. II	4·6	15	2	1·68	5	6	10·4	34	0
Austin									
Mini	3·05	10	$0\frac{1}{4}$	1·41	4	$7\frac{1}{2}$	8·55	28	0
1300	3·7	12	$2\frac{3}{4}$	1·54	5	$0\frac{1}{2}$	11·20	36	9
Maxi	4·05	13	3	1·625	5	4	10·3	33	9
3 litre de luxe	4·7	15	$5\frac{3}{4}$	1·695	5	$6\frac{3}{4}$	12·2	40	0
Bentley									
T Series	5·15	16	$11\frac{1}{2}$	1·8	5	11	11·60	38	0
Buick									
Riviera	5·2	17	$1\frac{1}{4}$	2·02	6	$7\frac{1}{4}$	14·25	46	9
Cadillac									
Eldorado	5·6	18	5	2·05	6	8	13·6	44	9
Fleetwood Broughan	5·8	19	$0\frac{1}{2}$	2·05	6	8	14·0	45	9
Chevrolet									
Corvette	4·65	15	$2\frac{1}{2}$	1·75	5	9	12·15	39	9
Caprice	5·5	18	0	2·03	6	$7\frac{3}{4}$	–		–
Chrysler									
300 Hardtop	5·7	18	$8\frac{1}{2}$	2·01	6	7	13·5	44	3
Daimler									
Sovereign	4·8	15	$9\frac{1}{2}$	1·77	5	$9\frac{3}{4}$	11·0	36	0
Limousine	5·0	16	$6\frac{1}{2}$	1·62	5	$3\frac{3}{4}$	12·8	42	0
Dodge									
Challenger	4·85	15	$11\frac{1}{4}$	1·94	6	$4\frac{1}{2}$	11·9	39	0
Charger	5·83	19	$1\frac{3}{4}$	2·01	6	7	12·4	44	0
Ford									
Escort	3·95	13	$0\frac{1}{2}$	1·57	5	$1\frac{3}{4}$	8·75	29	0
Capri	4·25	13	$11\frac{3}{4}$	1·645	5	$4\frac{3}{4}$	9·75	32	0
Corsair 2000E	4·5	14	$8\frac{1}{2}$	1·61	5	$3\frac{1}{2}$	11·15	36	6
Zodiac Mk. IV	4·72	15	$5\frac{3}{4}$	1·81	5	$11\frac{1}{4}$	10·5	34	6
Hillman									
Imp	3·82	12	7	1·53	5	$0\frac{1}{4}$	9·30	30	6
Hunter	4·3	14	$1\frac{1}{2}$	1·61	5	$3\frac{1}{2}$	10·4	34	0
Humber									
Sceptre	4·3	14	$1\frac{1}{2}$	1·645	5	$4\frac{3}{4}$	10·4	34	0
Jaguar									
XJ6—4·2 litre	4·8	15	$9\frac{1}{2}$	1·77	5	$9\frac{3}{4}$	11·0	36	0
420G	5·15	16	10	1·93	6	4	11·30	37	0
Mercedes Benz									
220	4·7	15	$4\frac{1}{2}$	1·77	5	$9\frac{3}{4}$	10·8	35	6
600	5·5	18	2	1·95	6	$4\frac{3}{4}$	12·4	40	6
M.G.									
Midget	3·48	11	$5\frac{1}{2}$	1·40	4	7	9·5	31	3
MGB	3·9	12	$9\frac{1}{4}$	1·525	5	0	9·75	32	0

TABLE II—*continued*

Dimensions of Cars, 1970 [2]

Make and Model	*Length* metres	ft	in	*Width* metres	ft	in	*Turning circle* metres	ft	in
Morris									
Minor 1000	3·75	12	4	1·55	5	1	10·05	33	0
Oxford	4·4	14	6	1·61	5	3½	11·3	37	0
Peugeot									
204	3·95	13	0	1·56	5	1½	9·45	31	0
504	4·5	14	8¾	1·69	5	6½	10·9	35	9
Pontiac									
Firebird	4·85	15	11	1·88	6	2	11·9	38	6
Grand Prix	5·3	17	6¼	1·925	6	3¾	12·0	39	3
Renault									
4	3·65	12	0	1·485	4	10½	8·7	28	6
8 and 10	4·0	13	1	1·485	4	10½	9·30	30	6
12	4·25	14	3	1·64	5	4½	10·0	32	9
Rolls-Royce									
Silver Shadow	5·18	16	11½	1·8	5	11	11·60	38	0
Phantom VI	6·0	19	10	1·75	6	7	14·90	48	9
Rover									
2000	4·5	14	10½	1·68	5	6	9·6	31	6
3·5	4·72	15	6½	1·78	5	10	12·2	40	0
Simca									
1100 GLS	3·95	12	11¼	1·58	5	2¼	11·0	36	0
1301 GL and 1501 Special	4·45	14	7½	1·575	5	2	9·75	32	0
Singer									
Chamois	3·54	11	7	1·53	5	0¼	9·30	30	6
Vogue	4·3	14	1½	1·61	5	3½	10·4	34	0
Sunbeam									
Rapier	4·45	14	6½	1·645	5	4¾	10·4	34	0
Triumph									
Herald 1200, 13/60 and Vitesse 2 litre Mk. II	3·9	12	9	1·525	5	0	7·64	25	0
2000	4·4	14	5¾	1·65	5	5	9·75	32	0
Vauxhall									
Viva and Viva GT	4·1	13	5	1·60	5	3	9·65	31	9
Victor 1600, VX 4/90 and Ventora II	4·5	14	8¾	1·70	5	7	10·15	33	3
Volkswagen									
1300	4·75	13	4¼	1·55	5	1	11·0	36	0
1600 TL	4·2	13	10½	1·60	5	3	11·30	37	0
Volvo									
131	4·45	14	7¼	1·62	5	3¾	9·6	31	6
164	4·7	15	5½	1·73	5	8	9·2	30	3
Wolseley									
18/85 Mk. II	4·22	13	10	1·70	5	7	11·30	37	0

British Parking Association Technical Committee are 4·75 m (15 ft 7 in) × 2·5 m (8 ft 2½ in).[3] The reduced length of 4·75 m (15 ft 7 in) would accommodate in length approximately 95 per cent of the cars in the United Kingdom at the present time (1970). The British Parking Association Technical Committee recommend that the width of a parking stall could be reduced to 2·30 m (7 ft 6 in) where a car park is used for long term parking, e.g. a staff car park for commuters where the motorist and passengers are not likely to be handling luggage, push chairs, parcels, etc., which they may do in a short term public car park.

The Allegemeiner Deutscher Automobil Club recommends a stall width of 2·30 m (7 ft 6½ in) for short term parking and 2·25 m (7 ft 4½ in) for long period parking, and a stall length of 5·0 m (16 ft 6 in). In the United States of America

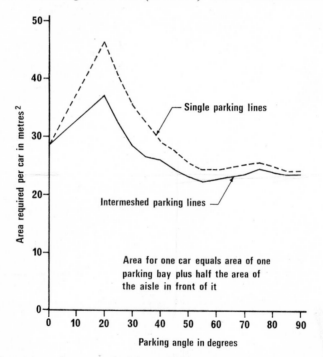

Fig. 9.1 Comparison of area required for parking one car. (*Reproduced from 'Parking', by Burrage and Mogran, by permission of Eno Foundation for Highway Traffic Control Inc., Saugatuck, Conn., USA.*)

the size of the parking stalls in common use is 5·0 m (18 ft 6 in) × 2·60 m (8 ft 6 in). Where the side of a parking stall adjoins a wall an extra width of 0·30 m (1 ft 0 in) should be allowed.

The aisle width recommended with 90° parking and one-way traffic is 6·0 m (20 ft 0 in). For two-way traffic the aisle width should be increased to 7·50 m (24 ft 0 in). With angle parking the width of the aisle may be reduced as shown in Table VIII in Chapter 10—Multi-storey Car Parks.

Cars may be parked by reversing into the parking stall or by driving forward. It is usually easier to drive forward, and reverse out, rather than the converse.

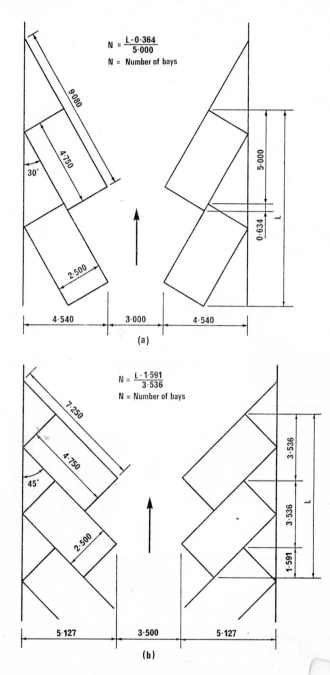

Fig. 9.2(*a*) and (*b*)   Dimensions (in metres) required for parking cars at ang'

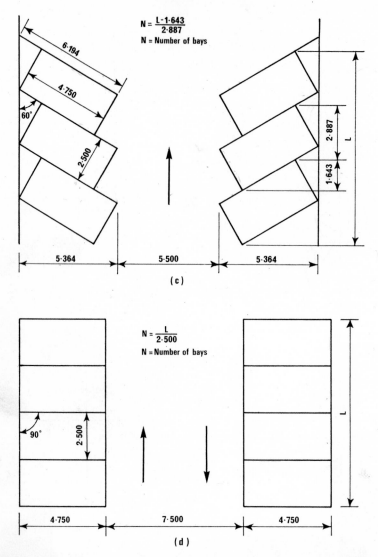

Fig. 9.2(c) and (d) Dimensions (in metres) required for parking cars at angles of 60° and 90°.

The angle of parking has an effect on the area of space required for each car. This is shown in the graph (Fig. 9.1). Parking at 90° to the direction of the aisle is the most economical, and parallel to the aisle the most uneconomical in space requirements. The choice of layout in a car park will depend on the shape and dimensions of the area available. Figures 9.2(a)–(d) show the dimensions required for parking cars at an angle of 30°, 45°, 60° and 90°, and Figs. 9.3(a) and (b) show the dimensions required for different interlocking layouts.

Layouts for an area 28·0 m × 30·0 m are shown in Figs. 9.4(a) to (h) using the

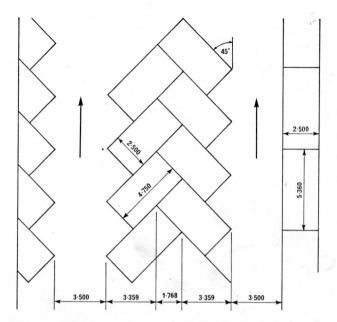

Fig. 9.3(*a*) Layout and dimensions (in metres) required for interlocked parking with traffic moving in one direction.

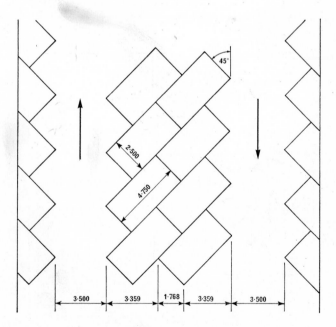

Fig. 9.3(*b*) Layout and dimensions (in metres) required for interlocked parking with traffic moving in two directions.

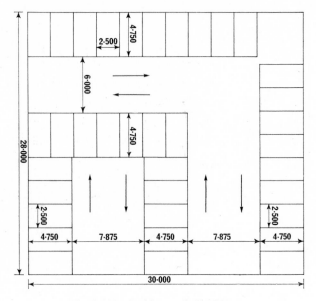

Fig. 9.4(*a*)   Parking stalls for 36 cars.

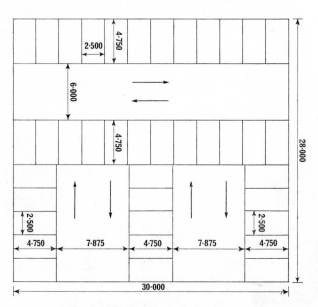

Fig. 9.4(*b*)   Parking stalls for 39 cars.

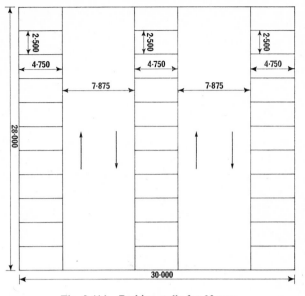

Fig. 9.4(*c*)   Parking stalls for 33 cars.

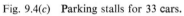

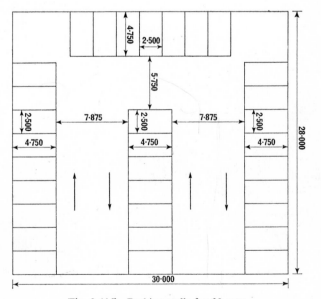

Fig. 9.4(*d*)   Parking stalls for 32 cars.

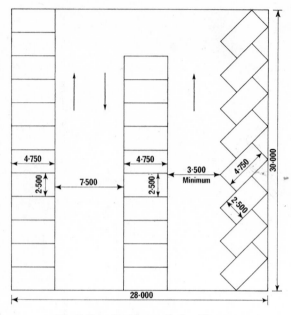

Fig. 9.4(*e*)   Parking stalls for 30 cars.

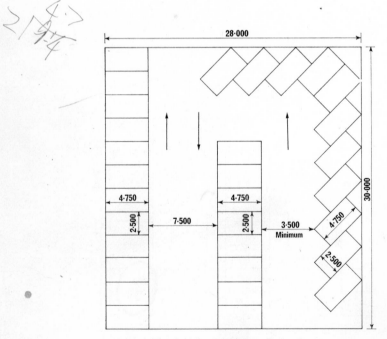

Fig. 9.4(*f*)   Parking stalls for 31 cars.

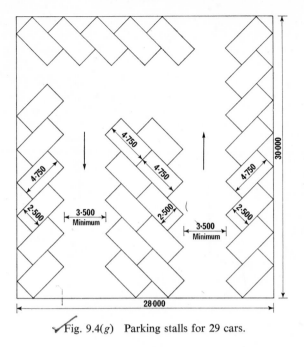

Fig. 9.4(g)   Parking stalls for 29 cars.

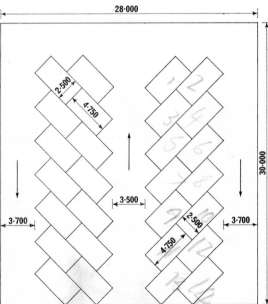

Fig. 9.4(h)   Parking stalls for 28 cars.

Fig. 9.4(a) to (h)   Diagrams showing the number of parking spaces for cars that can be provided in an area 28·0 m × 30·0 m. (All dimensions in metres.)

dimensions for spacing given in Figs. 9.2(*a*)–(*d*). It will be noted that there is an appreciable variation in the number of cars parked in the different layouts. It is desirable that the designer should draft out different layouts for any parking site to obtain the maximum number of parking places. It should also be noted that with 90° parking, a two-way traffic flow may be permitted in the aisles, but with angle parking the traffic flow must be limited to one direction. The flow of traffic in the aisles on the car park is important, and it may be necessary in a layout to give up a few parking places to facilitate ingress and egress.

In city centres, land is too expensive for large areas to be used for surface parking permanently, and it is in the suburban areas where they will be found

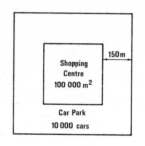

Fig. 9.5 Diagram showing walking distances in different arrangements for parking around a supermarket.

most suitable. An hotel or restaurant situated in the middle of a site with an ample number of parking spaces all around, or perhaps around three sides, would be regarded as ideal. Easy access, ample parking space and short walking distance make the car park most attractive. In the United States of America, and other countries, regional and suburban shopping centres have been built with large areas of surface car parking around them. It is now considered in the United States of America that the ratio of parking to shopping area should be 2·5 to 1, and some authorities recommend that the ratio should be 3 to 1. Shopping centres may have a floor area increasing to 100,000 m^2 (1,000,000 sq ft) and, therefore, a parking area of 300,000 m^2 (3,000,000 sq ft) would be

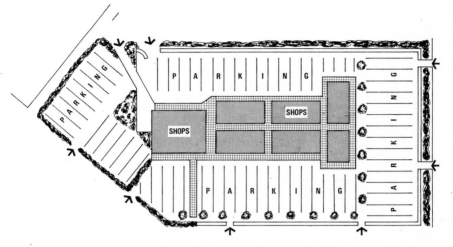

Fig. 9.6   Cheltenham, Philadelphia, USA Shopping Centre. Parking capacity 3850 cars.

Fig. 9.7   The Yorkdale Shopping Centre, Toronto, Canada, on 20th December, 1969. (*Reproduced by permission of Lockwood Survey Corporation Ltd., and Triton Centres Ltd., Toronto, Canada.*)

Fig. 9.8 The Northlands Shopping Centre, Southfield, Michigan, USA. (*Reproduced by permission of the Northlands Shopping Centre.*)

required. This would be so large that in order to reduce the walking distance as much as possible, it is necessary for the shops to be in the centre of the parking area (Fig. 9.5). This would give a depth of 150 m (500 ft) for car parking surrounding a 100,000 m² (1,000,000 sq ft) store. If the car park had to be situated on two opposite sides of the shopping centre it would extend for 460 m (1500 ft) and, if situated on one side only, it would extend for twice this distance or 920 m (3000 ft).

These parking areas are usually approached from expressways by well designed entrances and connecting lanes. They are planned in sections with a road around the boundaries. The areas are laid out into parking stalls, which are numbered to facilitate the easy location of a car when the driver comes to collect it (Figs. 9.6 to 9.8).

American ingenuity has also invented the 'drive-in' cinema with cars parked in concentric arcs of a quadrant in front of a screen. Here, the whole family, including the baby in a carry-cot, can remain in the car. Whilst the baby sleeps, parents can see the film.

FORECOURT PARKING

Many buildings such as town halls, public halls, theatres, cinemas, hotels and various places of entertainment, are planned with an entrance forecourt and there may or may not be some space available for car parking. The space available is likely to be very small compared with the number of cars used for visits to the building. To use the available space for car parking often involves a lot of backing and turning against the flow of traffic, which causes delay and congestion, and it is often better to provide a smaller forecourt with very few if any parking places. All visiting cars should have a free flow by driving in at one entrance, and after delivering the passengers, driving out at the exit, adequate parking arrangements being provided a short distance away.

SUBURBAN SHOPPING CAR PARKS

Suburban shopping centres should be provided with adequate off-street parking, and the best site is usually at the rear of the shops. A modern shopping centre should be grouped around a pedestrian way so that the shopper is segregated from moving vehicular traffic. Even when there is car parking space available, motorists are found parking their cars by the kerbside to avoid carrying heavy parcels, or to save time.

The walking distance around blocks of buildings can become quite tiresome especially for women when carrying heavy shopping bags and parcels. The distance to be walked from a car park to shops can often be reduced considerably if the car park is at the rear of the shops and a secondary shopping frontage with a public entrance is designed to face the car park. The shopper can then pass through the shop direct to the car, and so save a considerable carrying distance. This will make it easier and more simple to park in the car park rather than the street.

RURAL CAR PARKS

Whilst car parking has become a problem in the urban areas it has also created a problem in some rural districts, by the visitors to well-known beauty or picnic spots, and travellers stopping by the roadside for a picnic meal. There are many country roads without footpaths, which are places of scenic beauty. At weekends and on public holidays they are often lined on both sides with parked cars. These conditions force pedestrians to walk in the centre of the road in the line of moving traffic. There are situations where a loop road leading to a surface car park should be provided, and preferably screened from the road by trees or shrubs so that the cars would not be unsightly nor a potential danger to anyone.

With the development of Country Parks, Nature Reserves, Canal and Riverside Parks and Nature Trails, the provision of car parks in the countryside is becoming most important. It is essential that areas allocated for car parking should be well designed and landscaped to harmonise with the surrounding area (Fig. 9.9).

Fig. 9.9 Car park at the National Park Centre, Brockhole, on the shores of Lake Windermere in the Lake District National Park. The surface is of hollow concrete blocks permitting grass to grow in the interstices. (*Reproduced by permission of the Central Office of Information, London.*)

An example of the control of traffic and parking in the country may be seen in the Goyt Valley within the Peak National Park. Here, because of the large number of visitors at weekends, arrangements have been made for motorists to leave their cars in a car park, and proceed along the valley by mini-bus. No cars are permitted within the motorless zone between 10.0 am and 6.0 pm at weekends. Visitors arriving between these hours must park their cars at one of the four car parks at the edge of the valley, and then either walk into the valley or ride on a mini-bus. Each car park is supervised by a marshal with powers to direct traffic. Temporary chemical toilets have been provided at three of the car parks to supplement the flush toilets in the valley. Each mini-bus seats twelve people and follows a circular route, linking request stops in the valley and calling regularly at each car park.

Motor access through the valley is only permitted to those who require access to land in the valley, *i.e.* those carrying permits, as well as essential services such as police and firemen. Pedal cyclists, walkers and pony trekkers may use the roads in the valley, while the marshals at each car park exercise discretion in letting through private cars carrying very old, infirm or paralysed people who are unable to use the mini-bus service.

On many motorways suitable parking places have been well designed off the motorway and concealed behind trees. Strong wooden benches are fixed in the shade of the trees and, where possible, there is a water supply. These concealed parking places or laybys are just as necessary for other main traffic routes and on other roads where groups of cars are parked.

This is a parking need which has been neglected in many countries, and the motorist has had to rely on a level piece of grass verge or an empty layby when not in use for storing road metal.

SURFACING OF VEHICLE PARKS

Coated macadam is the material most generally used for the surfacing of vehicle parks. Having regard, however, to the particular problems which arise from parked vehicles and to the fact that the surfacing does not receive the same degree of compaction from the rolling action of traffic as it would under normal road usage, it is essential, in order to obtain the best results, to select the type or types of coated macadam most appropriate for the particular circumstances.

The main requirements of a surfacing for such areas are:

(*a*) it shall not indent or deform under the standing loads of parked vehicles,
(*b*) the surface shall be resistant to the softening effect of oil droppings.

The first requirement can be met by the use in the surfacing of a sufficiently strong binder, while the second can be dealt with by the use of a binder which is not softened by oil droppings or the selection of a material which is sufficiently dense or close-textured to prevent oil droppings penetrating the material to any serious extent.

In general, tar is more resistant than bitumen to softening by oil droppings, but close-textured material made with a relatively high-viscosity bitumen can have a satisfactory life if the contamination is not excessive.

In addition to having a surfacing, *i.e.* base course and wearing course, which will not deform in itself under the standing loads, it is important that the remainder of the construction, *i.e.* the base and sub-base, is adequate to distribute the standing and slow moving loads over a sufficient area of sub-grade. The Road Research Laboratory has shown that this type of traffic produces greater stresses in the sub-grade than the same weights when moving at normal speeds.

The construction and surfacing should, therefore, be selected according to the heaviest type of vehicle for which the parking area is to be provided and for the purpose of these recommendations vehicles have been divided into the following categories:

(*a*) private cars and light vans,

(b) medium lorries carrying up to, say, 5 tons,

(c) heavy lorries, articulated vehicles and buses.

Specifications and further information are available from The Asphalt and Coated Macadam Association, 25 Lower Belgrave Street, London. SW1.[4-18]

Concrete paving is a suitable material for surfacing car parks, and will give satisfactory service for very many years during which time maintenance will be negligible. It is especially suited to ground which has a poor bearing value.

Where sub-grades are composed of very firm and stable soils such as naturally occurring mixtures of sand and gravel which can be readily compacted, the provision of a base under the concrete paving is not necessary. More usually, however, a base is considered desirable since it provides a hard working platform over the site which not only protects the sub-grade but also ensures uniform support to the concrete paving. Subsequently, it gives protection to those sub-grades which are susceptible to frost action.

A base thickness of 75·0 mm (3 in) is usually adequate, although this should be increased to 150·0 mm (6 in) where the sub-grade consists of unstable soils such as soft clay and chalk, peat and soils of variable bearing capacity.

Materials suitable for based are hoggin (i.e. a natural gravel sand and clay mixture), lean concrete, cement stabilised soil, crushed stone and slag. Clinker and shale are also suitable provided they are well burned, hard, free from sulphur and suitably graded, whilst hardcore can be used if it is crushed to a maximum size of 50·0 mm (2 in). Large lumps of brick or concrete are unsatisfactory, and ashes are also unsuitable because they are generally unstable when wet.

The following tables give the recommended thicknesses for concrete paving on vehicle parking areas for various conditions (Table III); the mix proportions by weight for plain concrete (Table IV), and for air entrained concrete (Table V); the recommended weights of reinforcement and spacing of joints (Table VI), and the recommended dimensions and spacing of dowel bars (Table VII).[19,20]

TABLE III

Recommended Thicknesses of Concrete Paving

Subgrade Soil	Light Vehicles (Unladen weight of less than 1·5 tonnes (30 cwt))				Heavy Vehicles (Unladen weight of more than 1·5 tonnes (30 cwt))			
	Unreinforced (mm)	(in)	Reinforced (mm)	(in)	Unreinforced (mm)	(in)	Reinforced (mm)	(in)
Normal	150	6	125	5	200	8	175	7
Poor (e.g. very soft clay and soft chalk, peat, etc.)	175	7	150	6	225	9	200	8

TABLE IV

Mix Proportions by Weight for Plain Concrete

Maximum size of coarse aggregate, mm (in)		38 mm ($1\frac{1}{2}$ in)			19 mm ($\frac{3}{4}$ in)		
Slump, mm (in) (See note 1)		12–38 mm ($\frac{1}{2}$–$1\frac{1}{2}$ in)			12–38 mm ($\frac{1}{2}$–$1\frac{1}{2}$ in)		
Compacting factor (See note 1)		0·85–0·90			0·85–0·90		
Fine aggregate zone (BS 882) (9·19)		1	2	3	1	2	3
Dry weights of aggregate kg (lb) per 50 kg (112 lb) cement. (See note 2)	sand	147 kg 325 lb	136 kg 300 lb	125 kg 275 lb	125 kg 275 lb	113 kg 250 lb	102 kg 225 lb
	coarse	180 kg 400 lb	193 kg 425 lb	204 kg 450 lb	158 kg 350 lb	170 kg 375 lb	180 kg 400 lb

TABLE V

Mix Proportions by Weight for Air Entrained Concrete

Maximum size of coarse aggregate, mm (in)		38 mm ($1\frac{1}{2}$ in)			19 mm ($\frac{3}{4}$ in)		
Slump, mm (in) (See note 1)		12–38 mm ($\frac{1}{2}$–$1\frac{1}{2}$ in)			12–38 mm ($\frac{1}{2}$–$1\frac{1}{2}$ in)		
Compacting factor (See note 1)		0·85–0·90			0·85–0·90		
Fine aggregate zone (BS 882) (9·19)		1	2	3	1	2	3
Dry weights of aggregate kg (lb) per 50 kg (112 lb) cement. (See note 2)	sand	136 kg 300 lb	125 kg 275 lb	113 kg 250 lb	113 kg 250 lb	102 kg 225 lb	102 kg 225 lb
	coarse	170 kg 375 lb	180 kg 400 lb	193 kg 425 lb	147 kg 325 lb	158 kg 350 lb	158 kg 350 lb

Note 1: Slumps and compacting factors are quoted as a guide to workability, for use on sites where these qualities are measured.

Note 2: The proportion of sand to coarse aggregate may require slight adjustment though the total weight of sand and coarse aggregate should not be increased.

TABLE VI

Recommended Weights of Reinforcement and Spacing of Joints

Type of Vehicle	Slab Thickness	Minimum Weight of Reinforcement	Maximum Spacing of Transverse Joints
Light (unladen weight less than 1·5 tonnes (30 cwt))	125 or 150 mm (5 or 6 in)	1·6 kg (3½ lb)	12 m (40 ft)
	150 or 175 mm (6 or 7 in)	None	4·5 m (15 ft)
Heavy (unladen weight over 1·5 tonnes (30 cwt))	175 or 200 mm (7 or 8 in)	2·0 kg (4½ lb)	12 m (40 ft)
	200 or 225 mm (8 or 9 in)	None	4·5 m (15 ft)

TABLE VII

Recommended Dimensions and Spacing of Dowel Bars

Thickness of Slab	Dowel Bar		
	Diameter	Length	Spacing
150 and 175 mm (6 and 7 in)	13 mm (½ in)	500 mm (20 in)	300 mm (12 in)
200 and 225 mm (8 and 9 in)	19 mm (¾ in)	600 mm (24 in)	300 mm (12 in)

EXPANSION JOINTS

Expansion joints are only required in special cases as, for example, where the paved area meets adjoining buildings or walls. In these circumstances a separating medium of compressible material such as bitumen impregnated fibreboard or suitable chipboard about 25·0 mm (1 in) thick will be perfectly adequate.

FINISH ON CONCRETE SURFACES

Surfaces of concrete paved areas may have a 'tamped' finish, a 'sandpaper texture' or a brush finish texture. In certain cases it may be desirable to produce areas of concrete paving with a surface that contrasts with the normal concrete; this can be achieved by using coloured cements which enable a variety of surface finishes to be formed. Generally, coloured surfaces are used for aesthetic reasons, but they may also be used for practical purposes.

AMENITIES

The motor car in isolation may be well designed, beautifully finished and pleasing to look upon. When viewed *en masse* on a highway or on a parking ground it can be an ugly sight. When a large surface car park is empty it may have a depressing appearance of waste and desolation. This can probably be seen under the worst conditions when a demolished building site is used for car parking after carrying out the minimum amount of levelling work.

Surface car parks are unquestionably necessary and, therefore, some effort should be made when designing and constructing them to make them as attractive as possible, and harmonise them with the surrounding area. This can be done most successfully by planting trees, shrubs and, in special cases, flowers.

By planting individual trees on corners and odd pieces of land within the car park, the sight of the mass of cars can be broken up to advantage and the appearance of desolation will not be apparent when the car park is empty. Even if the planting does not completely screen the mass of cars from view, it gives colour, and a refreshing appearance of informality which distracts the attention of the pedestrian from the mass of chromium, steel, glass and cellulose.

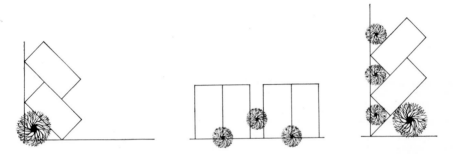

Fig. 9.10   Diagrams showing suitable places for planting trees in a car park.

It may be thought that adding these amenities to surface car parks reduces the parking area, and adds expense in layout, construction and maintenance. In some cases the parking area may be reduced or it may be possible to add extra land for planting trees and shrubs to form a screen.

It is possible, however, to carry out such planting without reducing the capacity of the car park, or interfering in any way with the flow of traffic. In most parks, after an economical layout has been prepared, there is some waste land, and even when as much of this as possible has been set aside for parking motor cycles there are often small areas of land which are inaccessible to a vehicle. These may be used to advantage for tree planting. Even with 90° parking which usually leaves the smallest amount of vacant space, the length of a car park does not always divide exactly by 2·50 m (8 feet) and there is often a spare strip in which one or two trees could be planted.

With a herring-bone layout there are small triangular areas which are useless for parking and ideal for tree planting (Fig. 9.10).

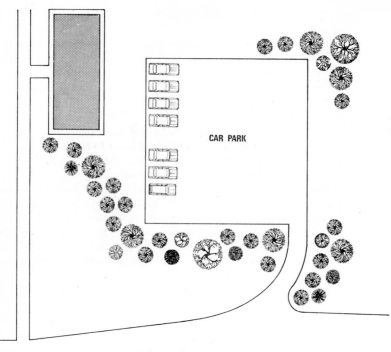

Fig. 9.11   Car park adjoining buildings suitably screened by a careful arrangement of tree and shrub planting.

An informal arrangement of groups of trees and shrubs massed to fit in with the landscape in a rural, semi-rural or suburban area can form an effective screen to a car park in such a way that it will be completely unnoticed except by people much above the level of the car park. Examples of this type of screening are shown in Figs. 9.11 and 9.12.

Variation in the level of the ground can be turned to advantage in screening a car park. A sunken site in a small valley, or low-lying ground, will be partially

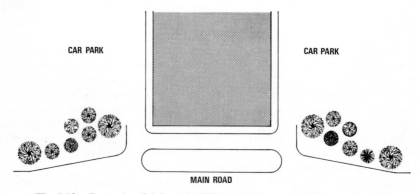

Fig. 9.12   Car park adjoining a building suitably screened from main road.

Fig. 9.13   Car park at road level screened by shrubs and trees.

Fig. 9.14   Car park below road level screened by bank and shrubs.

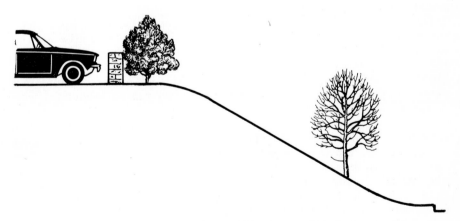

Fig. 9.15   Car park above road level screened by shrubs.

hidden from view and can be completely screened by the judicious planting of trees.

Figures 9.13 to 9.15 show how the eye line between a pedestrian on the road and a parked car can be broken by trees and shrubs, whether the car is parked above or below the road. Natural features and well-established trees should, as far as possible, be preserved. This is perhaps most important when large areas of land are being planned as car parks to accommodate several thousand cars.

Planting material for use in car parks should be chosen with care and caution. Forest trees should be planted where there is adequate space to allow their unrestricted development both above and below ground. Otherwise severe lopping will produce a grotesque subject, and the ramification of the roots can be a source of constant trouble to drains. Forest trees liable to shed their branches or be uprooted in gales, *e.g.* Elms, or to lose their branches in dry periods, *e.g.* Beech, should not be used.

The common Horse Chestnut, although majestic, should be omitted from planting schemes because the fruit, commonly known as 'conkers', provides a constant source of trouble from young children. The missiles shied at the trees to dislodge the fruit are liable to damage parked vehicles.

The form *Aesculus hippocastanum* variety *Flore pleno* having double flowers is sterile and does not set fruit. When this variety is available it may be planted without reservation.

The common Lime, *Tilia vulgaris*, can only be described as an offensive tree when associated with car parks. The sticky exudation of frass or honeydew, which drips from the leaves when the trees are attacked by an aphis, will cover cars parked beneath them with an objectionable gummy fluid not easy to remove. The exudation is likely to be very bad during dry summers.

Tilia euchlora and *Tilia petiolaris*, are almost insect proof and are both superb trees. Conifers, although very desirable, should only be planted where the soil and climate will permit their growth. In many respects they are ideal for screening because they give both summer and winter effect. Species prone to the production of large cones are best not planted where they will overhang parked vehicles, because the falling large cones, which have sharp protrusions, would be liable to damage vehicles.

Trees with drupaceous fruits, such as the Mulberry, the fruits from which will severely stain any material upon which they fall, should be avoided. The ubiquitous Yew, while not prone to shed its fruits, is the scene of improvident feasting by various birds, in particular blackbirds, who invariably suffer from diarrhoea after feeding upon the fleshy fruits. This has a caustic nature, and where Yews are adjacent to car parks, many cars will be bespattered with excrement in the late summer.

A list of trees which may be planted in and around car parks would be very extensive and will be governed by the soil, topography and climatic factors.

Where trees are planted in car parks they should be surrounded by a low wall or high kerb, and this should extend at least 1·0 m (3 ft 6 in) from the tree and stake. Many modern cars have a long overhang at the rear and unless an adequate distance is left between the tree and the kerb, the trees will be continually uprooted and damaged by the rear bumpers.

Each site for a car park will have its own peculiarities which should be studied, and an individual scheme designed to fit the site. Difficulties and peculiarities on a site can often be turned to advantage by exercising a little thought when preparing the design.

REFERENCES

1. 'Cars in Housing', Design Bulletin No. 12. Ministry of Housing and Local Government. HMSO, 1967.
2. International Buyer's Guide, 1970. *Autocar*, October, 1969, Vol. 131, No. 3843.
3. British Parking Association Technical Note No. 1. *Traffic Engineering & Control*. April, 1970, Vol. 11. No. 12.
4. 'Recommendations for the Construction and Surfacing of Vehicle Parking Areas', Asphalt and Coated Macadam Association, London.
5. 'Specification of Tar Macadam or Bitumen Macadam for Use in Road Bases', Asphalt and Coated Macadam Association, London.
6. 'Model Specification for Roads and Footpaths on Housing & Factory Estates and Parks', Asphalt and Coated Macadam Association, London.
7. 'Dense Base Course with Bitumen or Tar', Asphalt and Coated Macadam Association, London.
8. 'Dense Tar Surfacing', British Road Tar Association, London.
9. 'Protection of Sub-Grades & Granular Bases by Surface Dressing', Road Research Laboratory, Road Note No. 17. HMSO, London, 1953.
10. 'Construction of Housing Estate Roads using Granular Base and Sub-base Materials'. Road Research Laboratory, Road Note No. 20. HMSO, London, 1960.
11. 'Recommendations for Tar Surface Dressing', Road Research Laboratory, Road Note No. 1. HMSO, London, 1958.
12. 'A Guide to the Structural Design of Flexible & Rigid Pavements for New Roads', Road Research Laboratory, Road Note No. 29. HMSO, London, 1960.
13. 'Tars for Road Purposes', British Standard Specification No. 76. British Standards Institution, London, 1964.
14. 'Fine Cold Asphalt', British Standard Specification No. 1690. British Standards Institution, London, 1968.
15. 'Bitumen Macadam with Crushed Rock or Slag Aggregate', British Standard Specification No. 1621. British Standards Institution, London, 1961.
16. 'Tarmacadam "Tarpaving" for Footpaths, Playgrounds, etc.', British Standard Specification No. 1242. British Standards Institution, London, 1960.
17. 'Tarmacadam and Tar Carpets (Gravel Aggregate)', British Standard Specification No. 1241. British Standards Institution, London, 1959.
18. 'Tarmacadam with Crushed Rock or Slag Aggregates', British Standard Specification No. 802. British Standards Institution, London, 1967.
19. 'Aggregates from Natural Sources for Concrete (including Granolithic)', British Standard Specification No. 882. British Standards Institution, London, 1965.
20. 'Steel Fabric for the Reinforcement of Concrete', British Standard Specification No. 1221. British Standards Institution, London, 1964.

Chapter 10

Design of Multi-Storey Car Parks

There are four important factors to consider when designing a multi-storey car park. The first is the parking demand which must be ascertained locally, the second is simplicity and speed in parking and unparking, the third is the cost, and the fourth is that the building will harmonise with its surroundings.

It is becoming general opinion that five floors is a maximum height for a ramp type of garage as longer drives and ramps are unpopular with customers, and a total capacity of 500 to 750 cars is about an optimum figure if the time to recover the cars is not to be excessive. There are car parks that have a capacity much in excess of these figures, and it may be that there is no other alternative way of providing the parking accommodation where it is required.

Multi-storey car parks may be divided into three groups:

(*a*) customer parking,

(*b*) attendant parking,

(*c*) combined customer and attendant parking.

CUSTOMER PARKING

Customer parking in garages is becoming increasingly popular. As the motorist drives into the garage he is issued with a ticket, either by an attendant or by an automatic machine. Direction signs indicate the way to the parking place. On returning to collect the car, the motorist either pays the fee at the office on producing the ticket issued on entry, shows the receipt on his way out and drives away, or pays the fee at the exit.

The advantages of this system are:

(*a*) A large reservoir space is not required because there is no delay in waiting for the attendant to park the car.

(*b*) Customers may lock the car doors, which gives more security.

(*c*) A customer may have access to his car whilst parked.

(*d*) A smaller staff is required to operate the car park.

(e) At peak periods, time is saved by the motorist collecting his own car.

(f) There is no congestion on the ramps, as the cars come out in single file.

(g) It is less irritating to the motorist to be delayed in his car rather than to wait for an attendant to deliver his car.

The disadvantages are:

(a) More space is required in the aisles and parking bays.

(b) The ramps should be wider and less steep and preferably one-way.

(c) Some timid drivers are unhappy driving on ramps.

ATTENDANT PARKING

The attendant parking system has the advantage that a larger number of vehicles can be parked on a given floor area because an attendant can park cars closer together than customers would be expected to do. Some of this advantage is lost because it is necessary to have a reservoir where customers may leave their cars for the attendant to collect and drive to the parking place. The main disadvantage with this system is that an increased staff is required at peak periods if a serious delay in delivering the cars is to be avoided. Furthermore, it is difficult to get staff capable of driving any make of car and willing to undertake car parking duties. A shortage of staff can cause considerable delay, and irritation to the customer.

CUSTOMER AND ATTENDANT PARKING

Customer and attendant parking may be an advantage when the space for parking is restricted, and a floor attendant assists with the placing of the vehicle. With this system the customer drives the car up and down the ramps, and the floor attendant parks and unparks the car. With experienced attendants the cars can be parked closer together than can be permitted with customer parking, and less space is required. Attendants' time is not lost moving up and down from the ground floor, and as the customer delivers and collects the car from the floor on which it is parked no additional reservoir space is required on the ground floor, and the possibility of congestion is avoided. The arrangements for paying the parking fee and checking in and out may be the same as for the customer parking garages.

THE SURVEY

The methods of conducting a parking survey are described in Chapter 2. The size and siting of a multi-storey car park should be chosen in accordance with the parking requirements as revealed by the results of the parking survey, and the overall traffic and parking plan for the town or city. There is, however, certain detailed information that will be required for each site before a design for a car park is prepared. This may be the traffic volumes and arrangements on the adjoining roads, *i.e.*, whether one-way or two-way; the position of traffic signals; whether free street parking is permitted or parking meters are in use; the most suitable position for an entrance and exit and whether the car park is to be used for short term or long term parking, or both. This type of information will enable the designer to determine whether the car park will have to cater for very heavy traffic flows at peak periods or a steady flow throughout the day, and the effect that the traffic generated by the car park will have on the traffic flow on the adjoining streets. The advantage of having an ideal design for a car park and first class equipment is lost if vehicles are held up in the car park because they cannot join the traffic stream on the adjoining street at peak periods. For instance, consider the exit from a car park placed near a road junction controlled by traffic signals to the right of the exit. When there is a heavy flow of traffic in both directions, a motorist will find it difficult to make a right-hand turn from the car park, because on one phase there will be a heavy flow of traffic in both directions, and on the other phase there will be a queue coming from the left and building up behind the traffic signals. Under these conditions arrangements should be made for traffic leaving the car park to make a left turn only. In countries where traffic is driven on the right-hand side of the road, traffic leaving the car park should make a right turn only.

BASIC DATA

The size of the parking stall depends on the size of the car to be parked, and these vary in size considerably.[1] In Europe there are few classes of cars that are longer than 4·75 m (16 ft). They are very expensive and therefore there are comparatively few on the road. Therefore a stall length of 4·75 m (16 ft) has now become accepted and in practice is found to be quite adequate. The stall width has to accommodate the width of the car plus sufficient space to open the door to enable the driver and passengers to take their seats. Most European cars (probably 90%) are less than 1·75 m (5 ft 9 in) wide, and the British Leyland Mini is only 1·40 m (4 ft 7½ in) wide. The opening width required for a car door is 0·30 m–0·45 m (12 in–18 in). Therefore assuming that cars are all parked centrally in a stall 2·50 m (8 ft 0 in) wide, the space between cars will not be less than 0·75 m (2 ft 3 in), which is ample width to open a car door and gain access. There are arguments put forward that in the interests of economy the stall width could be reduced to 2·30 m (7 ft 6 in), which would give a space between cars not less than 0·55 m (1 ft 9 in), which again is ample width. In practice, however, motorists cannot be relied upon to park their cars exactly in the centre of a parking stall and most appear to be satisfied if they place the car somewhere between the lines marking out the stall. Whilst the driver of a car parked on or too near the boundary of his stall should have ample space to gain access to his car on the opposite side, the car in the adjoining stall may not be so favourably placed. Apart from being able to open a car door there is also a strong objection to being forced to brush one's clothes close to the body of the car which may be wet and/or mud splashed. Therefore it is wise not to be too economical in determining the stall widths, and in practice a width of 2·50 m (8 ft 0 in) has been found to be very satisfactory for garages in Europe. The British Parking

Association recommend that 2·30 m (7 ft 6 in) may be used in car parks used for long term parking, and 2·50 m (8 ft 2½ in precisely) for short stay parking, to allow for motorists handling luggage, parcels, pushchairs, etc. When stalls are marked out at an angle of less than 90° to the aisle, it is easier for a motorist to park or back out into the aisle. Nevertheless the same arguments about the space between cars for opening the car doors still apply.

In the United States of America the popular makes of cars are both longer and wider than in Europe. It is therefore recommended that the length of a stall should be 5·00 m (18 ft 6 in), and the width not less than 2·60 m (8 ft 6 in), but preferably 2·75 m (9 ft 0 in).

TURNING CIRCLE

The turning circle of cars varies from 7·64 m (25 ft 0 in) diameter for the Triumph Herald to 15·0 m (49 ft 0 in) for the Rolls Royce Phantom V, but the great majority of cars have a turning circle under 12·20 m (40 ft 0 in) diameter. Therefore in practice a turning circle 18·0 m (60 ft 0 in) diameter between kerbs will accommodate all cars.

GROUND CLEARANCE

The ground clearance on most cars is about 100 mm (4 in), and the wheelbases range from 2·13 m (7 ft 0 in) to 2·75 m (9 ft 0 in), increasing to 3·65 m (12 ft 0 in) for the Rolls Royce Phantom V. It is important to design the junction between the ramp and parking floor so that a clearance with the undercarriage of the car is maintained.

HEIGHT

Cars are usually under 1·80 m (6 ft 0 in) high, and minibuses go up to 2·15 m (7 ft 1 in) high. The minimum height should be 2·0 m (6 ft 6 in) but the most common practice is to have a clear height of 2·13 m (7 ft 0 in) from floor level to underside of beams. If minibuses are to be accommodated then the clear height should be 2·30 m (7 ft 6 in).[2]

AISLE WIDTH

For head in parking at 90° to the line of the aisle, a width of 6·0 m (20 ft 0 in) is considered to be adequate in the United Kingdom. This width of aisle will take car traffic in one direction, and 7·5 m (24 ft 0 in) in width is better for two direction traffic where pedestrians also use the aisle. The German motoring organisation (ADAC) recommends 5·0 m (16 ft 3 in), and in the United States a width of 6·70 m (22 ft 0 in) is considered necessary for traffic in one direction.

When a one-way traffic system is planned, cars may be parked at an angle of

70° with advantage to the motorist when parking and unparking. The aisle width may also be reduced.

Provided the stalls set at an angle are intermeshed there does not appear to be any great advantage over 90° parking from an economy aspect, but it is easier for a motorist to park and unpark from a stall set at an angle.

TABLE VIII

Parking Angle	Aisle Width		Bin Width allowing for Touch Rail	
	One Direction Traffic	Two Direction Traffic	One Direction Traffic	Two Direction Traffic
90°	6·0 m (20 ft)	7·5 m (24 ft)	15·7 m (52 ft 8 in)	17·2 m (56 ft 8 in)
70°	4·50 m (15 ft)		14·2 m (50 ft 8 in)	
45°	3·0 m (10 ft)		12·7 m (44 ft 4 in)	
			25·4 m (82 ft 8 in) (Double Bin)	

The important criteria are the size of the site, and the bin width that is permissible. For instance, 90° stalls 4·75 m (16 ft 0 in) long and an aisle width of 6·0 m (20 ft 0 in) plus 100 mm (4 in) for each of two touch rails, needs a bin width of 15·7 m (52 ft 8 in). For parking at other angles the dimensions required for aisles and bin widths are given in Table VIII.

RAMP SYSTEMS

It would be incorrect to say that any one ramp system is the best for all sites. Each site must be given individual consideration, taking into account the limitations and facilities available and the type of motor traffic the garage will have to serve.

Ramps may be divided into two classes (a) 'clearway ramps' and (b) 'parking ramps'. The 'clearway ramp' serves only to give access to and from the garage, whereas the 'parking ramp' gives access to and from the garage and to the parking stalls.

CONTINUOUS SLOPING FLOORS

Perhaps the simplest form of a parking structure is the continuous sloping floor at a gradient of 1 in 25 with two-way traffic using the aisles (Fig. 10.1). This system is economical in space, because the aisles are used for entry, exit and access to stalls. On entry the drivers pass the stalls and can take the first one that is vacant. If there are several floors, the travel route to the exit for cars parked on the upper floors can be long and tedious. Two-way systems within a garage have the great disadvantage of causing congestion and delay when substantial volumes of traffic are both entering and leaving the garage at the same

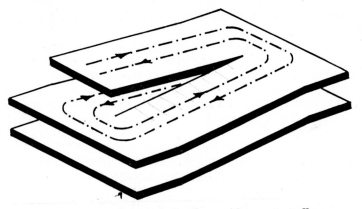

Fig. 10.1 Continuous sloping floors with two-way traffic.

time. This inconvenience is reduced if the bulk of the traffic is entering or leaving within a short period, say entering in the morning, and leaving in the evening. Nevertheless the capacity of this type of garage is limited, and before a decision on size is made a careful survey is necessary to ascertain that there will not be congestion at peak periods.

CONTINUOUS SLOPING FLOOR WITH 'CLEARWAY' EXIT

In order to eliminate congestion caused by two-way traffic in a garage, an exit 'clearway ramp' may be constructed leaving the sloping floor aisle to be used by incoming traffic only. The 'clearway ramp' could take the form of an outside ramp which is limited to structures long enough to accommodate a ramp at a gradient of 1 in 10 or a spiral ramp (Fig. 10.2). The latter could be attached to the end of a building, accommodated in one corner or the centre, according to the

Fig. 10.2 Sloping floor with spiral clearway exit.

layout adopted. The latter position is suitable for an underground car park. The 'clearway ramp' exit operates extremely well, and gives a quick exit for vehicles from all floors. It avoids any congestion with incoming traffic and the exit to the highway can be arranged at a point quite clear of the entrance to the garage from the highway. It is, of course, more expensive in construction and the ramps may require some under-surface heating to prevent icing during the winter months. The added expense of a spiral ramp is not justified for small garages, but for garages with a capacity of 400 or more cars it is worthy of consideration.

CONTINUOUS SLOPING FLOOR WITH CROSSING BETWEEN INTERLOCKING FLOORS

With this arrangement there is only one-way traffic on each floor because the floors are interlocking (Fig. 10.3). This means that each ramped floor

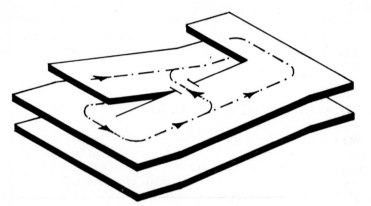

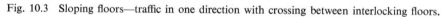

Fig. 10.3   Sloping floors—traffic in one direction with crossing between interlocking floors.

ascends or descends the height of two floors. Midway along the length of the ramped floors the up and down ramps cross and at this point a cross connection between the floors is made. This enables a car to move to the descending ramp from each rising floor, followed by a tedious drive along the ramps of all the descending floors. A disadvantage of this system is that drivers may have difficulty in finding an empty stall as half are on the 'up' ramp and the other half on the 'down' ramp. There may be a temptation for drivers failing to find an empty stall on the lower floors to move from the 'up' ramp to the 'down' ramp with no more success, and ultimately have to drive to the higher ramps causing unnecessary traffic on the aisles, and irritation to the drivers.

LEVEL FLOOR WITH STRAIGHT RAMPS

This system can be external on the side of the building (Fig. 10.4) or internal between floors. A wide ramp may also be provided for two-way traffic.

The entrance to the garage from an external ramp on the side of a building may present turning difficulties that can be overcome by eliminating parking stalls. The layout should be for a minimum of two bin widths. Straight ramps between floors dictate the length of the building. As with other external ramps under-surface heating will be required to prevent ice formation in winter. The gradients should not exceed 1 in 10.

For the internal ramp system, two separate ramps are required and as these should be located between rows of stalls, at least three bin widths are required plus the width of the ramps. The gradient of the ramps should not exceed 1 in

Fig. 10.4   Level floor with straight ramp.

10, with lower gradients at the junction with the upper and lower floors. Turning from the ramps into adjoining bays may be difficult and special attention should be given to this point in the design.

Straight ramps between level floors, whether external or internal, are of necessity rather long because they have to rise the full distance between floor levels. This makes circulation long and tedious and there is also considerable wasted space.

LEVEL FLOORS WITH SPIRAL RAMPS

In order to eliminate some of the disadvantages of straight ramps between level floors, the spiral ramp may be used, and arranged at opposite ends of the building, one for entrance and the other for exit (Fig. 10.5).

Another arrangement is the intertwined semi-circular ramp where each traffic stream is confined to its own ramp (Fig. 10.6). The entrance and exit points are arranged on opposite sides of the ramp tower.

The surface of all ramps must be fully superelevated, and it is necessary for information by means of signs giving the number of vacant stalls on each floor,

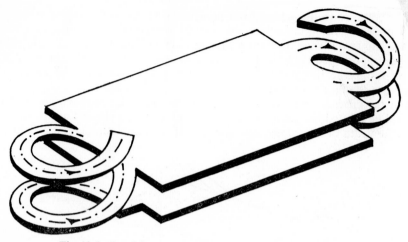

Fig. 10.5   Level floors with spiral ramps for entrance and exit.

Fig. 10.6   Intertwined semi-circular ramp for entrance and exit.

to be available to drivers before leaving the ramp; otherwise there may be much time lost and traffic generated unnecessarily.

STAGGERED FLOOR OR SPLIT LEVEL SYSTEMS

The staggered floor system is relatively simple in design and construction and fits well into a rectangular building. The advantage of this system is that it is only necessary to rise one half the total height between floors, which gives a short ramp and a turn through 180° to the next ramp. There are several alternative arrangements which may be made.

TWO-WAY RAMPS

This arrangement is illustrated in Fig. 10.7 and it will be seen that traffic moves in two directions on the ramps and also in the parking aisles. This, of

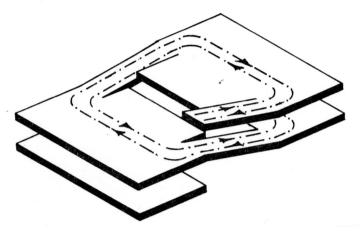

Fig. 10.7   Two-way ramp—traffic moves in two directions on floors and ramps.

course, is not good, especially in the aisles where cars will be entering and leaving the stalls with traffic flowing in two directions in addition to pedestrians. For two-way traffic a wider aisle is also necessary.

ONE-WAY RAMPS

In order to eliminate the congestion caused by two-way ramps and aisles, the ramps may be arranged as shown in Fig. 10.8, where the upstream

Fig. 10.8   One-way ramps with traffic segregated on floors and ramps.

traffic is separated from the downstream. It is possible to arrange the 'down' ramps to give a quick exit, and the 'up' ramps to circulate along the aisles and pass the maximum number of parking bays.

CONCENTRIC CIRCULATION

Another arrangement is to separate the up and down ramps as shown in Fig. 10.9 so that the flow of traffic in the aisles is in one direction only. This

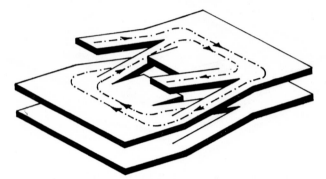

Fig. 10.9   Concentric circulation with traffic segregated on ramps.

means that there will be more moving traffic in the aisles than in the previous arrangement. It is possible to arrange the down ramps near together to give a quick exit, and the up ramps near each end of the building so that cars will pass the maximum number of parking bays.

THREE LEVEL STAGGERED FLOOR RAMP

This system uses three separate floors. The two end floors are at the same level and the centre floor is one half floor height above or below the two end floors (*see* Fig. 10.10). The advantage claimed is that 50 per cent less turns are

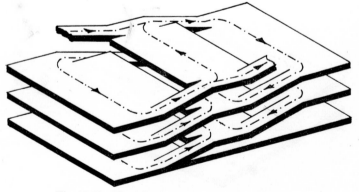

Fig. 10.10   Three level staggered floor ramp system.

required, but the disadvantage is that the end sections have access to an up or down ramp only, and therefore each car must be driven up one extra half floor on entering or leaving the car park. A staggered floor design requires two bin widths as a minimum, but more bin widths may be added and three gives a very efficient layout.

WARPED SLAB SYSTEM[3]

The warped slab type of multi-storey car park obviates the need for short steep ramps (*see* Fig. 10.11). It also permits a completely horizontal external slab

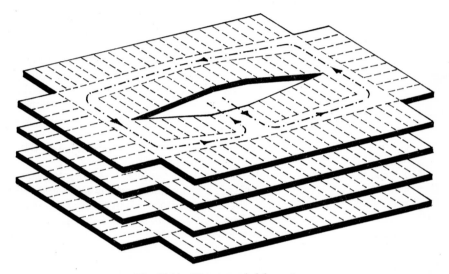

Fig. 10.11   The warped slabs system.

edge on all floors, thus giving a new freedom of choice for the architect when considering elevational treatment. The buttonhole arrangement in the middle of the building, which provides the interconnection between the parking floors, is achieved by warping or twisting the reinforced concrete floor slabs. This gives a similar circulation to that of a split level car park.

ROOF PARKING[4]

The roof of a building appears to be the obvious solution to the problem of providing additional space in a closely built-up area of a city. Whilst there will be increased cost for structural work there will not be additional claims on land, which should offset the expense of the structural work.

The cost of providing this accommodation is a most important factor and must be carefully considered. Firstly, there is the additional cost of providing a roof that will take a load of 2400 N/m^2 (50 lb per sq ft) (the design load for a floor of a multi-storey car park). Secondly, there is the cost of providing a suitable ramp. This will vary with the height of the building, and if the roof area of the building is small the cost of the ramp will be greater per car space than for a building with a large roof space. If the roofs of two or more buildings are linked together by bridges, then it should be possible to use one ramp for more than one building which again should reduce the cost of the ramp per car space, but there would be the additional cost of the bridges to allocate and add to the cost per car space. The extent to which this is an economical proposition depends on the area of the roofs and the span of the bridges.

A single-storey building will be a much more attractive proposition than one of several storeys, because of the cost of providing the ramp, but single-storey buildings in central business areas of cities are not common. This puts a limit on the possibilities of using roofs as car parks. It may be possible to use a sloping site to advantage in reducing the length of ramp to the roof of a building of one or more storeys high.

Multi-storey car parks are different from most business premises in so far as they will have a ramp or some mechanical lift system as far as the floor immediately below the roof which may be 2·0 m to 2·5 m (7 ft to 8 ft) above the top floor of the building. It would not be excessively expensive to continue the ramp or lift up to roof level and use the roof area for parking. This is often done when designing and building multi-storey car parks. Parapet walls are desirable around the edge of a roof park and in some cases may have to be as much as 2·0 m or 2·5 m (7 ft or 8 ft) high for fire protection to adjoining property.

Roof parking has been adopted in Bedford, Bradford, Corby, Coventry, Exeter and Wolverhampton in England, and quite extensively in several cities in Germany and the United States of America. In Coventry, a system of roof parks linked together at roof level and connected to multi-storey car parks has been provided in the new City Centre.

SITE EXPLORATION WORK

Most civil engineers today recognise the importance of preliminary exploratory work on the site before a structure is designed, and a thorough investigation of the ground conditions before detailed designs are prepared. Anyone with a slight appreciation of geology will recognise that this is an essential course to take. Car parks are often constructed in built-up areas where buildings have been demolished; where there may be areas of filling, made ground and the remains of old foundations, overlying the natural strata.

The actual work undertaken and the means and extent of investigation must of necessity be governed by local conditions. They may include exploratory test borings, test pits, examination of geological survey reports, examination of ground-water levels, existence of wells, examination of any local reports or knowledge of ground conditions that are available. Laboratory tests may be carried out, such as sieve analyses, triaxial compression tests, consolidation tests, chemical analyses and tests for the presence of sulphates.

A small percentage of time and money spent on this type of investigation can save an enormous amount of trouble and expense at a later date.

PRACTICAL CONSIDERATIONS IN DESIGN

The most important aspect of car park design is to ensure that when the car park is completed it can be operated efficiently. This may appear to be obvious and elementary, but it is often overlooked. It may mean that a few less parking stalls are provided, or that the most economical layout for columns is not adopted. These variations will increase the cost per car stall, which is the usual criterion when comparing designs for car parks. It is wise to look further than the initial capital cost, and consider the possible loss of revenue from a car park which has awkward corners to negotiate, poor sight lines, a long delay at the entrance and exit coupled with the possibility of a motorist causing damage to his car when entering or leaving a parking stall. These conditions cause irritation to a motorist, and the operator may be quite helpless because he cannot rectify faults which are basic to the design and construction of the building. A small increase in capital cost can soon be offset by increased revenue from a car park that is efficiently operated.

The following criteria should be considered when designing a car park:[5]

(a) When determining the spacing of columns the first consideration should be an efficient operational layout. It is also necessary to consider economy in design, but this should be the secondary consideration.

(b) The entrances and exits should be designed to give good visibility at all changes of direction both horizontal and vertical.

(c) It is preferable that motorists are given a fixed route after entering the car park. If there is more than one alternative route it is likely to cause confusion.

(d) Any awkwardly shaped areas which cannot be used as a safe parking stall should be raised 120 mm or 150 mm (5 or 6 in) in level and edged by a kerb.

(e) The maximum gradient of sloping floors used for parking should not exceed 1 in 25.

(f) The controlled entrance for a car park accommodating 500–600 cars should have at least two lanes and preferably three. The exit should have at least three lanes and preferably four, the higher figures being used where there is a high peak flow of traffic.

(g) Lavatory accommodation should be provided to serve staff and motorists.

(h) Stairs, landings and pedestrian ramps should be provided, and if a pedestrian ramp is integral with a vehicular ramp it should be separated by a barrier rail.

(j) If climatic conditions could cause icing on pedestrian ramps, etc., they should be heated.

(k) Lifts should be provided for more than two floors and, if possible, one lift per floor above the second floor level. This will enable each lift to operate between the entrance level and one other floor at peak periods.

(l) A lip should be provided at the top of each ramp at its junction with the parking floor. This is to prevent liquids flowing from the floor down the ramp, especially petrol, in case of an accident and/or fire.

(m) Ramps should not drain on to the parking floor.

(n) Drainage falls on decks should not be less than 1 in 50, and the floor finish should not leave any 'slack' places.

(*o*) The drainage falls must be created in the slab and not by adding graded screeds afterwards.

(*p*) A sufficient number of trapped gullies should be provided and rainwater pipes suitably sited to give easy access for rodding.

(*q*) Wherever possible, it is an advantage to provide space for at least two cars between entry barrier and the street, and for two or three cars between exit barrier and the street.

(*r*) It should be remembered that in a car park there will also be a large number of pedestrians, and their movements should be considered and facilities provided.

(*s*) Provision of movement joints is frequently required on large parking structures. These can be sources of disfigurement due to unsightly weathering, and embarrassment due to water leaking from floor to floor. Generally a soundly constructed concrete floor finish should be sufficiently waterproof for the intermediate floors. Very careful waterproofing should be provided for the roof parking area. It is advisable for the structural designer to specify the positions of expansion, contraction and day work joints, and to specify precisely the technique for forming each type.

(*t*) To improve the durability of ramps and ground floor slabs, air entrained concrete should be used as a protection against de-icing salts. The floor surface can be concrete of structural quality provided excess moisture is prevented by good mix design and compaction. Any excess surface laitence should in all cases be removed as part of the floor finishing operation. Finishing by power float assists in compacting the surface as a preliminary to forming indentations by roller or by machine grooving to produce a hard wearing non-slip floor.

METHODS OF CONSTRUCTION

(*a*) *IN-SITU* CONCRETE

Multi-storey car parks are structures which are suitable for construction in *in-situ* concrete reinforced with high tensile steel. In the United Kingdom the design loads are based on the Building Regulations Schedule 5, Clause 3, which states that floors used for the parking of vehicles not exceeding 2540 kg ($2\frac{1}{2}$ tons) gross weight should be designed to carry a minimum superimposed load of 2400 N/m^2 (50 lb per sq ft).

Generally the design should be on the basis of a flat slab or beam and slab *in situ* reinforced concrete structure, with a wearing surface of 50 mm (2 in) granolithic concrete cast integrally with the slab. Alternatively, a suitable hardener may be used instead of the granolithic surface. The positions of all construction joints should be specified and, if the building is large, expansion joints may be necessary. These should be carefully designed and constructed to avoid any leakage of water through them.

There has been a great deal of discussion on the advantages and disadvantages of clear span or supported structures on intermediate columns. From the designer's point of view the intermediate column design has the advantage. It is usually less expensive, there is less liability of cracks developing in the concrete beams, greater freedom of elevational treatment is possible, and the absence of heavy beams improves the internal appearance of the building. Intermediate columns could be arranged to give 3·0 m (10 ft) spans and an intermediate span of 10·0 m (32 ft) in a bin width of 15·5 m (52 ft). This arrangement would reduce any obstruction caused by the intermediate columns to a minimum. From the operator's point of view a clear span gives complete freedom to vary the layout of the parking floor. In practice this is limited to varying the width of the parking stall, and the need to do this is minimal.

Reinforced concrete car parks in the United Kingdom are usually designed in accordance with the British Standard Code of Practice 114—'The Structural Use of Concrete in Buildings'.[6]

In situ reinforced concrete is very suitable for the construction of multi-storey car parks and it is possible to design to fit a site of any shape or size; in urban areas where good aggregate is available, *in situ* construction is likely to offer the cheapest solution provided that the structural form is not required to provide 'bin' length spans. Some firms have developed the manufacture of standard prefabricated units. The use of simple standard shuttering has also received attention, and certain advantages are claimed.

Precast forms of construction are more favoured where large car parks are required which give an opportunity for filling rectangular sites with repetitions of a standard module. When an early completion date is very important, or the economics of a high site value during the period of construction has to be considered, then the precast form of construction might be favoured in order to reduce the construction period. In highly developed urban areas limited construction space may favour precast units.

The Lift Slab[7] method of construction is associated with flat slab design. It was developed in the United States of America in the 1950s.

The Lift Slab technique commences when the foundations have been laid and the ground floor slab cast. A resinous separating medium is then sprayed over the ground floor slab. This is to prevent bonding between the concrete. Precast concrete columns are then erected with the fabricated steel lifting collars threaded on. Collars for the first floor slab are then lowered, and the first floor slab is cast over the ground floor slab. The operation is repeated for subsequent slabs, and lifting can commence as soon as the roof slab has reached its specified strength. The slabs are lifted by hydraulic jacks with a capacity of approximately 69·0 tonnes (70 tons). The lift slab jacking system has an advanced, automatic synchronising, control mechanism which ensures that undue stresses are not induced in the slabs during lifting; lifting takes place at between 2 m (6 ft) and 3 m (10 ft) per hour.

The strain on the precast columns has to be taken into account when designing for a Lift Slab operation. The free standing columns are first restrained by fixing the roof slab temporarily at the top of the first section which allows more slabs to be lifted and parked under the roof slab. The lower floor slabs can then be lifted into position. When the columns are extended to the second section, the roof slab is again raised and the others follow. This procedure is repeated for the third section until all floor slabs are in place.

The advantages, provided that the site conditions and the design of the building are suitable for the Lift Slab type of construction, include speed and economy. The fact that all major concreting work is carried out at ground level avoids expensive shuttering and the need to hoist materials. Against this is the cost of hoisting the slabs with the hydraulic equipment.

British Lift Slab Ltd, Birmingham, operate and develop this method in the United Kingdom and Eire.

A system using *in situ* concrete is known as 'Ribspan', and may be described as an on-site industrialised building system which brings factory production methods to *in situ* construction (Fig. 10.12). It was primarily introduced to

Fig. 10.12   Illustration of fibreglass trough moulds used for Holst 'Ribspan' multi-storey car park floors. (*Reproduced by permission of Holst & Co. Ltd, Watford, England.*)

give the 15·7 m (52 ft 0 in) clear spans with minimum deck thickness for multi-storey car parks, but it can be applied to any building where long clear spans are required. It is basically a trough floor having 0·90 m (36 in) rib centres and the floor slab may be 75 mm (3 in) thick for one hour fire protection or 100 mm (4 in) thick for two hour fire protection. To meet the wide range of spans and loadings 'Ribspan' minor, 'Ribspan' standard and 'Ribspan' major have been introduced. For multi-storey car parks the long clear spans vary between 14·0 m and 16·0 m (47 ft 0 in and 52 ft 0 in).

High quality fibreglass trough shutters are used for fast repetitive use, and are moved steadily forward whilst the ribs remain on undisturbed supports throughout the curing period.

The advantages of this system are that the rib soffit board is cheap and can be used repeatedly. Vibration to the full depth of the rib with correctly placed reinforcement is easy. There is no need to use 10 mm ($\frac{3}{8}$ in) aggregates to obtain good finishes, and the fibreglass trough moulds cut out unsightly grout leaks and are easily struck without interference to rib soffit boards and props. They can be assembled from above or below, and being light they are easy to handle. Special units in fibreglass give a good appearance to the concrete surface and reduce grout leaks. The system is flexible and has a minimum number of components.

The 'Ribspan' trough flooring system has been developed by Holst & Co. Ltd, Watford, Herts.

(b) PREFABRICATED UNITS

Proprietary systems abound for the construction of floors and walls. Some are completely precast systems, others are composite using a precast unit at intervals.

An example of a precast system is the 'Bison'[8] multi-storey framed structure (Fig. 10.13). This structure is supported by walls 3·0 m (10 ft 0 in) to 3·65 m

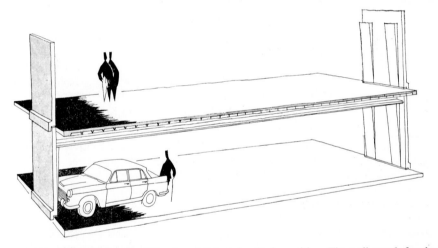

Fig. 10.13   Diagram showing 'Bison' prefabricated units in position. The wall panels for the upper floors rest on those below in the manner shown. There are parking spaces of 4·75 m (16 ft) on either side of the bay, thus formed, with an access lane 6·0 m (20 ft) wide in the centre.
(Reproduced by permission of Concrete Ltd, London.)

(12 ft 0 in) apart along the perimeter and between the parking stalls. The walls are precast units formed with corbals which provide a bearing for the pre-tension main beams spanning the width of the parking stalls, and these in turn carry the floor. The beams are 0·60 m (24 in) deep and are arranged in pairs supported by wall units 1·60 m (5 ft 3 in) wide. In certain cases only one beam is to be carried by the wall units, when the width may be reduced to 1·0 m (3 ft 3 in). The basic conception of the structural layout of the car park is connected with the development of the Prestressed Concrete Development Group bridge beams.

A beam 15·7 m (52 ft 0 in) span has a construction depth of 0·55 m (21 in) with beams at 1·80 m (6 ft 0 in) centres and 0·70 m (28 in) with beams at 2·5 m (8 ft 0 in) centres. On a 15·7 m (52 ft 0 in) span and a beam depth of 0·60 m (24 in) the total depth of beam and floor is 0·72 m (2 ft 4½ in). The height between floors is 2·85 m (9 ft 4 in) and the headroom below the beam is 2·13 m (7 ft 0 in).

The main beams support a Bison composite floor 110 mm (4½ in) thick, the top 25 mm (½ in) of which acts as a wearing surface. The ramps are standardised and run between the precast concrete cross walls which also provide transverse stability. The walls are kept back as far as possible from the access lanes, and have oval holes formed at sight level in order to improve visibility.

When the lower part of the car park is used for another purpose, such as shops, the construction can be varied, and the supporting walls are, in many cases, replaced by columns and panel edge beams. The standard pre-stressed beam and plank floor construction is generally retained.

The Bison method of construction has been developed by Concrete Ltd, London WC2.

Another system using precast reinforced concrete units for multi-storey car parks is known by the trade name 'Unipark'. There are two 'Unipark' systems. System No. 1 has three basic components:

(a) The slab, which is a double-tee section in reinforced concrete, is 7·30 m (24 ft 0 in) span between traverse beams. A reinforced topping is laid *in situ* after the slabs are erected.

(b) The beam is a double cantilever and arranged in pairs on each column. At a ramp position one standard beam is replaced by a ramp beam inclining either up or down.

(c) The columns are cast on octagonal steel base plates to which the reinforcing bars are welded.

System 2 is a two pinned portal frame designed to suit clear span parking requirements, which can accommodate unit parking depths from 14·50 m to 16·5 m (48 ft 0 in to 54 ft 0 in). The longitudinal spacing of frames is the same as for System 1 and the same floor units are used. The storey height is 2·75 m (9 ft 0 in) for both systems.

Whilst these two systems have been designed primarily to provide precast units for the conventional multi-storey car park, they lend themselves for use in quite a variety of situations and conditions. For instance, there must be many miles of railway track in cuttings in or near the built-up areas of our towns and cities which occupy a great deal of land additional to the track width. Two complete units of System 1 would span a double track and provide a deck for parking 14·50 m to 15·7 m (48 ft 0 in to 52 ft 0 in) wide as required (Fig. 10.14). Additional decks could be provided or, if circumstances permitted, a wider deck could be constructed. This is a type of construction which causes a minimum of interference with the working of the railway track when it is erected. For parking over railway stations the longer spans of System 2 may be more suitable. If this can be done over railways there may be roads which can be suitably bridged.

On existing housing estates where private garages have not been provided there is an increasing problem with cars parked on the highways. In some cases it is possible to provide a limited amount of surface parking accommodation on spare corners of land. A simple precast structure which could add an additional deck on the site would make a useful contribution towards satisfying the demand. It is of low construction, and could easily be screened by trees and shrubs if it was in view from dwelling houses or from the roads.

Again, on steep sloping sites much land is often wasted. System 1 units appear to be very suitable for car parks that are stepped up the slope (Fig. 10.15). The upper deck could either be used as a roof park or play area, whichever was required. The small shopping centres on the older estates are now finding difficulty in providing suitable parking facilities for their customers. These units are suitable for providing garages for vans and stores for shops on the ground floor, and parking for customers on the roof. A suitable place

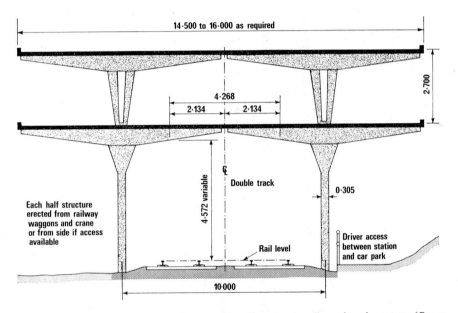

Fig. 10.14   Unipark units erected over a double railway track—dimensions in metres. (*Reproduced by permission of Unipark Ltd, Loughborough, Leicestershire, England.*)

for this is at the rear of shops, and could be provided in new development. In fact an integrated car park and shopping structure could be planned with rationalised column layouts suiting each floor.

Unipark Ltd, have their offices at Bishop Meadow Road, Loughborough, Leicestershire.

The Truscon Double Trustee Units, which are prestressed precast concrete units, are capable of catering for spans up to 18·0 m (58 ft 0 in) in a range of depths from 0·25 m to 0·60 m (10 in to 24 in), according to the span and loading conditions. The overall width of the unit is 1·20 m (4 ft 0 in) but the top slab can be adjusted where necessary to allow for covering the maximum amount possible of the whole area of the floor in precast construction. These units are

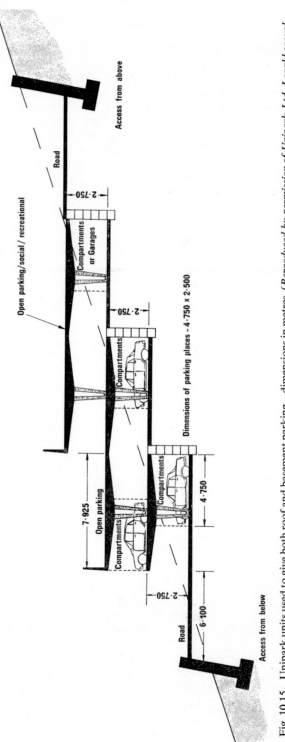

Fig. 10.15   Unipark units used to give both roof and basement parking—dimensions in metres. (*Reproduced by permission of Unipark Ltd, Loughborough, Leicestershire, England.*)

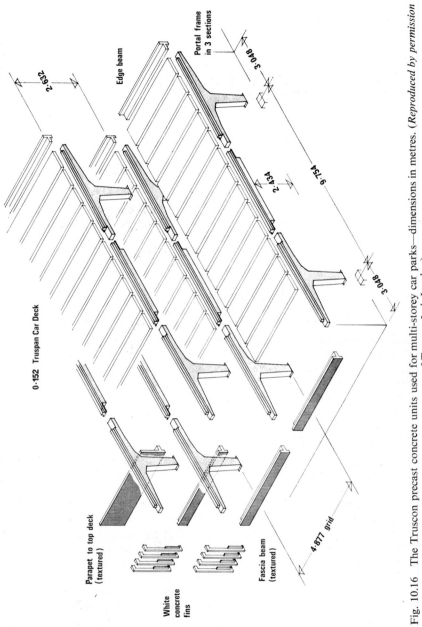

0·152 Truspan Car Deck

2·632

Edge beam

Portal frame
in 3 sections

3·048

2·434

9·754

3·048

Parapet to top deck
(textured)

White
concrete
fins

Fascia beam
(textured)

4·877 grid

Fig. 10.16   The Truscon precast concrete units used for multi-storey car parks—dimensions in metres. (*Reproduced by permission of Truscon Ltd, London.*)

particularly suitable for car parks for which a clear span up to 16·0 m (52 ft 6 in) is often required.

Truspan Units are prestressed precast units which may be used for floors, roofs and walls. They are designed for use in varying types of buildings and have been used in the construction of a multi-storey car park at Eccles, Lancashire. The standard width of the unit is 1·0 m (40 in) and can be made in depths of 100 mm, 150 mm, 200 mm or 250 mm (4 in, 6 in, 8 in, or 10 in). The casting beds are 137·0 m (450 ft 0 in) long, and the slabs are produced to the total length of the beds, and thereafter cut to the required lengths while still on the prestressing beds. The cores in the slabs are formed by steel cylinders.

Both the Truscon Double Trustee Unit and the Truspan Unit are manufactured by Truscon Ltd, 35–41, Lower Marsh, London SE1.

Other British firms who are known to be interested in precast concrete for multi-storey car parks are:

Anglian Building Products Ltd, Norwich.
Ralf Blatchford & Co. Ltd, Midsomer Norton, Somerset.
British 'Fram' Construction Co. (1911) Ltd, Pontypridd, Glam.
Cardeck Construction Ltd, Hayle, Cornwall.
Cementation Construction Ltd, Croydon, Surrey.
Costain Concrete Co. Ltd, London SW1.
Dow-Mac Concrete Ltd, Stamford, Lincs.
GKN Reinforcements Ltd, Smethwick 40, Staffs.
Fram Precast Concrete Ltd, Manchester 13.
Head Wrightson Teesdale Ltd, Thornaby-on-Tees.
Kaiser Floors Ltd, Maidenhead, Berks.
Omnia Concrete Sales Ltd, London EC1.
Pierhead Ltd, Liverpool 24.
Spanform Construction Ltd, Bromley, Kent.
Trent Concrete Ltd, Nottingham.
Yorkshire Hennebique Contracting Co. Ltd, York.

(c) STRUCTURAL STEELWORK

The results of research carried out in the United Kingdom at the Ministry of Technology and Fire Offices' Committee, and Joint Fire Research Organisation's Fire Research Stations, showed that if a car in a car park is on fire, and even if it burns out completely, the fire is unlikely to spread provided natural ventilation is available. Further there is no risk of lightweight non-combustible structures suffering from heat distortion or collapsing. This means that for steel framed multi-storey car parks it is not necessary to protect the steelwork from fire.

In the United Kingdom, the Department of the Environment allow a relaxation of Part E (Structural Fire Precautions) requirements of the Building Regulations in respect of multi-storey car parks in structural steelwork. In the United States of America, Building Code and Fire Insurance authorities endorse within reasonable size limitations the use of incombustible construction supported on exposed structural steel framing. Structural steel is therefore recognised as being suitable for the construction of car parks. Designs with spans up to 16·0 m (52 ft 6 in) across a parking bin without intermediate columns are possible. Whilst the designs are to a standard module, the spacing of the columns and beams can be varied, and the whole superstructure can be fabricated off-site. The decks and ramps are often of precast concrete. In some cases it is claimed that when used with a precast slab floor it is demountable, and can be dismantled and erected on a new site.

A system where this is claimed is known as the 'Tempark' Steel Framed Car Park. This is a completely prefabricated building of modular construction, comprising a steel frame with precast concrete decks. It may be built up in various shapes to create a complete elevated car park up to about five storeys high. It is claimed that the structure has an economic advantage because it can be completely dismantled and used again if it is not required as a permanent structure on its original site.

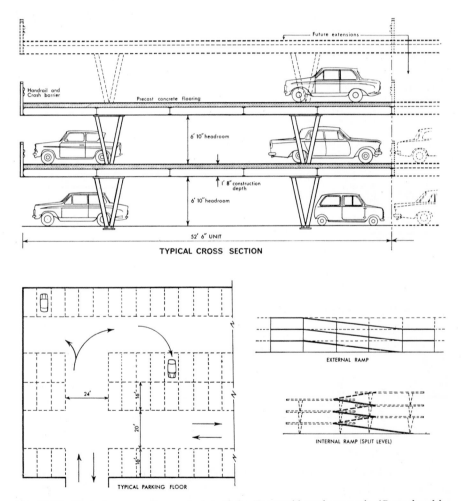

Fig. 10.17 Typical cross section and plan of the 'Tempark' steel car park. (*Reproduced by permission of R. M. Douglas (Contractors) Ltd, and Braithwaite & Co., Structural Ltd, London.*)

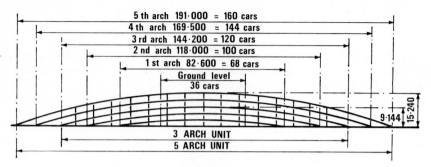

ELEVATION

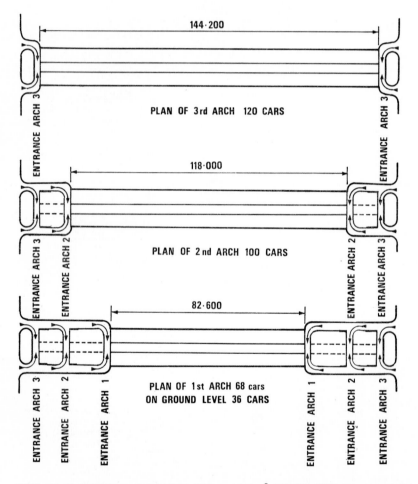

TOTAL NO. OF CARS ON 3 -ARCH SYSTEM - 324 AT 6·782 m² GROUND AREA PER CAR SPACE

TOTAL NO. OF CARS ON 5 - ARCH SYSTEM - 628 AT 4·831 m² GROUND AREA PER CAR SPACE

Fig. 10.18 Diagram showing the Wheelwright system of car parking—dimensions in metres. (*Reproduced by permission of John Lysaght's Bristol Works Ltd, Bristol.*)

The basic 'Tempark' unit (Fig. 10.17) is constructed from steel cantilever frames, connecting beams and precast concrete floor slabs, and provides an area of 15·7 m (52 ft 0 in) × 7·40 m (24 ft 6 in) on a column grid 8·50 m (28 ft 0 in) × 7·40 m (24 ft 6 in). Each unit takes six cars with an access road, and units can be placed end to end or side by side. The module is adaptable to provide the most suitable layout for any site. Upper floors can be superimposed at rises of 2·60 m (8 ft 6 in), giving a clear headroom of 2·1 m (6 ft 10 in); these floors are approached by external, straight or spiral ramps, and by internal straight ramps where a split level floor arrangement is employed. It can be arranged for extra floors to be added as parking requirements increase.

This system is sponsored by Braithwaite and Co. Ltd, West Bromwich.

A special type of design known as the 'Wheelwright' Self Parking Unit (Fig. 10.18) has been devised by Mr John Smith, FRIBA, of Heckmondwike, Yorkshire. The basic unit has three shallow arches, one above the other, and will house approximately 300 cars. The maximum height will be about 9·0 m (30 ft). The cars enter lower arches from the side, and the upper arch from the end. Each archway forms a sloping floor and cars park at 80° from the central drive. The ground area required per car space on a three arch unit is 6·7 m² (72·0 sq ft) and on a five arch unit 4·8 m² (52·08 sq ft). If used for parking only, the choice of site is very wide and it may even be built on an island site. The central roadway can be 5·30 m (17 ft 6 in) wide, and the overall length for a three tier unit is 125·0 m (410 ft 0 in). Slipperiness in very cold weather on the surface of a sloping floor may be overcome by a simple under-surface warming unit.

The foundations are the only part of the structure which need to be permanent. The superstructure can be completely prefabricated in suitable materials. The unit lends itself to architectural expression and may be incorporated into any scheme such as a shopping precinct, office block, stores, sports establishments or an airport.

The maximum economic unit is five tiers, housing 625 cars at a maximum height of 15·0 m (50 ft). The licence for the construction of Wheelwright Car Parks has been granted to John Lysaght Bristol Works Ltd, St Vincent's Works, Bristol, 2.

BUILDING REGULATIONS[9]

In the United Kingdom, the 'Building Regulations 1965' apply to England and Wales with the exception of the Inner London Boroughs, where the London Building Acts prevail.

Part E of the Regulations refers to structural fire precautions, and under Regulation E.2, multi-storey car parks are classed in Purpose Group VIII. This Purpose Group includes 'a place for the storage, deposit or parking of goods and materials (including vehicles)'. The limiting dimensions of buildings and compartments are stated in the Table to Regulation E.4, and in the larger multi-storey car parks compartmentation within the building becomes a requirement. Moreover, in the larger multi-storey car parks the elements of structure are required under Table A, Regulation E.5, to have a minimum period of fire resistance of four hours where the capacity of the building exceeds 21,000 m³ (750,000 cu ft); between 7000 m³ (250,000 cu ft) and 21,000 m³ (7500,00 cu ft), the fire resistance period is two hours. The application of Schedule 9 of Regulation E.7 in determining the distance required from the relevant boundary, requires separating distances so great in many cases that some of the smaller sites in urban areas become incapable of economic development.

It is generally accepted by the Fire Authorities that the fire risk in an open sided multi-storey car park is very slight especially when compared with the fire risk of a large warehouse or store which can be stacked with goods.

In a paper by G. J. Langdon-Thomas ARIBA, AADip, of the Fire Research Station, on 'Fire Protection Problems in Multi-storey Mechanical Car Parks',[11] he states:

'... statistics of the incidence of fires in motor vehicles in use and at rest show that the risk of fire is in the region of one per 1000 vehicles at rest per year.

When considering the fire risk associated with large numbers of motor vehicles, it is unwise to compare the risk to a series of parked cars with that of the large, extensive and expensive fires that have occurred in the motor industry. In the case of car factories, the materials of construction of the buildings often form a large part of the combustible material available to contribute to the fire. This contribution of combustible material, both in the structure and the contents of a building, is known as the fire load, and it is upon this fire load that the design of the structure to resist fire must be based. The fire load associated with the average motor vehicle consists of the car body, upholstery, tyres, oil and the petrol in the tank. For one vehicle these items may appear to present a considerable hazard, but in relation to the cubic content of the building, the amount of combustible material involved presents a comparatively low fire load, probably not exceeding 108,400 kcal/m^2 (40,000 Btu/ft^2) of floor area.

In the grading of building structures for fire resistance, the fire load is taken as the basis on which to assess the structural requirements. A fire resistance of one hour in the structure is required to withstand the burn-out of the contents of a building with a fire load not in excess of 275,000 kcal/m^2 (100,000 Btu/ft^2), and a two hour standard where the fire load exceeds 275,000 kcal/m^2 (100,000 Btu/ft^2) but is less than 550,000 kcal/m^2 (200,000 Btu/ft^2). It is likely that the type of building under consideration will have a total fire load well within the limits of 275,000 kcal/m^2 (100,000 Btu/ft^2) of floor area. Therefore the maximum fire resistance required in the structure may be taken as one hour.'

In March 1968, in the United Kingdom, the Minister of Housing and Local Government and the Secretary of State for Wales, issued a joint Circular[10] which gave notes for guidance on the Minister's attitude to relaxation of Part E requirements in respect of multi-storey car parks. These are as follows:

'6. For open sided multi-storey car parks which have no floor more than about 1·2 m (4 ft) below the surrounding ground level, the following are features which may well in the Minister's view support the case for relaxation of Part E requirements:

(1) Construction consisting wholly of non-combustible materials;

(2) For car parks exceeding 15·0 m (50 ft) in height, all elements of structure having a fire resistance of at least one hour; for car parks not exceeding 15·0 m (50 ft) in height, little fire resistance would generally be necessary, providing all the remaining criteria were satisfied;

General Note: The phrase 'little fire resistance' in respect of structure under 15·0 m (50 ft) in height permits unprotected steelwork to be used in all forms and sections likely to be required in practice.

(3) Where the car park is part of a building or immediately adjoins another building, artificial separation of the car park by compartment or separating walls having the fire resistance required by Regulation E.5 for the adjoining building or part, subject to a minimum of one hour for car parks exceeding 15·0 m (50 ft) in height or one-half hour for lower car parks.

General Note:[10] If a multi-storey car park adjoins other buildings either on one or both of its shorter sides, then waivers for exposed steel frames can generally be obtained, provided that the separating walls have a fire resistance of one-half hour.

(4) Adequate fire brigade access, combined with a separation distance from each side of the building to any boundary of the site or to the opposite side of any road that adjoins the site, and to the face of any building on the same site which is not attached to the car park calculated (as these were relevant boundaries) as follows:

(a) Where all elements of structure have a fire resistance of at least one hour: 9·0 m (30 ft) or any lesser distance that might result if Table I to Part II of Schedule 9 were to be applied.

(b) in all other cases: 9·0 m (30 ft).

General Note: Structures should be at least 9·0 m (30 ft) from the face of any building on the same site or from the boundary of the site, in which case there should be at least 9·0 m (30 ft) to the opposite side of the road.

(5) Permanent ventilation to the external air in the two opposing longer sides, the openings in each of the two sides having at each level an aggregate area of at least $2\frac{1}{2}\%$ of the area of the parking space at that level (making a total of at least 5% per floor) and being so distributed as to provide effective cross ventilation.

General Note: This requirement, relating to ventilation, would be easily met by most designs. For the limiting condition in the case of car parks which are square in plan, in which for example two opposite sides are two-thirds open and the height from floor to soffit of the perimeter beam is 2·30 m (7 ft 6 in), the maximum area permissible is 3715 m^2 (40,000 ft^2) per parking floor. In a rectangular car park, however, where the length is, for example, twice the width, the limiting area becomes 7430 m^2 (80,000 ft^2) per parking floor under similar ventilation conditions. It should be noted that additional ventilation can often be obtained by the use of steel mesh safety barriers, thus increasing the maximum permissible area.

(6) Adequate alternative means of escape, no parking space being further than 45·0 m (150 ft) from an escape stairway being separated from parking space by walls having fire resistance of at least one hour for car parks exceeding

15·0 m (50 ft) in height, or at least one-half for lower car parks; and any opening in these walls being fitted with self closing doors complying with Regulation E.11.'

LONDON BUILDING ACTS[13]

INNER LONDON BOROUGHS

The following are the relaxations which would normally be allowed (*see* Schedule 3—Section 20 of the London Building Acts (Amendment) Act 1939).

(*a*) the omission of a sprinkler installation;
(*b*) the omission of any restriction on cell sizes;
(*c*) the omission of mechanical ventilation, except in basements where adequate natural ventilation cannot be secured.

To secure the full relaxations, the open-sided multi-storey car park should comply with the following:

(1) have not less than 50% of its sides permanently open, the openings being distributed so as to provide adequate cross ventilation to all parts of the building;

(2) be not less than 9·0 m (30 ft) from other buildings unless a satisfactory standard of imperforate separation is provided therefrom, or alternatively, drenchers may be installed to protect any openings within 9·0 m (30 ft) of other buildings, but no openings will be permitted within 4·5 m (15 ft) of other buildings; openings may be permitted without protection where in the same plane as the face of an adjoining building if not less than 3·0 m (10 ft) distant therefrom;

(3) be positioned in respect to streets or upon an open site so that there is easy access for fire brigade appliances to a sufficient part of its perimeter to enable fire within any part of the structure to be attacked from the exterior;

(4) have sufficient staircases, enclosed or in protected positions, not more than 60·0 m (200 ft) apart for escape and fire fighting purposes. In the case of a structure exceeding 24·0 m (80 ft) in height to the topmost parking level, a fire lift may be necessary;

(5) have its main structural members protected to a two hour standard of fire resistance;

(6) any petrol service facilities to be external to the structure with a satisfactory standard of separation.

Paragraphs 1 and 2 of Section 20 of the London Building Acts (Amendment) Act, 1939, are as follows:

'20 (1) Unless the Council otherwise consent:

(*a*) no building shall be erected with a storey or part of a storey at a greater height than:

(i) 30·0 m (100 ft)
(ii) 24·0 m (80 ft) if the area of the building exceeds 930·0 m² (10,000 sq ft).

(b) no building of the warehouse class and no building or part of a building used for purposes of trade or manufacture shall be of a cubical extent exceeding 7000 m^3 (250,000 cu ft) unless it is divided by division walls in such manner that no division of the building or part of the building as the case may be is of cubical extent exceeding 7000 m^3 (250,000 cu ft).

Provided that the Council shall not withhold consent under paragraph (a) of this sub-section if they are satisfied that having regard to the proposed use to which the building is to be put proper arrangements will be made and maintained for lessening so far as is reasonably practicable danger from fire in the building.

(2) In granting consent under this section the Council may without prejudice to any other power to attach terms and conditions to the consent give the consent subject to conditions restricting the user of the building or part of the building or relating to the provision and maintenance of proper arrangements for lessening so far as is reasonably practicable danger from fire in the building or part of the building.'

GENERALLY

Both the enclosed and open-sided type of garage would have to be equipped with an adequate number of hose-reels and/or hand fire extinguishers and buckets of sand and any floor drainage would have to be passed through a petroleum interceptor. All electrical equipment would have to be of a type not liable to ignite inflammable vapour and any such equipment in storeys below ground level would have to be of the flame-proof type if installed within 1·2 m (4 ft) of the floor.

The storage and sale of petrol or other inflammable goods should be external to the building and would only be permitted where effective separation is provided between the car park and the storage or sale area. Similarly, any repair service area would have to be effectively separated from the car park and, if extensive, might require sprinkler protection.

An automatic sprinkler system would not usually be required in a garage building of lesser extent than 7000 m^3 (250,000 cu ft), except that if motor vehicles were garaged in any part of a building below ground level and that part had a floor area in excess of 465 m^2 (5000 sq ft), a sprinkler installation would be necessary therein.

LIGHTING

Lighting in multi-storey car parks is very important. There should be an absence of glare. It should be unnecessary to switch on headlamps, but the lighting should be of sufficient standard so as not to give a sense of driving into darkness when entering the car park in daytime (Fig. 10.19).

The British Standards Institution have published a Code of Practice for Street Lighting[14] which includes the lighting of car parks.

A recommended standard of lighting for the intermediate floors of a multi-storey car park is 50 lx (4·7 lumens per sq ft), but on ramps and corners this value should be increased to not less than 70 lx (6·5 lumens per sq ft). It is important to install a higher standard of lighting at the entrance to a car park which is at basement level and artificially lighted during the hours of daylight. In these circumstances it may be necessary to increase the standard of illumination to 150 lx (14·3 lumens per sq ft). On roofs used for parking, a standard of illumination of 20 lx (1·9 lumens per sq ft) is usually found to be sufficient.

In designing a lighting installation special attention should be given to the arrangement of the lighting points. It is advisable to arrange for the larger proportion of points to be installed directly over the aisles and for the parking

Fig. 10.19   Photograph showing a well lighted entrance to a multi-storey car park in Exeter, England.

stalls to be generally lighted by 'spill light' from these fittings. Care should be taken to ensure that there is sufficient light available over the parking stalls to ensure cars to be parked with safety (Fig. 10.20).

The lighting fittings should be constructed of corrosion resisting materials or be treated to resist corrosion, as in most cases they will be operating in conditions almost equivalent to those in the open air. In selecting fittings particular attention should be paid to the avoidance of dirt and moisture penetration to the apparatus and terminals.

It may be desirable to provide a standby system of lighting. This should be arranged to come into operation automatically in the event of failure of the public supply. A battery operated unit, automatically charged would be sufficient to light small tungsten lamps at strategic points. The equipment should be capable of providing continuous lighting for three hours. In locating the emergency lighting points attention should be given to lifts and staircases although the former may be out of action if the main electrical supply has failed.

Fig. 10.20 View of roof park at Heathrow (London) Airport at night. (*Reproduced by permission of L. G. Mouchel and Partners, Weybridge, Surrey, England.*)

Fig. 10.21 An example of signs used in multi-storey car parks.

Lighting in car parks is usually switched on for long periods which may be 24 hours in a day. The cost of energy consumed therefore may be quite substantial and it may well be that an installation that is higher in capital cost but has low running cost is the most economical one to install. Perhaps the ideal light source is the 1·5 m (5 ft) fluorescent tube which has a good colour rendering and an acceptable surface brightness when the fitting is equipped with a diffusing trough. It is shallow, reliable, easy to maintain and also economical.

SIGNS

Lighting and signing in car parks are closely related. Internally illuminated signs are quite vital for the successful operation of a car park (Fig. 10.21). There should be an adequate number of well lighted signs so that it is unnecessary to hold up traffic whilst enquiries are made. Parking places should be clearly defined by white lines; areas where vehicles should not stand or run over should be clearly marked by a raised kerb or diagonal lines; other floor markings and direction arrows should also be clearly marked. It is important to see that all these markings are kept clean and fresh. Unlike road markings they are not subjected to periodical rain washing.

HEATING[15]

Heating is not generally required in multi-storey car parks other than that required in offices and waiting rooms, and also where the ramps are exposed to the weather in districts subject to temperatures below freezing point. The most satisfactory way of heating ramps is by embedding heating elements within the top 50 mm (2 in) of the slab. There are at least two systems available. One consists of insulated cables operating at mains voltage, and the other consists of a steel mat and operating at a low voltage of 10–15 volts. The two systems operate with equal efficiency, but the mains voltage system is simple to install. The electrical loading is between 1·0 and 1·5 watts/m^2 (10 and 15 watts per sq ft). It can be operated at 'off peak' rates of energy and controlled by means of a thermostat to switch on/off at a temperature of say 1°C (34°F). A similar installation may be used in the treads of steps in staircases that are exposed.

VENTILATION[15]

The open-sided car park is becoming increasingly popular. This type of design may be ventilated solely by natural means if not less than 50% of the sides are permanently open, the openings being distributed so as to provide adequate cross ventilation to all parts of the building. The site and weather conditions should be taken into account and it may be that there would be little natural air movement on the lower floors of a car park sheltered by other buildings and/or trees. There may be a case in these circumstances for the installation of some mechanical ventilation plant for the lower floors. With the open side design, expense is reduced both in construction and in the provision of artificial ventilation. If the car park is enclosed, a mechanical ventilation system should be included capable of making six changes of air per hour at peak periods.

FIRE FIGHTING EQUIPMENT[12]

Fire fighting equipment should be provided in multi-storey car parks in accordance with requirements of the local authority and the Fire Prevention Section of the Fire Authority. The apparatus usually required consists of rising mains, hose reels, and hand equipment such as foam extinguishers.

Wet rising mains are usually provided on each floor near staircases if these are provided with smoke break doors. The length of hose reel is normally 18·0 m to 21·0 m (60 ft to 70 ft) and the jet will have an effective range of at least 6·0 m (20 ft). Therefore the effective range will be 24·0 m to 27·0 m (80 ft to 90 ft) and there should be sufficient provision for any part of the floor to be reached by the jet of water from a hose. The wet rising mains should be lagged and traced with an electric heating element and automatically controlled to protect from freezing. In a very large car park the Fire Authority may also require dry rising mains to be provided. The usual requirement is one 100 mm (4 in) riser and one 65 mm ($2\frac{1}{2}$ in) landing valve to each 930 m^2 (10,000 sq ft) of floor area.

LIFTS

Lifts in a car park are primarily for the use of people and therefore the type of person that has to be catered for should be studied. If the car park will be used largely by the shopping public with prams, children and parcels, then a larger lift will be required with a capacity of 10–13 persons. If used chiefly by adult commuters then a smaller lift will suffice, with a capacity of 8–10 persons. If the car park has a heavy peak load it is an advantage to have a lift operating between each floor and the ground floor. This avoids the lift stopping at each floor to unload one or two passengers and using much time. This may be considered to be too expensive but it does speed up the lift service between floors. Because multi-storey car parks are usually limited to 6–8 floors, it is not considered that high speed lifts, which are expensive, are justified.

TELEPHONES

At least one telephone is necessary and there should preferably be two, one for public use and one for car park staff. A car park attendant should be able to communicate with other car parks, and when a motorist finds himself at a full car park, the attendant should be able to give directions to other car parks where space is available.

AESTHETICS

As with many projects, a client instructs his engineer and/or architect to prepare a scheme for an isolated structure, in this case a multi-storey or underground car park. The site may be of suitable size and available. In common with other buildings a car park must be designed to harmonise with the surrounding buildings, but in addition it must be carefully planned to function efficiently with the traffic system. This is important in relation to traffic flows on the approach roads, and pedestrian traffic to and from the car park.

A multi-storey car park is essentially a functional building, and there is usually a great deal of emphasis on achieving a low cost per car space. This does not excuse the designer from achieving a pleasing architectural effect.

In evidence prepared on behalf of the University of Oxford against some details of the Oxford Development Plan, Professor Colin Buchanan, referring to multi-storey car parks, stated:[16]

'Only too often they are ugly in appearance, overpowering in scale and unpleasant in usage. I have yet to find a public multi-storey car park that makes an aesthetic contribution to the civic scene, or can be enjoyed in its own right as a piece of satisfying architecture. I have never heard of a multi-storey car park—and there must be many of them—being the subject of a Royal Institute of British Architects' Award. Nor have I found them floodlit at night as a contributory showpiece to a brighter and livelier town centre.

In my view this lacuna in civic design can be largely attributed to an unnecessary solicitude on the part of local authorities for the pockets of motorists, which results in these structures being whittled down to the cheapest possible design with the barest minimum of expenditure on finish, cladding and appurtenances. For most part these structures look exactly what they are—crude concrete frameworks. They may be acceptable when located in the commercial or industrial hinterlands to town centres, but I do not think they are appropriate when they trespass into areas of historic interest or appear in proximity to buildings which have been designed to quite different standards of cost and finish.'

There is no doubt that multi-storey car parks will form a large part of the new urban scene, and will be dominant features in towns and cities. Our role should be to ensure that these new functional buildings do not disrupt or mar, but rather enhance and complement, the existing functions of our towns. A car park building is generally composed of a series of slabs supported on columns to provide large areas of uninterrupted floor space. Very little weather protection is required and generally there is no need to roof the last floor. There is much flexibility in the design of reinforced concrete structures which give opportunities to achieve a pleasing architectural result. By carefully designing the structural elements of the building, many opportunities can be presented for a simple elevational treatment with vertical or horizontal lines, a suitable blending of brick, stone and concrete, and there are very many variations of concrete finishes that may be used. It is the finish of car park buildings that appears to suffer most in pruning to reduce costs.

The treatment of the site surrounding the building should not be overlooked. Landscaping can serve as an important means of relating the car park with other buildings, and is of special importance when used to relieve the severity of modern architectural buildings. Pedestrian access points, especially with underground car parks, give the opportunity to introduce some natural colour from shrubs and flowers. This can be a feature that is much appreciated.

It is also important to give attention and thought to the interior of the car park. Visitors to a town may find their first stopping place in the car park, and from here they will begin to form their impressions. Colour may be used to help identify the parking floors; cleanliness on the parking deck is important and especially in the toilets, staircases and lifts.

COST OF CAR PARKS

At the time of writing (December 1970) the cost of materials and wages in the United Kingdom is rising rapidly and this also applies to civil and structural engineering work. It is therefore difficult to compare costs of different designs and types of construction. Mr P. B. Wood, of W. V. Zinn and Associates, Consulting Civil and Structural Engineers, Epsom, Surrey,[17] gave a summary and breakdown of costs based on actual tenders and updated to 1970 cost figures. These figures are shown in Table IX. The figures have been adjusted to include in each case the cost of such items as foundations, lifts and cladding. The figures also allow for fire protection being provided.

The table also indicates the percentage split up of the cost in terms of structure, foundations (assuming $214 \cdot 5$ kN/m^2 (2 tons/sq ft) at $1 \cdot 0$ m (3 ft) below ground level except in the ramped car park where piling was used), cladding, etc. The cladding costs can significantly affect the total cost, a typical range being from £30 to £100 per car.

Clear span construction is shown to increase the cost per car space by £13, but ease of crane access may have an important bearing on cost and on congested sites may preclude the use of precast floor construction.

DESIGN AND TENDERING PROCEDURE[18]

The traditional practice in the United Kingdom for the construction of buildings and civil engineering works is for the engineer and/or architect to prepare the designs, contract drawings and other documents. Tenders are invited from experienced contractors, and the selected contractor carries out the construction of the works under the supervision of the engineer and/or architect. The client employs the engineer and/or architect and pays their professional fees. They in turn look after the client's interest. The professional staff employed directly by a local authority, Government Department or other public body act in the same way as the private practising engineer and/or architect, the client in this case being the public authority employing them. The professional fee is for work connected with the preparation of one final scheme, with drawings, specification and quantities prepared to meet the client's requirements, and each contractor

TABLE IX

Car Park for Approximately 500–600 Cars
Cost per Car

Type:	(1) Split Level		(2) Ramped	(3) Steel-work frame	(4) Warped slab
Section	(a) Balanced Cantilever	(b) Clear Span	Clear Span (Piled)		
	£ — %	£ — %	£ — %	£ — %	£ — %
Substructure	20 — 7	19 — 7	69 — 15	31 — 10	24 — 8
Superstructure	143 — 52	156 — 54	202 — 44	185 — 58	150 — 50
Drainage	6 — 2	4 — 1	5 — 1	4 — 1	6 — 2
Prelims	37 — 13	40 — 14	60 — 13	40 — 13	45 — 15
Lift Tower	5 — 2	5 — 2	10 — 2	– — –	– — –
Total Structure	211 — 76	224 — 78	346 — 75	263 — 82	225 — 75
Lighting	21 — 8	21 — 7	18 — 4		
Signs	2 — $\frac{1}{2}$	2 — $\frac{1}{2}$	5 — 1	57 — 18	75 — 25
Barriers and Handrailing	17 — 6	17 — 6	23 — 5		
Bay Marking	2 — $\frac{1}{2}$	2 — $\frac{1}{2}$	2 — $\frac{1}{2}$		
Lifts	21 — 8	21 — 7	46 — 10	– — –	– — –
Lighting (Lifts)	1 — $\frac{1}{2}$	1 — $\frac{1}{2}$	2 — $\frac{1}{2}$	– — –	– — –
Handrailing (Lift)	1 — $\frac{1}{2}$	1 — $\frac{1}{2}$	5 — 1	– — –	– — –
External Works	– — –	– — –	13 — 3	– — –	– — –
Total	65 — 24	65 — 22	114 — 25	57 — 18	75 — 25
GRAND TOTAL	276 — 100	289 — 100	460 — 100	320 — 100	300 — 100

EO Cladding   (0–70)   EO for Fire Protection   19   6

With more expensive cladding of £70 (EO)   346   339

(EO 20)

The above estimates of costs do not include the following items:

(a) Cost of Land Acquisition.
(b) Site Exploration Work.
(c) Fees payable to a Local Authority.
(d) Professional fees or expenses.
(e) Costs in respect of works carried out by Statutory Authorities, diversions, etc.

Reproduced from Paper by P. B. Wood, Car Parking Seminar Report, London, 1970.

prepares his tender on the basis of these documents. When the tenders are submitted the prices can be compared knowing that they are all for the same scheme and based on the same specification.

It is no doubt true to say that it is not every engineer and/or architect who is experienced in designing car parks, and that a specialist firm for this work would be preferable. If a firm needs help and advice there are people available who may be consulted, and I am sure a reputable firm would call for specialised advice when required.

An alternative system which has developed is the all-in service or 'package deal', whereby the builder or civil engineering contractor employs his own engineers and/or architects either directly or from firms in private practice. The contractor submits a complete design and tender to the client. For the client the operation is simple. He merely states that he wishes to build, say a multi-storey car park for 500 cars, on a selected site, and asks for a price from the

Fig. 10.22 Elevation and entrance to Churchill Square Car Park, Brighton, England. (*Reproduced by permission of National Car Parks Ltd, London.*)

contractor. The amount of detail given to the contractor can vary considerably and usually depends on whether or not the client is employing a professional adviser direct. If more than one tender is requested, then each tender submitted is on an individually prepared scheme—separate plans, specification and quantities have to be prepared by each contractor tendering although they may be in an abridged form. There may be three or four tenders submitted or as many as twenty, or even more. Each scheme submitted will be different—each tender figure will be different. The lowest tender may be based on the most economical design, and efficient workmanship. Alternatively it may be on the cheapest design and poorest specification. Tenders submitted in this way are difficult to analyse, and it is difficult to make a true comparison. More often than not the lowest tender is accepted whatever the merits might be.

With this system the professional services are engaged or employed by the contractor, and not the client, although the client will pay for them indirectly as professional services, or as overhead charges which are included in the contract. The money spent on professional services in preparing schemes and tenders which were unsuccessful has to be recovered by the contractor and must be included in overheads or such other charges, and recovered on successful tenders. Ultimately the client pays for this abortive professional work with the 'package deal' system.

Fig. 10.23 Parkhaus Savignystrasse, Frankfurt-am-Main, Germany. (*Reproduced by permission of Hoentief AG Frankfurt.*)

It is argued that the combination of the experience of the contractor and engineer and/or architect at the preparation stage of a scheme will produce a better design and probably a lower tender. There is a great deal of merit in making use of the contractor's practical experience, but there are ways of doing this which will also protect the client's interests. One is to discuss the scheme with the successful contractor and incorporate acceptable suggestions and modifications. Another is to select the contractor on a preliminary design and complete it in conjunction with the selected contractor.

BRIEF FOR 'PACKAGE DEAL' TENDERS

If the traditional practice in the United Kingdom for the design and construction of civil engineering and building works has been followed, there will be detailed drawings, a specification and bill of quantities available for the contractors and all tenders will be based on these documents. This practice, if followed rigidly, excludes firms who have developed a specialised method of construction particularly using prefabricated units. These firms could be included if the invitation to tender permitted a contractor to submit an alternative tender accompanied by drawings and specification for the specialised method of construction in addition to the tender based on the documents supplied to contractors. These documents would also form the brief for the alternative scheme.

If it is decided to invite 'package deal' tenders it is in the interest of the local authority or other client and the contractors for the requirements to be defined as precisely as possible. The basic information that should be available to contractors is:

(a) a site plan with levels and showing the means of access,
(b) a detailed report on ground conditions,
(c) the number of cars to be accommodated and the number of floors in the car park.

At this stage it may be decided to invite approximate estimates and a brief specification from any firm interested in the project. From these firms a selected list of five or six contractors could be prepared, who would be invited to submit a complete scheme and firm tender.

The client or local authority may decide not to invite preliminary tenders and specifications, but from information available to them they may decide to select five or six firms, to submit a firm scheme and tender. It is in the client's interest that the selected contractors should be given a very clear brief so that each firm will know precisely what is required and the standard of workmanship expected. This will be fair to the contractor and ultimately much more satisfactory to the client.

An outline of the information that should be included in the brief is as follows:

1. Information given for the preliminary tenders.
2. General and Special Conditions of Contract.
3. Time allowed for preparation of scheme and submission of tenders. (This time should be adequate for the contractor to prepare a carefully considered scheme).
4. Plans and drawings required.
5. Outline specification:

(a) standard of architectural design,
(b) principles of structural design, including loading, BS Codes of Practice, floor height, aisle width, stall size, ramp slopes, type of circulation,
(c) accommodation—car capacity, lavatories required, offices, stores, service and meter room, emergency exits, number of lifts,
(d) information on existing services that is available,
(e) provide and connect to public utility services,
(f) standard of floor; roof and wall finishes required,

(g) standard of sanitary fittings,
(h) fire precaution requirements,
(j) standard of electrical installation,
(k) provisional sums for landscaping, mechanical control equipment, illuminated and non-illuminated signs, and contingencies.

6. Time allowed for work to be carried out. (This should be adequate, and twelve months to build a car park for 500 cars is reasonable).

If a client or local authority cannot supply this information to a contractor, they should seek advice. It is important and in their interest that a minimum standard of design and construction should be specified. Otherwise low tenders may be submitted for sub-standard work which is unsatisfactory to the local authority if accepted and grossly unfair to other contractors tendering for work of a higher standard. It is often very difficult to compare 'package deal' tenders and, therefore, essential that they all comply with a clear basic standard of design and construction.

TOWN CENTRE REDEVELOPMENT SCHEMES

In many towns, redevelopment schemes in the central business area are being considered. These schemes give an opportunity to include multi-storey and/or underground car parks in the redeveloped area. One advantage is that car parking facilities can be provided near to a shopping centre, and another advantage is that ground level accommodation can be used for shopping and thereby draw a high rental. The upper or lower floors, which attract a much less rental, may be used for car parking.

It is, however, essential that these parking facilities form an integral part of the parking plan and policy for the town. The method of control, management and ownership of the car park should be considered at an early stage when schemes from prospective developers are being invited.

Whatever method of tendering may be selected, it is essential and in the interest of all parties that the client makes a firm and clear decision on the basic requirements, and that reasonable time is given for the contract to be carried out. It is very foolish for a client to waste time making up his or their mind and pressing the designer and contractor to speed up their work. This leads to unnecessary difficulties and troubles.

REFERENCES

1. British Parking Association Technical Committee, Technical Note No. 1. 'Metric Dimensions for Car Parks', *Traffic Engineering & Control*, April, 1970, Vol. 11, No. 12.
2. A. J. Information Library—'Car Parking Buildings', *The Architect's Journal*, 29th June 1966.
3. GLANVILLE, JOHN. 'The Warped Slab Car Park', *Civil Engineering & Public Works Review*, May 1969.

4. BERRY, GRANVILLE. 'Roof Top & Mechanical Parking'—Report of the Convention on the Problem of Parking. Institution of Municipal Engineers, 1960.
5. HUGHES, A. C. 'Design & Structural Aspects of Roof Top and Multi-storey Car Parks'. Paper given to Study Course, Barford, Warwick, Institution of Municipal Engineers. 1966.
6. British Standard Code of Practice. CP114 'Structural Use of Reinforced Concrete in Buildings', 1957 with amendments 1953/56/67. Part 2 (Metric) 1969. British Standards Institution, London.
7. BIDGOOD, R. 'Lift Slab Construction'. *Journal of the Junior Institution of Engineers*, 1963/64, Vol. 74, Pt. 8.
8. GIFFORD, F. W. 'Multi-storey Car Parks in Precast Concrete', *The Structural Engineer*, March 1963, vol. 41, No. 3.
9. 'Building Regulations 1965', HMSO, London.
10. 'Building Regulations 1965'—Multi-storey Car Parks, Circular 17/68 Ministry of Housing & Local Government, Circular 11/68 Welsh Office. HMSO, London.
11. LANGDON–THOMAS, G. J. 'Fire Protection Problems in Multi-storey Car Parks', *Civil Engineering*, June 1961, Vol. 56, No. 659.
12. Ministry of Technology & Fire Office Committee, 'Fire & Car Park Buildings', HMSO, London, 1968.
13. The London Buildings Acts (Amendment) Act, 1939.
14. 'Street Lighting, Lighting for Town & City Centres & Areas of Civic Importance', British Standard Code of Practice. CP1004. Part 9. British Standards Institution, London, 1969.
15. ADCOCK, S. F. 'Mechanical & Electrical Services Associated with Car Parks'. Paper given to Study Course, Barford, Warwick. Institution of Municipal Engineers, 1966.
16. BUCHANAN, C. Evidence given to Public Inquiry, Oxford, *Traffic Engineering & Control*. September 1970, vol. 12, No. 5.
17. WOOD, P. B. 'Cost Implications of Car Park Design'. Paper given at Car Parking Seminar, London, November 1970.
18. BRIERLEY, JOHN. 'Preparing the Brief & Planning for Construction'. Paper given at Car Parking Seminar, London, November 1970.

SUGGESTIONS FOR FURTHER READING

MANZONI, SIR HERBERT, 'Public Parking Garages', *Journal RIBA*, London. 3rd Series. March 1968, Vol. 65, No. 5.

Modern Developments in Reinforced Concrete—'Parking Garage Layouts', No. 24. Portland Cement Association, Chicago, Illinois, USA.

Report to Highways Research Board. 'Garage Design Criteria', *Highway Research Abstracts*. March 1960, Vol. 30, No. 3, Washington, DC.

DOUBLEDAY, E. H. 'Off Street Parking', *The Chartered Surveyor*, London, January 1961.

RICKER, E. R. 'The Traffic Design of Parking Garages', Eno Foundation for Highway Traffic Control, Saugatuck, Conn. USA.

'Construction Hazards & Protection of Garages', National Fire Protection Association, Boston, Mass. USA. 1968.

'Fire Hazard in Multi-storey Car Parks', Chamberlain Parking Systems Ltd, London, 1965.

Car Park Feature. *Civil Engineering*, London, December 1964.

RICH, R. C. 'Planning a Downtown Parking Deck', *Architectural Record*, USA. May 1965.

SEYMER, NIGEL. 'A Survey of Parking Garages', *International Road Safety & Traffic Review*.

SEYMER, NIGEL. 'Design of Parking Garages for European Needs', *International Road Safety & Traffic Review*, Autumn 1966.

BARR, W. G. 'How to Plan Parking Structures', *Consulting Engineer*, USA. September 1964.

BAKER, G. and FUNARO, B. 'Parking', Reinhold, 1958.

KLOSE, D. 'Multi-storey Car Parks & Garages', Architectural Press, London, 1965.

SILL, O. *et al.* 'Parkbauten', Bauverlag Wiesbaden, Germany, 1961 (in German).

ELLSON, P. B. 'Parking: Dynamic Capacities of Car Parks', Road Research Laboratory. Report LR221, London, 1969.

BELLCHAMBERS, D. M., BUTTON, R. J. and SUMMER, P. J. 'Parking: Effects of Stall Markings on the Positioning of Parked Cars', Road Research Laboratory. Report LR289, London, 1969.

Chapter 11

Examples of Multi-Storey and Roof Car Parks

A selection has been made of existing multi-storey and roof car parks to illus-trate the basic designs and ramp systems described in Chapter 10.

CONTINUOUS SLOPING FLOOR CAR PARKS AT BRISTOL AND LEICESTER

The multi-storey car park at Bristol (Fig. 11.1) accommodates about 560 cars on a site of approximately 3250 m² (35,000 sq ft), close to the proposed inner ring road at Lewins Mead. The construction is of beams and columns cast *in situ* with a reinforced concrete deck, and provides a gradually ascending roadway 7·3 m (24 ft) wide with parking stalls 4·75 m (16 ft) by 2·50 m (8 ft) on each side. The building is elliptical in shape based on axes of 63·0 m and 40·0 m (209 ft and 129 ft). A garage with fuel pumps, showrooms and workshops occupies the ground floor.

The overall width of the deck between balustrades is 17·0 m (56 ft) and the whole deck is tilted towards the inner well so that drainage points can be provided. Rainwater pipes are fitted to the walls of the central lift well. The tilting of the deck has produced a camber at the circular ends in the correct direction, but allows the whole roadway to be wetted when rain blows in from the outside. The gradient in the longitudinal direction is 1 in 32 on the straight, and at the outside of the kerb is about 1 in 60.

The Lee Circle Car Park at Leicester is designed as a double ramp with entrances at each end. Two towers are provided, each containing a staircase and two passenger lifts which give access to both ramps.

This car park will accommodate 1140 cars in six complete circuits of the building above first floor level. The ground floor is used as showrooms, work-shops and restaurant, with an extensive service forecourt equipped with 14 petrol pumps.

By having access at either end of the building it is possible to arrange for one access to serve circuits 1, 3 and 5, and the other circuits 2, 4 and 6. The car park is operated by a staff of four men, two of whom are collecting fees.

Fig. 11.1   View of entrance to Rupert Street Car Park, Bristol. (*Reproduced by permission of G. C. Mander and Partners, Bristol.*)

The Consulting Engineers for these car parks are G. C. Mander and Partners, of Bristol, and the Consulting Architects are R. Jelmeck-Karl, F.R.I.B.A., for the Bristol scheme, and Fitzroy Robinson and Partners, of London, for the Leicester scheme. The Contractor for both schemes was Wm. Cowlin and Sons Ltd, of Bristol.

CONTINUOUS SLOPING FLOOR WITH CLEARWAY EXIT
AT EXETER

This building which is situate at King William Street, Exeter (Figs. 11.2 and 11.3), is the result of a competitive design tender. The design brief was prepared by John Brierley, O.B.E., F.I.C.E., F.R.T.P.I., the City Engineer, and Vinton Hall, F.R.I.B.A., M.R.T.P.I., the City Architect.

The design is based on a continuous sloping floor forming eleven decks for incoming traffic and parking stalls. The exit from all parking areas is separated from incoming traffic and consists of an independent spiral ramp. The vehicular circulation from the entrance on the south side to the parking stalls and down the spiral exit ramp is in one direction only. This simple circulation ensures uninterrupted movement of vehicles within the building.

The pedestrian ways from the main entrance, lifts and the two subsidiary staircases are separated from the vehicular traffic. The toilets for both sexes are on the south side of the building with access from inside and outside the car park. There are 462 parking stalls in the park including the roof.

Aesthetically, advantage has been taken of the structural elements and method of construction to give balance between the vertical and horizontal lines. Infill panels are textured, and the interesting slope of the spiral ramp has been enhanced

Fig. 11.2 Interior view of King William Street Car Park, Exeter.

by the introduction of vertical ribs, and the stair-well enclosures are clad with brickwork.

The building is constructed in accordance with the Building Regulations 1965 and current Codes of Practice. The main frame, floors and spiral ramps are of reinforced concrete with each deck having a clear span of 16·0 m (52 ft) with 2·15 m (7 ft) headroom under beams, and an uninterrupted length of 60·0 m (200 ft).

Fig. 11.3 View of entrance to spiral exit ramp, King William Street Car Park, Exeter.

The foundations consist of mass strip concrete in open trenches extending down to firm sandstone marl. The decking sections were constructed integral with the principal supporting beams in sections 16·0 m (52 ft) by 4·75 m (16 ft), each section being completed during one working day. Steel mobile shuttering was used, and the curing of the concrete was accelerated by warm air circulation. This enabled the concrete to stand with minimal supports within 12 hours of casting and this made it possible to operate a continuous daily casting cycle, the curing of the concrete taking place during the hours of darkness.

The contract price was £158,930, giving a cost per car space of £344. The work was completed in February, 1969.

A representative cross section of the structure was load tested on completion to 25% above the design loadings. In all cases the structure withstood the stresses. The deflections and the resilience of the concrete produced amply satisfied the requirements of the design and appropriate Codes of Practice. The contractors for the scheme were EBC and Sleeman Ltd, Exeter, and their Consulting Engineers, L. G. Mouchel and Partners, Bath.

SLOPING FLOOR WITH CLEARWAY EXIT AT WATFORD

The site chosen for this car park (Figs. 11.4 and 11.5) is near the main shopping centre. It is known as The Shrubbery, and lies between Watford High Street and Rosslyn Road.

The four storey structure is rectangular on plan, with an external spiral descent ramp on the south side. Two-thirds of each floor area provide a flat parking space and one-third a ramped parking space at a slight gradient of 1 in 20. The electrically heated descent ramp has a gradient of 1 in 12 to provide speedy access to the two exit barriers. Two flights of stairs and two lifts serve all floors.

As a proportion of the space is reserved for invalid carriages, actual parking accommodation is marked out for 702 cars and 47 motor cycles. The parking area for each car is 4·72 m × 2·30 m (15 ft 6 in × 7 ft 6 in), and there is 2·30 m (7 ft 6 in) clear headroom below the soffits of the floor beams.

The access roads are 6·0 m (20 ft) wide and there is a one-way clockwise traffic circulation. Drivers of incoming vehicles will accordingly be able to see every available parking space to the right and left of them.

The car park is 100·0 m long × 32·0 m wide (323 ft 2 in long × 104 ft 10 in wide); the height to the roof top parking deck is 13·75 m (45 ft). The structural concrete frame is carried on spread footings, and consists of three longitudinal rows of reinforced concrete columns, spread at approximately 9·0 m (30 ft) centres, connected by edge beams 0·38 m (1 ft 3 in) wide by 0·70 m (2 ft 4 in) deep. The columns are 1·20 m (4 ft) wide and vary from 0·20 m to 0·25 (8 in to 10 in) in thickness.

The floors at each storey level span 15·5 m (51 ft) between the outer and centre columns and are constructed of *in situ* reinforced concrete by the Holst 'Ribspan' system, thus forming a monolithic structure. The floor units are of inverted channel section; the slab is 0·10 m (4 in) thick (giving a 2 hours fire resistance), and the integral rib units at 0·90 m (3 ft) centres, are 0·60 m (2 ft) deep by 0·15 m

Fig. 11.4   View of the Shrubbery Car Park, Watford, showing a typical layout with spiral exit. (*Reproduced by permission of Holst and Co. Ltd, Watford.*)

Fig. 11.5   View of main entrance at the front and fast exit spiral ramp at the Shrubbery Car Park, Watford. (*Reproduced by permission of Holst and Co. Ltd, Watford.*)

(5¾ in) thick at the soffit edges. *In situ* beams, 0·28 m (11 in) wide, are placed at right angles to the rib beams.

The concrete for the floors is placed in fibreglass trough forms with timber supports for the rib soffits. The forms are carried on a patent head jacking system which enables the forms to be removed for repetitive use without disturbing the rib supports.

The external surfaces of the building have been rendered with 'Mineralite' in contrasting colours—grey lustre for the columns and beam edges, white lustre for the roof deck parapet, and green lustre for the balustrades of alternate parking bays. The remaining parking bays will have steel framed wire meshed balustrades.

The overall cost per car space in 1965 was £275 including all site works, roads, drains and finishes.

The work was designed and constructed by Holst and Co. Ltd, Watford, under the direction of F. C. Sage, F.I.C.E., F.I.Mun.E., Borough Engineer and Surveyor, Watford.

CONTINUOUS SLOPING FLOOR CAR PARK WITH LINK BETWEEN INTERLOCKING FLOORS AT LONGBRIDGE, BIRMINGHAM

This car park was built for the Austin Motor Co. Ltd, now British Leyland (Austin-Morris) Ltd, to provide accommodation for up to 3300 cars awaiting delivery.

The structure is of reinforced column and slab construction (Fig. 11.6). It is 114·5 m (376 ft) long, 62·0 m (204 ft) wide and 22·0 m (72 ft) high. It is nine storeys high including the roof which is also used as a parking area. All parking floors are ramped, and a double spiral system of floors enables upward and downward movement of traffic to be completely segregated.

The flow of cars from the assembly lines is such that a single entrance is inadequate, and the ramps are therefore divided, with two entrances. This has the advantage that a one-way traffic system can be devised, and there are eight lines of parking stalls across the width of the building served by four aisles. Half of the aisles are used for up traffic, and half for down traffic, with level crossover links in the centre and at each end. The distance up the ramp from the entrance is about three-quarters of a mile. To reduce travelling time from the upper levels to the ground floor, two vehicle lifts have been provided for vehicles parked on the top three levels to be conveyed to and from the appropriate level by lift. Passenger lifts and staircases are provided at the four corners of the building.

Tests carried out on the car park reveal that a car permitted to roll unbraked down a gradient of 1 in 34 can gather a speed of 48 km/h (30 mph) on the ramps of about 106 m (350 ft) length, and that barriers are necessary to resist the impact of a car at this speed. The time taken to drive from the entrance to the furthest parking stall is 5 minutes at 16 km/h (10 mph).

Handling cars within such an immense building brings its own special problems. Unless some precise indexing system is operated the task of finding any

Fig. 11.6 View of model of continuous sloping floor car park for British Leyland (Austin-Morris) Ltd, at Birmingham, showing design of floor layout. (*Reproduced by permission of British Lift Slab Ltd, Birmingham.*)

one car could be equivalent to finding a needle in a haystack. Though an electronic control system may eventually be used, a straightforward visual method is now being used. The twin ramp system makes it a simple operation to divide the building into four zones. Each zone is denoted by a colour and each zone level by a number. Each parking stall can therefore be numbered, *e.g.* Red 4–60. A card index system in the office gives the location of every car. Directional and 'No Entry' signs; arrows and lines painted on the floors and ramps are also used to control traffic.

This building was erected by the 'Lift Slab' method of construction which is described in Chapter 10.

The Architects for the car park were Harry W. Weedon and Partners, Birmingham. The constructon was carried out by British Lift Slab Ltd, in conjunction with their parent company, Robert M. Douglas (Construction) Ltd, George Street, Birmingham.

MULTI-STOREY CAR PARK WITH LEVEL FLOOR AND STRAIGHT RAMPS AT LONDON (HEATHROW) AIRPORT

The specification for this car park (Figs. 11.7 and 11.8) was prepared by the United Kingdom Air Ministry and included a number of limiting conditions.

The site covered a section of a disused runway which could be used as the ground floor to the park, and to make the maximum use of the available space a flat floor design was chosen. In order to squeeze six floors into a height of 13·8 m (45 ft) and provide minimum headroom of 2·30 m (7 ft 6 in) the structural depth was limited to 45 cm (18 in).

The design of the park provides for cars to be parked at right angles to the aisles; the traffic circulation is arranged so that the entry and exit routes form

Fig. 11.7   View of multi-storey car park No. 1, with level floor and straight ramps, at London (Heathrow) Airport. (*Reproduced by permission of L. G. Mouchel and Partners, Weybridge, Surrey, England.*)

spiral type circuits rising through, and integral with the parking floors. The entry is at the north-west end of the building, and the exit at the opposite end. The circulation of all traffic is clockwise within the building and along one-way flow aisles only.

The floors are interconnected by single-way ramps having a gradient of 1 in 10. The up and down ramps for each floor are stacked one above the other.

Pedestrian access to the floors is by means of a lift and a stair block which project from the main building. Three lifts are provided, each having a capacity of twelve persons. There is also a small administrative suite of offices at ground level. There are two sets of emergency stairs, built with concrete shafts and fireproof doors.

The structure of the car park is of *in situ* reinforced concrete, because it was found to be cheaper than precast work. It consists of single-way spanning beams and slabs designed in accordance with British Standard Code of Practice 114. This design enabled a system of travelling table shutters to be used, each unit being rolled parallel to the line of the beams for re-use.

Control of entry and exit is by automatic equipment. A car counting system is installed which relays to the operating supervisor the number of car spaces available on each floor. The system is operated by two pairs of photo-electric cells mounted on each ramp, which have to be obscured to register a car passing. Drainage has been arranged by forming shallow valleys in the floors.

Fig. 11.8   Illuminated entrance to multi-storey car park No. 2 at London (Heathrow) Airport.
(Reproduced by permission of National Car Parks Ltd, London.)

Artificial illumination consists of fluorescent lighting fittings along the centre lines of all circulation aisles to give a minimum intensity of 32 lx (3 lumens per sq ft) at all points in the building. The roof lighting is by means of flood lamps mounted on lighting towers placed over the small brick buildings forming the upper entrance to the emergency stairs.

This car park has accommodation for 1145 cars and 20 coaches. The size of each parking stall is 5·0 m (17 ft) by 2·5 m (8 ft); the width of the aisles is 5·5 m (18 ft); the maximum gradient of ramps is 1 in 10 and the clear distance between columns on either side of the parking aisles is 8·0 m (26 ft). The cost of the car park was approximately £350,000 in 1963, giving a cost of £290 per car space.

The Contractors for this work were Taylor Woodrow Construction Ltd, the Consulting Engineers, L. G. Mouchel and Partners, and the Consultant Architect, Frederick Gibberd, C.B.E.

LEVEL FLOORS WITH 'CLEARWAY' ENTRANCE AND EXIT AT BRISTOL

This structure is known as the Parkway Car Park (Fig. 11.9), and is situated between Newfoundland Road and Wellington Road, about 230·0 m (250 yards) east of the Inner Circuit Road, and is the first of a series of car parks which will provide direct connections to the principal roads in the Broadmead district, and also a high speed direct connection with the proposed Parkway (M32) which links with the M4 and M5.

In the design particular attention was paid to the rapid and easy movement of cars and pedestrians in and out of this eight storey building. The time taken to travel from the entrance of the car park to the most distant parking stall and

Fig. 11.9 General view of Wellington Road Car Park, Bristol. (*Reproduced by permission of the City Engineer, Bristol.*)

vice versa can be as small as 1·50 minutes. This ease of movement is made possible by the provision of non-parking exterior helical entry and exit ramps, which connect with alternate floors of the car park. This means that under normal circumstances, to park a car or leave the building by car, only one or two parking floors need be used.

The capacity of the car park is 1067 cars accommodated on eight parking levels. Parking is provided off a two-way traffic aisle and each level is internally connected by parking ramps at the west side of the structure at a gradient of 1 in 22. The structure is formed of *in situ* concrete with slabs spanning in one direction supported by beams at 4·75 m (16 ft) centres. The beams are 17·0 m

(56 ft 0 in) long (half car park width) including a 3·0 m (11 ft 0 in) cantilever at the outer edge. The structural form adopted for the helical ramps consists of a 0·15 m (6 in) *in situ* slab supported on cantilever beams. The columns are on the inner face only.

Inside the car park, high speed 10 person passenger lifts connect with the eight parking levels and the ground floor pedestrian way which is completely segregated from the vehicular entry and exit routes. There are two entrances and three exits to the car park, and it is planned so that ultimately the helical ramp system will connect directly with an elevated urban motorway and another multi-storey car park.

The contract price for the car park was £560,000, giving a cost per car space of £525, in 1968.

The scheme was designed in the Department of the City Engineer, J B. Bennett, C.B.E., F.I.C.E., and the Contractors were Ernest Ireland (Contractors) Ltd, of Bath. Their Consulting Structural Engineers were Anthony Masters and Associates.

MULTI-STOREY CAR PARK WITH FLOORS FORMING A DOUBLE SPIRAL RAMP AT CROWELL ROAD, COWLEY CENTRE, OXFORD

This car park (Fig. 11.10) is based on the principle of the double spiral ramp, with 'odd' floors providing a ramp up, and 'even' floors a ramp down. Motorists

Fig. 11.10   View of Crowell Road Car Park, Cowley Centre, Oxford, England. (*Reproduced by permission of W. V. Zinn and Associates, Epsom, Surrey.*

on the up ramp who wish to transfer to the down ramp can do so very easily by turning on to the connecting floor running through the centre of the building. This car park has the following features:

(a) The circulation is entirely one-way. A motorist entering the car park from road level could (if he continued to go in the same direction) complete the spiral circuit, and arrive at road level once more.

(b) As far as possible column-free parking space has been provided. Most of the columns are placed on the outside face of the building, thereby becoming a feature of the elevational design.

(c) The car park has two entrances and two exits, on Crowell Road and Beauchamp Road.

(d) The site is almost square and provides a large turning circle with easy turns at the corners.

(e) The capacity is approximately 500 cars.

The design is an expression of the structure with varying concrete surface textures, and a minimum amount of applied decoration. A pedestrian bridge links the car park with the office block on the opposite side of Crowell Road. The cost of this car park built in 1965 was approximately £400 per car space.

The Architect for the structure was D. Murray, A.R.I.B.A., City Architect, Oxford, and the Consulting Civil and Structural Engineers were W. V. Zinn and Associates, Epsom, Surrey. The Main Contractor was John Laing Construction Ltd.

SPLIT LEVEL MULTI-STOREY CAR PARK FORMING PART OF THE MERRION CENTRE DEVELOPMENT, LEEDS

This building (Fig. 11.11) provides for:

A basement containing a 42-lane bowling alley; ground floor containing garage, service station and car showrooms, covering 9000 m² (30,000 sq ft) as well as shops and access points to the car park.

A supermarket of 4850 m² (16,000 sq ft) with an 850 seat cinema constructed over it will adjoin the building.

First, second and third floors and roof are devoted to car parking with a total capacity of 1100 cars.

The car park is a 'Bison' design with split level floors and ramp access. The parking areas are unobstructed by columns. The superstructure is composed of prestressed concrete beams with inverted 'T' section providing three bays, each with clear spans of 16·0 m (52 ft) and supported on columns and beams. The floor construction of the car park comprises prestressed concrete planks 65 mm (2½ in) thick and 0·70 m (2 ft 4 in) wide, and a 50 mm (2 in) cast *in situ* concrete topping which includes 12 mm (½ in) wearing surface.

There are two stair blocks which are precast, and a lift well constructed with precast walls. The treads of the stairs were left to receive granolithic topping on the site. The ramps ascend only 1·4 m (4 ft 8 in) instead of the floor to floor height of 2·85 m (9 ft 4 in). The clear headroom is 2·15 m (7 ft) and the slope of the ramp 1 in 7. This design was found to be economically comparable with the type of precast concrete construction used for the car park building at Fairfield Road, Croydon, but utilising columns and beams instead of load bearing walls.

The cost of the car park superstructure only, which was constructed by Concrete Ltd, was £220,000 in 1963.

The structure was erected for Town Centre Securities Ltd, sponsors, and lessees from Leeds City Council. The Architects were Gillenson and Barnett,

Fig. 11.11   View of multi-storey car park at Merrion Centre, Leeds, England. (*Reproduced by permission of Concrete Ltd, London.*)

and the General Contractors who worked in association with Concrete Ltd, were Sir Lindsay Parkinson and Co. Ltd.

SPLIT LEVEL MULTI-STOREY CAR PARK AT ST ANDREW'S STREET, NORWICH

St Andrew's Street multi-storey car park (Fig. 11.12) is a split level clear span structure with 550 car spaces.

The car park has 4½ floors and provision has been made for another complete floor to be added in the future. The building is 73·0 m (240 ft) long and 31·5 m (104 ft) wide. It is intended that the building should be extended in the direction of St Andrew's Street, and the development as a whole should be combined with moorings for pleasure craft on the River Wensum. The appearance of the elevation to St Andrew's Street is of a temporary nature only.

The building is founded on the driven *in situ* type of pile produced by Frankipile Ltd. The piles generally were 13·6 m (45 ft) long and 0·53 m (21 in) diameter with a bearing capacity of 82,000 kg (82 tons).

Fig. 11.12   View of entrance to St. Andrew's Street Car Park, Norwich. (*Reproduced by permission of the City Engineer, Norwich.*)

The outline drawings and specification were prepared by the City Engineer's Department, and the successful tenderer was Chamberlain Parking Systems Ltd. The tender was £168,751.

SPLIT LEVEL CAR PARK AT COVENT GARDEN, LEAMINGTON SPA

Leamington Spa's main car park is situated at the rear of the principal shopping street in the town. A multi-storey structure, which can accommodate 535 cars, and a surface park with 95 parking spaces have been combined on the site which measures 60·9 m (200 ft) by 106·7 m (350 ft). Entrance and exit, each with three lanes, are common to the multi-storey structure and the surface car park.

The multi-storey car park is of the split level type with a common circulatory system for cars entering and leaving the structure. The ramps are designed in such a way as to provide rapid egress. Entrance and exit are positioned at opposite ends of the car park, the cross fall on the site facilitating entrance at ground level and exit at first floor level.

The main structure is a clear span reinforced column, beam and slab construction. The 0·6 m (2 ft) deep beams which span 15·3 m (52 ft) are generally spaced at 4·5 m (14 ft 10 in) centres and the minimum headroom is 2·3 m (7 ft 6 in). Floors slope at 1 in 80 to the centre and ramps between floors slope at 1 in 8. All exterior ramps, both on the roof of the structure and at entrance and exit are electrically heated to prevent ice formation in winter months.

Precast cladding panels along all exterior elevations were used as permanent shuttering for the impact resisting *in situ* wall. As an additional safety measure, PVC covered, spring steel buffer stops, anchored to the concrete floors, have been provided in each parking bay.

Three staircases are incorporated in the structure together with attendants' offices and public toilets. Two lifts are available in the main entrance.

A feature of the structure is an enclosed bridge, constructed of precast concrete, carrying pedestrian traffic from third floor level of the car park across a road and shops to emerge on to the main shopping thoroughfare.

The total cost per parking space, including the cost of the pedestrian bridge was approximately £395. The building was designed and constructed by Car Parking Ltd, of Hayes, Middlesex, to specifications drawn up by R. G. W. Druitt, C.Eng., F.I.C.E., F.I.Mun.E., Dip.T.P., A.M.T.P.I., M.B.I.M., Borough Engineer and Surveyor, Leamington Spa.

SPLIT LEVEL MULTI-STOREY CAR PARK USING PRECAST UNITS AT CROYDON

This car park (Figs. 11.13 and 11.14) is of split level design comprising a six-storey section with two bays each 16·0 m (52 ft 8 in) wide and a five-storey

Fig. 11.13   Interior view of split level multi-storey car park, Fairfield Road, Croydon. (*Reproduced by permission of Concrete Ltd, London.*)

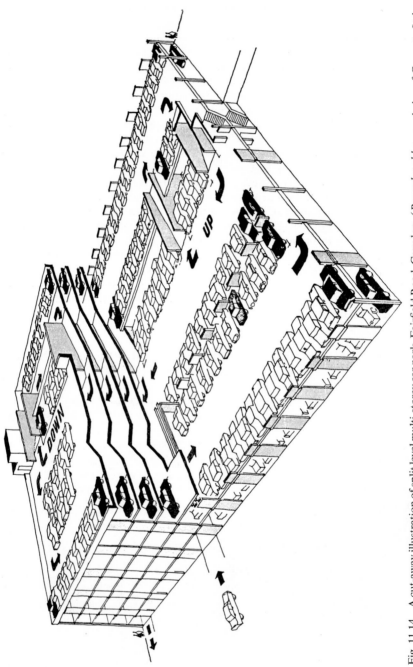

Fig. 11.14   A cut-away illustration of split level multi-storey car park, Fairfield Road, Croydon. (*Reproduced by permission of Concrete Ltd, London.*)

section with one bay of the same width. In each case the roof is counted as one floor. Each of the three bays runs the full length of the building, which is 66·0 m (218 ft) long.

The parking arrangement has been based on the square parking method with a space allowance of 4·75 m × 2·5 m (16 ft × 8 ft) per car. Traffic circulation is one-way with a lane 6·0 m (20 ft) wide down the centre of each bay. There is an allowance of 0·10 m (4 in) on either side of each bay for lightweight barriers and the total span is thus 16·0 m (52 ft 8 in). This arrangement provides a floor area completely free from structural obstructions.

The structure consists of prestressed inverted 'T' beams mounted in pairs on RC structural wall units. The wall units are of storey height and the beams rest on corbels cast in during manufacture. The outer wall units along the length of the bays are 1·60 m (5 ft 3 in) wide and 0·15 m (6 in) thick spaced at intervals of 3·10 m (10 ft 3 in). Each pair of beams is spaced at intervals of 4·72 m (15 ft 6 in), and the distance between each beam of a pair varies from 0·86 m to 1·0 m (2 ft 10 in to 3 ft 4 in). The internal walls between bays are of similar design with corbels on both sides. At the split level position, these are at different heights. Wall units set at right angles to the internal walls on either side of the ramps provide the lateral stiffening to the structure.

The beams are 0·60 m (2 ft) deep, made composite with a prestressed concrete plank floor topped with *in situ* concrete, the total depth being 0·72 m (2 ft 4½ in). The height between floors is 2·85 m (9 ft 4 in) and the headroom below beams is thus just under 2·15 m (7 ft).

There is a staircase at either end of the building and two passenger lifts at the northern end.

Strip footings were provided where wall units were used in construction and individual footings where columns were used. Owing to the excavations necessary in a 6·0 m (20 ft) high bank at the south end, a precast concrete retaining wall was made and erected by Concrete Ltd.

The external face of structural wall units is finished in grey Rubislaw granite exposed aggregate, edge beams in Criggion granite and the parapet is finished in white marble chippings.

The General Contractor was T. R. Roberts Ltd, who was responsible for site excavation and foundation. Concrete Ltd erected the main building and the precast retaining wall. The Consultant Architect was D. R. Beatty Pownall, F.R.I.B.A.

SPLIT LEVEL MULTI-STOREY CAR PARK AT CWMBRAN, SOUTH WALES

This car park (Fig. 11.15) is sited in the town centre and is entirely of concrete construction. The split level system of six suspended decks, linked by ramps at each end, has been used, and with the two ground decks accommodates a total of 449 cars. The floor area of the suspended decks is 9000 m² (96,200 sq ft), and that of the ground floor 2250 m² (24,050 sq ft). For the convenience of shoppers it is positioned immediately adjacent to the shopping centre and is to be connected by a pedestrian underpass. Eventually there is also to be a filling station included at the point of entry and exit, off Glyndwr Road. There is no charge and no supervision. The simple method of circulation enables all motorists to park without difficulty.

The car park is constructed in ramp form and makes use of the fall in the land from west to east. Each of the six *in situ* and suspended decks are designed on the Truscon banded plate system. They are 68·0 m (224 ft) long and 16·0 m (52 ft) wide and are each supported on two rows of *in situ* concrete columns set 9·75 m (32 ft) apart with a 3·05 m (10 ft) cantilever section each side.

The clear height between decks is 2·38 m (7 ft 10 in) with only one point— where the up ramp joins the top deck—of a lesser dimension, 2·26 m (7 ft 5 in). The sides of the building from the first to the top deck are enclosed by precast concrete panels incorporating vertical fins of white concrete.

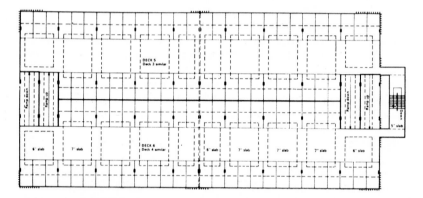

Fig. 11.15   Typical layout of Cwmbran No. 1 and No. 2 Car Parks. (*Reproduced by permission of Truscon Ltd, London.*)

The external limits of the top decks and ramps are defined by galvanised tubular steel hand railings, except for the topmost deck which is finished with an *in situ* concrete wall. Cantilevered from the south end of the building an *in situ* concrete pedestrian staircase provides access to all floors.

The staircases are reinforced concrete steps cantilevered from the spine wall with solid concrete balustrading to outer strings. Rough board marked concrete on the staircase side walls contrast with the precast concrete units elsewhere.

The concrete ramps and decks are finished with a granolithic concrete wearing surface, and the ground floor decks are divided by an *in situ* concrete retaining wall and finished with tarred macadam. Metal posts, protected by rubber, are placed at the perimeter of decks to prevent motorists backing up too far and damaging cladding units.

Lighting and water supply is provided on all floors and many of the ramps are heated electrically to prevent icing in winter.

The Architect for this structure was GordonRedfern, Dip. Arch., A.R.I.B.A., Chief Architect, Cwmbran Development Corporation, and the Main Contractors, Truscon Ltd, 35–41, Lower Marsh, London SE1.

SPLIT LEVEL MULTI-STOREY CAR PARK WITH SEPARATE 'UP' AND 'DOWN' RAMPS AT EASTGATE STREET, SOUTHAMPTON

This car park (Fig. 11.16) was designed by Lawrence Robertson, M.Sc., the City Engineer and Surveyor, in conjunction with British Lift Slab Ltd. It has a capacity of 713 vehicles.

The column and plate slab structure has 0·23 m (9 in) solid reinforced concrete slabs supported by 0·305 m by 0·305 m (12 in by 12 in) and 0·255 m by 0·255 m (10 in by 10 in) precast concrete columns. The structural grid is based on a four column layout with three spans across a parking bin and three 2·4 m (8 ft) parking bays between columns set 9·70 m (32 ft) apart.

Fig. 11.16   View of Eastgate Street split level multi-storey car park, Southampton. (*Reproduced by permission of British Lift Slab Ltd, Birmingham.*)

The precast concrete columns were erected in pockets formed in reinforced concrete cups to the piled foundations. After careful plumbing these were grouted up and the floor and roof slabs cast one upon another using the finished surface of the ground floor slab as the mould for the first floor and so on.

Hydraulically operated Lift Slab jacks, each having a 61,000 kg (60 tons) capacity were subsequently placed one on top of each column and the floors lifted and anchored in their final position. Fabricated steel lifting collars were cast into each slab around each column. These were used to take both the lifting and final anchoring forces; the final connection was made with forged steel connectors transmitting the load in direct bearing from the slabs to the columns.

The car park will accommodate 713 vehicles with right angled parking. The parking stalls are 4·75 m (16 ft) long by 2·50 m (8 ft) wide, the aisles are for one-way traffic; they are 6·0 m (20 ft) wide, and the ramps are on a slope of 1 in 8 and are a maximum of 3·2 m (10 ft 6 in) wide. Two pedestrian access shafts are provided; one contains a staircase and two lifts and the other a staircase.

Externally the elevation is in white coloured aluminium sheeting with a hand rail and vertical barrier to parking floors and facing brickwork to both access shafts.

The waivers from the Building Regulations which were obtained allowed:

(*a*) structural fire resistance of 2 hours,
(*b*) no compartment walls, and
(*c*) no protected areas in external elevations.

MULTI-STOREY CAR PARK WITH CONTINUOUS SLOPING FLOOR AND ONE-WAY TRAFFIC CIRCULATION AT WHITEFRIARS, CANTERBURY

This building is of framed reinforced *in situ* concrete construction on driven pile foundations (Fig. 11.17). The columns occur at 4·75 m (16 ft) centres and

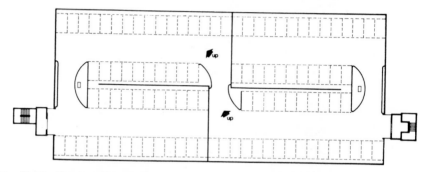

Fig. 11.17   Sketch layout of Watling Street multi-storey car park, Canterbury, England. (*Reproduced by permission of Truscon Ltd, London.*)

provide a clear span of 16·0 m (53 ft). The continuous ramp design chosen allows for a one-way traffic circulation to parking stalls at all levels. In addition there is a basement parking area with independent access and exit. There is parking accommodation for 604 vehicles.

The elevation treatment consists of exposed aggregate precast cladding units combined with fair faced concrete framework and steel balustrading. The two staircase and lift towers are of *in situ* concrete construction with sawn boarded finish, and form dominant features at either end of the building.

Public toilet facilities are incorporated at ground floor level and there is accommodation for staff and storage. In addition there is space for a large showroom at street level. The whole structure is set in an area which is paved and landscaped. This is the only covered car park which has been erected within the city walls.

The building was designed by D. Tomkinson, M.C.D., B.Arch., A.R.I.B.A., the City Architect of Canterbury, in association with the Consulting Civil and Structural Engineers, W. V. Zinn and Associates, Epsom, Surrey. The Main Contractor was Truscon Ltd, London SE1.

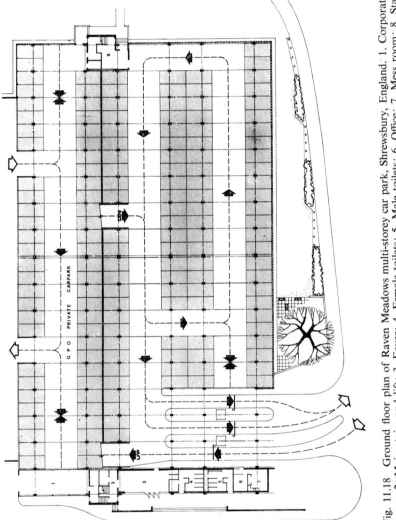

Fig. 11.18   Ground floor plan of Raven Meadows multi-storey car park, Shrewsbury, England. 1. Corporation stores; 2. Main stairs and lift; 3. Foyer; 4. Female toilets; 5. Male toilets; 6. Office; 7. Mess room; 8. Stairs. (*Reproduced by permission of Truscon Ltd, London.*)

MULTI-STOREY CAR PARK WITH INTERNAL QUICK RAMPED EXIT AT RAVEN MEADOWS, SHREWSBURY

This multi-storey car park (Fig. 11.18) accommodates 837 cars on four levels. The structure is built on piled foundations and consists of 9·70 m (32 ft) span precast concrete portal frames, each with two projecting 3·05 m (10 ft) cantilevers and constructed in three component parts joined at an arbitrary point of conflecture. Frames are erected on prepared bases at 4·75 m (16 ft) centres. The parking deck and ramps are built using 0·152 m (6 in) thick standard 'Truspan' units with a reinforced 0·05 m (2 in) thick *in situ* topping.

The perimeters of the parking decks are bounded with precast fascia beams textured on the outer face. At roof level the fascia beam is increased in height to form a parapet. Between the fascia beams at each level are fixed white concrete fins at 0·305 m (12 in) centres.

Access to the parking decks is by means of short ramps at an incline of 1 in 7 which are positioned to permit one-way traffic circulation and a quick exit on the down grade ramps. There is a pedestrian lift to alternate decks, and pedestrian staircases are provided at each end of the building. At the southern end of the building an access to Castle Street is provided by way of a pedestrian footbridge from fifth deck level. Toilet facilities are incorporated on the ground floor. This car park was built by Truscon Ltd, and designed by that company's Design Division in close collaboration with R. W. Gibb, C.Eng., M.I.C.E., the Borough Surveyor.

CAR PARK ON TRIANGULAR SITE WITH QUICK EXIT AT KEIGHLEY, YORKSHIRE

This building is known as the Damside Multi-storey Car Park and provides 509 parking stalls in the Keighley town centre (Figs. 11.19 and 11.20).

The shape of the triangular site made the layout a difficult problem. This was solved by constructing the building in three bays, two of them at right angles to each other and with level floors, and the third forming the hypotenuse providing a parking ramp at a gradient of 1 in 20. Short ramps at a gradient of 1 in 8 connect the bays. Vehicles entering the car park turn left and pass through the three bays in turn until a parking space is found. An exit spiral ramp at a gradient of 1 in 10 constructed partly in the well in the centre of the triangle provides a rapid exit for the cars. There are five floors including the roof and all the ramps at a gradient of more than 1 in 12 have been wired for electrical heating at the rate of 100 W/m² (10 watts per sq ft) and automatic control equipment installed to prevent icing in frosty weather.

Parking decks are 16·0 m (52 ft) clear span allowing for parking stalls 4·75 m × 2·50 m (16 ft × 8 ft) and an aisle 6·0 m (20 ft) wide. The floor was constructed of *in situ* concrete using the Holst Ribspan system. This is a rapid form of construction using special fibreglass moulds.

The parapet walls are in precast concrete with a 'Linenfold' finish to the external face. In order to improve the colour, 50 per cent white cement was used in the concrete for the external panels. Shadows on the vertical fluting of

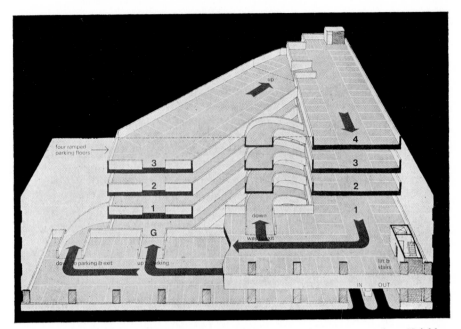

Fig. 11.19 Diagram showing planning arrangements in multi-storey car park at Keighley, England. (*Reproduced by permission of Holst and Co. Ltd, Watford.*)

Fig. 11.20 Interior view of multi-storey car park at Keighley, England. (*Reproduced by permission of Holst and Co. Ltd, Watford.*)

the face provide a pleasant texture. The lower part of the panel forms the external shuttering of the edge beams and floor. The exposed faces of the outer columns are finished in black Mineralite.

Adjacent to the vehicular entrance is a lift for 10 persons and a staircase well serving all floors. A secondary staircase has a footbridge link at first floor level to the road which provides the nearest approach to the town centre. Public conveniences are provided on the ground floor.

Construction was complicated by the restricted site and by a culvert crossing diagonally beneath the building. The columns were carried down through filled material to pad footings on rock capable of sustaining five tonnes per square foot. Several of the columns occur above the culvert and these were carried on heavy reinforced concrete bridging beams to concrete piers on each side of the culvert. Foundations were up to 6·0 m (20 ft) deep, and to avoid one being 10·5 m (35 ft) deep a concrete column was carried on a 2·75 m (9 ft) deep reinforced concrete cantilever over the culvert. The cost of the car park excluding land was £170,000, giving a cost per car space of £334, in 1967.

The work was initiated by R. Courtenay Gibson, M.I.C.E., the former Borough Engineer, and completed by his successor, J. D. Jennings, M.I.Mun.E. The Contractor was Holst and Co. Ltd, of Watford.

MULTI-STOREY CAR PARK INTEGRATED WITH A NEW SHOPPING CENTRE AT CHESTER

This scheme is in the centre of Chester. The new shopping centre includes the multi-storey car park, and connects with the Rows, which is the ancient tiered covered shopping area, and also with additional shopping precincts at other levels.

The accommodation in the car park (Figs. 11.21 and 11.22) is for approximately 600 cars, and it is connected by lift to each shopping level. One floor has a direct link with the Grosvenor Hotel and Ballroom which gives immediate access for motorists to the hotel and the shopping centre.

The car park is of the straight ramp, split level type with five storeys including roof parking. The structure is reinforced concrete with prestressed concrete I beams supported by 0·30 m × 0·30 m (12 in × 12 in) average reinforced concrete columns. The structural grid is derived from the shopping grid which is 6·0 m × 6·0 m (20 ft × 20 ft). This spacing is continued where car park columns are common to the shopping area, so that the external treatment both of shopping centre and car park is related. Reinforced concrete precast panels fixed by steel cleats form the perimeter walls. Galvanised steel standard anti-crash barriers protect the inside face of the external cladding.

The lift, halls and staircase are finished in concrete. The side elevation of the pedestrian lift and stairway is in facing brickwork panels inserted between storey height concrete beams.

The scheme was designed by Sir Percy Thomas and Son, Architects, and the Consulting Civil and Structural Engineers were W. V. Zinn and Associates, of Epsom and Manchester. The developers were the Grosvenor/Laing Development Co. Ltd.

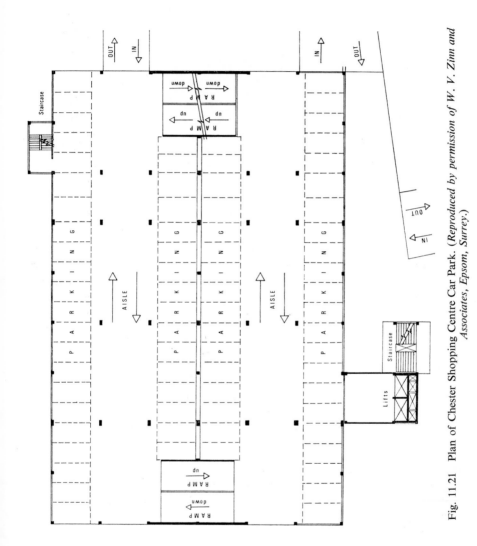

Fig. 11.21   Plan of Chester Shopping Centre Car Park. (*Reproduced by permission of W. V. Zinn and Associates, Epsom, Surrey.*)

Fig. 11.22   Interior view of Chester Shopping Centre Car Park. (*Reproduced by permission of W. V. Zinn and Associates, Epsom, Surrey.*)

INTERNAL LONGITUDINAL RAMPED MULTI-STOREY CAR PARK AT CÄCILIENSTRASSE, COLOGNE

This multi-storey car park (Figs. 11.23 and 11.24) is connected to the highways by one entrance and two exits. The crossing at the Kronengasse is regulated by signals. Departure from the car park to the east is only possible from the Kronengasse exit, but for departure to the west both exits may be used.

The entrance is controlled by an automatic barrier where parking tickets are issued. The exit barrier opens when a metal disc which was issued after payment of the parking fee at the ticket office, is inserted. Each parking stall is marked and numbered according to the floor it is on. The ground floor has a floor to ceiling height of 4·00 m (13 ft) and is suitable for lorries and tank vehicles.

Adjoining the petrol and diesel oil filling station there are two subsidiary toilets, showers and changing rooms for ladies and gentlemen. For customers there is one additional waiting room and two lavatories. For the convenience of customers there are two ticket offices at both Cäcilienstrasse and Kronengasse entrances. Two lifts are available for use by customers as well as staircases.

The longitudinal ramps are fitted into the middle of the car park, one for upstream and the other for downstream traffic. The width of each traffic lane is 3·5 m (11 ft 6 in) and they are separated by crash barriers. The gradient of the ramps is 1 in 7 to 1 in 8.

The car park is erected around a steel framework. It is connected with a departmental store which is situated on the main shopping street, Schildergasse, by a covered passage, and at ground level there is access for pedestrians to the shopping street, Schildergasse. The basement has mechanical ventilation. The installation is connected with 'Co-Gerate' appliances and operated automatically in an emergency. In case of fire the basement can be divided into two sections by sliding doors, and there are emergency staircases for both sections. The

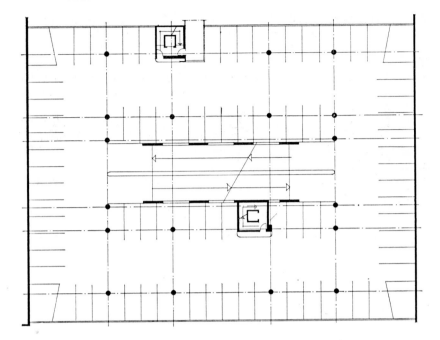

Fig. 11.23   Typical floor plan of Cäcilienstrasse multi-storey car park, Cologne, West Germany.
(Reproduced by permission of the City Engineer, Cologne.)

Fig. 11.24   View of Cäcilienstrasse multi-storey car park, Cologne, West Germany. *(Reproduced by permission of the City Engineer, Cologne.)*

headroom is 2·45 m (8 ft 0 in) which makes the basement accessible for mini-buses and vans. On the upper floors the floor to ceiling height is 2·15 m (7 ft 0 in).

The drainage of the roof parking area is directly connected to the public drainage system. The other floors are first drained to petrol separators. There is a controllable, self illuminated car park sign which indicates if the car park is 'full' or 'free'.

The car park, including the service station, is open day and night. The retail trade in Cologne has formed a Parking Association, and 50 Pfg (5p) are refunded on making a purchase of a certain value. This car park is associated with the Parking Association.

The parking fees in Deutchmarks (including the surplus value tax) are:

For the first two hours	— DM 1.10 (12p)
From the third hour onwards	— DM 1.60 (17p)
From the fourth hour onwards	— DM 2.10 (23p)
Up to the maximum	— DM 5.00 per day (55p)

The parking fee per day (excluding the surplus value tax)
For 3 days — DM 3.50 (38p) per day etc.

The monthly fee (excluding the surplus value tax) is DM 65.00 (£7·15) day and night.

The Architect for the scheme was J. Schmitz, 5 Koln-Deutz, Von-Sandt-Platz 11, and the information has been supplied by F. Brun, City Engineer, Cologne.

MULTI-STOREY CAR PARK IN COLOGNE WITH CONCENTRIC CIRCULATION ON THE SPLIT LEVEL SYSTEM

This site (Fig. 11.25) has the disadvantage of being triangular in shape with the exit and entrance on the Enggasse which is at the base of the triangle.

The entrance is controlled by an automatic barrier where the motorist receives the parking ticket. The exit barrier opens when a metal disc which was issued at the entrance on payment of a fee, is inserted into the machine. All parking stalls are marked and numbered according to the floor they are on. The ground floor has a ground to ceiling height of 3·50 m (13 ft 9 in). The basement and upper floors have a height of 2·15 m (8 ft 6 in).

On the ground floor is a petrol station as well as changing rooms for ladies and gentlemen, showers and lavatories. The pedestrian reaches the parking floors by using the lift or staircase. The gradient of the ramps is 1 in 8, and the width of each ramp is 3·50 m (13 ft 9 in).

The car park is erected round a steel frame. The two underground floors are ventilated mechanically, which operates automatically. On both underground floors and in parts of the ground floor, sprinkler apparatus has been installed.

Because of the situation of the car park, it is used mostly by long term parking customers, and the amount of short term parking is very small. The park is operated by a Parking Association and, together with the petrol station, is open day and night.

Fig. 11.25   View of multi-storey car park on Hunnenrücken, Cologne. (*Reproduced by permission of the City Engineer, Cologne.*)

The parking fee including the additional turnover tax is 0·50 DM (5½p) per hour. The charges for long term parking are arranged separately with the Bank and Insurance Company who built the car park. There are 383 parking stalls and the cost per parking stall is 7400 DM (£822). The difficult shape of the building has led to the relatively high cost.

MULTI-STOREY CAR PARK AT HOCKMORE STREET, COWLEY CENTRE, OXFORD

This car park (Fig. 11.26) is planned to structural bays of 6·7 m × 6·7 m (22 ft × 22 ft), and 6·7 m × 4·0 m (22 ft × 13 ft), using a single ramp system with cars moving in both directions up and down the same ramp. This system, though not ideal, was adopted because access was possible on only one side of the site. The cost of this car park was approximately £250 per car space in 1962.

The Architect was D. Murray, A.R.I.B.A., City Architect, Oxford, and the Consulting Civil and Structural Engineers were W. V. Zinn and Associates, Epsom, Surrey. The Main Contractor was John Laing Construction Ltd, London.

MULTI-STOREY CAR PARK FORMING PART OF COMPREHENSIVE DEVELOPMENT AT WHITCOMB STREET, LONDON WC2

The Whitcomb Street Garage forms part of a comprehensive development on a 1300 m² (⅓ acre) site near Leicester Square, London, which includes a podium block of plan dimensions 45·5 m × 36·5 m (150 ft × 120 ft), providing parking

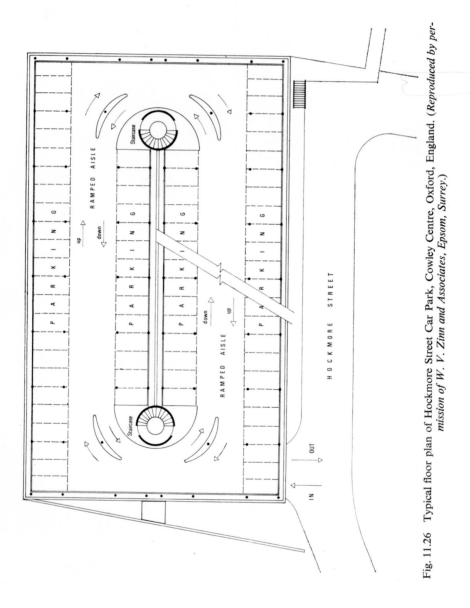

Fig. 11.26 Typical floor plan of Hockmore Street Car Park, Cowley Centre, Oxford, England. (*Reproduced by permission of W. V. Zinn and Associates, Epsom, Surrey.*)

spaces above and below ground level, together with shops and restaurant facilities. Rising above the podium is a tower block, seven storeys high containing flats and offices.

The garage has been designed for customer parking, using a split level ramp system with eight levels below ground and eight above ground, giving space for approximately 330 cars. The entrance and exit are controlled by electronic gates. A ticket dispenser and cashier's kiosk are located between the entry and departure lanes. All traffic circulation is in a clockwise direction.

There is a staircase and two passenger lifts giving access to all floors, and all basement levels are protected by sprinklers and a ventilation system. Smoke vents have been provided round the perimeter to all levels.

The garage was erected for the City of Westminster, and the Architects were Oscar Garry and Partners, in consultation with F. Cave, B.Sc., F.I.C.E., the City Engineer of Westminster. The Consulting Civil and Structural Engineers were W. V. Zinn and Associates, Epsom, Surrey.

WARPED SLAB CAR PARK

This design was first proposed by a North American Civil Engineer, E. M. Khoury. The shape of the parking floor has been derived from a flat slab of reinforced concrete, which has been slit along its centre line, and depressed and elevated along each side of the slit whilst the perimeter of the slab remains level.

Circulation between floors is provided at the central split where the up and down warps of opposing sides join. On entering the building the motorist drives on a one-way system around the ground floor on a constantly changing slope until arriving at the central connection to the first floor. He then proceeds in a similar manner until he finds a vacant parking stall. A rapid exit route may also be provided.

Because the perimeter of the floors is level, there is more freedom in the treatment of the elevation.

An example of this type of car park may be seen at Lichfield, England, and is illustrated in Figs. 11.27 and 11.28. It was designed and constructed by British Lift Slab Ltd, of Birmingham, to the basic design and specification of D. E. Lawrence, C.Eng., M.I.C.E., the City Engineer and Surveyor.

The column and plate slab structure has 0·28 m (11 in) solid reinforced concrete floor slabs supported by 0·35 m × 0·305 m (14 in × 12 in) and 0·305 m × 0·305 m (12 in × 12 in) precast concrete columns. The structural grid is based on a two column layout with three parking stalls between columns, generally 6·85 m (22 ft 6 in) apart. The precast concrete columns are erected in pockets formed in reinforced concrete bases. After plumbing these are grouted up and the floor and roof slabs are cast and jacked into position.

The elevations have precast balustrades with an exposed aggregate finish. The corners of the building have feature panels of facing brickwork which include two access shafts, and the south-west elevation facing the bus station has intermediate panels of facing brickwork.

The capacity of the car park is 479 vehicles on four floors with right angled parking. The cost per parking space is approximately £275, in 1970. This

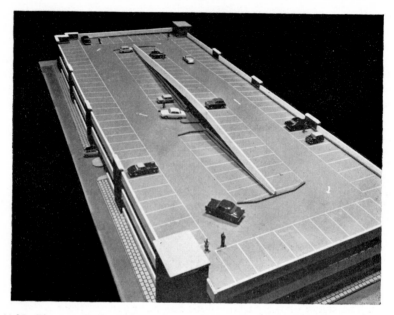

Fig. 11.27   Photograph of model of warped slab car park, Lichfield, England. (*Reproduced by permission of British Lift Slab Ltd, Birmingham.*)

Fig. 11.28   Interior view of warped slab car park, Lichfield, England. (*Reproduced by permission of British Lift Slab Ltd, Birmingham.*)

relatively low figure has been achieved by incorporating columns in the parking area instead of having clear spaces and by using the minimum acceptable space standards for a public car park. Parking stalls are 4·75 m (16 ft) long and 2·30 m (7 ft 6 in) wide, and the aisles, all for one-way traffic, are 6·09 m (20 ft) wide. The four one-way driveways across the central split are 3·65 m (12 ft) wide. Two are on a slope of 1 in 13 and two are level. Two pedestrian access shafts are provided each containing staircases.

MULTI-STOREY LOCK-UP GARAGES

A multi-storey building consisting of lock-up garages has been erected at the London Borough of Barking. This meets a growing need where high density housing has to be developed or, alternatively, on existing housing estates where it is not possible to erect individual garages.

These lock-up garages have been designed and patented by Parking Systems Ltd, West Norwood, London SE27. The system uses steel cased fire protected

Fig. 11.29   View of multi-storey lock-up garages, London Borough of Barking. (*Reproduced by permission of Parking Systems Ltd, Norwood, London.*)

columns, supporting a concrete deck and carrying wire mesh panels dividing the garages and 'up and over' doors. The arrangement of the floors is on the split level principle with separate ramps for up and down stream traffic.

The system is illustrated in Figs. 11.29 and 11.30 and it is claimed that the costs are approximately 10 per cent below the Ministry of Housing and Local Government allowance for garages.

Fig. 11.30 Interior view of multi-storey lock-up garages, London Borough of Barking. (*Reproduced by permission of Parking Systems Ltd, Norwood, London.*)

PARKING FACILITIES FOR OFFICE AND FACTORY STAFF IN LEICESTER

An example of the use of 'Unipark' prefabricated units may be seen as part of the business premises of N. Corah (St Margaret) Ltd, Leicester (Fig. 11.31). This is the first stage of a larger development, and provides office and factory accommodation on the ground floor, with two floors for parking above. The second stage of development includes converting the first floor for office and factory use (it has been designed for a suitable loading) and to add an additional two floors above the existing structure which will be for car parking. Access to this building is by ramp from an adjacent multi-storey car park.

This type of project is a possible solution for industrial organisations who find themselves with a limited area of land and increasing demands for productive operations and car parking.

The work was carried out by Unipark Ltd, Bishop Meadow Road, Loughborough, Leicestershire.

ROOF PARKING ON BUILDINGS OTHER THAN CAR PARKS, AT COVENTRY AND PORTSMOUTH, ENGLAND, AND DETROIT, USA

In Coventry, a system of roof car parks (Fig. 11.32) linked together at roof level, and connected to multi-storey car parks has been provided in the new

Fig. 11.31 Interior view of parking facilities provided over office and factory premises at Leicester, England. (*Reproduced by permission of Unipark Ltd, Loughborough, England.*)

City Centre. It is estimated that 3000 parking places are required in the immediate vicinity of the shopping area, and these are provided at roof level and in open deck multi-storey car parks connected together by bridges. The ramps to the roof and open deck car parks are exposed, and in order to overcome the dangers of ice and snow on a ramp, electrically heated panels have been embedded in the running surface of the ramps at a depth of 38 mm ($1\frac{1}{2}$ in). The heating panels

Fig. 11.32 Ramp leading to roof parking over Market Hall and multi-storey car park, Coventry, England. (*Reproduced by permission of the City Engineer, Coventry.*)

are automatically controlled, and are designed to come into operation in advance of ice formation and to remain switched on until the temperature has risen to a point where there is no danger of any ice formation. A similar installation is used in the steps of staircases used by pedestrians.

The lighting of the roof car parks in Coventry is by 80 watt mercury vapour discharge lamps mounted on 4·5 m (15 ft) high steel columns spaced approximately 12·0 m (40 ft) apart. The standard of lighting should be sufficient to enable cars to be driven with side lights only so that pedestrians and any obstructions and clearly visible.

The cost of roof parking in Coventry was £170 per car space in 1959, which includes concrete ramps, heating and lighting, but not the site value.

Fig. 11.33 Aerial view of roof parking in shopping precinct, Portsmouth. (*Reproduced by permission of 'The News', Portsmouth.*)

In Portsmouth, roof parking is used quite extensively in the shopping precinct. The roof parks are linked together and also with multi-storey car parks, as shown in the aerial photograph (Fig. 11.33).

In the Civic Centre, Detroit, Michigan, USA, the entire roof of the Exhibits Building, Cobo Hall, is devoted to parking, and 1217 parking stalls are provided (Fig. 11.34). Access to and from the roof is by means of a three lane spiral ramp directly connected to an Expressway. The central lane of the spiral ramp is used, depending on the direction of peak traffic flow, for up traffic in the morning and

Fig. 11.34   View of Cobo Hall Car Park, Detroit, Michigan, USA. Area 8 acres; capacity
1217 cars. (*Reproduced by permission of Detroit Parking Authority.*)

down traffic in the afternoon. Pedestrian access to the lower floors of the
building and the street is by means of lifts and stairs.

Another 600 cars can be parked in an underground garage below the Exhibition Building.

The Cobo Hall was built for the City of Detroit in 1960, and the Architects
were Giffels and Rossetti, Inc.

DEMOUNTABLE STEEL FRAMED CAR PARK AT CANAL STREET, NOTTINGHAM

An example of the use of structural steelwork for multi-storey car parks can
be seen at Canal Street, Nottingham (Figs. 11.35 and 11.36). Here a three-storey
structure which accommodates 152 cars has been erected under the direction of
the then City Engineer, F. M. Little, B.Sc.Tech., F.I.C.E. The site is small,
irregular in shape, near the City Centre and forms part of an area to be completely redeveloped within the next seven to ten years.

The main steelwork is encased to have a fire resistance of one hour and precast
concrete anti-convection fascia slabs provide resistance to fire spreading from

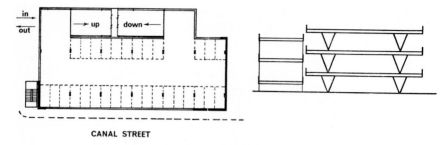

CANAL STREET

Fig. 11.35 Sketch layout plan of Tempark Car Park, Nottingham, England. (*Reproduced by permission of R. M. Douglas Ltd and Braithwaite and Co. Structural Ltd.*)

floor to floor. In addition, brick fire break walls resist the spread of fire to the staircase and from adjacent buildings. This building was erected before the adoption of the Building Regulations, 1965.

The ground is composed of silt overlying consolidated demolition rubble. Reinforced concrete bases 0·405 m (16 in) thick founded at a depth of 0·61 m (2 ft) were used. All foundation bolts were allowed to project about 0·15 m (6 in) to allow the structure to be adjusted in the event of subsidence. This was an essential precaution in view of the adoption of the high bearing pressure of one ton per square foot (110×10^3 N/m^2). This pressure though high was deemed reasonable for a temporary structure. The 1965 value of the structure available for re-use is estimated at £27,000. The loan period for that part of the structure available for re-use is 20 years, and for the remainder 9 years which is

Fig. 11.36 View of demountable steel car park at Canal Street, Nottingham. (*Reproduced by permission of R. M. Douglas Ltd and Braithwaite and Co. Structural Ltd.*)

the estimated time when the site will be required for permanent development.

When the Canal Street site is wanted for permanent development, it is intended that the whole structure will be dismantled for re-assembly on a new site or for storage pending a future need.

The scheme cost £51,000, or £335 per car space at 1965 values. This system of construction is known under the trade name of 'Tempark' and developed jointly by R. M. Douglas (Contractors) Ltd, and Braithwaite and Co. Structural Ltd.

'WHEELWRIGHT' ARCH CAR PARK, BIRMINGHAM

This is an interesting temporary structure (Fig. 11.37) which has been erected on cleared ground between Summer Row and Cambridge Street, behind the

Fig. 11.37   View of Wheelwright Car Park, Cambridge Street, Birmingham. (*Reproduced by permission of John Lysaghts Bristol Works Ltd, Bristol, England.*)

Civic Centre. This installation has been built to accommodate nearly 400 cars and the cost per car space was £224 (1964).

At the Summer Row car park a steel framework is used for the three-arch structure, together with 'Bison' wide slab decking, supplied and erected by Concrete Ltd. 'Bison' decking comprises prestressed units of 2·20 m (7 ft 2 in) × 0·15 m (6¼ in) thick, spanning 5·0 m (16 ft 6 in) between steel supports. A special requirement at Summer Row was that the structure should be demountable, a condition not normally associated with a concrete slab. Tests were carried out to prove that the 'Bison' wide slab could be speedily degrouted without damage and the sections lifted out for re-use elsewhere.

The 'Wheelwright' car park is marketed by John Lysaght's Bristol Works Ltd, who also designed, fabricated and erected the structural steelwork and hold the world rights. The Principal is the Wheelwright Parking Co. Ltd, Dewsbury, and the Sub-Contractors were Concrete Ltd, and Robert M. Douglas (Contractors) Ltd, Birmingham.

CAR PARK CONSTRUCTED OVER THE RAILWAY FOR JOSEPH LUCAS LTD, SHAFTMOOR LANE, BIRMINGHAM 1965–1966

The increasing number of employees travelling by car to and from the Shaftmoor Lane factory made it impossible for the company to provide sufficient off-street parking within the boundaries of the existing site, and the adjoining roads were becoming congested during the day with parked cars.

All attempts to acquire land adjacent to the factory proved unsuccessful and it was decided to investigate the possibility of creating space by constructing a double deck car park over the two track railway line which runs in a cutting

Fig. 11.38   View of staff car park in steelwork over railway at Shaftmoor Lane, Birmingham, for Joseph Lucas Ltd, England. (*Reproduced by permission of Clifford Tee and Gale, Architects, Birmingham.*)

along the east boundary of the site. British Railways' approval was obtained and a scheme produced for the parking of 340 cars (Fig. 11.38).

The width of the cutting made it possible to arrange an economical layout using standard 4·75 m × 2·50 m (16 ft × 8 ft) parking bays at right angles to both sides of two 6·0 m (20 ft) wide access lanes running the length of each deck. This arrangement enabled a 1·2 m (4 ft) module to be used with a 9·7 m × 9·7 m (32 ft × 32 ft) structural grid, and provided sufficient space at the top of the cutting for access ramps and staircases to the upper deck.

In order to reduce interference with British Rail services to a minimum, the erection programme was arranged in the following sequence:

1. Bored pile foundations at top of embankment and at track level—(no interference with British Rail services).

2. Erection of precast columns and longitudinal beams at one side of the track over a weekend period. British Rail closed one track during this period. A similar operation took place on the other side of the cutting on the following weekend, the adjacent track again being closed for this period.

3. Placing of precast deck units between longitudinal beams at side of track and ground beams at top of embankment, using cranes working from top of embankment—(no interference with British Rail services).

4. Placing of precast deck units over track—(operations suspended only when trains were passing).

The above operations having been completed, work was able to proceed irrespective of train movements, except that complete track occupation was required for two Sunday periods while the large end panels were put into place. The whole operation was under the control of a flagman provided by British Rail, who was in telephone communication with the stations immediately either side of the site.

A clearance of 5·6 m (18 ft 6 in) above track level was required by British Railways to allow for possible future electrification of this line and this resulted in the lower deck being about 0·45 m (18 in) above the natural ground level at at the top of the cutting. Because of the proximity of the adjacent houses it was considered desirable to keep the overall height of the structure to a minimum and this has been achieved by using *in situ* concrete flat slab with mushroom headed columns for the upper deck.

The 1·2 m (4 ft) planning module is expressed in the elevations by using 2·4 m (8 ft) wide fair faced precast concrete parapet units on the sides, ramps and staircases with balusters supporting the steel handrail at 1·2 m (4 ft) centres. At the ends the higher parapet units, required by British Railways, are 1·2 m (4 ft) wide and faced externally with 40 mm (1½ in) Criggion green granite aggregate to reduce the effect of smoke stains from passing trains, which were still steam driven at the time of construction. Engines are now diesel and this situation does not arise.

The access from Shaftmoor Lane is sited as far as possible from the bend in the road by the railway bridge and is provided with a small gatehouse which houses a works security officer and all electrical controls for the lighting. The ramp heating installations cut in automatically at a predetermined temperature. All land between the car park and Shaftmoor Lane is landscaped, as is an area between the boundary fence and the back of pavement which will at some future time be required for road widening. A specimen Beech tree was planted near the entrance to the car park and the amenities of the existing houses were preserved by the planting of semi-mature Whitebeam and Rowan trees along the strip of land between their rear boundary and the car park.

A second phase to accommodate 300 cars will be added if and when the need arises. The construction will be in all respects similar to the existing structure except for a minor adjustment in column spacing required to give adequate clear area to the platforms of Spring Road Halt railway station over which the extension would be built.

The cost per car space for Phase I was £455. While this may be considered expensive in relation to more orthodox car parks the cost to the company was justified on the following grounds:

(*a*) Unavailability of other suitable land.

(*b*) The proximity to the factory giving immediate pedestrian access but excluding private cars from the existing internal road system. Other factors affecting the cost were as follows:

1. The suspended lower deck and supporting stanchions would be unnecessary on a level site.
2. The need to design the project in a way that would preserve the amenities of the area in general and the houses on either side of Shaftmoor Lane in particular.
3. The payment of charges to British Rail for the provision of flagmen, track occupations and diversion of existing services.
4. The need to strictly control the pattern of concrete placing on the upper deck as the shuttering was supported from the lower deck, the design load of which was 100 lb per sq ft.
5. The necessity to pile the foundations at the top of the embankment to the level of the lower tracks.

The scheme was designed by the Birmingham Office of Architects Clifford Tee and Gale (Partner in charge—E. H. Greenwood, F.R.I.B.A.) in collaboration with Thomas Bedford and Partners, Structural Engineers; the Group Works Engineering Section of Joseph Lucas Industries; and the Chief Engineer of British Rail.

Chapter 12

Mechanical Car Parks

The first patent for the mechanical parking of cars dates back to 1906, but it is since the end of World War II that it has been developed as a profitable investment.

In the centre of cities where the demand for parking spaces is the greatest, building sites are usually very scarce and it may be that only small sites are available for development. A ramp car park requires a comparatively large site, certainly not less than 36·5 m (40 yards) square, so that the structure may be designed economically and obtain the maximum use from the ramp which occupies a large proportion of the garage space. To overcome these difficulties where land is scarce and the values very high, different types of mechanical parking have been devised, and since 1950 have been developed to meet modern requirements.

In order to understand and compare the different systems of mechanical parking, it is an advantage to classify them into the following groups:[1]

1. simple mechanical devices
2. horizontal movement only
3. stationary and moving elevators and stationary stalls
4. ferris wheel.

Mechanical garages can provide greater storage capacity than ramped garages in a small area, and it becomes more economical with a greater number of floors. Against this there is the expense of the regular maintenance of the mechanical and electrical plant.

Mechanical garages can be constructed with a distance from floor to ceiling of only 2·0 m (6 ft 6 in). A reservoir space should be provided adjacent to the garage where cars can wait before joining the elevators, otherwise waiting will take place in the street and cause congestion. A properly designed mechanical car park allows for the fluctuations of demand, and consequently will cope with peak periods delivering the number of cars necessary to deal with the influx of drivers. A garage designed for peak flows will be more expensive than one designed for a more even flow, but not excessively so. Whilst some parkers will have to wait longer than others for their cars on collection, it is claimed that at no time need this be more than a few minutes. In comparing the time for collection of cars in a mechanical car park with a self parking ramped garage, account must be taken of the time spent walking or in lifts in order to reach the car in a self parking garage, and also the time spent in queueing (if any) at the entrance and exit. The Greater London Council have published a Code of Practice for garages and car parks.[5]

SIMPLE MECHANICAL DEVICES

(a) ERF PARCAR SYSTEM

The ERF Parcar system is a simple mechanical device for placing one car above another. The motorist drives the car on to a platform inclined at an angle

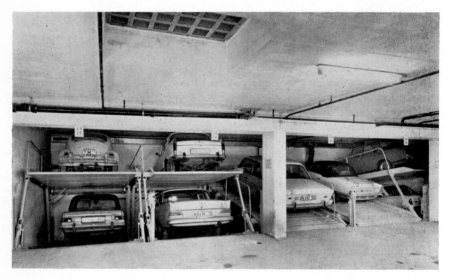

Fig. 12.1   View of the ERF Parcar system of parking. (*Reproduced by permission of Parcar Utilities Ltd, London.*)

of 11° and locks the car. By means of a push button control of the hydraulic power, the platform holding the car is raised, and the lower platform becomes available (Fig. 12.1). For unparking, either space can be made available by the push button control. This system can be used side by side for serial or unit garages, and no partition walls are necessary.

This equipment is manufactured in the United Kingdom by ERF Engineering Ltd, Leek New Road, Baddeley Green, Stoke-on-Trent, under licence from Klaus GmbH, Menningen, West Germany.

(b) SPACE-O-MATIC SYSTEM

The Space-O-Matic system is very similar to the ERF Parcar system, and serves the same purpose. The difference is in the design of the platform and the dimensions of the equipment (Figs. 12.2 and 12.3). The on-centre spacing is at

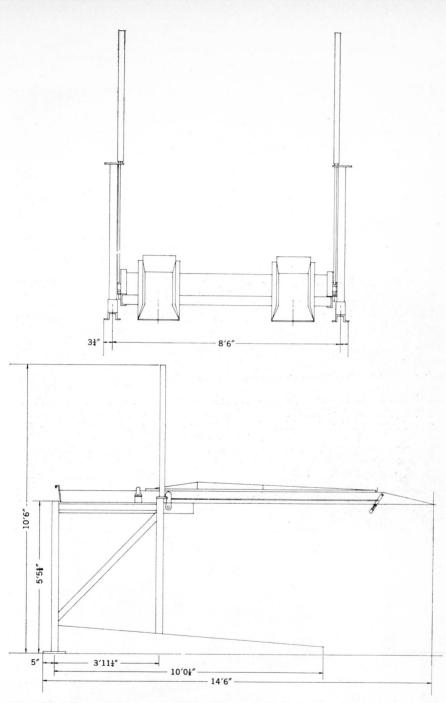

Fig. 12.2 Diagram giving dimensions of Space-O-Matic Parking Unit. (*Reproduced by permission of Space-O-Matic Parking (UK) Ltd.*)

On-centre spacing: standard spacing at 8 ft 6 in (other dimensions available on special order). *Clearance width:* 7 ft 9 in (inside). *Clearance height:* 5 ft 2 in (bottom space, inside). *Ceiling height required:* 10 ft 6 in. *Power actuation:* hydraulic system, electric drive, with mechanical locking. *Electric service:* 3 phase/5 or 10 hp (conversion to other power sources by special order). *Loading capacity:* 5 tons (10,000 lb—4536 kg). *Vehicles accepted:* all standard domestic and imported passenger cars. *Safety features:* fail-safe locking devices.

Fig. 12.3   View showing one of two banks of Space-O-Matic units in Brompton Place parking garage of Harrods Ltd, Knightsbridge, London. (*Reproduced by permission of Space-O-Matic Parking (UK) Ltd.*)

Fig. 12.4   View of double deck parking unit by Parking Systems Ltd. W, 8 ft (2·44 m); L, 18 ft (5·49 m); H, 13 ft (3·96 m); Y, 9 ft (2·74 m); Z, 4 ft (1·22 m); h, 6 ft 6 in (1·98 m); w, 7 ft 2 in (2·18 m). (*Reproduced by permission of Parking Systems Ltd, London, SE27.*)

2·58 m (8 ft 6 in); the clearance width 2·35 m (7 ft 9 in) (inside); the clearance
height 1·56 m (5 ft 2 in) (bottom space—inside); the ceiling height 3·18 m (10 ft
6 in), and the loading capacity 4536·0 kg (10,000 lb). The equipment will accept
all standard domestic passenger cars. The manufacturers are—Space-O-Matic
Parking (UK) Ltd, 253–255, Belgrave Gate, Leicester.

(c) PARKING SYSTEMS LTD TWO LEVEL PARKING UNIT

This parking unit is in the form of two hydraulically operated tilting platforms
so arranged that headroom requirements are kept to a minimum and any of

Fig. 12.5   View of Parking System's double deck parking unit with cars in down position.
(*Reproduced by permission of Parking Systems Ltd, London, SE27.*)

the two cars can be driven off without affecting the other. Hydraulic equipment
can operate batches of 6 to 8 cars and this form of two level parking, in costly
basement spaces, can show overall economies (Figs. 12.4 and 12.5).

The equipment is supplied by Parking Systems Ltd, 1, Ernest Avenue, West
Norwood, London SE27.

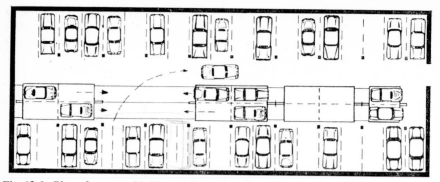

Fig. 12.6   Plan of garage with Plymoth Plates installed, showing how 14 extra cars may be parked by using these plates. (*Reproduced by permission of Plymoth Garage Plattor AB, Malmö, Sweden.*)

(d) THE PLYMOTH PLATE

In order to use for parking purposes some of the large amount of space allocated to access lanes in multi-storey garages, a method has been devised which provides shallow electrically operated plates which move along the access lanes. The plates, which are known as 'Plymoth' plates, may be of different sizes to accommodate one, two or four cars. If it is necessary to take a car from the parking place at right angles to the access lane, and it is obstructed by cars on the 'Plymoth' plate, a switch can be operated, and the plate is moved along the lane

Fig. 12.7   View of garage using Plymoth Plates. (*Reproduced by permission of Plymoth Garage Plattor AB, Malmö, Sweden.*)

clear of the car (Figs. 12.6 and 12.7). It is claimed that by adopting this system in a normal multi-storey car park the parking space will be increased from 20 per cent to 40 per cent; alternatively, when included in new construction, the cost per car space can be reduced by 15 to 30 per cent.

This system has not yet been installed in England, but it is operating in Germany and Scandinavia. It can be supplied by Plymoth Garage Plattor AB, Ostanvag 36, Malmö SV, Sweden, or in England by Elof Hansson Ltd, 32-36 Great Portland Street, London, W1.

HORIZONTAL MOVEMENT ONLY

(a) THE PEARCE AUTOPARK

In this system, orthodox lifts are used in conjunction with hand-operated trolleys. On arrival, a customer is received by an attendant in the reservoir on the ground floor; he is given a ticket, asked when he will require his car, and may depart in a few seconds. The car is then moved into a lift and raised to an upper floor. Here it is pushed by hand to a trolley, which is moved sideways to a vacant parking space. Meantime the lift has returned to the ground floor for another car. Two, three, or more lifts can be installed according to the size of the garage, and any one lift can be used to serve the whole of any parking floor, which is important during rush hours. As cars do not have to be manoeuvred into bays on the parking floors, the space saving is considerable.

When the customer calls for his car, he hands in his ticket at the pay office; whilst he pays his bill, the ticket authorising release is sent through a Lamson tube to the floor where the car is located and the reverse process of trolleys and lifts put in motion.

It is claimed that economy in manpower is effected by its being unnecessary to keep attendants on a parking floor unless cars are actually being moved to or from that particular floor. At peak hours it is necessary to man several floors, but at other times a comparatively small staff move from floor to floor. A system of coloured lights controls the location of personnel and lifts (Fig. 12.8).

It is claimed that a '540' Pearce Autopark with four lifts can deal with 250 cars per hour. The average time for delivery is two to three minutes or, at peak hours, five to six minutes.

The Autopark system normally includes services such as washing, polishing, greasing and minor repairs. Labour required in rush hours to assist with parking can be used for washing cars in the quieter periods.

The construction of the Pearce Autopark is basically a plain symmetrical reinforced concrete structure. Windows are not required, and ventilation is no problem because cars are not driven on the parking floors. The building area in relation to the number of cars parked is small, being less than 19 m² (200 sq ft) per car in a garage for 270 cars.

A garage constructed in Cornwall Street, Birmingham, in 1956, cost approximately £45,000, or under £250 per car space.

The building area required for a '540' Autopark of seven storeys, with ground floor used mainly for reception and the top floor for service, is approximately 40·0 m (130 ft) × 38·0 m (125 ft) or 1520 m² (1806 sq yd). Alternatively, a

Fig. 12.8   The Pearce Autopark showing cars being placed in position. (*Reproduced by permission of R. S. Pearce & Co. Ltd, Birmingham.*)

smaller type six-storey park with capacity for 270 cars could be built on an area 24·5 m (80 ft) × 36·5 m (120 ft) or 894·25 m² (1067 sq yd). Detailed plans must be prepared to suit particular sites.

The developers of the Pearce Autopark are R. S. Pearce and Co. Ltd, of Birmingham, 3.

(b) THE CARPACK SYSTEM

The Carpack system is a British development. The space required for parking is reduced to two-thirds of that required for normal parking, because two rows of cars can be parked adjoining each other.

The cars, other than those on the back row, are parked on movable platforms which are power driven to provide sideways movement. One space is left in each row of platforms, and by operating the sideways movement it is possible to gain access to any car without the assistance of an attendant.

The platforms run on a central guide wheel, and strips are set in the concrete screed with falls from the central rail to the gulleys, the additional headroom required being only 76·2 mm (3 in) (Fig. 12.9).

The layout requires an access aisle 7·3 m (24 ft 0 in) wide with columns at 4·87 m (16 ft 0 in) centres along the aisle and 4·87 m (16 ft 0 in) centres between the two rows of parking spaces which are 4·87 m (16 ft 0 in) deep.

This system may be seen in operation at Bow Bells House in the City of London. The equipment is marketed by Economic Parking Ltd, Francis Street, London SW1, and the winch, motor and drive is manufactured by Fuller Electric Ltd, Fulbourne Road, London E17.

Fig. 12.9   The Carpack system of mechanical parking. (*Reproduced by permission of Fuller Electric Ltd, London, E*17.)

STATIONARY AND MOVING ELEVATORS AND STATIONARY STALLS

THE AUTO-SILOPARK CAR PARKING SYSTEM

The Auto-Silopark mechanical car park was developed originally by Applied Research Development ARD AG of Zurich, in 1949.

The Silopark system is designed to make the maximum use of available space, and garages built to this system can park a given number of cars on a considerably smaller area than that which would be occupied by a ramp type multi-storey car park of similar capacity. It is claimed that this space saving can be as much as two-thirds, only one-third of the area being used by the Silopark.

The basic principle is to use high speed heavy lifts which are either arranged to move only in the vertical plane or both vertically and horizontally. This, together with the provision of platforms arranged to carry one or two cars at a time, allows considerable flexibility in design potential; either high and narrow or low and long garages can be designed and all intermediate stages can be accommodated. Similarly, the system enables garages to be designed which are entirely below ground, entirely above ground or partly below and partly above, and entry and exit can be positioned to suit the site requirement, either can be arranged at any level, and entry and exit can be on the same or on different levels. Special equipment designed and patented by the Silopark organisation is used to automatically align the car at the point of entry and to transfer the car on to the lift and to deposit or retrieve the car into or from the parking stalls (Fig. 12.10).

Fig. 12.10   Interior view of the Burlington Street Auto-Silopark Car Park, London. (*Reproduced by permission of Auto-Silopark (Great Britain) Ltd, London.*)

The structural element of the garage is composed of a series of stalls, of sufficient width to take one, two or three parked cars, arranged in rows opposite to one another across a central shaft in which the elevator platform travels. It can be constructed of reinforced concrete by any of the many methods now employed or as a steel structure and is straightforward in design; tolerances are well within the capabilities of any reputable building contractor.

When parking, the motorist drives his car in the forward direction into an entry bay, switches off the engine and is free to leave immediately, all subsequent operations are achieved mechanically. On collection, his car is delivered to him in an exit bay from which he can drive away, again in the forward direction. In a public Silopark garage, he pays for the time the car is parked, not for the time which it takes him to leave the car park after collecting his car.

Speed of operation is a feature of this equipment and it can be equated to suit the type of operation for which the garage is designed. A garage used mainly in peak periods will need to provide equipment to cope with the high input and output requirements, whilst one which is subject to a reasonably constant input and output, for example in shopping areas, can operate with a much higher number of cars per mechanical element. Thus, cost per car space for the mechanical equipment is dependent upon the use for which the garage is intended.

Silopark garages can be erected for as few as twenty cars up to any size requirement, there being no mechanical limitation on the number of cars which can be accommodated, only the physical size of the site and the height or depth to which the building may be restricted. In practice, care must be taken to ensure that the traffic facilities and roads around the car park can handle the flow of cars both into and out of the car park.

The smaller garages which would normally be for private use lend themselves to completely automatic operation, and, whilst it is possible to automate the larger, experience suggests that it is desirable to have some supervision in public garages to ensure that cars are not left in the entry bays in a condition unacceptable for parking. Silopark standard equipment is automatically operated, sequence locked, but all operations, with one exception, are preselected by an operator and initiated by push buttons, only unskilled labour being required. The one exception is the centering device which is actuated by the front wheels of the incoming car, and which completes its function within one and one-half seconds, before the driver has left his vehicle.

An example of the Auto-Silopark (stationary elevator with traversing cross carriages and two 'dollies' to carry two cars at a time) can be seen at Burlington Garage, Old Burlington Street, London W1; another example (moving elevator with two 'dollies' to handle two cars at a time) can be seen at Rochester Row, London SW1. Other examples may be seen in Belfast, Genoa, Hamburg, Johannesburg, Leeds, Milan, Munich, Nairobi, Paris, Zurich, etc.

This equipment may be supplied in the United Kingdom by Auto-Silopark (Great Britain) Ltd, 59–60, Jermyn Street, St James's, London SW1.

FERRIS WHEEL TYPE OF CAR PARK

(a) AU-RO PARKING SYSTEM

The Au-Ro Mechanical Parking System consists of an endless belt conveyor, automatically storing vehicles in the minimum space. The conveyor consists of a number of trays or pallets on which the vehicles are supported and these, not being connected with each other mechanically, are moved smoothly in either direction via rubber buffers located at each end of the pallet. Electric motors drive the conveyor through special gearing. The conveyor can be moved in either direction so that the required pallet or tray reaches the entrance or exit by the shortest distance (Fig. 12.11).

This system can be installed in the basements of existing buildings. Providing there is 3·9 m (12 ft 10 in) of headroom a car will occupy an average of 9·29 m² (100 sq ft) of floor space. This compares with 23·23 m² (250 sq ft) to 27·87 m² (300 sq ft) required for parking in the normal manner. The parking units can be supplied in any length for up to 60 vehicles per unit for both front and side entry. As the cost of the drive units is the same for any conveyor length it is

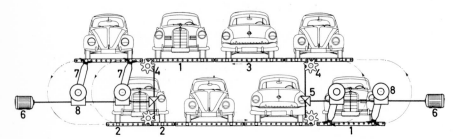

Fig. 12.11 The Au-Ro mechanical parking system. 1. Tray; 2. Rollers; 3. Rack; 4. Pinion; 5. Bevel gear; 6. Electric motor; 7. Levers for raising and lowering trays; 8. Worm gear.
(*Reproduced by permission of J. M. J. Maus Ltd, London.*)

most economical to install the longest possible unit. On the usual side entry type a width of 6·45 m (21 ft 3 in) accommodates the line, and typical lengths are 34·5 m (113 ft) for a 28 car belt, 51·0 m (168 ft) for a 44 car belt, and 63·0 m (223 ft) for a 60 car belt. The only access required to this area is a single or double width entry and exit, or entry and reversing space, and this may be either at the lower floor level or 2·3 m (7 ft 7 in) above at the top belt level. The Au-Ro Mechanical Parking System is marketed in England by J. M. J. Maus Ltd, Hammersmith, London, and manufactured by Fried. Krupp Maschinen- und Stahlbau, Rheinhausen, West Germany.

(b) KRUPP-PARK SYSTEM

The Krupp-Park system is an automatic pigeon-holing system for motor vehicles, which makes it possible to garage a maximum number of vehicles in a minimum of parking space. Parking platforms are arranged on two to six levels; the transfer of vehicles from one level to another is by vertical lifts at the ends of the installation.

When the installation starts up, the platform at the top level is lowered to the ground level, whilst the second lift raises its platform to the top level. Whilst this reciprocating movement is under way, all other parking compartments remain at rest.

Each working sequence thus comprises the raising and lowering of one compartment each at the ends of the conveyor and moving the upper and lower row by the width of one stall to the right or left. This process takes about 12 seconds (Fig. 12.12).

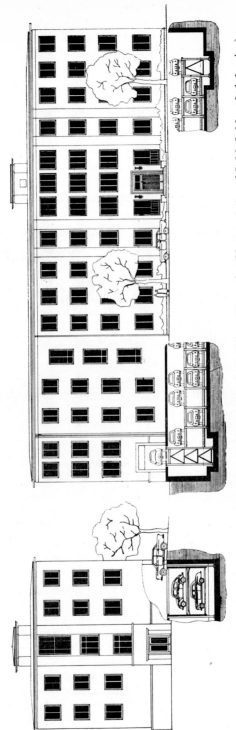

Fig. 12.12   Section showing the Krupp-Park System for parking under buildings. (*Reproduced by permission of J. M. J. Maus Ltd, London.*)

This equipment is adaptable to different types of vehicles. The parking platform width or length can easily be altered without affecting the basic design. The height of vehicles parked is equally immaterial, as the conveyor can be spaced to suit any headroom.

This equipment is manufactured by Fried. Krupp Maschinen- und Stahlbau Rheinhausen, West Germany. It is marketed in England by J. M. J. Maus Ltd, Hammersmith, London.

(c) BUTTERLEY WULPA LIFTPARK

The Butterley Wulpa Liftpark consists of a structure of standard steel sections with overall dimensions of 7·3 m × 6·0 m (24 ft × 20 ft) base and 26·75 m (88 ft) height. Within this structure 20 cabins are suspended upon two high duty

Fig. 12.13   View of entrance to the Butterley Lift Park parking unit. (*Reproduced by permission of The Butterley Co. Ltd, Ripley, Derby.*)

chains which are driven by a 45 hp motor through a reduction gear box and gear train. The cabins are each capable of carrying one vehicle up to a maximum length of 5·8 m (19 ft), and weight of 2032·1 kg (2 tons). The whole plant is operated from a control panel sited near the loading point, and barrier gates add to the safety precautions. This structure may be installed as a free standing unit or incorporated within a building scheme.

The car is driven on to a vacant cabin which is automatically stationed at ground level. Noting the number of his cabin, the driver goes to the control panel in the kiosk, and turns the appropriate key to 'park' which brings the nearest vacant cabin to ground level (Figs. 12.13 and 12.14). To recover the car, the driver inserts the key in the lock which he turns to 'unpark'. The car immediately descends to ground level. The key is then turned to 'vacant'; this allows the barrier gates to rise and the car to be driven away. Alternatively, an attendant can operate the Liftpark by means of push button controls. Several Liftparks have been installed in Germany and Italy and two in England—one at High

Fig. 12.14   The Butterley Lift Park—view of installation of three units in Milan. (*Reproduced by permission of The Butterley Co. Ltd, Ripley, Derby.*)

Street, South Norwood, London, and another at Ripley, Derby. The Liftpark is manufactured by The Butterley Company Ltd, Ripley.

PARKING SYSTEMS LTD VERTICAL AND HORIZONTAL MECHANICAL PARKING

Mechanical equipment has been developed which will lower a car through several floor levels, move it longitudinally along the floors and sideways to its final parked position. This is done completely automatically from the original drive-in position. A unit of this type has been fitted at No. 10, Queen Anne Street, London W1.

These mechanical units can be fitted with control equipment to operate the system in whatever way is most suitable to the user. Small units of twenty to thirty cars can be located exactly where required, no attendant is necessary, and a foolproof press button or key operated unit is available.

This equipment may be supplied and installed by Parking Systems Ltd, West Norwood, London SE27.

REFERENCES

1. SEYMER, NIGEL. 'Design of Parking Garages for European Needs'. *International Road Safety & Traffic Review*, Autumn 1966, Vol. XIV, No. 4.
2. Report to World Touring and Automobile Organisation (OTA), *International Road Safety & Traffic Review*, Autumn 1956, Vol. IV, No. 4.
3. SEYMER, NIGEL. 'A Survey of Parking Garages'. *International Road Safety & Traffic Review*, Autumn 1960, Vol. VIII, No. 4.
4. MANZONI, SIR HERBERT. 'Public Parking Garages'. *Journal RIBA*, 3rd Series, March 1958. Vol. 65, No. 5.
5. London Building Acts (Amendment) Act 1939, Section 20. Code of Practice for Buildings of Excess Height and/or Additional Cubical Extent. Greater London Council.

Chapter 13

Underground Car Parks

Underground car parks may be under a road, an open space or square in a city, the basement to an hotel, commercial building or garage. The lower floors of a multi-storey car park, if below ground, would come under this heading. Probably the majority of underground car parks are in areas where part of the expense of construction would have been incurred whether or not a car park had been constructed.

An underground car park is usually a very expensive proposition when all the cost of land, excavation and construction is charged to the car park. It is probably the most expensive method of providing parking accommodation. The work includes excavation, retaining walls, ramps, columns and suspended floors, ventilation, lighting, heating, fire prevention equipment, and maybe restoration of the ground surface. To offset some of the heavy expenditure, it may be possible for a local authority to allocate a site in the central business area of the city free of cost if the surface is restored to its original condition as an open space.

The Greater London Council have published a Code of Practice for garages and car parks.[1]

The design, gradient of ramps, spacing of columns and layout of parking spaces for underground car parks are similar to the requirements for multi-storey car parks described in Chapter 10.

DEEP BASEMENT CAR PARKS

In large and highly developed cities, it is uneconomic to use valuable land as a surface car park, neither is it always possible, either physically or economically, to build a multi-storey car park exactly where it is required.

When building on an expensive site the architect will no doubt wish to make more remunerative use of floor space with daylight access than using it for car parking, and the car parking requirements may be met by constructing a deep basement. Again, in cities where there are buildings of great historic interest or architectural value, the only permissible way of providing car parking space may

229

be in an underground car park. This could be under an existing building, an open space such as a 'square' or parkland or under a road.

Whilst the construction costs of underground car parks are high, nevertheless local authorities and private developers are being compelled to resort to this method of providing car parking space in densely developed city centres.

During the last half century there have been many radical developments in the design and construction of retaining walls and sheet piling. One development was pioneered by Dr H. Lorenz, of West Berlin, and Mr H. B. Fehlmann, of Zurich.[2] This method has been used almost exclusively for caissons on major civil engineering works, other than car parks, such as cellular quay walls, pumping stations, etc.

The use of the Lorenz/Fehlmann caissons for underground car parks is now being developed. When the caisson for the foundations of a large block of flats or offices is sunk into position, there is a large space below ground level which can be excavated. Ramps and car parking decks can be constructed in this space.

The economy of the Lorenz/Fehlmann method is obtained by the action taken to reduce the friction between the walls of the caisson and the surrounding soil during the process of sinking. A clay slurry, bentonite, is used to lubricate the wall surface as the caisson is eased into the ground. An advantage of using this method in city centres is that there is no noise like that associated with driving sheet piling.

This method is operated in the United Kingdom under licence by Foundation Engineering Ltd, London.

Another method of construction which is based on a technique developed by W. V. Zinn and Associates, Consulting Civil and Structural Engineers, of Epsom, Surrey, has been applied in a number of deep basements in the London area with conspicuous success.[3] They include the basements to the Royal Garden Hotel, the London Hilton Hotel, Leicester Square Car Park and the Winter Gardens Development, Drury Lane.

The system consists of the construction of a contiguous bored sheet pile wall round the perimeter of the site, the piling being designed and reinforced to withstand the effects of lateral earth pressure during subsequent construction, and to support the intermediate floor construction. The outer perimeter areas of the floors are constructed successively as excavation proceeds, and act as waling supports to the perimeter wall. Internal floor areas are constructed after completion of the excavation, commencing with the lower level (Fig. 13.1).

Construction by this method has many practical and economical advantages, principally as follows:

(i) All work carried out forms part of the permanent construction and the absence of all temporary struts leads to maximum economy of construction. Moreover, planning is not inhibited by the need to provide working space outside the line of the external walls, since by using these methods of construction there is no need to provide working space around the perimeter of the site, and the bored pile walls can be constructed on the actual line of the site boundary.

(ii) Since the bored piling which supports the excavation is itself supported at every level, both during construction and permanently, the risk of subsidence in the surrounding ground is reduced to negligible proportions and the normal hazard attaching to such deep basement construction is eliminated.

(iii) The rate of construction is governed only by the rate at which excavated material can be removed from the site.

(iv) If required, the method can be adapted to support construction above ground level without loss of economy, and by provision of suitable waling supports it is feasible for construction at the upper levels to proceed simultaneously with the basement construction. The cost of car parking can, to a considerable extent, be offset by saving in foundation costs for the super-structure building if this possibility is adopted.

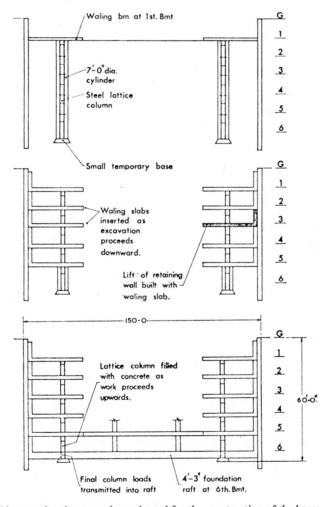

Fig. 13.1   Diagram showing procedure adopted for the construction of the basement car park at the Winter Gardens Theatre, Drury Lane, London, by W. V. Zinn and Associates. (*Reproduced by permission of W. V. Zinn and Associates, Epsom, Surrey.*)

The methods developed by W. V. Zinn and Associates are in some respects similar to those evolved by Mr N. E. M. Brydon, M.B.E., B.Sc., F.I.C.E., which have British Patent No. 940,500. W. V. Zinn and Associates have taken a licence from Mr Brydon entitling them and their clients to use his patent.

There are several other firms whose services are available for diaphragm construction work.[4]

UNDERGROUND CAR PARK AT IPSWICH

This car park forms part of the new Ipswich Civic Centre. It is 55·0 m (180 ft) in diameter and 15·0 m (46 ft) deep. It comprises a spiral ramp 17·0 m (56 ft) wide which, being supported on radial concrete beams, is free from vertical obstructions. The beams are inverted T-section and were precast and prestressed. The spiral ramp completes approximately three and a half turns and descends at an average gradient of 1 in 40. Accommodation is provided for 330 cars which may be parked radially against the walls which form the outer cylinder, and against the inner core, within which the pedestrian ramp is contained.

Motorists on leaving their cars, pass through fire resisting doors into the inner core, where there is a pedestrian spiral ramp 2·0 m (7 ft) wide and there are also stairs. The pedestrian spiral integrates with the car park spiral where both emerge through ground level on to the terraces which form the main approach to the Civic Centre. Over the inner core of the car park there is an ornamental pool and fountain. Rising through the inner core and emerging at one side of the pool, is a granite clad ventilation shaft which towers upwards for 12·0 m (40 ft). Attractive use has been made of precast concrete paving, flower containers and seats on the pedestrian terrace.

The construction of the car park began with a saucer-shaped excavation to +6·5 m (21 ft 6 in) OD, and from this level a circular ring of steel sheet piling 12·0 m (40 ft) deep with an internal diameter of 55·5 m (182 ft) was driven. The top of the ring of piles was supported by a circular reinforced concrete ring beam to which each pile was anchored. Excavation was continued to +2·25 m (7·35 ft) OD when a steel ring beam or waling was erected. Concrete packings were placed between the sheet piling and the ring beam, and the outer edge of the waling was supported by steel straps welded on to the sheet piling. The excavation was then continued down to the chalk on which the base slab was founded. In one area the chalk bed disappeared and 45 piles were placed to support the base slab.

To prevent the base floating prior to completion of the walls and ramps, 64 bored piles were placed in the central area, and anchored to the base slab which varied from 0·90 m (3 ft) to 1·35 m (4 ft 6 in) in thickness and was heavily reinforced. It was laid in sections and each joint was protected with a continuous system of 'Serviseal' water bars laid on the blinding layer.

The walls were designed to be constructed to their full height before the precast beams supporting the ramp were fixed. The outer walls were cast against the sheet piling with a nominal minimum thickness of 380 mm (15 in). Above the concrete ring beam the wall was shuttered both sides.

The precast concrete beams were inverted T-section and varied in weight from

6 to 12 tonnes. The lighter ones were pre-tensioned on a long line casting bed, while the heavier beams were post-tensioned. Each beam was supported on the outer wall in a pocket cast in the wall, and at the inner end, on a corbel cast on to the inner ring wall.

Each precast beam, which is on a level radial line and approximately 65·0 mm ($2\frac{1}{2}$ in) higher than the adjacent beam, supports 65·0 mm ($2\frac{1}{2}$ in) prestressed concrete planks which are level. A topping varying from 65·0 mm ($2\frac{1}{2}$ in) to 130 mm (5 in) thick was cast to form the ramp. The slab consisting of topping and planks, is designed to act compositely with the beams, which were propped at centre and quarter points during the casting and curing of the topping. When the floors were complete it was possible to backfill outside the outer wall above the concrete ring beam, additional thrust on the wall being taken through the floors to the centre core.

Where the structure emerges above ground, the helical form has been integrated in the layout, and levels of the terrace, in the centre of which, over the inner core of the car park is the fountain and ornamental pool.

The Architects for the car park were Vine and Vine, 1 Cecil Court, London Road, Enfield; the Consulting Engineers, R. F. Galbraith and Partners, 87, Manor Road, Wallington, Surrey; and the Main Contractors, Allen Fairhead and Sons Ltd, Sydney Road, Enfield, and J. Gerrard and Sons Ltd, Hadleigh Road, Ipswich.

PARK LANE UNDERGROUND CAR PARK, HYDE PARK, LONDON

The Hyde Park (Underground Parking) Act, 1961, enabled the Minister of Transport to grant to the Westminster City Council interests in and rights over an area in the north-eastern part of Hyde Park for the provision of underground parking facilities, together with a petrol station and other services commonly provided in parking places.

Tenders were invited by the Westminster City Council from a limited selection of contracts on a basic design prepared by the City Engineer. This incorporated the requirements of the Ministries and other public authorities concerned with the site, and was accompanied by a detailed specification of requirements. The contract provided for the contractor to detail the whole of the structure and the mechanical and electrical services within the framework of the basic design provided. Each contractor was allowed to submit an alternative tender based on his own design, but to comply with the requirements of the specification.

The car park measures 320·0 m (1050 ft) by 90·0 m (295 ft) and has a clear headroom of 2·30 m (7 ft 6 in) throughout with a general ceiling height of 2·60 m (8 ft 6 in). The length of the north tunnel providing vehicular and pedestrian ingress and egress is approximately 150 m (500 ft) and the similar eastern tunnel approach is 120 m (400 ft) in length. A pedestrian subway connecting to the public subway and underground railway at Marble Arch is approximately 150 m (500 ft) long.

Because of the large size of this car park, the problems encountered in providing adequate ventilation were considerable. Both vehicular tunnels are used as entries for fresh air and an additional supply of fresh air is provided to the centre of the car park by mechanical means. Large extract equipment is situated between these points to provide a good circulation of air in the car park. The total electrical horsepower required on the ventilation fan units is approximately 190 to achieve six complete air changes per hour. A 200 hp standby diesel generator is provided, which will start up automatically in case of a mains failure, and maintain half the normal ventilation rates together with emergency lighting. Independent supplies of fresh air are made to the offices, toilets and work rooms (Fig. 13.2).

Fig. 13.2   Interior view of Park Lane Garage, London. (*Reproduced by permission of Sir Robert McAlpine and Sons Ltd, London.*)

The design of the garage takes proper account of public safety by the provision of smoke-free escape corridors, emergency staircases, fire doors, water sprinklers and hose reels, etc. To meet the requirements of the Fire Brigade, 90 shafts have been constructed through the car park roof to the paths in the park over the car park. These shafts are fitted with specially designed covers which whilst being strong enough to carry a gun-carriage, may be broken by the Fire Brigade in the event of a fire, to permit the smoke to rise from the car park by natural convection. The escape corridors, which run the entire length of the car park, have a suspended ceiling set below the concrete roof, designed to reduce noise in the corridors. The walls are decorated in light clean colours, and independent supplies of fresh air should form a more pleasant and safe walk for the motorist reaching his car in this large structure. The garage also includes ancillary provisions in the form of car servicing bays, toilets, staff welfare facilities. The lighting in the garage is by fluorescent tubes in totally enclosed lanterns of glass fibre and plastic construction to give an average illumination at floor level of 33–44 lx (3–4 lumens per square foot). Each row of lamps across the car park is controlled by a separate switch so that a lower standard of lighting can be selected at the quieter times if desired. The same fitting is used in the vehicle tunnels to give a slightly higher standard of illumination. At the tunnel entrances extra fittings are provided to give a maximum lighting intensity of 200 lx (20 lumens per square foot) for day-time use in order to acclimatise the motorist to the brighter light.

In the pedestrian subways and corridors, the fluorescent lighting fittings are recessed into the suspended ceiling at 7·30 m (24 ft) centres along the 1·8 m (6 ft) wide corridors. This gives an average illumination of 54 lx (5 lumens per square foot). This standard of illumination is also provided on the open entrance and exit ramps. In the case of the northern approach, this is achieved by fluorescent tube fittings set into the retaining walls in special fittings. At the eastern

Fig. 13.3   Approach to entrance of Park Lane Garage, London. (*Reproduced by permission of Sir Robert McAlpine and Sons Ltd, London.*)

approach where the petrol station is situated, there are 2·4 m (8 ft) long fluorescent tubes let into the handrails set on top of the retaining walls. By these means, it has been possible to avoid introducing any new lamp column into the park (Fig. 13.3).

To avoid icing conditions on the open ramps, electrical heating cables have been incorporated into the concrete slabs. These provide two degrees of ramp heating, one of 50 watts/m^2 (5 watts per square foot), and the other of 100 watts/m^2 (10 watts per square foot), to be switched on automatically by the falling temperature.

The structure is of reinforced concrete placed *in situ*, except the columns and side walls of the car park which were precast on the site. The retaining walls for the eastern ramped approaches were formed by continuous rows of concrete cylinder piles. At the northern ramps, reinforced concrete walls were constructed within temporary steel sheet piling. The roof is 0·30 m (12 in) thick reinforced concrete flat slab construction, supported generally on 576 columns either 0·30 m × 0·30 m (12 in × 12 in) or 0·30 m × 0·45 m (12 in × 18 in). The columns are at 7·60 m (25 ft) centres longitudinally, which permits three cars to be parked between them easily without undue disturbance of traffic movement in the car park. Laterally the columns are set back from the 6·0 m (20 ft) wide aisle by being placed at 7·30 m (24 ft) centres with 4·87 m (16 ft) wide spans on either side set in the parking stalls.

The floor is constructed of 210 mm (8 in) thick reinforced concrete laid on a 80·0 mm (3 in) blending of concrete with column bases of average size 2·0 m × 2·0 m × 1·35 m (7 ft × 7 ft × 4 ft 6 in) deep. Floor drainage is provided in parallel rows across the garage at approximately 15·0 m (50 ft) centres which lead into pumping chambers set below the floor of the car park. At each pumping unit, duplicate pumps are provided with facilities to switch on the standby pump in the event of the duty pump failing. Additionally an overflow pipe to a low level storm overflow sewer situated some distance away in the park is provided as an added insurance against flooding in the garage.

The garage is designed to accommodate 1100 cars, and the contractor's tender was £1,051,915 in 1961.

The basic design was prepared by the City Engineer, City of Westminster, and the work was carried out by Sir Robert McAlpine and Sons Ltd, London.

UNDERGROUND CAR PARK AT MELLON SQUARE, PITTSBURG, USA

In 1951, a gift of $4,000,000 was presented to the City of Pittsburg by three Mellon family foundations for the purpose of acquiring all of the property in the block now known as Mellon Square, and constructing an underground car park with a public park on the surface. The City of Pittsburg leased sub-surface rights to the Public Parking Authority of Pittsburg, who in turn sub-leased the area to Mellon Square Garage Inc, a private corporation which agreed to design, construct and operate the garage under a 38 years leasehold. Title to the garage structure is vested in the Parking Authority. The financing of the project has been handled entirely by Mellon Square Garage Inc—the Parking Authority receiving an annual rental based on a percentage of gross income.

In the lease agreement the requirements for the car park are listed, the purpose for which it is to be used is outlined, and the maximum allowable parking fees are established. At the end of the term of the lease the operation of the garage will be turned over to the Pittsburg Parking Authority.

The underground car park provides 1040 parking spaces on six levels. There is direct access to three levels from two of the four surrounding streets. A self operating elevator and an escalator provide vertical access to the parking floors. As the level of one of the surrounding streets is 4·0 m (13 ft) higher than its parallel counterpart, the level of the park surface is approximately that of the higher street with steps leading down to the lower level.

The lower street (Smithfield Street) has excellent commercial frontage, and six retail stores have been constructed on the Smithfield Street frontage of the car park. The entrance and exit to the car park are in the parallel side streets.

One feature of the combined park and car park design is that the pedestrian footpaths have been carried in the park above car park entrances and exits, thereby eliminating pedestrian and vehicular interference (Fig. 13.4).

Users of the Mellon Square Car Park drive directly to the level on which they will park and are guided to a stall by an attendant. When returning to pick up his car, the motorist goes direct to his parking stall and drives out after paying a parking fee to the attendant. It is reported that incoming delays do not occur, and outgoing delays occur very infrequently at the car park exit points.

Fig. 13.4   Internal view of underground car park, Mellon Square, Pittsburgh, USA, showing access to rear of shops. (*Reproduced by permission of H. K. Ferguson Company, Cleveland, Ohio, USA.*)

The car park operates near to its optimum capacity, and accommodates between 1700 and 1850 cars on a weekday.

The car park was designed by H. K. Ferguson Co. and Morrison-Knudsen Co.

WINTER GARDEN THEATRE CAR PARK, LONDON
(Figs. 13.5 and 13.6)

The Winter Garden Development, Drury Lane, London, contains a theatre, shops, showrooms, banqueting hall, a ten-storey block of flats and a six-storey basement housing about 450 cars.

Here is an example where the contiguous bored sheet pile system was adopted to construct the basement for this development. To maintain complete support to adjoining buildings, streets and public services during construction of the unusually deep basement, it was decided to use the permanent floors as supports to retaining walls by constructing them in a downward sequence. A perimeter wall consisting of 0·48 m (19 in) diameter cast *in situ* concrete piles was constructed to a depth of approximately 20·0 m (67 ft) average, then 2·0 m (7 ft) diameter shafts were excavated to the full depth to accommodate structural steel columns with support floor slabs between the columns and perimeter piles at the various levels required. These waling slabs, whilst acting as part of the structural floors of the basement levels, support the concrete sheet pile walls until the perimeter

Fig. 13.5 Baseplate of steel shaft before lowering into position—Winter Gardens Theatre Car Park, London. (*Reproduced by permission of W. V. Zinn and Associates, Epsom, Surrey.*)

retaining walls, main foundations and other works have been completed. The top basement floor supporting the retaining walls is cast on solid ground, excavation to the first basement floor is then carried out and the floor constructed. This sequence is continued to foundation level.

The basement area has plan dimensions of approximately 56·5 m × 43·5 m (186 ft × 143 ft). The top level has a general storey height of 3·65 m (12 ft) and the remaining five levels have storey heights of 2·45 m (8 ft) approximately. Excavations for foundations extend to a depth of approximately 20·0 m (65 ft) below ground floor level.

There is no car parking at the top basement level which is used as a storage space and includes a loading bay served by means of a separate circular ramp which starts at ground floor level adjacent to the entrance of the car park.

The motorist collects his ticket at the entrance barrier and, missing out the top basement level, proceeds down a two-storey ramp to the first basement where he can park or carry on to any of the four basement levels below. He is not able to park on a section of the first basement which is taken up by plant rooms for electrical and mechanical services.

Fig. 13.6   Boring operation for Winter Gardens Theatre Car Park, London. (*Reproduced by permission of W. V. Zinn and Associates, Epsom, Surrey.*)

In view of the constricted nature of this site, it was decided that a single spiral ramp system should be used providing two way movement for access and egress with parking bays off the aisles, thereby avoiding the construction of a separate ramp system for access purposes.

On two sides of the car park the 6·7 m (22 ft) wide aisles are on a level grade, while on the other two sides the aisles fall through 1·2 m (4 ft) over their length on a ramp gradient of 1:26·5.

The motorist ascends in a clockwise direction and descends in an anti-clockwise direction. There are three ramps provided, and on the northern side the motorist has a choice of two ramps, while on the southern side there is only one ramp.

Parking bays are on a 6·4 m (21 ft) or 8·8 m (28 ft) grid providing three or four parking stalls in each bay. Where larger cars are required to be parked, one less car per bay will be accommodated, and sections of the car park are reserved for these cars.

Three staircases and one passenger lift for six persons are provided, with provision for a further lift if required. Water sprinkler, smoke extraction and ventilation systems are included.

The Architects for this development were Paul Tvrthovis in association with Sean Kenny and Chew and Percival. The Consulting Architects were Raymondon Spratley and Partners. The Consulting Civil and Structural Engineers, W. V. Zinn and Associates.

UNIVERSITY AVENUE UNDERGROUND CAR PARK, TORONTO
(Figs. 13.7 and 13.8)

The Parking Authority of Toronto was concerned about the lack of parking facilities in the University Avenue area of the south-west section of the central business district.

Fig. 13.7 Photograph of cut away model showing car park above underground railway. (*Reproduced by permission of the Toronto Parking Authority.*)

When the plans for the construction of the University Avenue Rapid Transit Subway were announced, they showed that the section between King Street and Front Street was to be constructed by the 'cut and fill' method. This involved the excavation of a deep trench on University Avenue, the construction of a subway tunnel on the floor of this trench, and back-filling with granular fill between the roof of the subway tunnel and street level.

The Parking Authority decided that by taking advantage of this situation and building an underground car park on the roof of the subway tunnel, and beneath the level of University Avenue, a considerable saving in construction costs could be made. The excavating was already done by the Toronto Transit Commission and did not have to be done by the Parking Authority. Instead of costing the Toronto Transit Commission a great deal of money to back-fill with expensive granular fill, this area could be back-filled with a car park.

With the co-operation of the Toronto Hydro Electric System, the Bell Telephone Company and other public service agencies, the Parking Authority was able to build the underground car park between King Street and Front

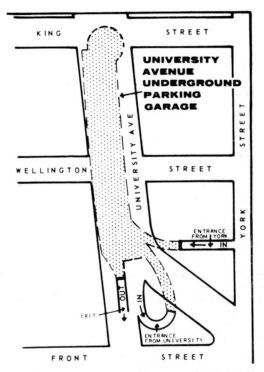

Fig. 13.8   Plan showing position of underground car park, University Avenue, Toronto, Canada. (*Reproduced by permission of the Toronto Parking Authority.*)

Street. The car park provides parking places for 325 vehicles. The total floor area of the two level car park is 9660·0 m² (105,000 sq ft). It has a clear span of 17·0 m (56 ft) and is equipped with an ultrasonic vehicle detector automatic car control system. It counts the cars in and out of the car park as well as indicating spaces available on either level. Illuminated signs controlling the entrance and exit of cars are automatically activated by this equipment. There is a four zone dry sprinkler system which together with chemical fire extinguishers equipped with alarm devices signalling when they are removed from their brackets, act as a protection against fire hazards. The car park is well ventilated, expelling air at the rate of 3000 m³/minute (105,000 cubic feet per minute) by means of three propeller type fans. A carbon-monoxide detection system monitoring key indicates when air has become contaminated, and automatically turns on the ventilation fans. Electrical snow melting equipment is buried in the exit and entrance vehicle ramps to keep them clear of snow at all times.

The Consulting Engineers were De Leuw, Cather and Company of Canada Ltd, and the General Contractors were Johnson–Perini–Kiewit.

ABINGDON STREET UNDERGROUND CAR PARK, LONDON, SW1

This underground car park was built for the Westminster City Council, and leased to National Car Parks Ltd, for operation. It is situated close to Parliament Square in Abingdon Street, opposite the Victoria Tower of the Houses of Parliament, adjacent to the precinct wall of Westminster Abbey, and is within 90·0 m (100 yards) of the River Thames. The site is approximately 76·0 m (250 ft) long by 42·0 m (140 ft) wide, and has been leased by the Westminster City Council from the Ministry of Public Buildings and Works, who have laid out a garden at street level over the structure.

Tenders were invited by the Council from a limited selection of Contractors on a basic design and a detailed specification for a two-storey car park prepared by the City Engineer. The contract called for the whole of the structure and mechanical and electrical services to be detailed by the tenderers within the framework of the basic design. Those invited were permitted to submit alternative tenders based on their own designs, but conforming with the basic specification which called for special and particular requirements to avoid noise and vibration during construction in this important location.

A tender submitted by Sir Robert McAlpine and Sons Ltd, was accepted. They used their patented 'arched retaining wall' system to retain the ground temporarily around the excavation; this involved the construction of 3·6 m (12 ft) long spans of reinforced concrete retaining wall between vertical precast concrete soldiers which were supported by heavy raking timbers. Inside the protection of this retaining wall the main garage was constructed using *in situ* reinforced concrete for the fabric of the building, after removal of some 19,000 m³ (25,000 cubic yards) of excavation.

The garage is entered from Gt College Street by a two-way open ramp with a 4·8 m (16 ft) wide carriageway and 1·8 m (6 ft) footway on one side and 0·9 m (3 ft) safety strip on the other side. The ramp is laid at a 1 in 10 gradient and is provided with electrical heating on automatic control so that either 50 or 100 watts per m² (5 or 10 watts per square foot) heating can be used to de-ice the surface. The two floors are connected by a covered 4·8 m (16 ft) wide vehicular ramp at a similar gradient. The columns at both levels are generally at 7·3 m (24 ft) centres, which allows for parking spaces 4·8 m × 2·4 m (16 ft × 8 ft) nominal size, with 6·0 m (20 ft) wide traffic lanes. The capacity of the garage is 200 cars if 'customer parked' and more if 'attendant parked'. The clear headroom throughout is 2·35 m (7 ft 9 in), and to achieve this the minimum clearance between floor and ceiling is 2·60 m (8 ft 6 in) to accommodate beams, lighting, sprinklers, etc.

The lower floor, which is laid to falls, was constructed in 200·0 mm (8 in) thick (minimum) reinforced concrete on 76·0 mm (3 in) blinding concrete

approximately 6·7 m (22 ft) below the adjacent road level, the floor being at
about standing ground water level. In order to construct the 3·0 m × 3·0 m
(10 ft × 10 ft) reinforced concrete bases to the columns and to allow for drainage, excavation, etc., it was necessary to dewater the site and some difficulty
and delay was experienced in constructing the drainage sump which was the
deepest part of the work. The suspended floor of the upper level is 254 mm
(10 in) thick *in situ* reinforced concrete thickened to give surface drainage falls,
and in common with all floor surfaces was treated with a surface hardener to

Fig. 13.9   View of entrance to Abingdon Street Car Park, Westminster, England. (*Reproduced
by permission of Sir Robert McAlpine and Sons Ltd, London.*)

reduce dust and finished with a light crimping roller. The roof is generally
300 mm (12 in) thick, increased to 380 mm (15 in) where situated under the
proposed widened part of Abingdon Street. The roof of the garage has been laid
to a transverse crossfall of about 300 mm (12 in) for drainage purposes and a
collecting drain provided on the Abingdon Street frontage.

    The design takes proper account of public safety by the provision of smoke-
free escape stairs and emergency exits, fire doors, roller shutters, automatic
water sprinklers and fire hose reels, etc. To enable the fire brigade to clear smoke
from either floor of the garage, independent breakable smoke vents have been
provided at surface level to each floor, and it was necessary for these to be
carefully positioned to fit into the garden layout above (Figs. 13.9 and 13.10).

    The ventilation system is designed to provide six air changes per hour through-
out the garage, this air change being induced by extracting stale air from the
garage into a 4·5 m (15 ft) high ventilation shaft in the Abbey Garden. Fresh air
is drawn down the ramp and through fresh air apertures in the ramp wall and

north face of the garage. The ventilation equipment consists of two 1·2 m (48 in) diameter axial flow fans connected in parallel and fixed on anti-vibration mountings. To avoid nuisance from noise, the two fans have been fitted with silencers and the exhaust vent is constructed of a 2·4 m (8 ft) diameter precast concrete tube which was forced by hydraulic rams beneath the Monastic Wall to discharge into the 1·5 m × 3·0 m (5 ft × 10 ft) ventilation shaft, thereby enabling air speeds to be kept at a low level. In the event of an electricity mains failure, the standby diesel generator will automatically operate and will supply power for one 1·2 m (48 in) diameter fan, as well as the emergency lighting.

The lighting throughout is by fluorescent tubes in totally enclosed shallow depth lanterns of fibre glass and plastic construction to give an average illumination at floor level of 32–43 lx (3–4 lumens per square foot). Each pair of alternate

Fig. 13.10   Interior view of Abingdon Street Car Park, Westminster, England. (*Reproduced by permission of Sir Robert McAlpine and Sons Ltd, London.*)

lines of lamps across the garage is controlled by a separate switch, so that a lower standard of lighting may be selected at quieter times if desired. The access ramp and area below the access portal are carefully graded so that a maximum intensity of lighting of 215 lx (20 lumens per square foot) is reached at the portal to acclimatise the motorist to daylight. Approximately one-third of the lamps are served by the emergency lighting circuit.

Other facilities provided include an office and waiting room; male and female toilets, built to public convenience standards; and also a mess room for the garage staff.

The drainage is by gravitation to the wet sump, all flow from the parking areas, etc., having passed through petrol interceptor chambers. Twin pumps lift the flow to a level well above the known sewer surcharge level to discharge by gravitation into the public sewer.

Means of escape have been provided so that occupants may leave the building either at the north end close to the Moat, or at the south end to Gt College Street, such emergency access being separated from the garage by roller shutters and smoke doors. There are also internal stairs connecting the two floors of the garage.

The work was carried out in 1963–64 and the contract price was £204,444.

UNDERGROUND CAR PARKS AT COLOGNE CATHEDRAL, WEST GERMANY

These car parks are situate to the south and west of Cologne Cathedral and are connected by a two-way aisle. At the sides of the aisle, parking stalls are provided. Because of the position of the Cathedral, the main entrance and exit are situate on the Bechergasse and Trankgasse. The surface over the underground car park is a pedestrian area with extensions to the main line Railway Station and the bus terminus. Roman remains which were discovered in the excavations, were partly included in the planning of the car park.

The entrance is controlled by an automatic barrier where parking tickets are distributed. The exit barrier opens after a metal disc is inserted, which is issued after the payment of a parking charge.

The parking floors have a floor to ceiling height of 2·15 m (6 ft 6 in).

The petrol station is on the first underground floor; next to it are the washing and service rooms, changing and waiting rooms and lavatories. For customers there are waiting rooms and lavatories in the Bechergasse and Trankgasse. The car park has five stairways that lead directly to the pedestrian way. From the Trankgasse, the customer can reach the underground station which is in the main line Railway Station. From the upper parking floor a pedestrian subway leads to the Cathedral Hotel.

The longitudinal ramps have a gradient of 14% (1 in 7) and the aisles have a width of 3·50 m (10 ft 6 in). The car park has been erected around a steel framework, and the roof is designed to carry any vehicles that are required for repair work to the Cathedral, or fire fighting.

The car park has a mechanically operated ventilation and air conditioning system.

The building is divided into three sections for fire prevention purposes, and both parking floors are provided with sprinkler appliances.

It is intended that the car park will be used for short-term parking with 100 reserved stalls for hotel guests.

The cost per parking stall is 14,000 DM (£1600) (1969), and the accommodation is for 613 cars.

The Architect for the work is Jac Schnitz, Architekt BDB, Köln-Deutz, Von-Sandt-Platz 11. The construction was carried out by the City of Cologne.

CAR PARK FOR THE HILTON HOTEL, PARK LANE, LONDON

The London Hilton Hotel occupies an island site bounded by Park Lane, Hertford Street, Stanhope Row and Petts Head Mews, with a frontage of 50·0 m (164 ft) to Park Lane, and a depth of approximately 95·0 m (310 ft).

Three basements are provided under the entire site and a fourth basement occurs under the main tower. These basements accommodate a grill room, plant rooms, kitchens, laundry, staff locker rooms and toilets, hotel storage and extensive car parking facilities, with two circular ramps providing access at the rear of the site.

The method used for the construction of the deep basement is described under 'Deep Basement Car Parks' on pages 230–232.

This car park provides accommodation for approximately 300 cars on three parking levels. On entering the car park from Hertford Street, cars can either be parked on the first floor (street level) or proceed down a spiral ramp, through the first basement, to park at the second basement level, or continue further down the ramp to park at the third basement level. Egress from the basements is by means of a separate spiral ramp.

The car park is operated on a concession basis by an independent company, and motorists may leave their cars at the entrance and, if required, the car park staff will park the car and deliver it on request later.

The Architects for this hotel were Lewis Soloman, Kaye and Partners, London, and the Consulting Civil and Structural Engineers were W. V. Zinn and Associates, Epsom, Surrey.

UNDERGROUND CAR PARK, NATHAN PHILLIPS SQUARE, TORONTO, CANADA

The Nathan Phillips Square Underground Car Park has a capacity for 2400 cars. It has four underground levels and is open 24 hours per day, and makes a substantial contribution to easing the considerable parking problems in the centre of downtown Toronto. The car park is located directly beneath Nathan

Fig. 13.11   Interior view of underground car park, Nathan Phillips Square, Toronto, Canada. (*Reproduced by permission of H. H. Ferguson Company, Cleveland, Ohio, USA.*)

Phillips Square and immediately in front of the New City Hall, with direct access into the City Hall as well as from entrances on Bay, Queen and Chestnut Streets. This car park has been built in two stages. The first stage was opened in 1958 with accommodation for 1300 cars, and the second stage has accommodation for 1100.

The structure is built in reinforced concrete, with a limited use of glazed bricks and concrete blocks in conjunction with the stairs and elevators (Fig. 13.11).

Ventilation is by means of supply fans which force air through long floor grilles on the south wall. This air is circulated throughout the building and

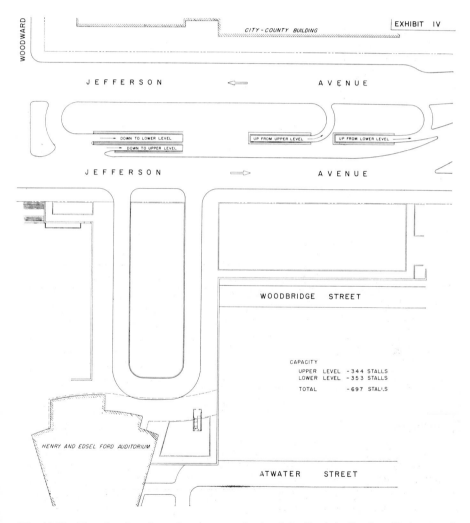

Fig. 13.12 Plan showing site and entrance and exit of the Ford Auditorium Underground Car Park, Detroit, Michigan, USA. (*Reproduced by permission of the Detroit Parking Authority.*)

exhausted on the west wall. The operation is continuous. The car park is provided with a heated standpipe system for fire protection in addition to a dry system of fully automatic sprinklers. To ensure the free flow of traffic during inclement weather, the entrance and exit ramps have been equipped with radiant heating for melting snow.

The car park is financed through Municipal debentures over a twenty-five year period and is required to be self-supporting.

FORD AUDITORIUM UNDERGROUND CAR PARK, DETROIT, MICHIGAN, USA

The Ford Auditorium underground car park consists of a two-level structure under the plaza of the Civic Centre between the new Ford Auditorium and the new City-County Building.

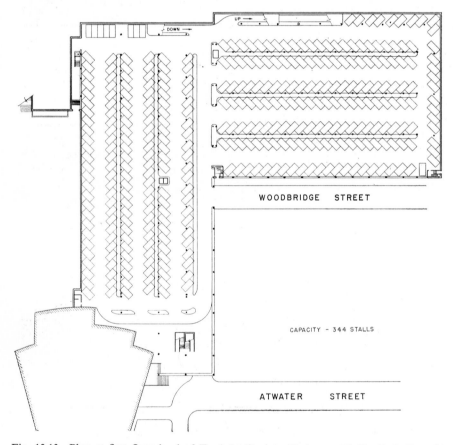

Fig. 13.13   Plan at first floor level of Ford Auditorium Underground Car Park, Detroit, Michigan, USA. (*Reproduced by permission of the Detroit Parking Authority.*)

It has a capacity of 697 parking stalls. Separate ramps are provided from each level for vehicular entrance and exit to Jefferson Avenue, which is the extension of the John C. Lodge Expressway. In addition, vehicular connection is provided between the upper level and Woodbridge Street and between the lower level and Atwater Street.

Direct pedestrian access is provided by means of escalators and stairs to the Ford Auditorium, and the plaza, Atwater and Woodbridge Streets. (Figs. 13.12 to 13.14).

The park is operated on the self parking basis, fees being collected at the cashier's window before unparking. About half the weekday parking is short term.

The site acquisition and construction costs were set by agreement between the Memorial Hall Commission, in overall charge of the Civic Centre, and the Municipal Parking Authority. The total of these costs amounts to $1,575,000 (£656,250) (1960).

Fig. 13.14 View showing roof car park over Cobo Hall and entrance to underground car park, Detroit, Michigan, USA. (*Reproduced by permission of the Detroit Parking Authority.*)

GRAND CIRCUS PARK UNDERGROUND CAR PARK, DETROIT, MICHIGAN, USA

This underground car park is located under Grand Circus Park, which is bounded by Adams and Park Avenues and Witherell Street. The car park is in

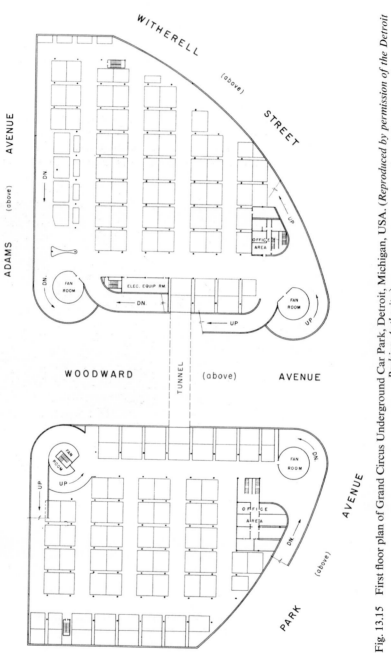

Fig. 13.15   First floor plan of Grand Circus Underground Car Park, Detroit, Michigan, USA. (*Reproduced by permission of the Detroit Parking Authority.*)

two sections separated by Woodward Avenue, the easterly one having three levels and the westerly one, two levels. The capacity is 1043 parking stalls.

The easterly section has entrance ramps from Adams and Woodward Avenues, and exit ramps to Woodward Avenue and Witherell Street. The westerly section has an entrance ramp from Park Avenue and an exit ramp to Adams Avenue. Pedestrian access is by means of escalators and stairs from the Park area (Figs. 13.15 and 13.16).

Fig. 13.16   View of Grand Circus, Detroit, USA, showing entrances and exits to underground car park. (*Reproduced by permission of the Detroit Parking Authority.*)

The parking fees for this car park in 1965 were as follows:

35 cents (15p) 1st hour
30 cents (12½p) each additional hour
$1.50 (62½p)—maximum day rate (6 am–6 pm)
90 cents (37½p)—maximum evening rate (5 pm–2 am)

Approximately two-thirds of the weekday parking is short term. The car park is operated on a partial self parking basis, with the motorist directed to the proper floor, where the car is parked and unparked by attendants as required. Parking fees are collected at the cashier's window before unparking.

The car park was designed by H. K. Ferguson Engineering Company.

UNDERGROUND CAR PARK, CHAMPS-ELYSÉES/AVENUE GEORGE V, PARIS

This car park, which is appropriately named, occupies the full width of the carriageway of l'Avenue George V and gives a clear width of 13·5 m (44 ft 3 in) at each level. This arrangement has been adopted in order to preserve the trees which border the avenue. The nature of the ground, however, permits the width to extend to 14 m (46 ft) at lower levels. There are six parking floors in the car park.

The length of the car park is 350 m (1150 ft) from the footpath south of the Avenue des Champs Elysées to the cross-roads at Avenues George V and Pierre-Ier de Serbie.

The ingress and egress for vehicles has been arranged via a subway. The entrance is situate in the Avenue des Champs Elysées between la rue Galilée and la rue de Bassano, and the exit near the lower part of Avenue George V.

The restriction on space in the car park makes it necessary to connect the different floor levels by helical tracks. The entrance is on even numbered floors and the exit on odd numbered floors. At the opposite end to the entrance of the car park, another helical track serves to give access between floors.

The exterior diameter of the helical track is 17 m (55 ft 9 in). This gives a satisfactory turning radius, and reasonable gradients. The average gradient of the access at the side of Avenue des Champs Elysées is 13 % and the gradient on the exit track on the side of Avenue Pierre-Ier de Serbie is 6·5 %. There are 216 parking stalls on each floor, and there are six floors. The pedestrian accesses have been placed in Avenue George V.

From the structural point of view the work is constructed between two lateral walls connected by beams 13·5 m (44 ft 3 in) span, without intermediate supports. The clear height under the beams is 2 m (6 ft 6 in).

The ventilation system makes six changes of air per hour with a battery of 12 ventilation fans. The lighting is by means of fluorescent fittings fixed to the ceiling between the beams. The lighting has been calculated to give a light intensity of 3 lx on the circulation floors and 15 lx on the sloping floors.

Protection against fire has been given special attention. Arrangements are made for each floor to be isolated from the other floors, and from the exterior, by fireproof doors which operate automatically and cut off all access by vehicles and pedestrians. In addition there is a fireproof wall and door which closes each floor into two parts. On the columns are dry mains which can be quickly connected to the main public water supply.

There is an arrangement of signs which give clear directions to motorists and pedestrians.

At the entrance to the access corridor, the vehicles are separated between users of the car park, which are directed to the right, and motorists requiring motor fuel, which is open to both users and non-users of the car park.

Users of the car park stop before an automatic barrier and they are put into three classes:

(a) Clients for parking on a time basis, who take a ticket from a machine on the right, this operation opening the barrier.

(*b*) Period ticket holders, who have places reserved for them, and occupy from one-quarter to one-third of the parking places. These motorists present their ticket to the electronic machine, the ticket being valid for a limited period.

(*c*) Shareholders of the car park who use the fifth and sixth floors. They have a permanent entrance card which is presented to another electronic machine.

The one-way circulating system is marked by arrows painted on the floors. The aisles and parking stalls are also marked out in paint.

The licence holders for the car park are Societe des Parkings des Champs-Elysées, Societe des Garages des Champs-Elysées, and GFD. 'Total'. The work was carried out by Grands Travaux de Marseille, Paris.

REFERENCES

1. London Building Acts (Amendment) Act 1939, Section 20. Code of Practice for Buildings of Excess Height and/or Additional Cubical Extent. Greater London Council.
2. Construction Progress, No. 7, December 1967. Research & Development Committee, Richard Costain Ltd, London.
3. ZINN, W. V. 'Economical Construction of Deep Basements', *Civil Engineering & Public Works Review*, March 1968.
4. 'Structural Diaphragm Walls', Supplement to *The Consulting Engineer*, London. June 1969.

Chapter 14

Parking of Commercial Vehicles

In a report[1] made on behalf of the Ministry of Transport and Civil Aviation in 1958, the following table shows the percentage increase in the volume of goods carried by road since 1952.

TABLE X

Inland Goods Transport
1952 *and* 1958

	Thousand Million Ton Miles		Per Cent of Ton Miles	
	1952	1958	1952	1958
Road	18·8	23·1	46	56
Rail	22·4	18·3	54	44
Total	41·2	41·4	100	100

Reproduced by permission of the Controller,
Her Majesty's Stationery Office, London.

The report states 'There was an increase of nearly one-quarter in the quantity of goods carried by road. The railway figures for 1958 . . . are depressed largely owing to the decline in iron and steel production, and the fall in the consumption of coal. This has also reduced the level of inland goods traffic to a level a little higher than that of 1952. Nevertheless even when allowance is made for the special circumstances in 1958 it is clear that whatever unit of measurement is used, road transport is now the major means of inland carriage of goods.' In 1968, the Ministry of Transport published a Summary Report on Transport for Industry and Table XI shows the share of each mode in total tons and ton miles generated by all industrial activity.

In addition to the increase in the quantity of goods carried by road there is a trend towards the use of heavier lorries. An article in *The Guardian*[3] in 1970 stated 'Whereas in the past ten years the number of cars on British roads has

TABLE XI

Share of Each Mode in Total Transport, 1968

Mode	Tons	Ton Miles
Own road transport	49	29
Road haulage	34	32
Rail	12	22
Coastal shipping	3	16
Pipelines	2	1
Total	100	100

Reproduced by permission of the Controller,
Her Majesty's Stationery Office, London.

more than doubled, goods vehicles have increased by less than a quarter, in spite of the freight tonnage going up all the time.'

This is where the benefits of a swing to heavier lorries are to be seen. If a greater load can be carried on each lorry, then fewer lorries are needed on the roads to transport a given quantity of freight. Carrying a greater load on each movement is cheaper. It is true, of course, that transport costs are rising just as most other costs are. If, however, a greater load can be carried per journey there is at least a chance that cost rises can be contained.

A 10-tonner can transport each ton of its load for 8 per cent less cost than can an 8-tonner. A 6-wheeler can save 12 per cent compared with a 4-wheeler. A 32 tonne (32 ton) gross articulated vehicle, the heaviest allowed at present, can save 11 per cent compared with vehicles running at the pre-1964 limit of 24 tonnes (24 tons) gross; although the cost of operating is much greater, 20 tonnes (20 tons) can be carried instead of 16 tonnes (16 tons).

This article further states: 'Only one type of projected lorry—one towing a separate multi-wheeled trailer, as is popular on the continent, and having an overall gross weight of 50 to 56 tons range—can produce big savings (up to 20 per cent in fact).'

'Quite apart from economics there is now a pressing need for higher gross weights simply to transport all the unit loads beginning to come into the country. The United States shipping lines, in particular are concentrating on 12·0 m (40 ft) long containers (the popular international sizes are 6·0 m (20 ft), 9·0 m (30 ft) and 12·0 m (40 ft). These can gross in themselves up to 30 tonnes (30 tons).'

'The railways too, are now gearing themselves to accept 12·0 m (40 ft) containers. This is fine for the long distance hauls. But these containers still have to be collected from or delivered to the terminals by road. If there are no vehicles to take these loads then the whole system of containerisation, with its accompanying economic benefits, is severely disrupted.'

The transport of goods by road has now become the major mode of transport for goods. Unlike the motor car, the requirements for parking are not limited to the terminus. This may be at the docks, distribution depot, or factory yard, where the responsibility for loading and unloading facilities rests with the company concerned with the goods and transport. The problem is the provision of overnight parking for these vehicles often loaded with valuable goods; and the provision of sleeping and catering facilities for the drivers, either near a terminus, or at an intermediate stage on the journey.

In the absence of suitable off-street parking places, heavy goods vehicles are parked overnight in quiet residential streets near the driver's sleeping accommodation. This creates another problem as it interferes considerably with local amenities and disturbs the residents when the vehicles are driven away in the very early morning. Because of the objections from local residents, the providers of sleeping accommodation are finding it more and more difficult to obtain planning permission for extension of these facilities.

The police are often reluctant to take steps to remove commercial vehicles from residential streets, on the basis that it is safer for the vehicles to be parked in these streets than on the main highway if there is no adequate off-street provision for the parking of these vehicles. There is also the problem of pilfering and stealing goods on vehicles left unattended on a carriageway. In 1970, the total number of cases of thefts from lorries in the Metropolitan Police District amounted to 4017 valued at £1,566,698. Whilst this was less than in 1969, the value and number of cases of robberies from vehicles left in streets rose slightly.

Therefore the situation is that the transport of goods by road is increasing, and if the weight of the load is not permitted to increase in the United Kingdom beyond its present limit of 32 tonnes (32 tons) gross, the proportion of heavy loads is likely to increase, and there is an increasing need for security arrangements to be available. In many towns and cities there is a real need for a programme co-ordinating lorry parks, overnight driver accommodation and catering facilities.

A lorry driver can lead a very lonely life, and when he stops for the night his need is to meet and be with people. He also needs to be near his lorry, so that he can make an early start the next morning, often before public transport is available. Parking on the street in a residential area may satisfy the driver's requirements, but this has the obvious disadvantages already referred to.

The site of a lorry park should have easy access to the motor road or trunk road network and avoid the traffic volumes in and near town centres. It should be near suitable overnight accommodation and not too far away from suitable social activities in the town. Unless these conditions can be satisfied it may be difficult to encourage drivers to use the facilities provided for overnight parking of lorries.

Local authorities faced with this problem should first examine the reasons for overnight parking in any particular area. Factors they should evaluate include the close proximity of docks, industrial areas, markets, etc.; lack of proper parking facilities; companies operating without sufficient depot space; non-availability of land for depots; lack of public transport to parking areas on outskirts for drivers who have to make an early start; lack of public transport in reverse direction for those who finish late at night; greater security if driver is near vehicle; peak hour loading bans which necessitate a driver coming overnight if he is to unload before they apply; increased number of vehicles having to park because of decreased drivers' hours; and drivers who have to stop to take statutory breaks.

Surface parking described in Chapter 9 will be the type most commonly used, but because of the great variation in size of goods vehicles it will not be possible to arrange a layout of standard parking stalls as for a car park. Nevertheless, an orderly arrangement for parking should be designed so as to give free ingress and egress for any vehicle at any time. Figure 14.1 shows heavy vehicles parked in an orderly manner in a park which is used as a car park during the day and a heavy vehicle park at night. The white lined layout is for the day-time parking of cars. The foundation and surfacing for a park used for heavy vehicles must have adequate strength to carry the heavy loads.

Fig. 14.1   Heavy commercial vehicle park at Marsh Barton, Exeter.

Security of parked commercial vehicles is of great importance, and an essential service that should be provided for lorry parks. A local authority may not be able to provide this service directly, but arrangements could be made with an agency to provide the security service or a partnership arrangement for the operation of the car park together with a security service.

The cost of providing and operating purpose designed lorry parks, together with a security service, should be recovered by the local authority by charging an economic parking fee. This is purely a commercial undertaking and no reason at all why an economic fee should not be charged.

In most cases there is a sound economic reason for parking a lorry. If it is to be prohibited on the road, then provision must be made off the road. Local authorities have been given powers to acquire land and provide parking facilities.

Perfection cannot be achieved overnight, and designated street parking places may be required in the short term, but one way or another convenient accommodation must be found before bans on street parking are introduced.

REFERENCES

1. 'Transport of Goods by Road', Report of a sample survey made in 1958. HMSO, London, 1959.
2. 'Transport for Industry', A study of the determinants of demand for transport in manufacturing industry conducted for the Ministry of Transport. HMSO, London, 1968.
3. DICKSON-SIMPSON, J. 'The Case for the Larger Lorry', *The Guardian*, 18th September, 1970.
4. 'Lorry Parking', Report of the Working Party on the Parking of Lorries. HMSO, London, 1971.

Chapter 15

Automatic Parking Equipment

The control of cars entering and leaving a car park is an operation for which automatic equipment may be used. There are several types of apparatus, from a simple ticket issuing machine to electronic equipment for the control of variable charges, which will meet the requirements of most car parks.

GODWIN WARREN AUTOMATIC PARKING SYSTEMS

The 'Fixed Charge' automatic equipment can control one or more entrances and exits. No fee paying tickets are issued but arrangements are made for admitting season ticket holders.

The equipment at the entrance consists of an electronic loop detector to open the barrier, a barrier unit, a red neon 'FULL' sign mounted on top of a pedestal, and an electronic detector to close the barrier after entry. At the exit the equipment consists of a 'Fixed Charge' coin machine (to which a season ticket acceptance unit may be fitted if required), a barrier unit, and an electronic loop detector. All this equipment may be erected on concrete plinths or on steel prefabricated island sections which are pre-wired, and ready for immediate use.

If required, the equipment can be arranged to operate for both season ticket holders and fee paying motorists. If reserved places are required for season ticket holders, a ticket unit at the entrance will allow season ticket holders to gain admittance to their reserved spaces even when the 'FULL' sign on the barrier pedestal is illuminated. At the exit the use of the season ticket raises the barrier arm, allowing free exit.

When the fee paying motorist enters the car park, he passes over a presence detector which automatically raises the barrier. When the vehicle has passed over the detector the barrier is automatically lowered.

Should cars be entering one immediately behind the other, the passage of following cars in front of the presence detector cancels the closing action set up by the previous vehicle, and the barrier only makes a 10° movement from the vertical for counting purposes. This arrangement allows motorists to enter in a continuous line with a minimum of delay.

On leaving the park, the fee paying motorist draws up in front of the coin machine, and having inserted the correct coinage, the barrier rises, permitting the vehicle to leave the park. After the vehicle has passed over the presence detector the barrier is automatically lowered into position.

Two counters are provided. One 'Add/Subtract' counter to register the number of stalls available at any time, and to control the entrance barrier and the 'FULL' signs, and one 'Total' counter for audit.

The Variable Charge Automatic Equipment is for use where charges are based on the length of parking time; it requires one attendant at each exit to collect the parking fees, and operate the barrier arm. Season ticket holders may also be accommodated.

At each entrance the equipment required is an electronic loop detector, automatic ticket issuer, barrier unit and 'FULL' sign, electronic loop detector to lower barrier and, if required, a season ticket acceptance unit.

Fig. 15.1   The Godwin Warren 'Variable Charge' equipment at entrance to car park. (*Reproduced by permission of Godwin Warren Engineering Ltd, Bristol, England.*)

Motorists who are season ticket holders insert a ticket in the season ticket acceptance unit when entering the car park, which is located before the ticket issuing machine at the entrance. This cancels the issue of a ticket and raises the barrier. Afterwards the arrangements are the same as for the Fixed Charge car parks.

When a fee paying motorist enters the car park a time and date stamped ticket is issued automatically from a ticket dispenser. The removal of this ticket raises the barrier. The vehicle enters the park and when it has passed over the presence detector the barrier is automatically lowered into position (Fig. 15.1). On leaving the park the motorist hands his ticket to the attendant who inserts it into a Ratell bench machine which records the fee due, gives change if required, and the barrier is raised by push button control. The counting arrangements are the same as for the Fixed Charge equipment (Fig. 15.2).

The Fully Automatic Variable Charge Computerised Equipment calculates the fee due, collects the money and gives change. It can be added to Fixed or Variable Charge equipment of any make. This replaces the need for an attendant.

When the motorist enters the car park he takes a conventional car parking ticket from a ticket dispenser and on the ticket a four figure code number is

Fig. 15.2   The Godwin Warren 'Variable Charge' equipment at exit from car park. (*Reproduced by permission of Godwin Warren Engineering Ltd, Bristol, England.*)

stamped. When the motorist drives to the exit he communicates his ticket number to a machine by pressing a series of proximity switches (Fig. 15.3). The machine displays the fee due, and on receipt of the money raises the barrier. Alternatively, when the motorist returns to the car park, he may pay whilst on foot, and the computer memory retains his number so as to open an exit barrier on pressing the same number on the switches at the exit within a permitted time. It is also possible to position two stations for payment from vehicles in one exit lane in series with a single barrier. Two motorists may thus pay at one time, and the machine regulates the barrier accordingly. A further variation enables a cashier to take the money and give change while the machine and coded tickets are used for fee calculation, audit control and, if required, actuating the exit barriers. There are facilities in all pay-from-vehicle machines for motorists who have lost their tickets to pay the maximum fee (Figs. 15.4(*a*), (*b*) and (*c*)).

A warning bell and light inform the supervisor if the supply of change is low (Fig. 15.5). If change runs out, or if the change dispenser fails to issue change for any reason, a 'No Change Given' sign replaces the 'Change Given' sign, and the rest of the system operates in the no change mode. A battery supplies the clock if there is a power failure, and the memory store of the computer remains

Fig. 15.3 The Godwin Warren 'Variable Charge' computerised equipment at exit from car park. (*Reproduced by permission of Godwin Warren Engineering Ltd, Bristol, England.*)

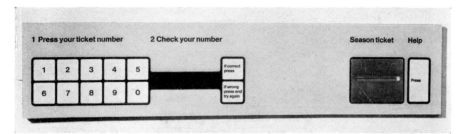

Fig. 15.4(*a*)   The Godwin Warren 'Variable Charge' computerised equipment operation panel at exit terminal. (*Reproduced by permission of Godwin Warren Engineering Ltd, Bristol, England.*)

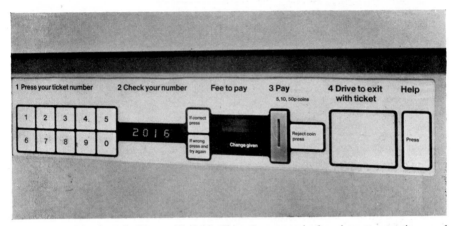

Fig. 15.4(*b*)   The Godwin Warren 'Variable Charge' computerised equipment operation panel when payment is on foot. (*Reproduced by permission of Godwin Warren Engineering Ltd, Bristol, England.*)

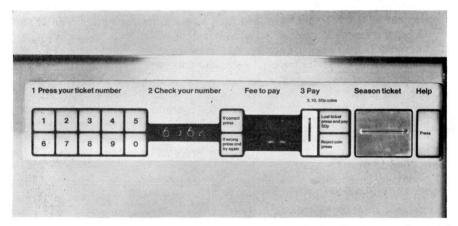

Fig. 15.4(*c*)   The Godwin Warren 'Variable Charge' computerised equipment operation panel when payment is from car. (*Reproduced by permission of Godwin Warren Engineering Ltd. Bristol, England.*)

Fig. 15.5   The Godwin Warren Control Panel. (*Reproduced by permission of Godwin Warren Engineering Ltd, Bristol, England.*)

intact. The tariff can be structured in any way in units of 5p, and units of one hour on a peg board. An audit counter shows the cumulative fees due for reconciliation with the cash collected, less the change used.

Fully automatic equipment has been developed for private parking systems which admits entry by using a forge-proof pass card or season ticket. The equipment at the entrance consists of a unit to raise the barrier arm when a valid ticket is inserted, a barrier pedestal complete with arm, and a loop detector to lower the barrier arm after entry. At the exit there is a loop detector to raise the barrier arm, a barrier pedestal complete with arm, and a loop detector to lower the barrier arm.

The unit at the entrance will allow ticket holders to gain admittance to a reserved area, and to leave by the automatic operation of the vehicle detectors.

The Rising Step Barrier rises from and lowers into the ground. By using rising steps in place of barrier arms, damage by vandals is prevented. The robust construction and absence of a barrier arm prevents unauthorised use of a car park (Fig. 15.6).

Another alternative to a barrier arm is a set of five hinged collapsible plates which are 114 mm ($4\frac{1}{2}$ in) high. They are depressed by the weight of a vehicle driven over them in the correct direction, but will resist a vehicle trying to enter in the wrong direction (Fig. 15.7).

The Godwin Warren Automatic Control Equipment is supplied by Godwin Warren Engineering Ltd, Emery Road, Bristol BS4 5PW, England.

Fig. 15.6 The Godwin Warren Rising Step Barrier. (*Reproduced by permission of Godwin Warren Engineering Ltd, Bristol, England.*)

METIOR SYSTEM OF AUTOMATIC PARKING

The Metior System of Automatic Parking consists of an assembly of mechanical and electronic units controlled from one central station. It is basically a fully automatic car parking system in which tokens are used for short period parking in place of the more usual ticket. Punched parking cards are used for long period parking.

Entry to the car park is halted by a barrier until the motorist (if parking for a short period) takes a coded token from the automatic machine or (if parking for a long period) has inserted his punched parking card in the card reader. The barrier opens, and remains open until the vehicle has passed.

Fig. 15.7 The Godwin Warren Collapsible Plate Barrier. (*Reproduced by permission of Godwin Warren Engineering Ltd, Bristol, England.*)

Fig. 15.8(*a*)   The pedestrian entrance to a car park controlled by the Metior System of automatic parking control. (*Reproduced by permission of Parking Systems Ltd, West Norwood, London.*)

Fig. 15.8(*b*)   The payment unit of the Metior System of automatic parking control. (*Reproduced by permission of Parking Systems Ltd, West Norwood, London.*)

When the short term parker returns to collect his vehicle he has to pass the payment point, where there is the payment unit and a bank-note exchanger which provides the required coins (Fig. 15.8c). The entry token is coded, the times of entry and exit are registered from it, and the amount to be paid is calculated. The motorist drops his entry token into the slot of the payment unit, and the amount due is flashed on the indicator. The motorist places the coins in the pay slot, and receives in return an exit token. The exit is closed by a barrier which opens after the motorist has inserted his exit token or his punched parking card.

The control panel is normally placed in the control room where it is manned

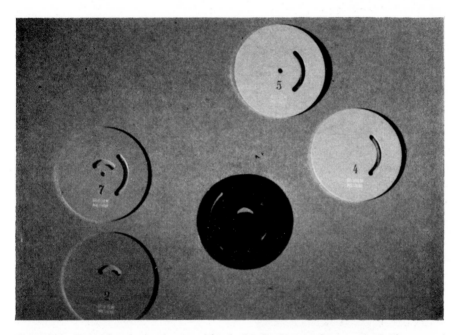

Fig. 15.8(c)   Examples of exit tokens used for the Metior System of automatic parking control. (*Reproduced by permission of Parking Systems Ltd, West Norwood, London.*)

by one person who supervises drive in, exit and payment points. The panel is provided with different alarm functions, and two-way voice contact is maintained between people at the automatic equipment and the controller. Television cameras give continuous inspection of primary points within the building (Fig. 15.9).

There is a recorder with the punched parking card reader on which is recorded the in and out time, and identity of the holder. There are two types of recorders, clear-text and puncher tape. The puncher tape records all data required for feeding to the data machine for use on invoices to the motorist. The tariff may be adjusted at the central control as required. Traffic is directed to and around the parking decks to vacant stalls by illuminated traffic signs. The directing devices may be fully or semi-automatically controlled.

Fig. 15.9(*a*)   External view of control room used at Skärholmen, Sweden, equipped with the Metior System of automatic parking control. (*Reproduced by permission of Parking Systems Ltd, West Norwood, London.*)

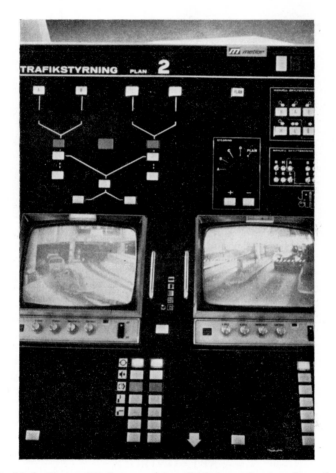

Fig. 15.9(*b*)   Metior System TV Screens used at Skärholmen, Sweden. (*Reproduced by permission of Parking Systems Ltd, West Norwood, London.*)

Fig. 15.9(c)   Metior System Control Panels used at Skärholmen, Sweden. (*Reproduced by permission of Parking Systems Ltd, West Norwood, London.*)

An alternative semi-automatic system may be substituted for the fully auto-matic. The entrance and exit controls would remain unchanged but a manual cashier would replace the automatic payment unit and bank-note exchanger.

This fully automatic equipment has been installed at Skärholmen, near Stockholm, Sweden.[1] Here a control tower has been built in which is housed the central control room. From this position the operator has uninterrupted visibility of the whole of the top deck, and the approach roads, and by closed circuit television of the lower decks, exit and entry points and payment stations. There are eleven entrances and exits to the car park which can accommodate 4000 cars.

This equipment is supplied by Parking Systems Ltd, West Norwood, London SE27.

APT CONTROLS

The equipment that is available under the trade name APT Controls consists of several units which may be installed in different combinations to give the type of control required for the operation of a car park.

The Auto Parking Gate unit consists of a steel pedestal which contains a small electric motor, and a thermostatically controlled heater to assure opera-tions under any weather conditions. The gate area is 0·9 m (36 in) high and 2·43 m (8 ft 0 in) long or any other length as required. The unit is designed to operate with other control units in the system, or direct control of the gate can be made with simple 'up' and 'down' switches (Fig. 15.10).

The Multiple Coin Unit can be used with one, two, three or four coins of different value, season tickets or tokens. It is housed in a steel case, and the mechanism to accept or reject coinage is entirely separate from the cash vault. A heater is built in. The motorist can operate the unit without moving from the driving seat. A coin return button allows all money to be recovered by the motorist up to the time of final acceptance by the unit.

The Ticket Dispenser and Synchronised Out Clock are available in both computing and non-computing models. This unit is placed at the entrance to the car park, and there is no need for an attendant. The computing dispenser issues tickets showing day, hour, minute and a rate line (in red) which indicates

Fig. 15.10 The APT Automatic Parking Gate Unit. (*Reproduced by permission of APT Controls Ltd, London.*)

parking charge when stamped (in blue) by the synchronised companion Out Clock. The non-computing dispenser issues tickets showing hour, minute, month and day at time of entrance, and the Out Clock imprints the same data at time of exit. The cashier at the exit computes the charge.

The Paymatic Fully Automatic Parking System is designed to enable a car park with any number of entries and exits to operate on a variable charge basis, completely unattended. The system allows for the charge to be varied according to the time of day or day of the week, and to collect the exact amount due, irrespective of the length of stay, up to a maximum of 80 days.

The motorist on entering the car park will pass over a detector which will sense the presence of the vehicle, and cause a ticket to be issued by the automatic ticket dispenser. The ticket will have the time and date of issue in figures, and in a specially designed punched hole code. The entry barrier will raise automatically as the ticket is taken.

When the motorist wishes to leave the car park he takes his ticket to any one of several reader units which are situate at convenient points within the car park. The code punched is a double symmetrical form permitting the ticket to be inserted either side up, and either end first. On inserting the ticket the total parking fee due will be indicated on an illuminated panel; on payment, a second ticket is automatically issued, which is valid for 15 minutes to enable the motorist to collect his car and proceed to an exit gate. At the exit the motorist will insert

Fig. 15.11　A control panel used with the Paymatic fully automatic parking system. (*Reproduced by permission of APT Controls Ltd, London.*)

the ticket into a second reader unit and, providing he is within the 15 minutes period, the gate will open. If it is outside this period, but within 30 minutes of the ticket being issued, then the reader instructs a coin unit, also in the exit reader, to open the gate, provided a penalty fee is inserted. Should the motorist be over 30 minutes late or be attempting to exit with an entry ticket, the ticket is returned to him and he has to return to a payment station. His ticket is then re-read, and a further charge made on the basis of the time elapsed, and a second exit ticket is issued to him. Should a queue occur at an exit point which would cause the motorist to incur a penalty through no fault of his own, a detector situated in the exit lane will sense the queue and extend the fee exit period in incremental steps equal to the length of time the loop is occupied by a stationary vehicle (Fig. 15.11).

Whilst a punch card method of operation is described, the system is suitable for operation with any form of impression on the ticket such as magnetic characters, optical recognition or any other such method.

APT Controls are supplied by APT Controls Ltd, 77-81 Scrubbs Lane, London NW10.

VENNER PARKING CONTROL EQUIPMENT

The simplest piece of automatic control equipment for car parks is the movable barrier arm. The equipment manufactured by 'Venner' is known as the Venner Parking Gate Console. The barrier arm and console are sited at the entrance and exit of the car park to control the passage of vehicles entering and leaving. It is suitable for use on open or covered sites under widely varying climatic and atmospheric conditions. The weatherproof case of the console is fitted with a thermostatically controlled heater, which prevents dewing and maintains an optimum working temperature.

The barrier is normally at rest in the horizontal position across the service road, and can be operated by any one of five different methods.

(a) by the driver of a vehicle taking a time and date stamped ticket from an automatic ticket dispenser;

(b) by the insertion of a coin into a coin mechanism;

(c) by inserting a season ticket into a scanner;

(d) by the insertion of a key into a key switch;

(e) by an attendant manually operating a push-button.

With the exception of (e) all operations can be performed by a driver of a vehicle from the driving seat.

When actuated by any of the five methods, the barrier arm rises to the vertical position which permits the passage of a vehicle. The barrier arm then automatically returns to the horizontal position as the vehicle passes a specified safe distance beyond the console. The time taken for the barrier to move from the horizontal to the vertical or vice versa is two seconds (Fig. 15.12).

The barrier arm is driven by a 0·37 kW ($\frac{1}{2}$ hp) motor through a gear box to a crank motion, and the motor drive may be made to reverse direction immediately.

The Venner Automatic Ticket Dispenser is suitable for use on open or covered sites, the case being waterproof and fitted with an internal heater which maintains the tickets in a dry condition. The usual position for a ticket dispenser is at the entrance to a car park in advance of the automatic barrier. As the car approaches, its presence is detected electronically, and the ticket dispenser issues a time and date stamped ticket which remains half protruding from the slot. The motorist, from his normal driving position, withdraws and retains the ticket. Whilst the ticket remains protruding from the slot, a bell rings and a

Fig. 15.12 The Venner Gate Console and Barrier Arm. (*Reproduced by permission of AMF International Ltd, Venner Division, New Malden, Surrey, England.*)

flashing sign reading 'TAKE TICKET' operates automatically. The action of taking the ticket causes the automatic barrier to rise and permits entry to the car park.

When the vehicle is at a safe distance beyond the entrance, the barrier automatically descends to the horizontal position. This is accomplished as the passage of the vehicle is detected by an electronic controller. Should a car stop under the barrier, the barrier will not descend, but will remain up until the vehicle has moved sufficiently forward to operate the 'closing' mechanism.

When there is a stream of cars at close intervals, the barrier descends as each car traverses the 'closing' mechanism, but immediately reverts to the vertical as each following motorist takes a ticket. This gives a rate of entry to the car park of 10 cars per minute. If a motorist in a stream of cars attempts to enter without taking a ticket, the barrier will descend in front of him, and this prevents illicit entry.

The capacity of this machine is 5000 tickets, and it is usually reloaded with a pack of 2000 tickets.

The Venner Automatic Cointroller Unit is a coin operated mechanism which closes an electrical switch when the appropriate coin or coins are inserted. From this initial operation, a sequence of electrical switchings is produced making the Cointroller suitable for controlling automatic parking barriers. This equipment would normally be sited at the car park entrance and used to operate the barrier. On inserting the specified coinage, the barrier rises to permit entry, and when the vehicle has proceeded to the predetermined 'clear' point, the barrier returns automatically behind the car to the closed horizontal position.

On leaving the car park, the motorist proceeds to the exit barrier passing over the concealed 'sensing' loop which detects electronically the approaching vehicle, and automatically raises the barrier. When the car has passed the 'clear' point, the barrier returns to the horizontal position and the exit is automatically closed.

This equipment may be supplied for (a) a fixed tariff, (b) variable tariff (mechanical), and (c) variable tariff (electrical). The fixed tariff Cointroller has a simple mechanical action, and is normally supplied to operate on a single coin either 2·5p, 5p or 10p, but may also be supplied for dual coin operation, e.g. $2 \times 2·5p$, $1 \times 5p$, $2 \times 5p$, or a 10p piece. The mechanism of this unit caters for a 'fixed tariff' only. If tariff alterations are required, the mechanism has to be changed.

The variable tariff Cointroller (mechanical) may be adjusted on site by changing the position of the thumb screw to cater for any tariff from 2·5p to 62·5p in 2·5p steps, no extra parts being required. The coin slot will accept 2·5 p, 5p and 10p pieces, and any combination of these coins may be used to satisfy the required tariff.

The variable tariff Cointroller (electrical) has exactly the same coin accepter characteristics, and performs the same function as the mechanical unit, but the tariff may be changed at any time as desired by the operation of an electrical change-over switch (Fig. 15.13).

When season ticket facilities are required in addition to fixed or variable tariff systems, or are to be used by themselves to control parking gates, a Card Controller will give these facilities.

The system operates by issuing each contract parker with a specially coded plastic card, which he retains for the period of his contract. When the motorist arrives at the entrance to the car park he inserts his card into the slot in the front of the Entry Card Controller. If the card is correct and in current use the entry gate will open and will automatically close again when the vehicle has entered. When leaving the park, the motorist inserts his card into the Exit Card Controller, and the gate will open, closing again when the vehicle has left. If the card is not correct the gate will not open (Fig. 15.14).

The Venner Cashier's Clock is housed in a heavy gauge metal case. The unit is electrically powered by a synchronous motor, and being mains frequency controlled will keep perfect timing under normal weather conditions. The unit is normally sited in the attendant's kiosk adjacent to the 'exit' barrier of an automatically controlled car park. The timing mechanism is synchronised by setting it to the same time as the 'ticket dispenser' clock at the entrance to the

Fig. 15.13   The Venner Automatic Cointroller Unit. (*Reproduced by permission of AMF International Ltd, Venner Division, New Malden, Surrey, England.*)

car park where a time/date stamped ticket is automatically issued to gain access to the park. On exit the motorist surrenders his parking ticket to the attendant who inserts it into his Cashier's Clock for franking. The action of feeding the ticket between the guides automatically activates the date/time stamp which prints out immediately above the 'entry' stamp so that an audit check of the amount chargeable is readily available (Fig. 15.15).

It is helpful to know the number of stalls that are vacant in a car park, and when the car park is full. This information can be made available by a differential

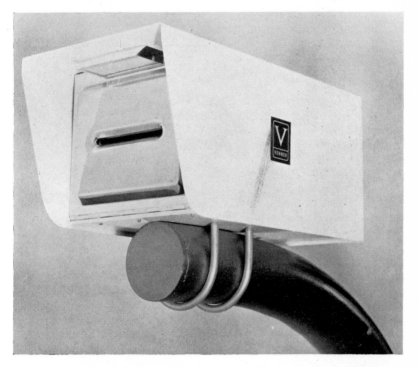

Fig. 15.14   The Venner Card Control Unit. (*Reproduced by permission of AMF International Ltd, Venner Division, New Malden, Surrey, England.*)

counter which is an electro-mechanical machine. Impulses are fed to the counter from the entrance and exit as vehicles enter and leave the car park. A vehicle entering subtracts one digit, and a vehicle leaving adds one digit. The counter is pre-set to the maximum number of parking stalls available. When all these stalls are filled, a micro-switch on the counter operates a relay which locks the entrance gate and ticket dispenser, and switches on the illuminated 'PARK FULL' sign. This effectively prevents any cars entering the park. When a car leaves the park and a stall is made available, the sign is switched off automatically, and all the mechanism is operable (Fig. 15.16).

This equipment is manufactured and supplied by AMF International Ltd, Venner Division, New Malden, Surrey, England.

Fig. 15.15 The Venner Cashier's Clock with Simplex Ratell Dial. (*Reproduced by permission of AMF International Ltd, Venner Division, New Malden, Surrey, England.*)

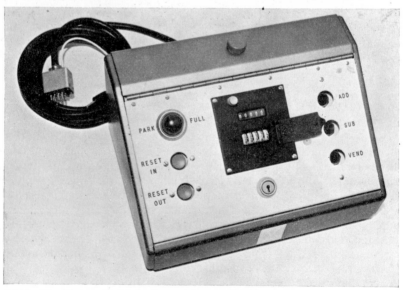

Fig. 15.16 The Venner Cashier's Control Box and Differential Counter. (*Reproduced by permission of AMF International Ltd, Venner Division, New Malden, Surrey, England.*)

PARCOA AUTOMATIC PARKING EQUIPMENT

This equipment is designed for the control of unattended surface car parks and the partial control of multi-level car parks. The equipment includes the following units:

The Gate Control Unit consists of a continental type level crossing gate, together with the control mechanism housed in a pressed steel casing. The housings are weatherproof, and the front and rear panels are easily removable for servicing and maintenance.

The opening or closing may be initiated in several ways by a separate unit such as coin or token mechanism—card key lock, time dated ticket dispenser—treadle—detector coil or remote control. As the car approaches the barrier one

Fig. 15.17   The Parcoa fully automatic single two-way gate system at Jodrell Bank, Cheshire. Entrance is by means of security pass key, and exit is free. (*Reproduced by permission of Parking Developments Ltd, London.*)

piece of the above mechanism is brought into operation either by inserting a coin or taking a ticket from a dispenser, or some other action, which actuates the gate mechanism, allowing the car to proceed to the car park. As the vehicle passes over a second treadle in the drive, the gate closes automatically and is set for the next car. A reversing model gate will reverse rotation instantly if an opening signal is received whilst the barrier is in the closing cycle. This feature saves time when there is a continuous line of cars waiting to enter the car park.

The gate unit can be supplied with a folding barrier arm for use in inside car parks with restricted ceiling heights (Fig. 15.17).

The coin unit is suitable for fixed charge car parks. It will accept single coins or up to three different ones making up the appropriate parking charge. The insertion of the coins automatically operates the gate unit. To accommodate contract customers a card key lock may be incorporated in the unit. The card key is a flat plastic magnetically coded card which, when inserted in the appropriate slot, operates the card key lock, and automatically opens the gate.

When the attendant removes the cash vault from the coin unit, it automatically locks and the vault can only be opened by a special four-way key (Fig. 15.18).

The Time-Dated Ticket Dispenser has been developed for variable charge parking, and is used in conjunction with an attendant at the exit. The incoming vehicles activate a detector which, in turn, illuminates the 'TAKE TICKET' sign and sounds a buzzer. The ticket is then automatically issued, bearing the precise time and date of arrival at the car park. The removal of the ticket from the dispenser causes the gate arm to rise automatically. When a motorist is

Fig. 15.18   The Parcoa Coin Unit. (*Reproduced by permission of Parking Developments Ltd, London.*)

ready to leave, the cashier at the exit records expired time, and collects the correct charge. When tickets in the magazine reach a low level, the 'LOW LEVEL' light is switched on or off depending on the operator's preference, and remains on or off until the supply of tickets is increased. An 'Empty' buzzer signal is given when the magazine runs out of tickets. A hinged door, with lock, is located in the lower section of the unit for access to the ticket magazine and control panel (Fig. 15.19).

A ticket issuing system has been designed for a 'free parking' service in conjunction with local merchants. The same procedure is used as for the Time-Dated Ticket Dispenser. The motorist automatically receives a ticket which he exchanges at a shop or theatre for a free exit token. If the car owner fails to visit the shop or theatre he must pay for parking by inserting a coin (or coins) in place of a token in the coin unit at the exit gate.

The Capacity Counter is used in conjunction with each of the above units. It gives a complete control of capacity in the car park. The unit will not allow any more cars to enter than there are stalls. Each operation is automatically counted, and when the car park is full it illuminates a 'FULL' sign at the entrance, and will not allow any further entries until it is relieved by the exit of a car through the exit gates.

The Control Console may be used with the Time-Dated Ticket Dispenser. It is normally housed in the attendant's kiosk, and is the co-ordinating centre

Fig. 15.19   The Parcoa Time Dated Ticket Dispenser and Season Ticket Unit. (*Reproduced by permission of Parking Developments Ltd, London.*)

for all physical controls, and provides for comprehensive auditing and accounting.

A 'Ticket Low' light indicates that the supply of tickets in the ticket dispenser needs replenishment. The 'ticket issue counter' records the number of tickets issued by the ticket dispenser; the ticket issue button enables the ticket dispenser to be operated manually by the attendant should a vehicle fail to actuate the necessary signal; the 'season in' and 'season out' counters record the number of 'card key lock' operations in and out respectively. The capacity counter and 'PARK FULL' light provides electronic computation of vehicles entering and leaving the park.

The Parcoa equipment is supplied by Parking Developments Ltd, Kent House, Market Place, London W1.

AUTOMATIC TICKET ISSUING MACHINES (Fig. 15.20)

There is a need for a simple and inexpensive means of controlling parking on small car parks in cities and towns. If there is no parking control of these sites they are quickly filled by commuters' cars; manual control is too costly for the small amount of income received and the normal automatic equipment used for larger car parks is also too costly and cannot be justified.

Fig. 15.20   The Automatic Ticket Issuing Machine (Mains Operated). (*Reproduced by permission of Automaticket Ltd, London.*)

The Automaticket Parking Control System consists of an automatic ticket issuing machine which is usually erected near the entrance or other suitable position in a small car park. On inserting the correct coin value into the machine a car parking ticket is automatically delivered, stamped with the time and date of issue. There is an adhesive section of the ticket so that it can be displayed on the car windscreen. This enables the traffic warden or attendant to observe the essential information such as parking time and the date. This machine can be used to control special car parking areas for residents.

This machine is known as the Autoslot Ticket Parking Machine, and is provided with three coin entry points of different values to provide for the maximum flexibility, and the elimination of change giving problems. It is designed to receive coins in any combination and any quantity up to a pre-determined amount. The coins are received through electric checking devices and are held in temporary suspension until the correct value has been inserted into the machine.

Fig. 15.21   The Universal Ticket Issuing Parking Meter. (*Reproduced by permission of Universal Parking Meter Co. Ltd, Tonbridge, Kent.*)

The machine is loaded with 1000 tickets, and the number used is indicated externally. If this reading is ignored a warning light will show when 60% of the supply has been used. If for any reason the machine is allowed to exhaust its supply of tickets it will refuse to accept coinage. Temporary failure of the electricity supply will not affect this equipment as it is operated on 24 volt batteries. These are on charge at all times.

The installation of this type of parking control equipment is subject to the regulations and procedure as for other traffic orders (Reference 5, Chapter 5).

This equipment is manufactured by Automaticket Ltd, 197, Wardour Street, London W1.

The Universal Ticket Issuing Parking Meter (Fig. 15.21) has been designed to provide a means of controlling 20 or 30 parking stalls from one machine. It is housed in a welded steel case 0·685 m (2 ft 3 in) × 0·254 m (10 in) × 0·324 m (12¾ in) and is fixed on one or two vertical poles at a convenient height for use by the motorist from the car seat or as a pedestrian. The mechanism and time stamp may be removed from the case quickly and another one inserted.

The mechanism has a basic frame supporting the coin system, a paper supply roll and a paper delivery system. Inside there is a printing solenoid which operates the hammer of the movement when it is in position, and prints the ticket before delivery. There is a single coin rejector, and a coin guideway which delivers the

Fig. 15.22   The ticket issued from the Universal Ticket Issuing Parking Meter. (*Reproduced by permission of Universal Parking Meter Co. Ltd, Tonbridge, Kent.*)

coin past the rotary micro-switch, and then to a coin box. The momentary closing of the micro-switch causes the relay on the relay board to close, and to initiate the cycle which prints the ticket by means of the solenoid, and then ejects the ticket beneath the two rubber rollers. When the ticket is ejected the mechanism switches off ready for the next cycle. Should a failure occur, an overload device at the back of the machine closes down the machine until it receives attention, and re-set by pressing the re-set button. In the event of failure, or power supply failure, the coin slot at the front of the case automatically closes, and a green pilot light goes out.

On the ticket are two peelable adhesive strips of which one may be removed to attach the ticket to the windscreen. The first figure on the ticket (Fig. 15.22) denotes the number of the week from 1 to 52, the second character is the abbreviation for the day of the week, followed by the large hour figure and small minute figure. Other information may be printed on the ticket such as the name of the car park, but it is advisable to keep additional information to a minimum so that the time stamp shows up clearly for examination. This equipment is supplied by the Universal Parking Meter Co. Ltd, Vale Road, Tonbridge, Kent, England.

The automatic parking equipment described in this chapter is a selection of the type of equipment that is available. There are other firms who manufacture similar equipment in other countries.

Names of firms who supply parking control equipment:

Western Industries, Inc,
3742 West 36th Place,
Chicago, Illinois, USA

Davis Controls Ltd,
4251 Dundas Street,
West, Toronto, Ontario, Canada

Communication Systems Ltd,
20, Eastbourne Terrace,
London W2

J. Simpson & Son Ltd,
Moreton Works,
Luton, Bedfordshire, England

Simplex Time Recorder Co. Ltd,
57–59, Clifton Street,
London EC2

Auto Parks, Inc,
762 Lancaster Pike,
Devon, PA, USA

Fisher-Karpark Ltd,
Brearley Works,
Luddendenfoot, Halifax, Yorkshire, England

Automatic Parking Devices, Inc,
16422 W. McNichols Road,
Detroit, Michigan, USA

Cincinnati Time Recorder Co.,
1733 Central Avenue,
Cincinnati, Ohio, USA

Card Key Systems, Inc,
5930 West Jefferson Boulevard,
Los Angeles, California, USA

REFERENCE

1. GLANVILLE, JOHN. 'Lessons from Skärholmen', *Highways and Traffic Engineering*, October 1970.

Chapter 16

Car Parking for Special Events

Special events such as exhibitions, agricultural shows and football matches create a special car parking problem. These events may be held once per week or even once per year and at that time will need a very large area of land temporarily for car and coach parking. It is essential that the land should be available when required for car parking and some other use found at other times.

A major agricultural show, exhibition or sports event in Great Britain probably attracts more cars in a single day than any other event. Since the Second World War, the provision of suitable car parking arrangements has become a major problem, and each year the demand for parking space increases in approximately the same proportions as the number of cars licensed.

Pre-planning and good organisation are essential if traffic is to flow freely, and continuously. Experience shows that in the years immediately after the war, when petrol was rationed and the number of cars on the roads was not more than a quarter of the number in 1970, there were serious traffic jams on the roads leading to show and exhibition grounds, and sometimes chaotic conditions were created through inexperience and an absence of planning. Fifty years ago it was only necessary to provide the site for the show or exhibition, but today provision may have to be made for the parking of 15,000–20,000 cars at one time. This number of cars requires 30–40 ha (75–100 acres) of reasonably flat land for use as car parks, which is often difficult to find within a reasonable distance of a show or exhibition ground.

The following are important points which should be observed when planning car parking facilities:

1. If possible the car parks should be situated on two, three or four sides of the showground, so that the police, the Automobile Association and Royal Automobile Club patrols, can route the cars coming from all directions in such a manner as to prevent the lines of traffic crossing.
2. The site of the show or exhibition should, if possible, be surrounded by roads.
3. The entrances to the car parks should be at least 12·0 m (40 ft) to 15·0 m (50 ft) wide, so that traffic can be taken off the roads into the car park at the maximum speed.

4. Three, four, or even five separate lanes should run from the entrance into the car parks to a length of 18·0 m (60 ft).
5. The parking fee should be taken at the end of the lane, and not at the entrance to the field. This method avoids delay in parking cars caused by collecting fees. As soon as one lane is filled, cars are run into the next lane, and thus a continuous movement of cars into the car park is maintained.
6. In wet weather, the place where the ground becomes churned up most is at the entrances to the car parks. This may become so bad that cars cannot move under their own power. It is wise to construct a tarmacadam apron from the road through the entrance and extend it a distance of 9·0 m (30 ft) into the car park.
7. If the car park is large and can serve traffic coming in two directions, it is wise to have two entrances into the field so that traffic coming from two directions can enter the car park without joining or crossing another line of traffic. This is important.
8. Once cars are in the park they must be parked quickly to a clearly defined plan. There are firms with wide experience in large scale car parking, and it is wise to arrange for one of the specialist firms to undertake this work.
9. It is essential that the car parking firm should provide sufficient staff to ensure that cars are parked as quickly as they arrive at peak periods. Shortage of staff will defeat any organisation.
10. It should be remembered that the aim of the organisers of the show or exhibition should be to get the visitors travelling by car into the car park quickly, and then from the car park to the entrance of the show in the shortest possible time.

If these suggestions are carried out, coupled with the co-operation of the Police and the Motoring Associations, it should not be difficult to maintain an even flow of traffic, which is essential for large scale parking.

It is not always possible to get sufficient land for car parks adjacent to a showground. This was the experience when the Bath and West and Southern Counties Society held their show in Exeter in 1954. An area of level land was found approximately 2·5 km to 3·0 km (1½ to 2 miles) from the showground, to which traffic from the east was directed. The local transport department arranged a shuttle service of buses to run throughout the period of the show, from the car park to the showground entrance. On leaving their cars in the car park, visitors boarded the buses, and were driven free of charge direct to the main entrance. It should be emphasised that the buses should not be kept waiting until they are full. It is most annoying to have to wait an indefinite time near the end of a journey. This new departure received great praise from the motorists using the car park, so much so that motorists coming from other directions tried to use the car park served by a shuttle service of buses.

Another innovation was introduced when the same Society held a show in Plymouth in 1958, before the bridge over the River Tamar was built. People from Cornwall could only reach the show by the Torpoint Ferry, or by road via Tavistock, which was a detour of 48·0 km (30 miles). Torpoint Ferry could not cope with the increased volume of traffic caused by the show, and if all the traffic from Cornwall had to pass through Tavistock it would cause traffic blocks in that town. Arrangements were made for the Society to have its own private ferry service, and three ferry boats were obtained from a local firm.

Playing fields at Torpoint were used as a car park, from which visitors were transported by a shuttle service of buses to the Torpoint Ferry. Here they boarded one of the three ferry boats, and were taken across the river to Devonport. On arriving at Devonport, another shuttle service of buses was available to transport passengers direct to the main entrance of the show. The time taken

Fig. 16.1   Aerial view of car parking arrangements for a race meeting at Cheltenham Racecourse, England. (*Reproduced by permission of National Car Parks Ltd, London.*)

to reach the showground from the Torpoint car park was exactly 15 minutes. This service cost the Society approximately £800. It is thought that this facility encouraged many more people to attend the show from Cornwall, and was a great relief to the traffic in Tavistock.

Although the number of cars on the roads is increasing, the traffic to shows and other similar events can be dealt with efficiently provided an efficient organisation is set up to deal with it. The main object should be to get visitors to the showground suffering from as little fatigue as possible. For those travelling by car it is necessary that they should be able to park their cars as quickly as possible and get into the showground with a minimum delay. At the end of the day they should be able to get into their cars and be on their way home as quickly as possible.

Football matches and similar events present a special problem. They draw very large numbers of people together for a very short period. Usually parking spreads over a large area, including official private car parks, spare land, roads and streets as far as the police will allow. A fortunate arrangement, if it can be made, is to use parking space that is used during normal working hours and vacant at other times, otherwise the cost of providing sufficient off-street parking could be quite prohibitive.

There are firms available who have the experience and trained staff who will undertake the planning, organisation and staffing of car parking arrangements for all kinds of exhibitions, golf tournaments, sporting events, agricultural shows, race meetings, etc. These firms have mobile teams and can undertake this work anywhere in the country.

Chapter 17

Security on Car Parks

Security on car parks is of vital and equal importance for the motorist and the management. The term security is interpreted in its widest sense, ranging from petty pilfering, to frauds of magnitude; it also includes auditing and even cleanliness, tidiness and politeness. It may be thought that the latter items would not come within the scope of security, but dirtiness, untidiness and rudeness are in fact the beginning of crime and if not stopped at the outset will certainly develop into increased laxity and eventually crime.

The regular police force has little or no power over the standards and morals of the people, and in the normal course of their duty do not patrol private premises. Experience indicates that the maintenance of security in car parks is an important factor, and is the responsibility of the management. Therefore in order to fulfil this responsibility the management need people who have experience of criminal investigation and have had a specialised CID training. Ex police officers who have had this particular type of experience are most suitable people to undertake this work. They know the organisation and methods used in the police force, and are able to promote liaison with the police, local government and airport authorities. In this way much crime is prevented and detected. The primary object of a private security organisation must be the same as that of a regular police force, *viz*. the prevention and detection of crime.

Many are the cases where people concerned with parking cars have learned, too late and by costly experience, of the dangers involved. There are, however, still many motorists who seek out a parking place on a piece of spare ground or on grass verges, in the wrong belief that they will save money. Whilst they save a parking fee they may find their cars have been damaged by unknown persons. There are many ways of committing a crime concerned with the parking of cars. Money is the only commodity transacted, and when an attendant is under pressure due to a heavy flow of traffic to and from the car park, money is sometimes handled very quickly. Added to this is the protection of a constant flow of cars which are a valuable asset. The temptations are enormous and constant.

Considerable sums of money may be spent in repairs to equipment in car parks damaged by vandals. This often includes safe breaking, lighting a fire in the car park and burning furniture, smashing windows, destroying confidential papers, damaging ticket machines and other automatic equipment, tearing down electrical wiring, breaking switches and starter panels, smashing equipment in toilets and breaking into lifts.

Security officers cannot keep all car parks under observation at all times, but the knowledge that a car park is watched by a security force is sufficient to deter vandals, and the cost of repairs to equipment and buildings can be reduced considerably.

It is usual practice for a car park proprietor to state that no responsibility can be accepted for losses or damage to cars and other personal property, but there is a moral onus on the proprietor to provide a service which will substantially prevent the possibility of this loss or damage and detect those responsible. This is essential for good relationship with the motorist, and to establish confidence that his car is reasonably secure when parked in a fee paying car park. The knowledge that a car is covered by an independent security service must attract business and give satisfaction to the motorist who uses the car park. Where there is little or no security service, serious troubles arise, both for the motorist and the proprietor of any car park. It is only by the most strict expert control that the motorist can be assured of a genuine effort to guard and protect what is usually to him a very valuable possession. Much of this responsibility falls on the car parking managers and staff, but their day to day responsibilities and frequent peak pressures are such that carelessness can creep in and crime begins to grow. Without proper security these matters can become so serious as to be the downfall of those responsible for certain car parking operations. Proprietors try to keep parking fees as low as possible, and the cost of a security service may be omitted for economic reasons, but by economising in this way the danger of loss or damage or theft can increase and prove the policy to be false.

It is known that theft of, or from, cars, and damage to vehicles on car parks is substantially less than with those left unattended on the street, but this should not be looked upon with complacency. When it does occur on a car park it should be investigated by the security service with the co-operation of the police, which will often prevent further larcenies. When immediate action is taken in this way a series of petty or major thefts become virtually unknown.

Even the motorist cannot always be trusted. Small tips to attendants for little favours received, tend to lead to other favours, such as not paying the correct fee, which tempts both parties (motorist and attendant) into committing what is really a conspiracy to defraud.

There is often a tendency to allow large sums of money to accumulate on car parks or in offices. This can and must be avoided. Routine visits to the banks, collection of monies from various parks and retaining in offices or even small safes, needs to be watched regularly and varied.

Over the years more and more involved machinery and electrical systems for recording times and numbers of vehicles on car parks have been introduced, each new idea being better than the previous one, but no perfect instrument has yet been introduced which can properly control the human element handling these systems. Barrier equipment, automatic counting machines (independent of the barriers), numbered tickets with time and date stamps of entry and exit, railings, fences and even multi-storey car parks specially designed for security, have all in their turn revealed weaknesses from the security angle. Barriers have been crashed, or found to be too short, thereby allowing cars to bypass them, breakdown of mechanical and electrical equipment allows for barriers to be hand operated, which, though necessary, introduces additional temptations to the attendant to record incorrect receipts. Jamming and electrical breakdowns of ticket machines occur frequently, thereby producing a wastage of tickets with dangerous consequences. Gaps in fences are created on surface car parks, allowing entry and exit to those not desiring to pay the official charge, and there is always the one person who waits until the attendant has gone home before retrieving his car from the car park. Time sheets, car record sheets showing details of vehicles on any park, forms showing number of tickets issued and monies paid, should also be closely scrutinised with the many other problems of security. Season ticket holders too frequently park their own cars and then hand their season ticket to another person to use unlawfully. Vandalism and wanton damage are also kept at a low level by liaison between the security officers and the police.

The motorist will often challenge the accuracy of his time of entry, exit or the change given to him. Frequently these matters may be due to mechanical or human error; on the other hand, these disputes may be deliberate attempts to avoid proper payment, or of being overcharged. All these complaints can be independently investigated, resulting in firm action being taken when necessary.

Official auditors and accountants are never really satisfied with explanations of genuine breakdowns, whether they be mechanical or human error. Attendants are not usually well established businessmen, or indeed, persons with considerable clerical experience, and genuine mistakes are bound to arise. Nevertheless, it is necessary for a security service to distinguish between mis-appropriation and genuine error. The motorist does not readily appreciate this and invariably claims he has been defrauded. Here again, experienced security officers are able to decide after investigation what action is necessary. The angry motorist is invariably satisfied when the result of a full investigation has been explained to him. He then realises that security is as much for his benefit as that of the proprietor or public authority. Much has been said about the devil the motorist becomes in matters appertaining to his car. He is a much oppressed person and it takes very little to make him really aggravated, and it is proper to say that he has a right to the best security possible.

The whole aspect of car parking for outside events, such as temporary shows, functions and certain race meetings, where space is allocated for car parking, creates very special problems for security. Here, of course, all the technical equipment of barriers, ticket machines, counting devices, etc., as used on sophisticated multi-storey car parks, cannot be used for obvious reasons. Frequently these areas can only be temporarily roped off, which again provides specific problems. Visual counts of cars present and checks on tickets issued and monies received, are all important. The very nature of any temporary operation brings about dangers and difficulties which have to be overcome. Quite frequently the organisers of these parking arrangements take their own staff by transport to sites all over the country to operate the outside events parking system. It is an expensive item, but for security purposes, very necessary.

Closed circuit television cameras and similar equipment for security purposes on car parks have not yet proved to be very practical, particularly on multi-storey car parks. Lorry parks are becoming more and more an established feature of the parking operations and it surely will not be long before security will find it necessary to employ these methods in preventing and detecting crime. Special alarm systems and guard dogs would also be necessary to complete security in this field, but the day has yet to come where a lorry parking scheme includes insurance of a valuable cargo and road transport.

A security service must be entirely independent in its approach to its work. The officers are not only detectives capable of doing the fullest investigation, but should be extremely knowledgeable on audits and accounts, taking inquiries into these aspects much further than the auditor or accountant. Once established this sort of investigation reveals mostly petty cases but there can be no doubt that if not discovered early, those cases of petty pilfering become enormous frauds and thefts. It may be that some authorities may not wish to employ security officers directly on their staff and would prefer to engage a firm experienced in this work.

Just as car parking has become part of our daily lives, unquestionably the future will bring about tremendous increases in the problems, and any security service will have to expand to cope with the situation.

Chapter 18

Parking Economics

The motorist has no legal right to park his car on the highway except where certain parts of the highway have been set apart for that purpose. This is not a new law. We can read about coach drivers of the last century being reminded that the Queen's Highway was not a stable yard. Parking on the highway is a privilege which has been conceded over the years when it caused little interference with the main function of the road, *viz.*, the passage of moving traffic. For most roads in central areas of towns the full width of the road is now required for its main function, and it is necessary to withdraw the privilege.

In 1936, the Chancellor of the Exchequer in the United Kingdom, announced that the Road Fund was no longer to receive as a right the bulk of the proceeds of motor vehicle taxation, but the whole of the tax, as well as the fuel tax, was to be paid into the Exchequer, and grants would be voted annually to the Road Fund through the Civil Estimates according to its requirements. This statement made it quite clear that motoring taxes were to form part of the general taxation. The Road Fund was finally abolished in 1955. As with beer, wines and spirits, there is no claim for the revenue derived from the taxation to be spent on hotels and public houses, so with motor taxation there is no claim for it to be spent of roads and car parks.

In spite of this statement, the motorist and many people connected with motoring still compare the taxes they pay by virtue of being a motorist with the service they receive in using roads and parking facilities. A car at a purchase price of £1000 giving 30 miles per gallon of petrol consumed, and an average annual mileage of 10,000, may be taken as a fair example. The purchase tax will be £250 which, spread over a seven year life, equals £36 per annum. The petrol tax is 23p (4/6d) per gallon, and 333 gallons would be consumed in travelling 10,000 miles, which equals an expenditure of £75. The licence duty is £25 per annum. The driving licence is 25p (5/-) per annum. This makes a total annual taxation of £136·25, or based on 10,000 miles per annum 1·36p per mile travelled. This figure compares very favourably with the tolls on the few toll roads and bridges in the United Kingdom and the United States. In addition, the motorist like any other ratepayer and taxpayer, makes his contribution towards the lighting, cleansing and maintenance of roads, and the control of traffic by police, partly financed locally and partly by the Exchequer. Like other people the motorist receives the same benefits from these services as other residents. Therefore for the additional tax of 1·36p per mile the motorist has the privilege of travelling on any highway in his own country or abroad.

In 1965, the Automobile Association in the United Kingdom commissioned Regional Planning Research Ltd, to carry out a survey of parking in nine chosen towns of differing character and with different problems. The towns, chosen for their size, location and hinterland, and for their varying traffic and parking problems, were Edinburgh, Cardiff, Bolton, Dublin, Leamington Spa, Nottingham, Newbury, Norwich and Torquay. All are important shopping centres. The results of this survey were published in the report entitled 'Parking—Who Pays?'.[1] The survey was carried out in the spring of 1965 with the aim of providing an adequate background of reliable information on motorists' parking needs coupled with indications of how they can be met. 'Until now', says the Foreword, 'all discussion has been based on ideas and prejudices formed from limited experiences or purely theoretical propositions.'

The essence of the report is contained in Part 2, where it sets out to find the answer to the questions: Who Pays Now? What would motorists pay? and Better Parking—How?

The report states that at the present time the provision of car parking facilities in our town centres is divided between a number of agencies. Car parks may be provided by the large stores, primarily for the convenience of their customers, by cinemas and others for their patrons. Charges may be levied in some; in others parking may be free. There are also commercially operated and privately owned car parks, where a charge is invariably made, possibly on a sliding scale according to hours parked, but the bulk of car parking spaces is inevitably provided by the local authority, mostly 'on-street' in either controlled or un-restricted areas, but also 'off-street' in open site or multi-storey car parks. The majority of 'on-street' parking is free although there is a growing tendency for charges to be made in controlled areas as well as in open site 'off-street' car parks.

The indication is that charges levied by local authorities are much less than those levied by private car park operators. This supposes that the latter will not charge below the economic price.

To the question, What would motorists pay? there is no general agreement reached from the survey. There is still a hard core of motorists who are opposed to all payments for parking. There are also those businessmen who realise the importance of parking facilities in the business area, but consider it to be the community's responsibility.

On the value of parking to trade in the central business area, it is calculated that in Edinburgh every 1 per cent reduction in the number of car shoppers represents an annual loss of net profit to central area shopkeepers of over £9500 and eventual loss in rate income as the result of reduced sales; in Cardiff it is estimated to be more than £5600; in Norwich more than £4000; and in Newbury more than £2500. In terms of weekly trade to shopkeepers, every 1 per cent drop in shopping traffic means a loss of over £2600 in Edinburgh; £1500 in Cardiff; £1100 in Norwich, and £616 in Newbury. On the other hand, the report shows that if better parking facilities were made available more than the present number of motorists would be prepared to pay to park.

The survey found that although the majority of motorists were opposed to paying more than they did, nevertheless between 33 per cent and 48 per cent of drivers were prepared to pay higher charges for better facilities; and where the journey purpose was shopping, between 39 per cent and 59 per cent were prepared to pay more. The greatest willingness to pay more was found in places with most free parking—implying that those who were used to paying nothing would, on balance, be prepared to pay something.

A most important finding of the survey is the proportion of motorists who avoid their local town centre because of the difficulty of parking. These figures range from 11 per cent in Newbury to 20 per cent in Torquay. The economic effects of motorists being forced away from town centres could be disastrous, and local authorities must become alive to the consequences of inadequate parking facilities and an absence of a clear and positive policy for parking.

In answer to the third question, Better Parking—How? the report looks into the possibilities of providing adequate parking facilities and makes the point that motorists are unlikely to be prepared to pay the whole of the cost involved. Nor would it be reasonable to expect them to bear the whole cost. Equally it would be unreasonable to load the entire financial responsibility on to the general body of ratepayers when businesses in the central area stand to benefit considerably from motorists' visits. The report comes to the conclusion that: 'a rational basis can be devised whereby costs of parking provision are shared between motorists generally, the business community who benefit most directly from the facilities of motorists being able to come to the town centre by car, and the local authority which also has a stake in maintaining the centre's vitality.'

It is recognised and stated that motorists, as the direct beneficiaries, will in future have to bear a larger proportion of the costs of improved facilities of the street and, taking Cardiff as an example, suggests that the ratio of cost bearing might be in the region of 86 per cent on motorists, 11 per cent on central area businesses and 3 per cent on the rest of the local ratepayers. The suggestion for the future is that: 'local authorities, in their role as planning administrator, should pay special attention not only to the assessment of actual parking demand in the town centres, but equally to the social cost/benefits which the provision of "off-street" parking facilities implies, and to the appropriate distribution of the financial burden of this provision under particular local circumstances.'

The conclusions drawn from this survey are very sound, balanced and reasonable. They will form an excellent basis for a local authority to formulate a clear and progressive policy on parking.

There is one practical difficulty connected with the contribution from businesses in the central area. There is no legislation in the United Kingdom which enables a local authority to call upon business firms to make a financial contribution towards the cost of providing a public car park, although agreement can be made under special circumstances where the local authority is the ground landlord. A local authority may also accept a gift for this purpose. There are indications that many firms would be willing to make a financial contribution if permitted. In the absence of suitable legislation the motorist is left as the only benefactor to whom a fee can be charged. This must be an economic fee unless the local authority is prepared to subsidise car parking in a town. If they do make this decision, they must be the owners of the car park. If the car parks are owned and operated by private firms, an economic fee must be charged as a private firm must make a profit to keep in business.

The conclusion to be drawn from this examination is that the motorist must pay the greater part if not the whole of the economic cost of parking in the central area of a town.

COST OF CAR PARKS

It would be quite misleading to write in general terms on the cost of providing parking accommodation, because the cost of land is a large and important

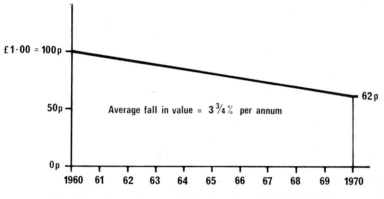

Fig. 18.1 Graph showing fall in the value of £1, 1960–1970.

variable factor. There may also be a large variation in the cost of the structure depending on the position of the building in relation to other buildings and the aesthetic treatment required for the elevations. In a period of inflation it is most difficult to compare prices and, therefore, Fig. 18.1 has been included which shows the falling value of the pound from 1960–1970.

In a paper[2] given to the British Parking Association Seminar in April, 1970, Mr G. D. Brigham, F.R.I.C.S. City Estates Officer, Leicester, gave the following example on the assessment of viability of a car park scheme. For the purpose of the example he made the following assumptions:

(a) Number of car spaces to be provided   500

(b) Cost of construction per car space   £320

(c) Average rental value per car space (probably ranging from £25 to £50 per annum)   £40 p.a.

(d) Capital value of site   £100,000

Without the benefit of any supporting commercial development, the calculations would probably be:

Estimate of capital outlay

Building cost: 500 car spaces at £320	£160,000
Add development on costs (professional fees, finance, contingencies, etc.) allow 25%	40,000
Site value	100,000
	——
Estimated total capital outlay	£300,000

Estimated value of completed development

Rental value of car park—500 car spaces at average rent of £40 per space	£20,000	
Capitalised at 10%	× 10	£200,000
	——	——
Short fall		£100,000

It is readily apparent that this scheme is in need of additional income in order to achieve an acceptable level of viability from a private investor's point of view.

An escalating ground rent would reduce the deficit by, say, £20,000, leaving a short fall of £80,000 to be met by other means. Suppose that the following additional uses could be incorporated in the scheme of development: a petrol filling station, a ground floor showroom, and a small block of offices of 1000 m^2 (10,000 ft^2). The following calculations illustrate how the sought-after viability could be achieved:

Petrol filling station

Estimated rental value of site	£2,500 p.a.
Capitalised at 10%	× 10
Value of Petrol Filling Station Site	£25,000

Showroom 800 m^2 (8000 ft^2) gross area

Lettable area of, say, 750 m^2 (7500 ft^2).		
Estimated rental value, say, 750 m^2 @ £10/m^2 (7500 ft^2 @ £1/ft^2)		£7,500 p.a.
Capitalised at 10%		× 10
		——
Value of completed development less		£75,000
Less building cost 800 m^2 @ £40/m^2 (8000 ft^2 @ £4/ft^2)	£32,000	
Development on cost @ 25%	8,000	40,000
	——	——
'Profit' element		£35,000

Offices 1000 m^2 (*10,000 ft*^{2}) *gross area*
Net lettable area of, say, 850 m^2 (8500 ft^2)

Estimated rental value, say, 850 m^2 @ £10/m^2 (8500 ft^2 @ £1/ft^2)		£8,500
Capitalised at 10%		× 10
Value of completed development		£85,000
Less building cost 1000 m^2 @ £55/m^2 (10,000 ft^2 @ £5·50/ft^2)	£55,000	
Development on cost @ 25% .	15,000	70,000
'Profit' element		£15,000
Total 'profit' element from commercial development		£75,000

The estimated short fall of £80,000 has almost been cancelled out. A saving of £5000 could probably be made elsewhere which would leave a scheme which is viable and should attract investment of private capital.

The four examples which follow are taken from a paper[3] given to the Institution of Highway Engineers in 1964, by A. F. Holt, then Borough Engineer of Croydon.

STANDARD MULTI-STOREY CAR PARK FOR 750 CARS (1964)

1. *Capital costs*

	£
Land: approx. 1 acre	100,000
Building cost: 750 @ £350 per car space	262,500
Total	362,500

Cost per car space $\dfrac{362,500}{750} = £485$

2. *Annual costs*

	£
Loan charges: land 60 years @ 5¾%	5,960
building 30 years @ 5¾%	18,500
Wages of attendants (two shifts each of 3 men plus extra attendant on Saturdays and Christmas, superannuation, holiday reliefs, sick reliefs, uniforms, etc.)	6,500
Cleaning	1,000
Lighting	1,000
Stationery, telephones, etc.	250
Repairs and maintenance	1,500
Rates and insurance	2,400
Establishment and miscellaneous charges, say,	1,500
	38,610

Income required per car space per annum

$\dfrac{£38,610}{750} = £51·50$ (say, £1 per week).

This expenditure of £1 per week is made up as follows:

	p	s	d
Loan charges	64	12	9
Wages of attendants	16	3	4
Rates and insurance	6	1	3
Cleaning, lighting and stationery, etc.	6	1	2
Repairs and maintenance	4		9
Establishment and miscellaneous charges	4		9
	100p	20	0

Note:

The capital cost of £350 per car space allows for a sophisticated design with careful elevational treatment, access formed at two levels, lifts, and some site complications. It also includes for design staff and clerk of works salaries.

SURFACE CAR PARK FOR 750 CARS

The car park serves commuters, shoppers and evening users. The site is on the edge of the business area with land at £30,000 per acre.

1. *Capital costs*   £

   Land: $3\frac{1}{2}$ acres   105,000
   Demolition, surfacing, lighting, etc.   30,000
                                                                          _____
                                                                          £135,000

   Cost per car space $\dfrac{135,000}{750} = £225$

2. *Annual costs*   £

   Loan charges on land: 60 years @ $5\frac{3}{4}\%$ 6,250
   Loan charges on works: 20 years @ $5\frac{3}{4}\%$ 2,560
   Wages of attendants (2 shifts/day)   4,800
   Cleaning and lighting   120
   Stationery and telephones   250
   Repairs   500
   Rates and insurance   2,000
   Establishment and miscellaneous charges   500
                                                                          _____
                                                                          £16,980

   Income required per car space per annum

   $= \dfrac{16,980}{750} = £22 \cdot 50$ per annum

   say, 44p (8s 9d) per week.

Note:

The cost of wages could be halved if attendants during the day only are required. It could be reduced even further if a fixed charge be made (instead of a charge varying with the time) as an automatic gate could then be used.

SURFACE CAR PARK FOR 250 CARS

1. *Capital costs* £

Land: 1·2 acres	12,000
Demolition and surfacing	7,500
	£19,500

$$\text{Cost per car space} = \frac{19,500}{250} = £80$$

2. *Annual costs* £

Loan charges on land: 60 years @ $5\frac{3}{4}\%$	730
Loan charges on works: 20 years @ $5\frac{3}{4}\%$	640
Wages of attendants	1,300
Cleaning and lighting	40
Stationery and telephones	75
Repairs	100
Rates and insurance	500
Establishment and miscellaneous charges	100
	£3,485

Income required per car space per annum:

$$= \frac{3,485}{250} = £14·00$$

say, 28p (5s 6d) per week.

Note:

If this car park is used mainly by all day parkers, it is practical to reduce substantially the wages of attendants by providing an attendant from 7.30 am to 9.30 am only Monday to Friday, and making a fixed charge. Alternatively, a 'Trust the Motorist' scheme could be introduced in which case the income required would be 18p (3s 6d) per week.

UNDERGROUND CAR PARK FOR 600 CARS

It is assumed that no land costs need to be charged to the project as the area above the car park may be used for other development. This is not a completely valid assumption as any building above an underground car park will almost certainly cost more because of extra foundation costs. Even a town park above an underground car park will suffer from the impracticability of growing trees.

1. *Capital costs*   £

   Building and services   600,000

2. *Annual costs*

   Loan charges on buildings and services @ $5\frac{3}{4}\%$ 42,500
   Wages of attendants
   Cleaning
   Lighting and ventilation plant
   Stationery, telephones, etc.   17,450
   Repairs
   Rates and insurance
   Establishment and miscellaneous charges
                                                                                 ———————
                                                                                £59,950

   Income required per car space per annum:

   $$= \frac{59,950}{600} = £100$$

   say, £2·00 per week.

MULTI-STOREY CAR PARK AT EXETER, COMPLETED 1969, FOR 461 CARS

1. *Capital costs*   £

   Building and equipment   163,000
   Land   42,500
                                                                                 ———————
                                                                                205,500

   Cost per car space: $\dfrac{205,500}{461} = £446$

2. *Annual costs*   £

   Loan charges: Buildings, etc.   14,568
                 Land   3,743
   Wages plus sick pay, uniform, etc.   3,717
   Securicor Patrol   293
   Maintenance and cleaning   2,535
   Lighting and heating   1,560
   Rates   3,539
   Establishment charges   1,915
                                                                                 ———————
                                               Total   £31,870

   Income required per car space per annum

   $$= \frac{31,870}{461} = £69 \text{ per annum, or } £1·33 \text{ per week.}$$

   Income for the first year of operation — £9,638.

The fees charged were 5p for the first two hours and 5p per hour afterwards to a maximum of 25p per day; they are now 5p per hour to the same maximum.

The income is low because the car park was not used to capacity during the first year and the fees are low; there is no other income from lettings. The loss on this car park is balanced by the profits on other car parks, and the final car parking account balances approximately.

SURFACE CAR PARKS AT EXETER, 1969

(1) CAR PARK CAPACITY 92 CARS

Parking fees 5p for first two hours and 5p per hour afterwards; maximum charge 25p per day.

Manual control.

Annual cost per car space — £42.

Annual income per car space — £57.

Income	£	Expenditure	£
Parking fees	5,250	Maintenance	3,823
		Loan charges	50
	£5,250		£3,873

Profit — £1,377

(2) CAR PARK CAPACITY 208 CARS

Parking fees 5p for first two hours and 5p per hour afterwards; maximum charge 25p per day.

Manual control.

Annual cost per car space — £33·50.

Annual income per car space — £61.

Income	£	Expenditure	£
Parking fees	12,650	Maintenance	6,303
		Loan charges	650
	£12,650		£6,953

Profit — £5,697

(3) CAR PARK CAPACITY 250 CARS

Parking fee 5p per day or part of day.

Automatic control.

Annual cost per car space — £7.

Average annual income per car space — £9·75.

Income		Expenditure	£
Parking fees	2,425	Maintenance	1,738
	£2,425		£1,738

Profit — £687

An examination of the income and expenditure of multi-storey car parks shows that an income of 25p per car space per day is required if the car park is to be self supporting. Lower fees may be charged if other income can be obtained from lettings on the ground floor, a petrol filling station or if the profits on surface car parks are used to offset the loss on the multi-storey car parks.

PARKING FEE ZONES

It is a generally accepted practice to charge the highest price for the best seats at a theatre or concert. The most desirable sites in a town centre are usually the most expensive. The principle of supply and demand operates. Parking places in the heart of a city (*i.e.* central business area) are in the greatest demand, they are on the most expensive land and therefore a higher fee is justified. Because they are in the greatest demand each parking space should be used by as many motorists as possible in a day (*i.e.* short term parking) and the fees should be designed to encourage this. It will probably be necessary to zone a central business area in a large town into two or three price zones, the most expensive one being at the centre, the next expensive a short distance out, and the less expensive still a further distance away. The parking time could also be extended in the less expensive zones. Price zoning could apply equally to on-street and off-street parking.

In a group of towns or a conurbation there may be more than one high priced zone necessary.

PARKING METERS

Many suggestions have been made for a policy on parking meter fees. One is to adjust the charges up or down to equate the supply and demand for street parking space. Another is to make adjustments to attract 85% ultilisation. There are many other variations in time and price; many are based on what is considered to be a reasonable charge for parking over a limited period. If it is cheaper to park on the street for 4 hours than in an off-street car park, we must expect the motorist to park on the street if there is space available.

Ideally, on-street parking should be related to off-street parking. In principle in the central areas, on-street parking could be used for short periods of $\frac{1}{2}$ hour or 1 hour, and off-street car parks for longer periods. The fees could be arranged to encourage this type of use. It is foolish to be dogmatic about this as there are so many varying conditions and circumstances. In practice there is likely to be a greater demand for short period street parking than can be satisfied and it can only be reduced artificially by increasing the meter fees, which would encourage motorists to use off-street car parks and/or create another parking problem outside the meter zone. The policy may also be complicated by the lack of sufficient off-street car parks. It may also be considered desirable to have higher fees in the centre of a business area and lower fees on the fringe. Two provincial cities introduced differential charges based on distance from city centre.

Newcastle-upon-Tyne (population 270,000).
Inner zone — 2·5p (6d) for ½ hour
Middle zone — 2·5p (6d) for 1 hour
Outer zone — 2·5p (6d) for 2 hours
Cambridge (population 95,000).
Inner zone — 2·5p (6d) for ½ hour
Outer zone — 2·5p (6d) for 1 hour

Plymouth introduced a basic charge of 1·25p (3d) for ½ hour with the option of 2·5p (6d) for 1 hour.

The standard charge for parking in London until 1965 was at the rate of 2·5p (6d) for 1 hour. Most meters gave the option of one or two hours of parking (the motorist must decide in advance which he wants—it is illegal to come back and pay for the second hour). A few long term meters give 4 hours for 10p (2s 0d) and 5 hours for 12·5p (2s 6d) or 10 hours for 25p (5s 0d). These charges are generally lower than the charges for off-street parking.

COST OF STREET PARKING

(a) Assuming land costs £125/m² (£100/yd²)
Meter space 6·0 m (20 ft) × 2·0 m (7 ft) = 12 m² (15 yd²) capital value £1500.

Assume 10% return	= £150 per annum.
Rate element on rent	50
Cost of maintenance	10
Cleaning and lighting	10
Providing, maintaining and operating parking meters	60 per meter/p.a.
	£280 per annum.

Based on 6 day week, daily rental $= \dfrac{£280}{312} = 90\text{p}$.

Hourly rental based on 10 hour day = 9p per hour.

Without meter daily rental $= \dfrac{£220}{312} = 70\text{p}$.

Hourly rental based on 10 hour day = 7p per hour.

(b) Assuming meter space has a capital value of £750.

Assume 10% return	= £75 per annum
Rate element on rent	25
Cost of maintenance	10
Cleaning and lighting	10
	£120 per annum

Daily rental @ 6 days/week $= \dfrac{£120}{312} = 39\text{p}$.

Hourly rental based on 10 hour day = 3·9p, say 4p.

The total revenue and expenditure on meters is shown in Table XII.[4]

TABLE XII

Parking Meter Schemes
Reproduced from RAC Survey of Parking Meter Schemes 1968[4]

Local Authority	Period of Scheme Covered	Total Income	Expenditure on Operational Costs, etc.	Surplus Available for Provision or Maintenance of Car Parks	Deficit
		£	£	£	£
Birmingham	1963/67	219,462	200,511	18,951	—
Brighton	1962/67	241,589	176,733	64,856	—
Bristol	1961/67	219,632	170,303	49,329	—
Cambridge	1964/68	142,000	103,000	39,000	—
Camden	1960/67	1,006,200	723,100	283,100	—
Croydon	1961/67	231,341	200,585	30,756	—
Edinburgh	1962/67	147,775	82,850	64,925	—
Glasgow	1965/67	103,834	88,582	15,252	—
Greenwich	1961/67	62,228	80,120	—	17,829
Hackney	1961/67	85,653	93,402	—	7,749
Islington	1961/67	119,951	160,778	—	40,827
Kingston-on-Thames	1961/67	125,095	110,347	14,748	—
Leeds	1965/68	246,806	194,138	52,668	—
Liverpool	1965/67	143,235	129,643	13,592	—
City of London	1961/67	453,542	342,245	111,297	—
Luton	1965/68	80,752	59,764	20,988	—
Maidstone	1964/67	41,272	27,528	13,744	—
Manchester	1961/68	549,200	356,600	192,600	—
Newcastle-on-Tyne	1963/67	257,895	168,671	89,224	—
Plymouth	1963/67	72,946	54,740	18,206	—
Southampton*	1967/68	50,000	39,275	10,725	—
Southend-on-Sea	1962/67	145,507	119,292	26,215	—
Tower Hamlets	1965/67	15,496	21,379	—	5,883
Westminster	1958/67	3,803,288	2,265,021	1,538,267	—
Worthing	July 1966	Not available	Not available	—	—
TOTAL		8,564,699	5,968,607	2,668,443	72,351

* Estimated figures provided by local authority. Note: Hull (Feb. 1968), Kensington and Chelsea (Jan. 1968), Merton (Apl. 1967), Redbridge (March 1967), Sheffield (Nov. 1967). Wolverhampton (Nov. 1967), Perth (1967), Havering (Nov. 1967) also operate meter schemes but were omitted from the survey owing to short period of operation.

There does not appear to be any sound reason why the motorist should not pay an economic fee for parking in the central business areas of towns and cities. It may not be possible for every car park to be profitable but when grouped together the car parking in a central business area should be viable. If it is not, we cannot expect the standard of service that is required for an efficient parking scheme, and if private enterprise is to operate, they must be in a position to make a profit.

With the exception of Westminster in the United Kingdom, parking meters do not make a large surplus of money. They are perhaps more useful in imposing a restraining influence on the motorist and in establishing orderliness rather than providing money for building 'off-street' car parks.

REFERENCES

1. 'Parking: Who Pays?' A survey by Regional Planning Research Ltd, commissioned by The Automobile Association, London, 1967.
2. BRIGHAM, G. D. 'Provision of Multi-Storey Car Parks: Local Authorities and the Developer', Report of British Parking Association Seminar, April 1970.
3. HOLT, A. F. 'Comparative Costs of Car Parks', Paper given to Institution of Highway Engineers, 1964.
4. Royal Automobile Club. Survey of Parking Meter Schemes, 1968.

Chapter 19

Parking Policy

Traffic is the life blood of a modern city. Traffic which needs to move should be given the facilities to do so. Traffic which needs to be stationary should as far as is possible be provided with off-street parking facilities, relying for very short periods only on on-street parking in those places where it will not impede the flow of traffic. The purpose of a traffic management and parking policy should be to use the facilities available to the best advantage.

The management of stationary vehicles is just as important as management of moving vehicles. A parked car by the kerbside reduces the traffic capacity of the road, and an accumulation of them will choke the road. A very large concentration of parked vehicles off the street could generate traffic at peak periods, and cause congestion on the traffic routes. The important influence that effective control of the stationary vehicle has on life in the central business area of a town is not yet fully appreciated. The time that a car is stationary is very great compared with the time that it is in motion. If it is assumed that the average mileage of a car is 10,000 miles per annum, and the average speed is 25 mph, then the total travelling time is 400 hours out of 8760 hours in the year. If the car is in a private garage for 75 per cent of its life, it still has to be parked in town or country for four times as many hours as when it is moving.

The control of parking both 'on' and 'off' the street is for the sole purpose of helping the motorist to make the best use of all the space that can be made available for moving and parked vehicles. It will help drivers by giving clear indication where waiting and parking is, and is not, permissible. It will help in the use of vehicles for business, pleasure, and the distribution of goods. It will help to reduce road accidents and improve the environment by introducing orderliness in place of untidy and indiscriminate parking. As far as it is possible a parking policy should be positive and, when it is essential to be restrictive, the restrictions should be applied only where and when it is in the general interest.

RESPONSIBILITY

The United States of America is about a generation ahead of European countries in the use of the motor vehicle. Many of their problems are similar to the problems that will arise in European countries and we are fortunate in being able to benefit from the experience of traffic engineers in the United States. But, the solution to a problem in one country is not necessarily the solution in another, nor is the solution for one town necessarily the solution for another town. There are, however, certain basic principles which can be used as a foundation on which to build a policy for controlling the parked vehicle.

In the United Kingdom, successive Governments have made it quite clear that they regard the local authority as the responsible authority for car parking. Local authorities have extensive powers to provide car parking facilities of all kinds in their area. These powers are permissive, and the responsibility for using them rests with the local authority. There is nothing to prevent private firms establishing car parks, provided they comply with local town planning requirements and Building Regulations.

Local authorities are in a unique position for controlling parking in towns. Their interest spreads over the whole area of the town, and they are concerned with the general prosperity of the area as distinct from one particular district, or one section, or one business. They are equally interested in 'off-street' parking, 'on-street' parking, traffic management and traffic control. Their concern is the motorist as well as the pedestrian. They can decide to make traffic and parking surveys, assess the requirements of moving and stationary traffic, now and in the future. Furthermore, they have powers to acquire property by compulsory purchase, if necessary.

If the local authority is the only authority that can exercise a comprehensive control over parking in a town, who then should provide the parking facilities? Should it be left to private enterprise, should the local authority undertake this work directly, or should they delegate their powers to an agency?

In many towns in the United States, private enterprise has provided a large proportion of the 'off-street' parking facilities. In the United Kingdom there is a tendency for local authorities to delay taking the initiative in providing 'off-street' parking facilities, in the hope that a private firm will come along and provide it.

The British Road Federation commissioned Research Services Ltd, to make a National Survey on Car Parking,[1] based on information provided by all County Boroughs and Boroughs in England and Wales with a population over 10,000, and in Scotland all Cities and Burghs over this population, together with certain other selected towns. The Report was published in November 1961, and the analysis of the replies set out in the tables of the Report were disquieting. Excluding the Metropolitan Boroughs, the Report revealed that of the authorities surveyed, 42 per cent neither made nor had they in hand, a study of the ultimate parking requirements of their areas. Of the remainder, 28 per cent had gone further than making a study and had incorporated the results in their development plans.

In 1964, the British Road Federation published a Report[2] on a further study by Research Services Ltd. This report was equally disquieting. It revealed that between 1961 and 1963, the number of parking places per head of population in the United Kingdom had increased only by 12 per cent, whereas the car population had increased by 23 per cent. The survey also showed that there was a

Fig. 19.1   An example of the built up area of a city dominated by car parks.

decided drift away from parking meters. Many authorities who were considering their installation at the time of the 1961 survey had dropped the idea.

In 1968, a further report was published[3] which stated:

'Since 1964, when the last survey was carried out, there have been a number of marked improvements. Nearly half the towns were then providing less than 10 parking places for every 1000 of their population. Now only a quarter do so. At the time too, only 52 per cent had made a thorough study of the demand that could be expected in the years ahead as the level of car ownership reached its peak. Now 64 per cent have done so, or are in process of carrying out such a study.'

'All this is encouraging but it is only one aspect of the findings. Taken as a whole, the survey clearly shows that there are still far too many local authorities who have not yet started to tackle the problem with the decision and imagination it requires. Sixty-four per cent may have carried out a study of future parking needs, but this still leaves more than one in three who have yet no real concept of how traffic in their town centre will develop and how it will affect the lives of those who live there. Even among those who have carried out the necessary studies, a considerable number have not yet decided on the course of action they should take.'

In the United States of America and Canada, high parking fees have made surface car parks fronting on streets in downtown shopping areas a profitable proposition. But this has completely ruined the street architecture and some streets are appropriately called 'gasoline alley' (Fig. 19.1).

If adequate parking facilities are to be provided, and they should be, and if they are not to have a serious detrimental effect on the environment, then they should be effectively controlled by the planning authority and managed as a viable undertaking. In other words the motorist must be prepared to pay for the facilities he uses. Furthermore, car parking facilities and policy must be related to the peak hour traffic volumes and capacity of roads leading to and from the central business area. Only in this way can a satisfactory solution to the parking problems in our towns be achieved.

UNIFIED CONTROL

Parking in a town or city is different from other business activities in so far as it has an influence either directly or indirectly on other activities in a central business area. Parking facilities are the terminus for journeys by car. If adequate facilities for parking a car are not provided, the use of the terminus is limited, and business activities in the surrounding area are limited.

With moving traffic we accept the discipline of driving on the 'left' or 'right' side of the road as determined by the government of the country; we also accept the discipline of traffic control signals, of one-way streets and road signs and markings. These disciplines are for the benefit of the road user, to permit traffic to flow more smoothly and in greater safety. It is also necessary to have similar disciplines for the stationary vehicle, and for the same reasons. These disciplines may be restrictions on street parking and areas where short term parking only is encouraged in off-street car parks. If the road network and the parking facilities are adequate to meet any demand for parking whether for long or short term, then restrictions may be unnecessary, but this is only likely to occur in the smaller towns, and most towns either now or in the future will have to deal with a parking problem. When this arises and no disciplines for parking are imposed on the motorist, then the policy becomes 'first come first served'. Amongst the first to come are the commuters who park for long periods and the parking places are filled when the motorist who requires short term parking arrives. These are the shoppers and business callers who are essential for the business life of a city.

In order to allocate areas for short and long term parking, and impose a discipline on motorists, there must be some unified control over parking in the town. Otherwise private car park proprietors would be able to encourage long term parking in areas reserved for short term parking, and consequently undermine and defeat the objective of the local authority. Therefore it is important that parking facilities in a central business area should be planned and controlled to serve the interests of the town and public. This means some form of unified control.

Unified control may be exercised by the local authority alone. As highway authority they are responsible for the control of on-street parking, and by taking the initiative in providing off-street parking they can control the bulk of the parking facilities in the central business area of the town. In the initial stages, when most parking facilities are on surface car parks, this is without doubt a wise policy, and if the parking facilities provided by private firms are small compared with the whole, they need not have any serious detrimental effect on the parking policy. Parking may be divided into two sections: (a) on-street parking which must be controlled by the highway authority, and any income will be from parking meter fees if these have been installed, and (b) off-street parking which is a business enterprise. In its simplest form the local authority provides the capital to build a multi-storey car park, and the ground floor may be let as shops or for some other use that is more remunerative than car parking. There may be periods when there are restrictions on the capital investment that a local authority is permitted to undertake, and the provision of car parking may be given a lower priority than other works. This may be quite deliberate because private capital is available for car park development, whereas other local authority work has to rely on capital raised directly by the local authority. Private capital may be used for comprehensive pieces of development of which a multi-storey or underground car park forms part and the developers will expect that it will serve their piece of development. It is important that these private enterprise parking facilities should be integrated with the parking policy for the town. Such proposals for property development will increase, and as this is a business enterprise it may be that the local authority would wish to enter into an agreement with a private firm to undertake responsibility for organising and managing the whole of their off-street parking facilities on their behalf. Such opportunities are available, but it is important that any arrangements agreed should be on a partnership basis with the local authority; the local authority being responsible for the on-street parking; the private firm for the off-street parking, and both parties working together in accordance with the comprehensive parking policy.

If a local authority wishes to engage private firms with capital to invest in car parks, it is most important that this arrangement should comply with the overall comprehensive parking plan. It should not develop as a number of isolated car parks working independently, and maybe in conflict with one another and the local authority's parking policy. If local authorities permit parking facilities to develop outside or in the absence of a parking policy, the time will come when they find it necessary to adopt a clear policy and bring parking under their control. The longer this is delayed the more difficult it will be to achieve a sound workable policy.

In the United States of America, Canada, and other countries, many cities have found it desirable to establish Parking Authorities. In the United States of America there is extensive State legislation with some differences between the powers given to local authorities by different States. The primary purpose of establishing a Parking Authority is clearly stated in an ordinance of the City of Grand Rapids, Michigan[4] '. . . to effectuate and properly regulate and control parking in the city and provide necessary off-street public parking facilities to make such regulation and control effective, it is necessary and expedient that automobile parking facilities owned or operated by the City of Grand Rapids including specifically all street parking facilities where parking meters are now located, for the purpose of limiting parking, and the municipal parking facilities to be acquired for "off-street" public parking purposes, be combined into a single automobile parking system to be known as the Grand Rapids Automobile Parking System and operated as a separate function of the City of Grand Rapids under the general supervision and control of the Automobile Parking Authority of said City, or such other Municipal Agency or office as may be hereafter designated by the City Commission'.

The ordinance further authorises the acquisition and construction of designated parking structures; all revenues from any facilities, kerb or 'off street', are deemed to constitute revenues of the entire system. The Parking Authority has nine members: the Mayor, City Manager, and seven businessmen serving without salary. There were three principles followed in selecting these men: (1) integrity and financial standing beyond question, (2) no direct interest in real estate near any possible parking site, (3) a record of non-political civic service.

In many cities in the United States, one of the reasons for establishing a Parking Authority has been the necessity to remove parking from political conflict and control. The majority of people in the United States are firm believers in private enterprise, and many Parking Authorities have leased sites for car parks to private firms, or when the building has been erected by the Authority it is often operated by a private firm. It is often essential for the Parking Authority to acquire the site because they alone have powers of eminent domain (i.e. compulsory purchase). These Parking Authorities are usually managed on strict business methods and a profit motive. Their success appears to be judged on the annual balance sheet.

In the United Kingdom, at the time of writing (April 1971), there is no legislation for the creation of Parking Authorities. It may be that an alternative to a Parking Authority in the United Kingdom would be for local authorities to co-operate with private firms for the management of car parks on a partner-ship basis.

The Greater London Council, under the Transport (London) Act, 1969, Section 36,[5] has powers to control 'off-street' parking by means of a licence granted by the Council to the operators of an 'off-street' car park, and the car park can only be operated in accordance with the terms and conditions of the licence. As far as is known to date (April 1971) these powers have not been applied.

PARKING STANDARDS FOR NEW DEVELOPMENT

In the United Kingdom, a planning authority has power under the Town and Country Planning Act, 1962, to require the developer of new property to make some contribution towards the provision of adequate car parking space in the neighbourhood of new development. The logic of this policy is that all developers would accept responsibility for the parking generated by their development.

The Greater London Council and its predecessor, the London County Council, along with other County Councils and County Borough Councils, acting as Planning Authorities, have adopted parking standards for new develop-ment within their areas.[6] These Planning Authorities imposed an obligation on intending developers to provide a specific amount of parking space with certain new buildings. In the United States similar regulations have been adopted by the most important towns and are known as 'zoning ordinances'.

Table XIII shows typical requirements for parking provision for new develop-ment in the United States of America and the United Kingdom.

TABLE XIII

Table Showing Typical Minimum Requirements for Parking Provision in New Development in the United States of America and the United Kingdom

Type of Development	USA Zoning Ordinances	UK Car Parking Standards
Dwelling house	1/1 dwelling	1/1 dwelling
Flats	1/1 dwelling	1/1 dwelling
Offices	1/18·0 m² (200 ft²) gross floor area	1/28·0 m² (300 ft²) or 1/2 employees
Large retail stores	1/18·0 m² (200 ft²) 1/185·0 m² (2000 ft²) gross floor area	1/92·0 m² (1000 ft²) plus space for loading and garaging business vehicles
Hotels	1/3 guest rooms	1/3 guest rooms, or varied according to needs
Hospitals	1/4 beds	1/4 beds plus accommodation for essential staff
Industry	1/2·5 employees	1/62·0 m² (750 ft²)
Theatres	1/10 seats	1/10 seats plus accommodation for essential staff

An examination of these 'parking standards' or 'zoning ordinances' immediately prompts certain questions. These are:

(a) Is it day time parking or permanent garaging that is required?
(b) Is it contended that the parking requirements will meet all the parking needs, *viz.* staff, visitors and customers?
(c) Is it intended that parking requirements are for the whole staff?
(d) Is the parking accommodation for the immediate demand? If so, what provision is made for the increasing demand that must be forthcoming in the future?
(e) Has consideration been given to land values?

The effect of these regulations has been to provide a substantial amount of car parking accommodation for new development in town and city centres. This accommodation is usually reserved for occupiers, users or visitors to the building concerned and is not usually available for other users, and closed outside working hours. Furthermore, when it is becoming necessary to restrict traffic entering the city to operational traffic and short term business traffic by parking controls, motorists using private car parks connected with buildings cannot be controlled. This in turn defeats the object of a local authority in attempting to relate parking in a city centre to the road capacity. Therefore it is not practicable to require provision for private parking connected with individual pieces of development in the central business areas of towns and cities, other than that required for loading and unloading, and also a limited amount for essential users. Regulations similar to those in Table XIII should be applied outside the central business area.

In a joint report by the United Kingdom Ministry of Housing and Local Government and Ministry of Transport (now Department of the Environment), it is stated:[7]

'Because land in town centres is valuable, its use for small, separate private car parks is seldom likely to be of the best use to which it can be put from the point of view of the community. Several local authorities have been able to conclude arrangements with developers whereby the latter make financial contributions towards the cost of providing spaces in public car parks as an alternative to providing parking space on site.'

'This solution will often be to the advantage both of the developer and the public. The developer will be absolved from the need to devote valuable space within his building or its curtilage to the less remunerative function of car parking; the public will get a car park which is open at all hours and available for their use. Where, therefore, the planning authority would normally require by condition that development should include provision for the parking of cars, it may be that the developer will prefer to make a contribution towards the cost of car parking facilities provided by the authority. If that is so, Section 268 of the Local Government Act, 1933, or Section 340 of the Local Government (Scotland) Act, 1947, would enable the authority to accept the gift and devote it to car parking purposes. Parking spaces so provided must be available to the public at large and cannot be earmarked for the particular use of a developer.'

'It should be understood that arrangements of this kind must be entirely voluntary. It would be wrong to seek to impose them as a requirement in a planning permission or to withhold a planning permission on the ground that the developer was unwilling to enter into such an arrangement.'

This may be seen as a way out of the dilemma, but it is extremely unsatisfactory. On the one hand the local authority is not allowed to sell planning permissions, yet it is freely offered a gift which is related to the parking spaces required, and this is taken into account to determine whether planning permission should be granted. A solution to this problem in the central area would be for the local authority to provide the public car parks that are required and charge an economic fee for parking, the developer to provide only the parking facilities required for the operation of the business either on the premises or within the curtilage of the buildings. The local authority would still be free to receive a gift of money to devote to more parking facilities, but it should not be related to planning permission where there is residential development in a central area. Space for garages would be required as distinct from parking spaces. This requirement could quite justifiably be regarded as operational.

Where commercial development is outside the city centre and is an isolated building or a small group of buildings, the developer would normally be responsible for providing parking spaces in accordance with the standards adopted by the local authority for the type of development. Where, however, the development is part of a shopping centre or major commercial zone, the provision of separate facilities by each developer would not be practicable, and the same general approach as described for the city centre could be adopted, and ensure that the parking areas came under the control of the local authority.

The basic requirement for new residential development is that there shall be one car space provided for each dwelling, and this could be a garage, a standing space, a car port, or a reserved area for future garage development. For the more expensive houses these facilities should be duplicated to serve two cars.

BASIC PRINCIPLES OF A PARKING POLICY

It is of course quite impossible to outline a policy which would be applicable to all towns, large or small, in different countries. The circumstances and problems vary enormously and the policy for each town must be developed individually.

In formulating a policy the objective should always be in sight. The broad objective for any town should be to maintain a free flow of traffic on roads allocated for traffic; to maintain free and safe movement of pedestrians and, if necessary, provide pedestrian shopping streets; to control street parking so as not to interfere with the free movement of traffic; to provide off-street parking to meet the demand in accordance with feeder road capacities and, if necessary, control in such a way as to ensure that parking facilities are available for short term parking in the central business area at all times; to make arrangements for loading and unloading vehicles so as to cause a minimum of interference with vehicular traffic and pedestrians, and to organise and manage all the parking facilities efficiently and economically. By the exercise of a few simple disciplines, establish a degree of orderliness in a town, in order to use the motor car and enjoy the advantages it brings in the freedom of movement, with a minimum detrimental impact on the environment. In other words, use the motor car to improve the quality of life, and not to destroy it.

The different methods and equipment that may be used to achieve this end are described in the chapters of this book. It is the responsibility of the policy maker to select the appropriate methods and equipment, and combine them into a plan suitable to the area under consideration.

PUBLIC RELATIONS

Everybody who is able to move from their home is involved with traffic. They may be old people who become agitated when attempting to cross a road, school children, blind persons or just able bodied pedestrians jostling with one another in the business and shopping centre of a town. They may be cyclists, motor cyclists, motorists, disabled motorists, bus passengers or drivers of buses and commercial vehicles. Whoever they may be they cannot avoid being involved in traffic whether in town or country. Traffic management is a comparatively new term for an old exercise which means the control of traffic, both pedestrian and vehicular. This is necessary to make the most efficient and safe use of our roads.

If everybody is involved then everybody should be informed of what the responsible authorities are trying to do and of what is expected from the public. On the other hand the authorities should be informed of the difficulties that the public experience and their reaction to the proposals made by the authorities. Much strife, conflict and heartache is generated by the lack of understanding between interested parties. The lack of understanding leads to suspicion; suspicion leads to opposition; opposition to conflict; and prolonged conflict can dissipate the time and energy of both parties, until in the end no one succeeds.

Our task therefore is to use whatever legitimate methods of communication are available in order to reach some understanding of traffic and parking problems and proposals. Everybody is involved, and there are many conflicting interests.

Parking is an important section of traffic management and it is a particularly difficult problem because superficially it appears to be taking something from people rather than giving something to people, although its purpose is to permit a greater number of people to enjoy and take advantage of the facilities that motor vehicles can provide. The traffic and parking problem has gradually grown during the present century, from the time when pedestrians and a few people who were motorists had the complete freedom of our highways. The sheer number of vehicles has made it necessary to impose some regulations. To some this may be an inconvenience, to others it may have a serious effect on a business. For instance, a business that has relied to a large extent on trade from passing motorists may find a big drop in trade by 'No Waiting' regulations.

Yet, traffic must be controlled and managed. In some of our cities the volumes of traffic have already created very serious conditions, and the prospects of doubling the number of licenced vehicles on the roads during the next twenty years is quite frightening. Everyone will suffer in some way or other.

How then can we tackle this problem of communication? How can we steer a course through this tangled skein of conflicting interests and arrive at a satisfactory solution? It is imperative that it is tackled. We must tackle it and succeed.

Different nations have differing temperaments and national characteristics and therefore different methods of communication, and tactics must be used. The people of the United Kingdom, which is an old democracy, dislike dictatorship of any kind. If dictatorship is applied even in a small way it is likely to bring a revolt. On the other hand, when it is seen that it is necessary for some action to be taken, even if it is unpleasant, appears to be inconvenient, or is taking away a long standing privilege, it is usually accepted. This often means that slow progress is made, and whilst the professional man concerned can foresee the action that is necessary, he has to wait until it is apparent to the public. Traffic and parking regulations bring forth typical reactions. In the first place before there is general understanding there is strong opposition. Later, when the benefits have been experienced, there are requests for them to be extended. Therefore it is well worth while taking time and trouble to explain new proposals to the public, through the press, radio, exhibitions, meetings, lectures or discussion groups. All means and methods of communication are well worth while if they help to achieve understanding.

REFERENCES

1. 'Car Parking—A National Survey', British Road Federation, London, 1961.
2. 'Car Parking—A National Survey', British Road Federation, London, 1964.
3. 'Car Parking 1968', British Road Federation, London, 1968.
4. City of Grand Rapids Ordinance No. 1205, 1947.
5. Transport (London) Act, 1969. HMSO, London, 1969.
6. OWENS, D. 'A Survey of some Parking Standards adopted by County Boroughs in England & Wales', Road Research Laboratory Technical Note TN308, May 1968.
7. Planning Bulletin No. 7. 'Parking in Town Centres'. HMSO, 1965.

Chapter 20

Disposal of Abandoned Vehicles

The publicity given to European Conservation 1970 has awakened the public conscience to the necessity of protecting and preserving the environment. Wherever motor vehicles are in use there will be at some time unwanted vehicles. These are found on city streets, in vacant parking places and on highway verges. They are increasing in number, and their detrimental effect on the environment wherever it may be is also increasing.

In the United States from 5 to 5·5 million cars are abandoned each year, and in the United Kingdom the total is about 1 million. There are several reasons which contribute to the abandonment of a vehicle. One is the regular checks by State and Local Authorities for roadworthiness of cars, high cost of repairs, towing away charges, vandalism and lack of information on how to dispose of a worn out vehicle.

In an article by Eileen M. Harloff, she states:[1]

'The general rule in most countries is that if the owner of an abandoned vehicle can be traced, he and not the authority concerned is responsible for defraying the costs of having it removed to a breaker's yard or otherwise disposed of. In Stockholm and many other cities, the owner in addition receives a fine for having illegally stored his abandoned property on the public streets. The experience of Pittsburg, Pennsylvania, was not however very encouraging: of the first five people heard for their offence, four were unemployed, and two had just been released from hospital. Pittsburg officials have concluded that the man who abandons a car is usually in the worst economic position to pay a fine.'

'For the most part, the owner of a car reported to be abandoned is never found, despite extensive efforts by the police to locate him. It is at this stage, in fact, that the real costs to the city, or to the State in the case of Austria, arise. Once the fact of anonymity of ownership is established or an owner has not removed the vehicle within an allotted period of time, the abandoned car is removed to an established storage place. Before this occurs, a complete description is made of the condition of the car, and in Amsterdam a photograph is taken of it as well. The negative is kept on the file, so that in the event of an owner appearing, it can be proved that his property was in a condition requiring removal. In that city, it has more than once occurred that a motor car in good condition was left on the street during a lengthy absence of the owner. Before his return the vehicle had been enthusiastically turned into a wreck by the local youth.'

'Many cities have their own equipment for removing vehicles to the established storage depot. In the United States it is not unusual for this to be done by a private firm on contract, once a request for removal has been made by the local police. This stage, too, involves the local authority in extensive costs, especially in those places where space of any kind is at a premium. Consider the length of storage time, which may range from one to six months, and the increasing number of vehicles being stored, and it will be seen that such costs are not negligible.'

'It is usual practice that vehicles which have been stored for the required length of time by the responsible authority shall be sold in an attempt to recover some of the costs incurred in investigation of ownership, towing charges, and storage and disposal costs. On the whole, this is a money losing affair. Sales generally take the form of public auctions. Before a public sale in Amsterdam, as in other cities of Holland, a commission assesses the value of the vehicles before they are auctioned to the highest bidder. In The Hague, there is a rule that any buyer at such an auction who proceeds to abandon the vehicle he has bought shall be prohibited from taking part in any future auction. Should the amount bid for the derelict cars—in some cases they are roadworthy vehicles—be insufficient to defray the total costs involved, the city may then enter a bid to the amount incurred. In this event, the city may sell the vehicle in any way it wishes, which is usually to a scrap yard.'

'Whereas the typical method of disposal of abandoned motor cars is through sale or public auctions, the expense involved in this process, combined with low prices for scrap metal, has led many cities to search for a new way of handling this problem. In Stockholm, Gothenburg and Malmö for example, abandoned vehicles may be disposed of by sale through competitive bids on an annual contract basis to licensed scrap merchants. Experience in Chicago, which follows the same procedure, has shown that this method of disposal has resulted in fast removal of cars from storage depots, and has helped immeasurably towards defraying the costs involved in handling the vehicles. The main point of this programme is that cars appraised at less than $100 (£42) can be sold to the city's contractor at a set price rather than through public auction at a variable price. It is vital that each contractor engaged by the city, through the means of public bidding, be able to pick up 100 cars per day, as established in his contract. Were this provision not made, the contractor would not remove any cars in a period when scrap steel prices were at a low level.'

'In other American cities, derelict cars are being used to reinforce river banks against erosion or to provide artificial underwater reefs to attract fish. The latter use, however, entails the risk that fish will be poisoned by rusty water, thus creating a water pollution hazard. The New York Sanitation Department buries scrap vehicles, which cannot be sold, at land fill sites. There has even been a suggestion that abandoned vehicles be rehabilitated and used in a "cars for peace" programme.'

'Especially where private enterprise does not find the disposal of derelict cars sufficiently profitable, larger cities may purchase their own car crushing and baling machines.'

In the United Kingdom, the position with regard to abandoned vehicles is similar to that in other countries. In 1950, just over 100,000 old motor vehicles left the road, in 1965 the figure was just over 1,000,000, and in 1970, 1,500,000.

In 1967, the Civic Amenities Act[2] was passed by Parliament, and Part III of this Act deals with the removal and disposal of abandoned vehicles and other bulky refuse. The Act imposes a duty upon local authorities to provide places where refuse may be deposited by the public, it outlaws dumping with heavy penalties and requires local authorities to remove abandoned motor vehicles and to make arrangements for their disposal.[3]

The maximum penalties for dumping a motor vehicle (or parts of a dismantled motor vehicle) are: £100 for the first offence and £200 or 3 months imprisonment or both for a second or subsequent conviction.

Local authorities are now required to remove any vehicle which appears to have been abandoned anywhere in the open air or on any part of a highway, subject to certain conditions as follows:

(a) If the vehicle is on private land it cannot be removed if the occupier of that land objects.

(b) If the vehicle is not on a road and in such a position that the cost of its removal to the nearest convenient carriageway would be 'unreasonably high'.

(c) If the vehicle is fit only for scrapping, a notice must be posted on it for seven days before it is removed to the effect that when it is removed it will be destroyed.

Vehicles are classified as either 'wrecks' or 'runners'. In the case of a vehicle other than a 'wreck', the owner, if he can be traced, must be notified, and the vehicle kept in safe custody by the local authority either until the owner retrieves it or, if he does not respond, until a prescribed period has elapsed after the notice was served on him. This prescribed period will not be more than 28 days. If a vehicle whether a 'wreck' or a 'runner' has a current road fund licence it may not be destroyed or sold until that licence has expired.

If a local authority wishes to dispose of removed vehicles by dismantling, crushing or any other suitable method, it is empowered to obtain and operate the necessary equipment. A Council may also sell its unwanted vehicles for resale or as scrap.

If the owner of a vehicle which has been removed but not disposed of by a local authority wishes to reclaim it, he may do so within a prescribed period provided that he pays the local authority for its removal and storage. If within one year after the sale of a vehicle by a local authority (either as a 'runner' or as scrap) the owner seeks compensation, he is entitled to the proceeds of the sale less the charges for its removal, storage and disposal.[4]

SUMMARY OF PROCEDURE FOR THE REMOVAL AND DISPOSAL OF MOTOR VEHICLES IN THE UNITED KINGDOM

PROCEDURE IN THE CASE OF 'WRECKS'

A. *Where abandoned on Council land*

1. AFFIX a notice to the vehicle stating that it is proposed to remove it at the expiration of 7 DAYS.
2. DESTRUCTION:
   (i) NO CURRENT LICENCE displayed, then AT ANY TIME AFTER REMOVAL.
   (ii) CURRENT LICENCE/S displayed, then AT ANY TIME AFTER LICENCE EXPIRY DATE.
3. GIVE NOTICE OF DESTRUCTION.

B. *Where abandoned on Private land*

1. SERVE NOTICE on OCCUPIER of the land stating that it is proposed to remove it at the expiration of 15 DAYS.
2. DESTRUCTION:
   (i) NO CURRENT LICENCE displayed, then AT ANY TIME AFTER REMOVAL.
   (ii) CURRENT LICENCE/S displayed, then AT ANY TIME AFTER LICENCE EXPIRY DATE.
3. GIVE NOTICE OF DESTRUCTION.

PROCEDURE IN THE CASE OF 'RUNNERS'

2 stages: (I) BEFORE removal and (II) AFTER removal.

I. BEFORE REMOVAL

1. Serve notice on occupier of the land.
   Addressee:
   The person who appears to be the occupier either *by name* or by the description of 'The Occupier' of (*description*) land.
   Method of delivery: (where there is an apparent occupier of the land)
   (i) *handing it to the person* who appears to be the Occupier;
   (ii) *leaving it* at his usual or last known place of abode;
   (iii) *sending it* by registered post or recorded delivery service, addressed to him at his usual or last known place of abode;
   (iv) if the apparent Occupier is an incorporated company or body, by delivering it to the Secretary or Clerk of the Company or body at the registered or principal office or by sending it by registered post or recorded delivery service addressed to the Secretary or Clerk.
   (*where no apparent occupier of the land*)
   (v) posting in an envelope marked clearly 'Important—This Communication affects your property', to the land by registered post or recorded delivery service or by delivering it, so marked, to some person on the land, or by affixing it, so marked, to some object on the land.

2. OBJECTIONS:
If the apparent Occupier on whom notice has been served wishes to object, the objection must be IN WRITING and either sent by post or left at the Council's Offices. The objection must be lodged within 15 days from date of service of Notice. THE VEHICLE CANNOT BE REMOVED IF AN OBJECTION IS RECEIVED.

II. AFTER REMOVAL
1. IF APPARENT OWNER OF VEHICLE IS KNOWN—serve Notice.
2. STEPS TO BE TAKEN TO FIND THE OWNER:
A. *Vehicle has GB registration mark:*
    (i) Apply to the Authority with which the vehicle was last registered giving details and requesting them to ascertain from their records the name and address of the person by whom the vehicle is kept and used.
    (ii) Send copies of application under A(i) to: (*a*) Chief Constable, (*b*) Hire Purchase Information Ltd.
    (iii) If name and address of a person who may be the owner is received then serve Notice upon him.
B. *Vehicle has any other registration mark*—Refer to Town Clerk's Department.
C. *Vehicle has no registration mark*—Send application under A(i) to Chief Constable.

3. *If an Owner is found as a result of inquiries:*
Serve notice upon him to remove the vehicle within 21 days. Service of the notice should be carried out in ONE of the following ways:
    (*a*) *delivery to the person* who appears to be the owner;
    (*b*) *leaving it* at his usual or last known place of abode;
    (*c*) *posting it* by registered post or recorded delivery, addressed to him at his usual or last known place of abode;
    (*d*) *if it is an incorporated company or body,* by delivering it to the Secretary or Clerk of the Company or body at their registered or principal office or posting by registered post or recorded delivery addressed to the Secretary or Clerk of the Company or body at that office.

4. *An owner subsequently turning up to claim the vehicle:*
If a person satisfies the Authority that he is the owner of a vehicle which is in custody and pays the amounts due in respect of removal and storage, he shall be permitted to remove it. He must remove it within 7 days from the date he satisfied the Council that he is the owner.

III. DISPOSAL
1. *Time:* Any time after taking the prescribed steps to find a person appearing to be the owner and EITHER (i) failed to trace a person; OR (ii) the person has failed to comply with a Notice served on him requiring him to remove the vehicle within the prescribed period; PROVIDED any licence in force in respect of the vehicle has expired.

2. *Information to be given after disposal:*
   Notice of disposal should be sent as follows:
   A. IF GB REGISTRATION MARK to:
      (*a*) the Authority with which vehicle was registered;
      (*b*) Chief Constable;
      (*c*) Hire Purchase Information Ltd.
   B. ANY OTHER REGISTRATION MARK: refer to Town Clerk's Department.
   C. IF NO REGISTRATION MARK: to Chief Constable.
   D. ANY VEHICLE: send notice to any person who appears to the Authority to have been the owner of the vehicle immediately before it was disposed of.

IV. RECOVERY OF EXPENSES

CHARGES:

For REMOVING vehicles—£4.
For STORING vehicles—50p for each period of 24 hours or part thereof. The period is reckoned from *noon* on the day following the day on which vehicle was removed.
For DISPOSING of vehicles—£2.
LIABILITY to pay the Council's charges:
The Council can recover these charges as a simple contract debt from any 'person responsible', *i.e.*
(*a*) OWNER at the time the vehicle was left in the place whence it was removed UNLESS he can prove he was not concerned and did not know;
(*b*) *Person putting the vehicle* in that place;
(*c*) *Person convicted* under S.19, Civic Amenities Act, 1967.

IMPORTANT

V. PROCEEDS OF SALE

If before the expiry of ONE YEAR with effect from the date of sale of the vehicle by the Council, any person proves that at the time of its sale he was the owner, the Council shall pay over the difference between the sale proceeds and cost of removal, storage and disposal. If seemingly there are one or more owners, the Council shall treat such one of them as the owner as it shall think fit.

METHODS OF DISPOSAL

There are different methods of disposing of unwanted cars, and the choice of method depends on the quantity, circumstances and facilities for disposal.[4]

(*a*) Tipping: This method is probably most used in rural areas where only a small number of cars are available for disposal. It is better if the cars are flattened and if any saleable parts are removed. In New York and Sweden, unwanted cars have been dumped in the sea.

(*b*) Dismantling: This method is usually carried on by local car breakers, earning an income from spare parts. The final disposal of car bodies may be by cutting up and compressing in small baling plants or by taking to a large shredding plant.

(*c*) Burning: If this is carried out in the open it can be objectionable and would no doubt be condemned by the local authority for polluting the atmosphere and creating a nuisance. The only satisfactory method is by incinerators equipped with smoke collection equipment, which is rather costly. Normally, to be economic an incinerator must be large enough to take about thirty cars through a long furnace where they are rotated to allow ashes and dirt to fall off.

(*d*) Shredding: This is a recent development, and a large plant is necessary for the complete operation to be economic. The large conurbations are usually suitable areas for this method of disposal to be successful, where transport costs of the disused car can be kept low.

INCINERATION[5]

As with most other mechanical plants, the size of an incinerator must be related to the amount of material to be processed, and for it to be an economic proposition a steady supply of material is required to justify the high expenditure on plant and ancillary equipment.

A refractory lined furnace containing rails or rollers is necessary for loading and unloading. Loading may be on a single line placing one car behind another, or two deep. The arrangements for charging and discharging may be of the 'batch' type or a 'continuous' type. With the former, one set of doors serves the dual purpose of charging and discharging, while the 'continuous' type has doors at each end, and permits one-way operation.

A combustion time of 30 minutes is required to ensure combustion with a furnace temperature of 870°C (1600°F). It is also necessary to burn fuel under controlled conditions, and liquid or gaseous fuels are most adaptable for use in incinerators.

From a public health point of view it is the treatment of the gases after they leave the combustion chamber that is most important. In order to reduce the pollution to the permitted standards required by the local authority Public Health departments, it is necessary to install an efficient after-burner which is brought into use with the furnace burners, and also dust arresting equipment.

CRUSHING AND SHREDDING PLANTS

The scrap metal industrialists have not been slow to foresee the potential business in buying and selling disused cars, and different types of plant have been developed to deal with the growing waste product.[6]

A baling press manufactured by Fawcett Preston Ltd, of Bromborough, England, whose baling press business has been subsequently acquired by Fletcher and Steward Ltd, of Derby, has been developed to produce from the average car body eight bales of uncontaminated steel, each 28·3 dm^3 (12 in^3) in size and having a total weight of 600 kg (12 cwt). Together with salvaged mechanical items this was estimated to produce a return of between £8 and £10 (1966). Non-metallic constituents had first to be burned out and the vehicle cut up with oxy-acetylene torches. Two men, it was stated, could handle six to eight cars in an 8 hour day.

Another piece of plant is the PSC 376 'Scrapmaster' car crusher, of American origin, but later built by Sheppard & Sons Ltd, of Bridgend, Glamorgan, S. Wales. This machine is 12·0 m (40 ft) long and weighs 40 tonnes (40 tons). It is capable of handling 18 cars per day, reducing each to a bale measuring 0·60 m × 0·30 m × 0·55 m (24 in × 12 in × 22 in). Berds Commercial Motors Ltd, Stratford-upon-Avon, England, have mounted the plant on a multi-wheel semi-articulated trailer chassis drawn by a 200 hp AEC 'Mammoth' tractor, with a view to touring local authority areas and rendering a car disposal service.

Fig. 20.1   A general view of the Proler–Cohen fragmentation factory in Willesden. This factory can process up to 1500 scrap cars per day, producing up to 1000 tons (or tonnes) of clean steel scrap. (*Reproduced by permission of The George Cohen 600 Group Ltd, London.*)

These two pieces of equipment offer local authorities plant which can be conveniently installed on a Council's own site, or may be conveyed from site to site dealing with accumulations of cars. In the case of the 'Scrapmaster', the cars must be assembled in sufficiently large numbers to make a visit by such a massive plant a viable proposition. This could be resolved by a consortium of local authorities bringing their derelict vehicles to a central site.

A modern shredding plant has been developed since 1958 by the Proler Steel Corporation, of Houston, Texas, USA. The first plant was erected in Houston and followed by similar installations in Kansas City, Los Angeles, Chicago, Boston, New York, Philadelphia and St Louis. In 1967, the George Cohen 600 Group, through its newly formed subsidiary, Proler–Cohen Ltd, opened the first Proler–Cohen scrap car shredding plant at Willesden, in North-West London. This plant follows closely the plants erected in the United States (Fig. 20.1).

The Proler process is a continuous fully automatic operation. Cars and other forms of scrap are picked up by a crane equipped with a cactus grab and are placed upon an apron conveyor, which may be from 2·43 m (8 feet) to 4·5 m (15 feet) wide (Fig. 20.2).

Fig. 20.2   Cars being taken to the top of the Proler scrap fragmentation factory on a 2·43 m (8 ft) wide apron conveyor, and dropped some 12·0 m (40 ft) into the disintegrator. (*Reproduced by permission of The George Cohen* 600 *Group Ltd, London.*)

The cars are dropped off the apron into the mill—a drop of some 12·0 m (40 feet). Within 15 seconds they are shredded into pieces about the size of a man's hand. These small pieces travel on an oscillating conveyor while the impurities, upholstery, rubber, glass, etc., continue on a lower conveyor to a separate dumping chute.

The process is completed in a condensing mill, where the clean scrap is

Fig. 20.3   Cars being delivered at the Proler factory. Many of the cars are flattened to help reduce transport costs. Up to 25 cars can be carried on a 10·0 m (33 ft) trailer. (*Reproduced by permission of The George Cohen* 600 *Group Ltd, London.*)

reduced to fist size pieces, before being conveyed to an overhead chute which drops them into waiting trucks or lorries.

The time taken from a car being placed on the conveyor to the time it emerges as clean scrap is a few minutes.

The scrap that emerges is a homogeneous-type, heavy melting scrap, chemically constant and physically dense. It weighs about 1000 kg/m^3 (65 lb per cubic foot) and can be moved by magnets, grabs or conveyors. It is small enough to be stored in hoppers, and it is claimed that it can be used in all types of steel making furnaces (Fig. 20.4).

The Proler process is the culmination of the extensive research made by the

Fig. 20.4   A typical fragment of Proler steel scrap compared with a match box. (*Reproduced by permission of The George Cohen* 600 *Group Ltd, London.*)

Proler Steel Corporation to find a method of returning sheet steel, used in the motor and consumer goods industries, to its original state of clean, low carbon material.

REFERENCES

1. HARLOFF, EILEEN M. 'Problem of Abandoned Vehicles', *Local Government Throughout the World*, March–May 1966.
2. Civic Amenities Act, 1967. HMSO, London.
3. Civic Amenities Act, 1967. Joint Circular from the Ministry of Housing and Local Government (Circ. 55/67), Ministry of Transport (Circ. GT1/18/01), Welsh Office (Circ. 49/67), HMSO, London.
4. 'Disposal of Unwanted Vehicles', Civic Trust Conference on Civic Amenities Act, 1967. October 1967. Civic Trust, London.
5. DOWNING, G. F. 'Incinerators for Scrap Cars', *Municipal Engineering*, London. 20th May 1966.
6. 'Developments in the Disposal of Old Motor Vehicles', *The Surveyor and Municipal Engineer*, 28th May 1966.

Chapter 21

Future Developments for Car Parking

Most of the developed countries have now accepted a realistic forecast for the increased use of the motor vehicle. This is in the region of 1·3 to 1·5 people per car. By applying traffic management measures, imposing traffic regulations, together with building a limited amount of new urban roads and car parks, traffic problems have been tackled and varying amounts of success have been achieved. Car parking accommodation in central areas has to be related to the capacity of the feeder roads, and this is probably less accommodation than that required by motorists. Some cities have now reached the position where they have to develop a restraining influence on cars entering the central business areas. In the future the parking problem will not be confined to central business areas; it is already developing on the University campus, airports, and trading estates.

At this stage some positive thought should be given to the new and changing pattern of urban life which is being influenced very largely by the motor vehicle. Everyone would like to see towns and cities where people can move about freely and safely. Everyone would like to use his car as and when he chooses. The real problem is how to maintain and improve a civilised urban life with an ever increasing motor car population, and within the framework of a democratic society. Can we solve the problem by the application of technology and engineering science, by building more and better roads, more and bigger car parks? All these measures are necessary but something more is required before a satisfactory answer to the problem is achieved.

What then is the answer? What is this changing pattern of urban life to which we have to adjust? Firstly, something has to be discovered about the life of the motorist and non-motorist by getting into the motorist's seat, not the seat of our own car but the seat of the doctor, the commuter, the shopper, the businessman, and understanding their genuine problems as distinct from mere prejudices, habits, and a determination not be to involved in any kind of change.

Consider some examples as illustrations. In the United Kingdom during the last 50 years or so, most domestic property has been built at a low density per acre, and we now have our large suburban estates extending as much as several miles from town or city centre. For many people life on these estates has been convenient and attractive when a car has been available, and reliance on public transport has been unnecessary.

The imposition of parking restrictions in a town or city centre can cause serious and far reaching problems for commuting motorists. These difficulties are not solved by suggesting that the commuters use public transport which may or may not be available at the time required. The use of public transport must be encouraged and improved as much as possible, but at the same time it must be recognised that the motor car is a very convenient machine for door to door transport in all weathers. It will not be abandoned or superseded easily.

Now examine the needs of the shopper. The housewife who uses a car for shopping. There appear to be two modern trends in household shopping. One is the development of the self-service stores and impulse buying. Some housewives make frequent visits to the stores and buy a few articles each time, others make visits less frequently and buy goods in bulk. The other development is for improved domestic facilities for food storage, including perishable food, and the financial advantages that are offered by traders for bulk buying. These developments, when extended, could have an important effect on the traffic and parking problem. Here is a field for research. How will impulse buying in self-service stores affect the traffic and parking problem? How and to what extent will bulk buying develop and where will the facilities be provided? When more housewives use a car for shopping, would an hourly parcel service between stores and car parks be practicable and serve a useful purpose?

With the development of modern means of communication and closed circuit television, a new pattern of business life is developing and many journeys between offices may not be necessary. Instead of a small group of men converging on an office in a city centre, contact could be made between them in their offices simultaneously by modern methods of communication, and the discussion take place without the use of transport. An examination of the business organisation and its establishment may reveal that it is unnecessary to employ the whole staff within the central area, and that a small suite of offices is all that would be necessary, the remainder of the staff being accommodated on an administrative estate where adequate facilities for parking would be available. Again, modern means of communication and closed circuit television would establish adequate contact between staff in different offices.

One further point is that when using a car one should be conscious of social responsibility to the quality of community life. The accident problem, quite rightly, has received, and is continuing to receive, a great deal of attention. An examination of car use and parking reveals that many cars are used unnecessarily. This of course adds to our traffic and parking problems, and causes inconvenience and frustration to other motorists. This is a national problem and requires a vigorous publicity campaign.

Statistics such as those produced in a Report on a Land Use/Transport Survey provides very valuable information by which a road network can be planned. The development of the computer has made it possible to produce in a comparatively short time information on a scale that could not have been imagined a few years ago. There is, however, still something missing, and that is the human factor. The individual motorist's reaction to all the changes that are taking place in urban life. This is very important, and could have a vital influence on planning. This is the field in which our researches should now be developed.

Recently there has been a great deal of publicity about public participation. Holding public meetings where planning proposals are explained; exhibitions of plans, photographs and models, and invitations to the public to submit comments, and ask questions. Basically this contact with the public is good, nevertheless it is bound by its nature to be superficial and cannot reveal a deep understanding of the true requirements of the public. One fundamental reason is that few people have tried to rationalise their requirements in urban life with those of the community. Perhaps the nearest approach that can be made to acquiring this knowledge is by first studying the motorists' difficulties and problems. This is essential knowledge in the search for a satisfactory solution to the traffic and parking problems.

People who are able to look back 40 years in local government work will recall the great changes that have taken place in urban life since 1930. It will also be appreciated how difficult it would have been in 1930 to plan accurately for 1970, and how unacceptable those plans would have been had they been based on an accurate forecast. It was no less difficult in 1970 to plan for the next 40 years to 2010, and it must be accepted that any long term plans made today must be subject to revision at 5 or at the most 10 yearly intervals. This is when we need this deeper research into human problems and difficulties that are developing in our changing urban life, and maybe specially trained research workers will be required for this type of work.

RESTRAINT OF TRAFFIC IN CENTRAL BUSINESS AREAS

The formulation of a policy of restraint is a problem which many towns will have to consider in the future. It must have as its basis the maintenance of economic stability within the town, and this presupposes the establishment of a priority amongst the competing classes of road users.

The amount of restraint that will be necessary will be very variable and cannot be related directly to the size of the town. For instance, a town with a population of 100,000 which is the centre of a county or similar area for administration, shopping, trade distribution, education and professional services, will have a very different traffic problem to an industrial town with the same population. In the former, the restraint necessary may be 50 per cent of the potential demand, whereas in the latter, restraint may be unnecessary.

If there has to be restraint then the cut must fall in the first place on vehicles which are used for journeys which are optional, viz., journeys to work which could be undertaken on public transport. These are the journeys which are the least necessary for the business life of a town centre. Vehicles used for essential commercial, industrial and business traffic which include vehicles for delivery and supplying goods, and cars for shoppers, visitors and business clients, are essential for the business life of a town, and these are the ones which should be accommodated with parking facilities and road capacity at peak traffic periods.

The real problem, of course, is the implementation of restraint, and for this it is necessary to explore several avenues. The first and obvious for consideration is the land use. Are there any business premises which are bringing employees into the area which could be better accommodated elsewhere? Are shoppers being brought into the town centre for day to day shopping which could be supplied by suburban shopping areas? Shopping is changing from the small private trader to the large store, such as Marks & Spencer, Boots, Woolworths, British Home Stores, and the many supermarket firms. These firms usually have their stores in the large shopping centres where the local authority's Market Hall is also situated. Inevitably they draw people to the central shopping area where there is a wider range of goods and often at a lower price than in the suburban shops. The benefit that can be obtained from the development of suburban shopping centres may be marginal, but nevertheless it should be explored. Is it possible to extend the shopping periods? The general trend in employment is for shorter working time, and shop assistants look for the same working conditions from their employers as do other employees. Shift systems are not always easy to staff, but with determined effort and co-operation between employers and employees they can be arranged.

It is, of course, very easy to take a broad view, and say commuters need not use their cars if an alternative means of transport is available. This is often true but not always. As the use of the motor car has increased, people have been offered a much wider range of choice for their residence. They have moved from densely built up urban areas to the sprawling suburbs and the country villages, and in many cases they are entirely dependent on private transport. These people will not take kindly to restraint on commuters. They will either have to change their residence, place of employment, or use a combination of public and private transport for their journey to work. Inconveniences of this kind may bring pressure on employers to provide parking facilities. This, they may not be able to do in the town centre, but could be done at a convenient site elsewhere and, if necessary, provide a private coach to complete the journey to work. Alternatively, it could lead them to examine the necessity to house the whole of their staff in the central area. Would it be more convenient and economical to have a small suite of offices in the centre of the town, and the bulk of the staff on an administrative estate where ample parking facilities could be provided? Modern means of communication and closed circuit television could make this quite possible and efficient. Female staff find town centre employment convenient for shopping at lunch time, but this is a matter which can be organised either privately or by providing facilities on an administrative estate.

The Smeed Report on Road Pricing[1] is a revolutionary document. It outlines for the first time the technical practicability of charging for congestion by using meters in cars which would come into operation when a vehicle passes over the boundary into the high priced territory.

The terms of reference given to Dr Smeed and his panel were: 'to study and report on the technical feasibility of various methods for improving the pricing system relating to the use of roads, and on relevant economic considerations'. The Report shows that the panel have carried out their work thoroughly, and have made a strong case for road pricing.

When considering this problem of congestion, we must recognise that the scale in the Greater London area is quite different from provincial cities. What may be a necessary and acceptable solution for London may not be the solution for other cities.

The proposition the panel put forward is that 'journeys should not be made if they are valued at less than the costs or losses they cause to other people; similarly, journeys should not be restrained if they are valued at more than the costs they cause.' This is basically sound and quite simple, but when one observes the behaviour of motorists in our cities, the question that immediately comes to mind is: how many motorists will stop to consider the cost of their journey to other people?

The Report gives some tentative estimates made by the Road Research Laboratory for Central London which show that the congestion costs imposed by a typical car on other vehicles rise from 2p (4d) per 1·6 km (1 mile) at speeds of 32 km/h (20 mph) to 10p (2s 0d) per 1·6 km (1 mile) at 19 km/h (12 mph) and 30p (6s 0d) per 1·6 km (1 mile) at 13 km/h (8 mph). The costs imposed by heavy vehicles are often two or three times higher.

The panel considered different methods of charging, such as the differential fuel tax, the poll tax on employees in congested areas, the parking tax and a system of daily licences. They came to the conclusion that superior results are potentially obtainable from direct pricing systems. They described six meter systems—two manual and four automatic—which with development could probably be made effective. It is also estimated that in urban areas a meter system could yield economic benefits of £100 m to £150 m per year under present traffic conditions. The most important difficulties which the congestion tax presents appear to come outside the terms of reference. The first is the effect that the tax will have on business in the central business area of the city. A very great amount of capital is invested in these areas by local authorities and business houses. A depreciation in trade and rateable value will have a serious financial effect on both the local authority and businesses. This may not apply to London, but it certainly would apply to many provincial cities. If the tax is small then it is not likely to have much effect on congestion or business. Therefore, for it to be effective the tax must be substantial.

The panel posed the question: 'Would the restraint of traffic by high charges have a more adverse effect on cities than would restraint by congestion or by other means?' The answer is that there are other means which would have less adverse effects on provincial cities than high road prices, but this may not apply equally to London. There are systems of control which, if adopted, will enable the professional, business and cultural life in a central area of a city to be live and prosperous without creating excessive traffic congestion. An alternative to the congestion tax is parking control. This has received some detailed consideration in Appendix 4 of the report. The consideration is limited to a fixed charge, or a variable charge at a uniform rate per hour. Under these conditions the panel concludes that the net benefits of parking tax are about 40 per cent of what is claimed for a pricing solution.

In a provincial city the segregation of essential and optional traffic can be achieved by parking control. If the parking fees for central area car parks are small for the first two hours of parking, and thereafter rise quickly so as to deter long term parking, the bulk of the commuters will either use the car parks outside the central area or use public transport. If traffic in the central area is limited to essential traffic and street parking is efficiently controlled, then the congestion problem is largely overcome. The report quite rightly points out that if congestion is relieved in this way, more through traffic is encouraged to enter the central area and offset the benefits achieved. This may be correct if no other action is taken, but by traffic management methods through traffic can be prevented from using the central area roads.

An advantage of this method is that it gives facilities for the professional and business life of the central area of a city to prosper. Modest parking fees for short periods are found by experience not to be a deterrent to business, and adequate car parking facilities are a great asset in a business area.

Perhaps the largest and most successful park and ride scheme in operation is in Greater London. Here, large numbers of commuters drive or are driven to the suburban underground railway stations and they complete their journey to town by public transport. Here there are certain definite advantages—one is that the number of passengers is so large that there is a very frequent train service, and waiting at the stations is under cover.

Park and ride schemes in provincial towns have not been very successful, but as the traffic and parking problems become more and more difficult, no doubt park and ride schemes will have to be adopted.

The restraint of traffic in a central business area is a very difficult and delicate operation. There is no one simple solution and each city will have to devise its own solution to the problem. In the United Kingdom, the Smeed Panel suggested that a 30p (6s 0d) per day parking charge (1962) would be 40 per cent effective in Central London and reduce peak hour traffic by 7 per cent with a resultant 2·4 km/h ($1\frac{1}{2}$ mph) increase in vehicular speeds. A charge of 5p (1s 0d) per hour would reduce peak hour traffic by 25–33 per cent. In Liverpool, a survey indicated that parking charges of 1·25p, 2·5p and 5p (3d, 6d and 1s 0d) per hour would reduce car commuters by 13·4 per cent, 34·4 per cent and 47·5 per cent respectively. There is no doubt that some restraint can be achieved by price control for parking. We have also to look for other methods such as improved public transport facilities and also the removal of the necessity to travel to the central area by transferring from the central area a large part or the whole of businesses which can function equally well, if not better, in other less congested areas of the city. Within limits it is better to reduce the necessity for a motorist to bring his car into the city centre rather than by imposing restrictions which prevent him from so doing, as the demand for parking space in city central areas is likely to be greater than the space available, and frequently there will be times of the day when all parking spaces are occupied. If traffic still flows into the central area under these conditions it will cause unnecessary congestion which could have a serious detrimental effect, especially at peak periods. On the other hand, no motorist will be pleased if he has to park his car some distance from the central area unnecessarily, and finds that he has wasted time by completing his journey on foot or by public transport.

We have reached the stage where the motorist's vision is being overtaxed, his eyes are given too much work to do in the central area of traffic-congested towns. He has to be alert for traffic signals, pedestrian crossings, direction signs, parking regulations, one-way streets, halt, give way, no left or right turning and all other mandatory and informative signs. It is also necessary to concentrate on all moving traffic whether it is crossing, overtaking, or weaving into the traffic stream, and the unexpected actions of selfish, impatient and careless motorists. Pedestrians have to be watched, especially at street junctions. Under adverse weather conditions of rain, ice, snow, fog, and sometimes a setting sun, the task of the driver is made much more difficult. The motorist cannot be expected to cope visually with the increasing multiplicity of information given by signs and signals which are part of the motoring scene.

As a first step towards the simplification of signs directing traffic to car parks, the occupancy of a group of car parks could be monitored, and their states indicated on signs which would assist motorists in choosing a convenient park. A control centre could be located together with counting equipment at one of the car parks. Loop detector units at the entrance and exit of the car parks send pulses to a counter on the passage of a car. The counter could be arranged to give a 'full' indication at, say, three different levels of occupancy, e.g. 90 per cent, 93 per cent and 96 per cent according to the position of the signs. Those further away from the car park will give a 'full' indication at an earlier time than the nearer signs. This should prevent the park filling up completely between the time a driver passes a sign indicating a car park with vacant spaces and the time he arrives at the park. On-street parking spaces available could be assessed on a statistical basis. The signs on the approach roads to the city centre could be very simple, and it might help if primary colours were used, e.g. blue when space is available, and red when full. For transmission, it is most likely that rented GPO lines could be used, although a combination of rented and private lines may be possible if the latter are already available between any car parks or signs, or the distances are very short.

Whilst this arrangement assists the motorist by directing him to a car park where space is available, it still relies on his vision. It is necessary to relieve the pressure on the motorist's vision, and at the same time convey to him 'up-to-the-minute' information on the car parking position in a city. This will vary for different days and different times of the day. For instance, if at mid-day all parking space in a city centre is occupied, and motorists are still driving towards the city, they should be informed of the situation and given directions indicating where there is a car park with accommodation available, and maybe they will have to finish their journey by public transport. The main point is that the motorist is given some authentic advanced information on the situation and advised on how to reach his destination. He must not be left in a situation where he does not know what to do. This causes congestion, delays, accidents and a waste of the motorist's time, which he will find irritating and frustrating.

From a central parking control, information could be broadcast to motorists who are either approaching or within the city, giving 'up-to-the-minute' information and directions for parking. This would clarify the position for the motorist and prevent him from making unnecessary journeys to the city centre.

To give this service it would be necessary to have broadcasting equipment for a short range, say, to the city boundary, and for each vehicle to have a simple transistor radio receiver installed. For the smaller cities or towns the same wavelength could be used, the radio switched on when approaching a city and the information would be forthcoming when the motorist came within the range of the broadcast. In larger cities and conurbations it may be necessary to divide the area into, say, four quadrants, each having a separate wavelength. A motorist driving within the city boundary may also wish to know whether or not it is practicable to use his car for a local journey. This equipment need not be limited in use for the broadcast of information on parking—it could also be used to give information on diversions, traffic situation, ice, snow, flooding and fog conditions and any other information that may be helpful to the motorist.

The cost of providing this service to the motorist would be quite reasonable, and car parks could be connected to the central control by GPO lines. It would be necessary to have some additional legislation, and co-operation between the police force and the local authority would be essential.

At the risk of stating the obvious, we know that traffic volumes are overtaking the construction programme for urban primary distributor roads. There is ample evidence that *ad hoc* methods of dealing with the moving and stationary vehicle are no solution to the problem. We must adopt more comprehensive and sophisticated methods of controlling and directing vehicles in our central business areas. This is as essential now as it will be in the future when our urban primary distributor road networks have been constructed.

REFERENCE

1. 'Road Pricing—The Economic and Technical Possibilities', HMSO, London, 1964.

Index